COMPUTER PROGRAMMING
IN
FORTRAN
THE
EASY
WAY

BY

Lawrence S. Leff

Assistant Principal and
Chairman, Department of Mathematics
Franklin D. Roosevelt High School
Brooklyn, New York

AND

Arlene Podos

Lecturer in Data Processing
Queensborough Community College
Bayside, New York

Barron's Educational Series, Inc.

All inquiries should be addressed to:
Barron's Educational Series, Inc.
250 Wireless Boulevard
Hauppauge, New York 11788

Library of Congress Catalog Card No. 84-18526

International Standard Book No. 0-8120-2800-7

Library of Congress Cataloging in Publication Data
Leff, Lawrence S.
   Computer programming in Fortran the easy way.

   Includes index.
   1. FORTRAN (Computer program language)   I. Podos,
Arlene.   II. Title.
QA76.73.F25L435   1984   001.64'24   84-18526
ISBN 0-8120-2800-7

PRINTED IN THE UNITED STATES OF AMERICA
23   100   987654

Dedication

To my husband, Don, my sons, Steve and Jeff, my mother, Shirley Drimmer, and my best friend, Beverly Rosendorf.

Arlene Podos

Acknowledgments

We would like to thank the staff of the University Computer Center of the City University of New York for providing us with the technical and hardware support which allowed us to illustrate Fortran concepts using the popular WATFIV compiler.

Rex Franciotti, Director of Computer and Communications at Adelphi University, and Charles Wilcox, Academic Systems Analyst at Adelphi University, made it possible for us to present the major features of Fortran 77 using a PRIME 850 computer.

Melchiore LaSala of Queensborough Community College provided encouragement and support. Ms. Beverly Rosendorf helped to shape the manuscript by making many valuable suggestions.

A Special Word of Thanks to . . .

Our editor, Joan Cipriano. Joan's confidence and energies helped to make this book a reality.

Contents

Introduction

Fortran (<u>For</u>mula <u>Tran</u>slation) was first introduced by IBM in the late 1950s. With the availability of "newer" programming languages such as PL/1 and Pascal, why study Fortran? The main reason is that no other high-level language is as powerful and versatile in handling computationally based problems, yet as easy to learn. From a computer's standpoint, Fortran is an efficient language. A Fortran compiler (the program that translates your Fortran program into the computer's own native machine language) is small compared to some other compilers, such as those for Cobol and PL/1; additionally, Fortran programs execute rapidly. Fortran offers a wide variety of built-in mathematical functions that may be referenced in a program. The availability of specialized mathematical and statistical Fortran library programs that can be "plugged" into the programs you write is another compelling advantage of the language.

As a result of Fortran's long history, and of some weaknesses in the original version, Fortran has experienced a number of significant revisions. In 1966 the American National Standards Institute (ANSI) issued a standardized version of Fortran that came to be known as Fortran IV. Recognizing certain limitations of the ANSI Fortran standard, the University of Waterloo in Ontario developed a student-oriented version of Fortran called WATFOR (<u>Wat</u>erloo <u>For</u>tran). WATFIV, an enhanced version of WATFOR, remains a very popular Fortran dialect that is used in many college-level Fortran programming courses.

The most recent standardized version of Fortran was defined by ANSI in 1977 and is referred to as Fortran 77. The Fortran 77 standard clarified some ambiguities contained in the 1966 implementation while adopting many of the language extensions introduced by WATFOR and WATFIV. Programs written in Fortran IV will generally run with little or no modification on systems based on Fortran 77. The converse is not necessarily true, however; not all programs that run successfully on Fortran 77 systems will execute on computers that use the earlier standard. Fortran 77 is better suited than Fortran IV for use in an interactive (terminal-oriented) environment. The Fortran versions available with some desktop computers tend to be a subset of the Fortran 77 standard.

The designers of Fortran 77 have introduced features to make the language more compatible with accepted principles of sound program design and construction that have come to be known as structured programming. Improved capabilities in manipulating nonnumeric data, as well as in processing external files maintained on secondary storage media such as magnetic tape and disk, also distinguish Fortran 77 from its earlier Fortran relatives.

Because of the additional features offered by Fortran 77 and the continued popularity of WATFIV on college campuses, the presentation in this book gives ample consideration to each of these Fortran implementations.

Preface

You as reader and we as authors have a major goal in common: that you learn how to write original Fortran programs. In preparing this book we did not assume that you have any previous knowledge of computers or of programming, or of any mathematics beyond high school algebra. Our goal was to produce a book that would make Fortran accessible to all individuals regardless of their computer or mathematics backgrounds. Much of our energy has been devoted to illustrating how to compose original Fortran programs. This book should therefore prove attractive to you whether you are studying the subject on your own, or are enrolled in an introductory course in Fortran on either the high school or the college level.

Although the major features of Fortran are discussed and illustrated, the book is not intended to serve as a language reference manual. Instead, you will find clear and thorough explanations, supported by a wide variety of illustrative material and sample programs. Practice exercises and examples have been interspersed throughout the development of each chapter. These will provide you with an opportunity to test your understanding of the concepts presented before continuing further. Each chapter concludes with a generous supply of review exercises. Sample program solutions for selected exercises will be found at the back of the book.

Throughout the presentation, particular attention has been given to fundamental computer and programming concepts that are independent of the grammatical requirements of the Fortran language. Chapter 1, for example, provides an overview of basic concepts related to computer hardware and organization and introduces some aspects of problem solving and structured programming. An ongoing theme of our development of Fortran is that programs should be easy to read and change, and that steps can be taken to increase the reliability of a program. Keeping these principles in mind will not only be helpful in your work with Fortran, but will also stand you in good stead when studying other computer languages.

This book is based on the most widely used features of Fortran 77 and WATFIV. Throughout the presentation, differences between Fortran IV, WATFIV, and Fortran 77 are noted so that the book may be used to advantage regardless of the version of Fortran that is available with your computer system. These differences have been collected and summarized in an appendix conveniently located at the back of the book. Since each version of Fortran as implemented on a particular computer system will vary somewhat from other Fortrans in its features and the language extensions it offers, you should use this book in conjunction with the language reference manual that accompanies your Fortran computer system.

LAWRENCE S. LEFF
ARLENE D. PODOS

August 1984

CHAPTER 1

Computer Fundamentals

COMPUTER AXIOM

If you want a computer to do something, you must tell it not only *what* must be done, but also *how* it is to be done.

COROLLARY

Once you tell a computer to do something, the computer will do it regardless of whether the action makes sense.

1.1 What Is a Computer Program?

How would a chef communicate, to a person who has never baked before, the procedure for preparing a cheesecake? The recipe that might be given is similar in concept to a computer program. A computer program consists of a step-by-step list of instructions that is designed to achieve a goal. Providing a person who understands only French with a list of instructions written in Russian will accomplish little. Similarly, the list of instructions that make up a computer program must be expressed in a language that the computer can understand.

A *computer program* is a step-by-step list of instructions written in a language that a computer can understand and designed to achieve a specific goal.

The instructions contained in a computer program must be written in a language common to the human programmer and the machine. It is extremely difficult for a person to learn the computer's "native" language, appropriately referred to as *machine language*. It is even more difficult for the computer to be taught a natural language such as English. We must, therefore, seek a compromise. Whereas a natural language such as English has rules like "*i* before *e* EXCEPT after *c* . . . and EXCEPT in words like *weird* and *foreign* . . . ," unambiguous computer languages with no grammatical exceptions have been developed that are part symbolic and part English-like. Some computer languages resemble English more than others. Cobol, for instance, is a business-oriented language having a sentence and paragraph structure that uses a large assortment of reserved English words to designate specific operations. Fortran, on the other hand, is concise and algebra-like in appearance, making it particularly useful in mathematical, engineering, and scientific applications.

Computer programs, regardless of the language they are written in, represent the *software* component of a computer system. All the "nuts and bolts" equipment that is associated with a computer (for example, the wires, electronic circuits, and mechanical devices) is referred to as the *hardware* component of a computer system. Software provides the instructions necessary to direct the operation of the hardware toward the achievement of some goal.

Our primary concern in our development of Fortran will be to learn to write meaningful Fortran programs that will permit us to use the computer as a problem solving tool. Additionally, we shall stress good programming habits that are transferable to the study of other programming languages. Our formal study of Fortran begins in Chapter 2. The present chapter will explore some fundamental computer hardware and software concepts.

To facilitate the discussion that follows, some preliminary terms are defined in Table 1.1.

Table 1.1 Some Computer Terms

character:	A letter (A–Z); digit (0–9); punctuation mark; special symbol ($, *, /, etc.); a single blank space.
data:	Any collection of facts and numbers.
operation:	A specific task, such as an *arithmetic operation* (for example, addition, subtraction, multiplication, division); a *comparison operation*, in which two data values are compared and the first is determined to be less than, equal to, or greater than the second data value; a *copy operation*, in which a value appearing in one location is duplicated so that it appears also in a second location.
processing:	The manipulation of data in a purposeful way that typically involves combinations of the operations listed previously.
instruction:	An unambiguous command that specifies the type of operation to be performed and the data involved in the operation. "Add data value X to data value Y and call the result SUM" is an example of an instruction. The terms *instruction* and *statement* are used interchangeably.
coding:	The representation of instructions in a particular programming language. The instruction given above would be coded in Fortran as follows: $$SUM = X + Y$$
execute:	To carry out an instruction or a set of instructions.

1.2 What Can a Computer Do?

Is a computer faster than a speeding bullet? Yes. Is a computer capable of performing more work, in the same amount of time, than the people working in a tall office building? Yes. Can a computer *think*? There is much about the architecture of a computer system that invites comparison with the human brain. Both respond to stimuli, called *input*; both can remember instructions and data by storing them in *memory* centers; both can *process* stored data by performing calculations and by making logical comparisons; both are equipped to communicate or *output* information. In short, both the human mind and the computer are information processors, capable of performing the four basic functions characteristic of all data processing systems: *input, processing, storage,* and *output*. Computers, however, are capable of learning and performing only by using rote methods, being inflexibly directed by a set of program instructions that must be stored in memory before processing can begin. The program, of course, must be developed by a person.

THINKING VERSUS FOLLOWING INSTRUCTIONS

In order to assemble a model airplane or a "knocked down" piece of furniture, the accompanying list of directions must be strictly followed. Such a list of directions is an example of an algorithm.

An *algorithm* is a straightforward, "recipe" method for solving a particular type of problem. Stated more formally, an algorithm is a set of procedures and operations, organized in the sequence in which they are to be performed, that will produce a solution to a given problem in a specific number of steps. Algorithms can be devised for baking a cake, for explaining how to travel to a friend's house, and for solving an algebraic equation, to name just a few possibilities.

Is there an algorithm for winning at chess? No, since an algorithm cannot be stated before the chess match begins that will always guarantee that a given player will win. One may, however, develop general strategies that will increase the chances of success. This type of approach is characterized by "educated" guessing performed in some systematic fashion and is referred to as *heuristics*. Algorithmic and heuristic approaches may be considered to be opposites. Algorithms are specified in advance and clearly define the steps necessary to reach a solution to a given problem. In a heuristic approach, the exact method of solution is not known at the outset; only a general approach is known that may be improved upon or replaced by another method as the solution process progresses. Using an appropriate algorithm to solve a problem guarantees that a solution will be found eventually. The use of heuristics offers no such assurances; a heuristic approach may or may not ultimately prove successful.

People are capable of devising and following both algorithmic and heuristic approaches; the latter we tend to associate with "creative thinking," problem solving, and the ability to make leaps in drawing logical inferences. Computers, on the other hand, must follow instructions in robot-like fashion; that is, in order to "solve" a problem, the computer must be provided, in advance, with the precise method for solving it. A *computer program* is used to instruct a computer in not only what must be done, but also how the task is to be accomplished. The computer program used to "solve" a problem or perform a processing task must specify the algorithm to be followed that will lead to the desired result.

Where does an algorithm that solves a particular problem come from? The programmer, of course. The algorithm may consist of an obvious sequence of procedures; it may be a modification of a familiar algorithm that has been previously developed; or it may have to be invented by you as the programmer. Sometimes there is more than one algorithm that leads to a solution to a problem. When this occurs, you should try to select the one that is the most straightforward. Once the algorithm is specified, it must be coded into an appropriate computer language such as Fortran. You should keep in mind that there are some problems for which algorithmic solutions do not exist. Heuristic approaches may be appropriate in these instances. Consideration of such problems, however, is beyond the scope of this presentation.

Let's illustrate some of the concepts presented above by considering a specific problem. Suppose that the problem is to solve the equation

$$3z + 2 = 14$$

A *heuristic* approach to solving this problem may take the form of the following trial and error process:

$$
\begin{aligned}
&\text{try } z = 1: && 3 \cdot 1 + 2 \neq 14. \\
&\text{try } z = 2: && 3 \cdot 2 + 2 \neq 14. \\
&\text{try } z = 3: && 3 \cdot 3 + 2 \neq 14. \\
&\text{try } z = 4: && 3 \cdot 4 + 2 = 14. \quad \text{Success, } z = 4!
\end{aligned}
$$

This problem can also be solved by using an algorithm taught in elementary algebra classes.

Step 1. Subtract 2 from each side of the equation:

$$3z + 2 - 2 = 14 - 2$$
or
$$3z = 12$$

Step 2. Divide each side of the equation by 3:

$$\frac{3z}{3} = \frac{12}{3}$$
or
$$z = 4$$

In designing a computer solution to this problem, an *algorithmic* approach would be used. It would be inefficient to design a program that works only for the *particular* equation $3z + 2 = 14$. Instead, the preceding algorithm can be modified so that it solves the entire family of equations which take the form $Az + B = C$. The desired algorithm must allow for different values for A, B, and C (in our example, $A = 3$, $B = 2$, and $C = 14$) to be supplied, and then must determine and print the corresponding value of z. The following algorithm is based on the fact that

$$z = \frac{C - B}{A} \quad \text{(provided that A is not equal to zero)}$$

Step 1. Enter three values; assign the first value to A, the second value to B, and the third value to C.

Step 2. Calculate $C - B$.

Step 3. Divide the result obtained in Step 2 by the current value of A.

Step 4. Print the result obtained in Step 3.

For given values of A, B, and C ($A \neq 0$), this algorithm allows *any* equation of the form $Az + B = C$ to be solved. It is also in a form that can be easily translated into an actual computer language. In addition, the algorithm can be refined to enable the computer to solve a series of equations having this form. Every computer language has a program statement that corresponds to Step 5:

Step 5. Go back to Step 1.

Much productive research is currently being performed in the area of artificial intelligence, a branch of computer science that is concerned with how computers can be programmed to imitate human intelligence. Artificial intelligence seeks to go beyond a computer's usefulness in implementing a straightforward algorithmic solution to a problem. Researchers in artificial intelligence are engaged in trying to enable a computer to:

- translate from one natural language (for example, French) into another natural language (for example, Italian)
- understand a commonly used language such as English
- learn from its past experiences
- apply heuristic strategies and logical patterns of thought to solving problems for which an algorithm is not provided or does not exist

WHY ARE COMPUTERS USED?

If computers are not capable of "thinking," why do we depend so heavily on them? The answer is that computers are faster, more reliable, and more accurate than any individual person or group of people. Whereas the efforts of people are prone to careless (that is, "human") errors, computers process information with uncompromising accuracy. In general, computers do not make mistakes; they merely follow instructions. The speed of computers has greatly reduced the amount of time needed to accomplish tasks. As an example, computers have made space exploration a reality. The calculations necessary to design, launch, and monitor the flight of a spacecraft would take one or more lifetimes if performed manually.

Computers are also used as electronic librarians, capable of storing vast amounts of information and then selectively retrieving a particular item in a fraction of a second. This ability of computers allows a business organization to stay on top of the piles and piles of information and statistics that it accumulates and uses in conducting its daily affairs. Our increasingly cashless society is made possible by computers. Computers permit an individual's credit account to be kept current so that it is possible to walk into a store and complete a credit purchase in a matter of minutes, including the time required for the store clerk to receive authorization from the credit card company. As many of us know only too well, the computer is also relentlessly persistent in sending out bills.

Interestingly, computers are often used to perform relatively simple processing tasks, but are asked to repeat them (that is, repeat the corresponding set of program instructions) a great number of times. Since computers are incapable of becoming bored or distracted, and are extremely fast, they are ideally suited to performing repetitive types of jobs. For example, the calculations involved in producing a payroll are relatively simple. Although the number of employees may be very large, the *method* of calculation for all workers is the same. What may vary is the number of hours worked, the hourly wage, and the number of dependents. When a computer processes a payroll, therefore, it performs the same set of relatively simple operations, but must repeat them for each employee according to the data supplied for each individual worker.

1.3 The Nature of a Computer

A computer *system* includes three major types of components: an input device, the computer, and an output device. An input device sends previously prepared program instructions and data to the computer. The computer operates on the data by following the supplied list of program instructions. When the computer encounters an instruction that commands it to show its work to the outside world, it transmits the appropriate information to an output device. In smaller computer systems (for example, some microcomputer systems), the input and output devices (abbreviated as I/O devices) may be housed in the same box as the computer. A typewriter-like keyboard would represent an input device, while a television-like (CRT) display screen would represent an output device. In larger computer systems, I/O devices are usually separated physically from the computer but attached to it by special cables. Larger computer systems generally have several different input and output devices attached to the computer.

The computer itself (that is, the computer minus any I/O devices) is sometimes referred to as the computer *mainframe*. A mainframe consists of two distinct units: a *main memory unit* and a *central processing unit* (CPU). Picture a college professor of mathematics solving a problem on the chalkboard in a classroom. The classroom would be analogous to the computer mainframe box; the chalkboard that temporarily stores information may be likened to the memory unit; the professor, who during the problem solving process controls the temporary storage and use of information on the chalkboard and who eventually produces an answer, corresponds to the CPU.

Throughout program execution, the memory section does not perform any processing functions. It passively stores instructions and data that are needed during processing. It is the CPU that takes charge. The CPU interprets the stored program of instructions and performs the required data manipulations. In addition, the CPU coordinates all I/O operations, making certain each device connected to the computer works in harmony with the other components so that the individual devices function smoothly as an integrated system. See Figure 1.1.

The CPU itself has two different sections: a *control unit* and an *arithmetic logic unit* (ALU). The control unit manages the execution of the program. It fetches from the memory unit each stored program instruction and interprets the instruction. The complex flow of data within the computer is coordinated by the control unit in much the same way that a traffic officer directs automobile and pedestrian traffic at a busy intersection.

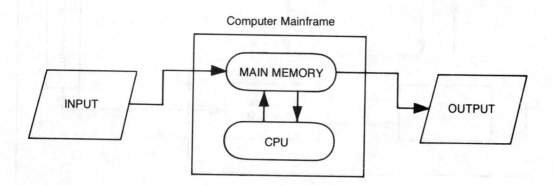

Figure 1.1 Basic Components of a Computer System. Note that, before data and program instructions can be operated on by the CPU, they must be stored in memory. Any information that is to be routed to an output device must be present in memory.

Neither main memory nor the control unit is capable of performing processing tasks such as arithmetic operations. The control unit delegates these chores to the ALU. All arithmetic calculations and logical comparisons are performed by the ALU, which, under the supervision of the control unit,

- fetches data from main memory
- performs the necessary data manipulations in temporary work-storage locations called *registers*
- transmits the results from the registers to main memory, where the results are stored until they are needed for another processing operation or until an output operation is performed

The relationships among the various units are illustrated in Figure 1.2.

So far, the computer may not seem much different from a hand-held calculator. A calculator has an input device in the form of its keyboard. The LED display screen or paper output tape serves as an output device. Most calculators not only can perform arithmetic operations but also, like a computer, are able to "remember" a data value. A "Memory" key on the calculator permits the user to temporarily store a data value and then to recall it when needed. A computer, however, differs from a calculator in several important respects:

- In order to effect each individual operation on the calculator, an appropriate set of keys must be pressed. To repeat the process, the same sequence of keys must again be pressed by the user. A computer, however, has the ability to internally store a list of program instructions and then to *direct its own operation* by implementing each stored instruction, thereby eliminating the need for human intervention. As long as the program remains stored in memory, it may be repeatedly executed by the computer (CPU) at electronic speeds.
- A computer has the ability to compare two data values and, based on the results of the comparison, to execute a specified instruction or group of instructions found within the stored program of instructions. It is this capability that gives computers their "decision-making" ability.
- The speed of a computer also distinguishes it from other types of calculating devices. A large modern computer, for example, is capable of performing more

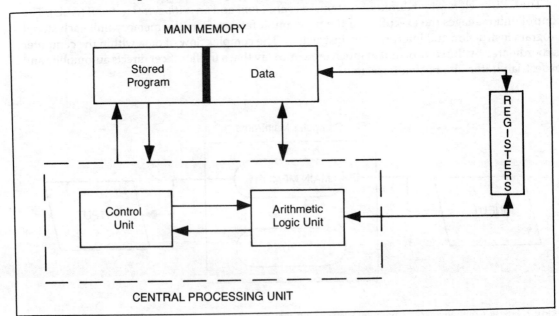

Figure 1.2 The "Computer." Input and output devices would be attached to the computer, forming a computer *system*.

than 10 million arithmetic operations per second and can execute several million instructions per second. The most powerful computers have operating speeds that are measured in terms of *nanoseconds* (billionths of a second) and are capable of executing as many as 200 million instructions per second.

1.4 Input and Output Devices

If one were to "knock-down" a computer and examine what's inside, one would find a bunch of wires, electronic circuit boards, various solid state (transistor) devices, and other such related electronic parts. It seems reasonable that, if a computer is to "understand" program instructions and data, these must first be converted into an electronic form. We have just described the major function of an *input device:* to capture data from an input *medium* and then reduce them to electronic impulses that are suitable for computer consumption. The distinction between device and medium is an important one. A *medium* on which music and songs are recorded, for example, is the familiar platter-like, long-playing vinyl record disk; the *device* that plays the record (interprets the information encoded on the record grooves) is the phonograph stylus/player.

In preparing a computer program, a programmer may write it on an ordinary piece of paper. The coded program, however, must then be prepared for computer input using a suitable medium. If a typewriter-like data entry device is being used, all that need be done is to type the instructions and data using a prescribed format. If a punch card system is being used, each program language instruction must be typed onto an IBM punch card, which serves as the input medium. The cards containing the program are then "read" by a card reader, which represents the input device.

Generally speaking, output devices serve two major functions:

1. They represent computer output in a human-readable form. A CRT display monitor and a printer that writes output on a paper medium are examples of output devices that accomplish this function. The printer produces *hard* copy output (paper), while the CRT screen offers *soft* copy.
2. They store information externally in a machine-readable form so that it may be used as computer input at some later time. Magnetic tape and magnetic disks are routinely used for this purpose. A payroll program, for example, may be stored on tape until it is needed for producing a payroll during the next payroll period. When the program is needed, the tape is read and a copy of the program is transmitted into the main memory of the computer.

TIME-SHARING VERSUS BATCH PROCESSING

Any I/O device that is part of a computer system so that it is able to communicate directly with the CPU is said to be *online*. A *terminal* is an I/O device that is capable of both sending and receiving data from a computer. A device that has a keyboard for data entry and an attached CRT display screen to show output is probably the most familiar type of terminal.

You will probably be submitting your program to the computer in either a *time-sharing* or a *batch processing mode.* In a batch processing system, the computer installation will accumulate jobs and execute them at the convenience of the installation. Typically, jobs submitted in a batch processing environment are stacked and grouped by type of job or by priority level ("importance"). At established time intervals, the jobs that have been piling up are executed. Although sometimes inconvenient from the user's point of view (you may have to wait a significant amount of time until your job is processed), batch processing may increase the efficiency of the computer installation. Changes to be made to an employee payroll file, for example, are usually accumulated and processed as a batch.

In a time-sharing system, users are serviced on a "first come, first served" basis. Time-sharing is characterized by having a number of different online terminal users share the resources of the same computer during the same interval of time. The computer services each online user in "round-robin" fashion by allocating to each user an equal "slice" of CPU time. If a particular job does not execute completely during its allotted time, its execution is suspended and then resumed after the CPU has turned its attention to each of the remaining users. Although the computer may be working on a number of different jobs, the speed of the computer makes it appear that the computer is dedicated to doing the work for a particular user.

Historically, batch processing systems were based on the use of punch cards. Today, CRT terminals may be used to submit to a computer a job that will be executed in either a batch processing or a time-sharing mode. *Turnaround* time (the time that elapses from submission of a job to receipt of computer output) is greater in batch processing systems. Time-sharing systems offer turnaround times that are typically measured in seconds (or minutes), while jobs submitted in a batch processing environment may have turnaround times of several hours or even a full workday. Actual times, of course, will vary considerably from installation to installation.

SECONDARY STORAGE

Although a person may have a very good memory, there is a limit to how much information he or she can accurately recall. Therefore people often rely on external media such as paper or books to store information that is not currently needed or is of such great volume that it exceeds the memory capacity of the brain. Because of economic and other practical considerations, the main memory unit of a computer is also limited in its storage capacity. For this reason a computer requires access to an auxiliary or secondary storage device that supplements the storage capacity of main memory. Magnetic tape and magnetic disk drive units are two of the most widely used secondary storage devices.

A tape drive unit is similar in appearance and operation to the familiar reel-to-reel tape recorder/player used to record and play music in the homes of many hi-fi enthusiasts. A phonograph turntable is roughly analogous to a disk drive. Each has provision for a platter-like disk to be placed on a rotating spindle. As the disk rotates, a mechanism attached to an "arm" reads information that has been previously encoded on the surface of the disk. A phonograph arm uses a stylus/cartridge assembly, while a disk drive arm is equipped with a "read/write" head that permits data to be either read from the disk surface or "written to" (that is, recorded on) the disk. Both tape and disk have a surface coating that allows data to be represented as patterns of magnetized spots.

Secondary storage devices such as tape and disk drives serve two major functions:

1. They provide for the *temporary* storage of data that may be needed during a current processing operation.
2. They provide for the *permanent* storage of data that may be required in a future processing operation. Because of their enormous storage capacities, secondary storage devices are sometimes referred to as *mass storage devices.*

Although tape and disk drives are referred to as secondary (auxiliary) storage devices, they are also considered to be input/output devices. Data and programs may be copied ("read") from a tape or disk and loaded into main memory. Information residing in main memory may be transmitted to and saved on ("written to") a secondary storage medium.

A larger computer system will typically have a variety of input and output devices attached to it, including:

- one or more punch card readers
- several online terminals, which the central computer "hosts"
- one or more high-speed printers for hard paper copy
- a device that can read OCR (optical character recognition) documents
- several tape drive units
- an array of disk drives

In addition, other types of secondary storage devices are in use, including the magnetic drum and the mass storage (cartridge tape) device. Some computer systems also include provision for producing COM (computer output microfilm). The banking industry depends heavily on MICR (magnetic ink character recognition) document readers.

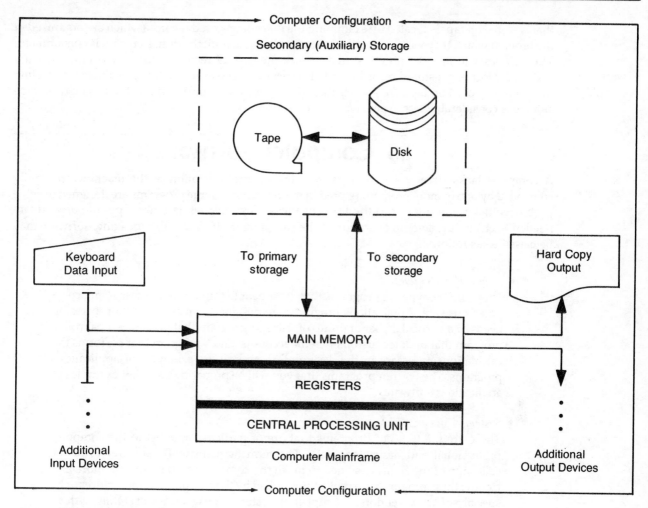

Figure 1.3 A Schematic of a Computer Configuration. Secondary storage devices may receive or transmit data and program instructions from or to the computer's main memory. A secondary storage device typically offers from 10 to over 100 times the storage capacity of main memory. Secondary storage devices offer lower cost per unit of stored data than does main memory. Main memory, however, offers faster data *access* times. In other words, data and program instructions stored in main memory can be located by the CPU much more rapidly than information stored on a tape or disk.

A computer mainframe and its externally connected devices (called computer *peripherals*) are referred to collectively as a *computer configuration*. Computer configurations tend to reflect the needs of the particular organizations that are being serviced and will generally vary from one computer installation to another. See Figure 1.3.

DIRECT VERSUS SEQUENTIAL ACCESS

The design of a disk drive allows information to be stored and then retrieved from any spot on the disk platter. To help visualize this concept, imagine playing an ordinary record disk. It is possible to play any song on the record disk by lifting the phonograph arm and positioning it on the desired groove or track. For example, it is not necessary to listen to the first two songs on a long-playing record disk in order to locate and play the third song. This ability to reach a particular song without examining the songs that come before it is referred to as *direct* or *random accessing*. Information stored on disk can be directly (or randomly) accessed. The main memory of a computer, which is usually based on semiconductor technology, also permits stored data items to be located directly (see also Section 2.1 of Chapter 2).

Since tape travels in one direction during an input or output operation, information must be stored and retrieved following a sequential order. A particular unit of information (called a *record*) that is stored on tape is located by examining the preceding stored records (which are organized in the order in which they were originally written to the tape) until the desired record is encountered. Thus, in order to find the fiftieth stored record, the first 49 records must be examined. Such a system for locating a stored record is called *sequential access.* Although access times for locating information stored on tape are greater than those for finding information stored on a disk, tape storage is considerably less expensive than disk memory.

1.5 Computer Software

A computer lacks "free will." All aspects of the internal operation of the machine are rigidly controlled by one or more programs stored in main memory. Some programs are designed to solve problems that are of interest to the users of these programs, while other types of software are needed to ensure the smooth operation of the computer itself. Generally speaking, software may be classified as follows:

- *Applications Software*
  These are the types of programs that most people think of when discussing computer software. Applications programs are designed to meet the data processing needs of a particular user or group of users. A program that processes a payroll, a program that updates customer credit accounts, and a program that performs the calculations necessary in the design of an aircraft are examples of applications programs. The Fortran programs that you will be preparing are other examples of applications software.

- *Systems Software*
  These are the types of programs that are of particular interest to the computer professional and design engineer. The term "systems software" refers to the collection of programs designed to make the computer system operate more efficiently; these programs are typically supplied by the computer manufacturer or by special software vendors. Examples of systems software are *operating systems programs.* Operating systems software are indispensable to the operation of a computer and are found in personal microcomputers as well as in large multimillion-dollar computer systems. Operating systems software have the overall responsibility of supervising and coordinating the internal activities of the computer while allocating and managing the computer's resources (for example, disk drives, tape devices, and printers).

- *Language Translators*
  Language translators are *programs* which serve a function similar to that of a foreign language interpreter at the United Nations. Without the presence of a translator, Basic, Fortran, and Cobol are just as foreign to the computer as English, French, and Italian. A computer understands only one language—its own internal machine language code, which varies from one machine to the next. A special computer program is used that converts the original program, which is written in a user-oriented programming language (called the SOURCE program), into the equivalent machine language code (called the OBJECT program). The language translation process is an internal machine activity, with each source language requiring its own special language translator program, called a *compiler.* Figure 1.4 shows the compilation process in which a Fortran source program is being translated into an equivalent machine language program before it can be executed. (In most computer systems the machine language object program must be processed by another program, either a program loader or linkage-editor, which establishes the final address in main memory that the program will have when it is executed.)

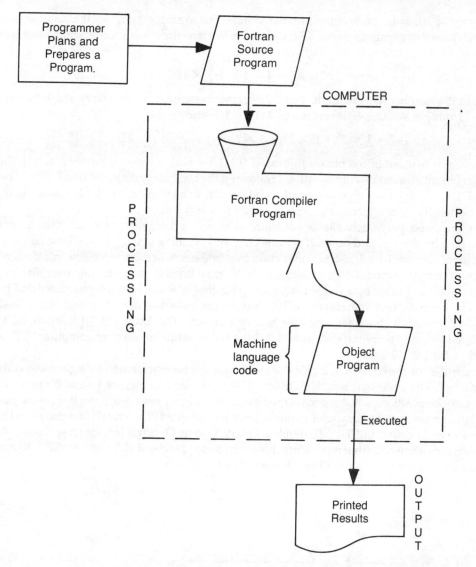

Figure 1.4 The Compilation Process. The Fortran compiler is usually stored on a disk and brought into main memory only when needed. The object program usually must be processed by another program (linkage-editor or program loader) before it can be executed.

1.6 Internal Data Representation and Memory

How does a computer recognize the difference between a pair of numbers such as 89 and 98, or between the letters "X" and "Y"? A computer is, after all, merely an integrated collection of electronic circuits held together by wires and circuit boards. These electronic components must, in some fashion, represent and store data.

Electronic circuit components are two-state devices in the same sense that a light bulb is a two-state device: it is either ON or OFF; current flows or current does *not* flow. It seems reasonable that computers must use sequences of ON and OFF circuits to represent data. Unfortunately, the number system that we are most familiar with, the decimal system, is not consistent with the two-state nature of electronic circuits. The decimal number system uses *ten* distinct digits (0, 1, 2, . . . , 9) to represent numeric values. There is, however, a number system that parallels the two-state operating condition of electronic circuits.

This number system, called the *binary* number system, is based on *two* digits, 0 and 1; no other digits are permitted. With this scheme, numbers are expressed in terms of powers of 2 rather than as powers of 10, as in the decimal number system. For example, consider the number 47. In the decimal (base-10) number system, 47 may be expressed as the sum of descending powers of 10 as follows:

$$47 = \underline{4} \times 10^1 + \underline{7} \times 10^0$$

Thus, in the number 47, the digits 4 and 7 represent coefficients of powers of 10. In the binary (base-2) number system, 47 is written as 1 0 1 1 1 1 since

$$47 = \underline{1} \times 2^5 + \underline{0} \times 2^4 + \underline{1} \times 2^3 + \underline{1} \times 2^2 + \underline{1} \times 2^1 + \underline{1} \times 2^0$$

To prevent confusion of the binary number 1 0 1 1 1 1 with a decimal number having the same digits, a binary number is written with a 2 following the last binary digit and one-half line below it: $1\ 0\ 1\ 1\ 1\ 1_2$. Each binary digit, a 0 or a 1, is referred to as a *bit*. All data that are stored in memory must ultimately be represented as strings of bits (0's and 1's).

We indicated previously that a program written in a language such as Fortran cannot be understood by the computer until it is translated into machine language. Machine language is an all-numeric, binary-based instructional code that is determined by the electronic design of the particular computer model. In translating an individual English character into machine language, the computer is guided by a translation code table that is internal to the computer and is determined by the computer manufacturer. This translation table uses one of several established codes that assign to each character a unique binary number. The letter "H," for example, may be translated by one computer system as 1 1 0 0 1 0 0 0, while in another computer "H" may be coded as 1 0 1 0 1 0 0 0.

Regardless of the computer, a character will typically be represented by eight consecutive bits, called a *byte*. Thus, one byte equals eight bits. The particular sequence of 1's and 0's that will fill up these eight bit positions will depend on the character being represented, as well as on the particular translation code that the computer manufacturer has adopted. The translation code used by IBM, for example, is called EBCDIC (Extended Binary Coded Decimal Interchange Code). Another popular translation code that represents characters as sequences of eight bits is ASCII-8 (American Standard Code for Information Interchange). See Figure 1.5.

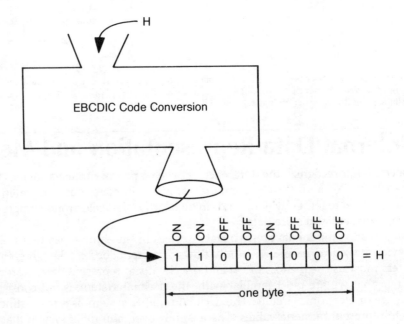

Figure 1.5 Converting the Letter "H" Using EBCDIC. Each bit position of the byte representation of H corresponds to an electronic component that is either ON or OFF. Since a byte typically represents a single character, it is common to find these terms used interchangeably.

MEMORY CAPACITY

The memory capacity of a computer is usually expressed in terms of the number of characters it can store. The unit of measurement that is commonly used is one kilobyte of 1Kbytes, where "1K bytes" equals "1,000 bytes" of storage. Actually, 1K = 1,024 bytes, where 1,024 is the power of 2 (2^{10}) that is closest to 1,000. A computer with a stated memory capacity of 512K is capable of storing 512 × 1,024 bytes = 524,288 bytes (characters). At one time, the storage capacity of a computer was a useful criterion in helping to distinguish between different "sizes" of computers. Today, however, many desktop computer systems have main memory capacities and computing powers that were found a decade ago only in large computer systems which occupied a full-sized room.

1.7 The Hierarchy of Computer Languages

There are three levels of computer languages: machine, assembly, and high-level. Machine language is characterized by its all-numeric, binary-based structure and its concern with how the particular computer to be used has been designed to store and manipulate data. In the early days of computers, machine language programming was the only available means for expressing program instructions.

Because machine language programming is cumbersome, time consuming, error prone, and dependent on the particular machine being used, high-level programming languages were developed. Basic, Fortran, Cobol, and Pascal are just a few examples of high-level languages. All high-level languages bear some resemblance to English, do not require any special knowledge of the internal operation of the computer, and vary in their use of mathematical shorthand.

Each high-level language is translated into machine language by its own special compiler. To conserve space in main memory, compilers are typically stored on disk (or diskette) and are called into memory from the disk drive only when needed. Large computer systems typically maintain a variety of compilers.

An assembly level language is very similar to machine language except that it uses mnemonics (meaningful alphabetic abbreviations) to refer to computer operations, instead of a long string of binary numbers. For example, in the IBM System/370 computer the machine language code that instructs the computer to add the contents of two memory work registers is 0 0 0 1 1 0 1 0. In assembly language, this operation would be coded as AR. Assembly language is a "low-level" language since it is "close" to machine language.

MACROINSTRUCTIONS: ONE INTO MANY

In order to calculate the sum of two data values stored in main memory, represented by A and B, the machine or assembly language programmer would typically write a set of coded instructions that would accomplish the following:

1. Copy the value of A from main memory into a work register.
2. Copy the value of B from main memory into another work register.
3. Add the contents of the registers, storing the sum in a register.
4. Move the result to a location in main memory called SUM.

In machine or assembly language, the processing required to add two numbers takes at least four distinct instructions. In Fortran, the single statement SUM = A + B accomplishes the same addition operation. The Fortran compiler then translates the statement into the corresponding set of machine language instructions. A statement such as SUM = A + B is an example of a *macroinstruction* since it generates many machine language instructions. All high-level languages are based on this macroinstruction approach, which leads to a number of significant advantages:

- The programming process is simplified. Fewer program instructions are needed as compared to machine and assembly language. High-level languages can also be made to resemble an English or symbolically oriented language.
- The programmer need not have any special understanding of how the machine works.

- Many high-level languages have been standardized by organizations such as the American National Standards Institute (ANSI), making it possible to write compilers for the major high-level languages that are compatible with different computers. For example, a program written in ANSI Fortran 77 that runs successfully on an IBM mainframe computer will also run successfully with very little or no modification on a CONTROL DATA Cyber computer that has its own ANSI Fortran 77 compiler. (This feature is sometimes referred to as *program portability*.)

HIGH-LEVEL VERSUS ASSEMBLY LANGUAGE

Assembly language is potentially more powerful than any of the high-level languages. An assembly language program is translated into machine language faster and executes more rapidly than a comparable program coded in a high-level language. With a high-level language, the programmer is confined to the features defined by the instruction set offered by the particular compiler being used. Since each assembly language instruction typically generates a single machine language instruction, the assembly language programmer can take full advantage of all of the computer's capabilities.

On the negative side, programming in assembly language is difficult to learn, extremely tedious, time consuming, and prone to error. Programs written in assembly language are difficult and costly to modify and are not portable, being machine dependent. As a result, high-level programming languages are generally applied to solving user problems (that is, developing applications programs), while assembly-level languages are used to help control and monitor machine operations (that is, developing systems software).

1.8 Representing Numbers and Data Precision

In storing numbers in memory, computers distinguish between *integer* values and *real* (also called *floating-point*) values. An integer is a whole number that can be either negative, positive, or zero: -3, 234, and 0 are examples of integer values. A real value has a decimal or fractional part and is written with a decimal point: -2.03, 98.6, and 57.0 are examples of real values. The real value 57.0 may be equivalently expressed as 57., where the trailing zero has been deleted but the decimal point retained.

COMMON ERRORS TO AVOID

1. Values such as 9 and 9. may *not* be used interchangeably. The value 9 is stored as an integer value, while 9. is internally represented as a real value.
2. Numbers may *not* be written with any explanatory symbols (other than a decimal point):

Incorrect	Correct
6,183	6183
$119.25	119.25
75%	0.75

E-NOTATION

Scientific notation is a compact method for representing very large and very small numbers. In scientific notation a positive number is expressed as a decimal number between 1 and 10 multiplied by a power of 10:

Number	Scientific Notation
1230000.	1.23×10^6
0.00000000706	7.06×10^{-9}

Notice that the exponent (power of 10) represents the number of decimal positions the decimal point must be moved in order to obtain a decimal number between 1 and 10. If the original number is less than 1 (that is, the decimal point must be moved to the *right*), then the exponent will be a negative integer.

Computers display "very large" and "very small" numbers in a form of scientific notation called *E-notation*. In E-notation the power of 10 is written using an E immediately followed by an integer that represents the exponent. For example, 10^{12} would be expressed as $E+12$ (the + sign is optional), while 10^{-7} would be expressed as $E-07$ (the 0 is optional).

Suppose that in a hypothetical computer all numbers less than 0.01 or greater than 999999999 are printed in E-form (the actual limits will depend on the particular computer).

Data Value	Scientific Notation	Value Displayed
1223334444	1.223334444×10^9	1.223334444E+09
0.009807	9.807×10^{-3}	9.807E−03
−0.0000546	-5.46×10^{-5}	−5.46E−05
117.5	—	117.5

DATA PRECISION

Suppose that a computer is asked to calculate 2.0 divided by 3.0. What number would be stored as the quotient?

$$\frac{2.0}{3.0} = 0.666666666 \ldots$$

The three periods indicate that the digit 6 repeats endlessly. All computers, regardless of their size, must impose a limit on the number of significant digits of a number that can be stored in memory. The upper limit varies from machine to machine and is referred to as the data *precision* of a computer.

Computers generally represent integers with greater precision than real values. A medium-precision computer will typically be able to store integer values having a maximum of 10 significant digits and real values having 8 significant digits. Higher and lower levels of precision are not uncommon. Check the appropriate manuals, or ask personnel at the computer installation for information about the precision of the computer that you will be using.

If a precision of 8 significant digits for real values is assumed, how would our hypothetical computer store 0.666666666 . . . ?

.6 6 6 6 6 6 6 6 |6
                ↙
        Ninth
        digit

(*Note:* The leading zero in 0.666666666 . . . is not significant.)

The ninth digit cannot be stored. The computer will delete the 6 in one of two ways: by *truncation* or by *rounding-off.* In truncation, the ninth 6 will simply be chopped off. In rounding-off, since the 6 is 5 or more, the ninth 6 will be deleted but the digit that immediately precedes it will be increased by 1:

.6 6 6 6 6 6 6 ̶6̶
Truncation

.6 6 6 6 6 6 6 ⁷̶6̶
Rounding-off

The following table offers some additional examples of determining the value that can be stored, assuming that the computer operates with a precision of 8 for real values and a precision of 10 for integer values:

	Stored Value	
Number	Truncation	Rounding-off
31999444777	3199944477	3199944478
87103.1694	87103.169	87103.170
0.600413782	.60041378	.60041378
9876543210	9876543210	9876543210

In addition to placing a limit on the number of significant digits a stored value may retain, each computer places an upper and a lower limit on the magnitude of the number that can be stored. In an IBM System/370 computer, for example, the largest integer value that can be stored is 2,147,483,647, and the smallest integer value that can be stored is −2,147,483,648. Any attempt to store a value larger than this maximum value results in an *overflow* error. An *underflow* error results from trying to store a value less than the minimum value. You should check the appropriate manuals to find out what the acceptable limits are on the computer that you will be using.

1.9 The Field-Record-File Concept

On September 23, 1984, Peter Q. Public purchases a pair of men's slacks for $34.95, including sales tax. The sales clerk uses a preprinted sales receipt form to write up the purchase. To make the form easy to process, information must be entered in specified blocks of reserved columns, called FIELDS. See Figure 1.6.

A *field* can be classified by the types of characters it may include. A field that may hold only digits (and blanks) is called a *numeric* field. The amount of sale field (columns 51−56) is an example of a numeric field. An *alphanumeric* field may contain all digits, all letters, all special characters, or any combination of these. The street address field (columns 22−40) is an example of an alphanumeric field.

The maximum number of characters a field may contain is called the *width* of the field. The width of the account no. field is 4 since there is provision for exactly four characters to be entered. Not all fields have the same width. The width of the amount of sale field is 6.

In the customer's first name field (columns 1−10), the first name Peter does not occupy all the column positions in the field. When the width of an alphanumeric field exceeds the number of letters in the data item that will be entered into the field, the first letter must be placed in the *leftmost* column position of the field. This is referred to as *left-justification*. Notice that in the amount of sale field (columns 51−56), the first column is left blank. When entering digits into a numeric field, the last digit of the number must occupy the *rightmost* column position. This is called *right-justification*. Figure 1.7 contrasts right- and left-justification for numeric and alphanumeric data.

All the fields on the sales receipt form describe a single purchase made by the same individual; that is, all fields involve either the item purchased or the individual making the purchase. Since all the fields are related, we may refer to the fields collectively as a RECORD. A *record* is any set of related fields. The day's collection of sales receipt forms would be referred to as a FILE. A *file* is a group of related records.

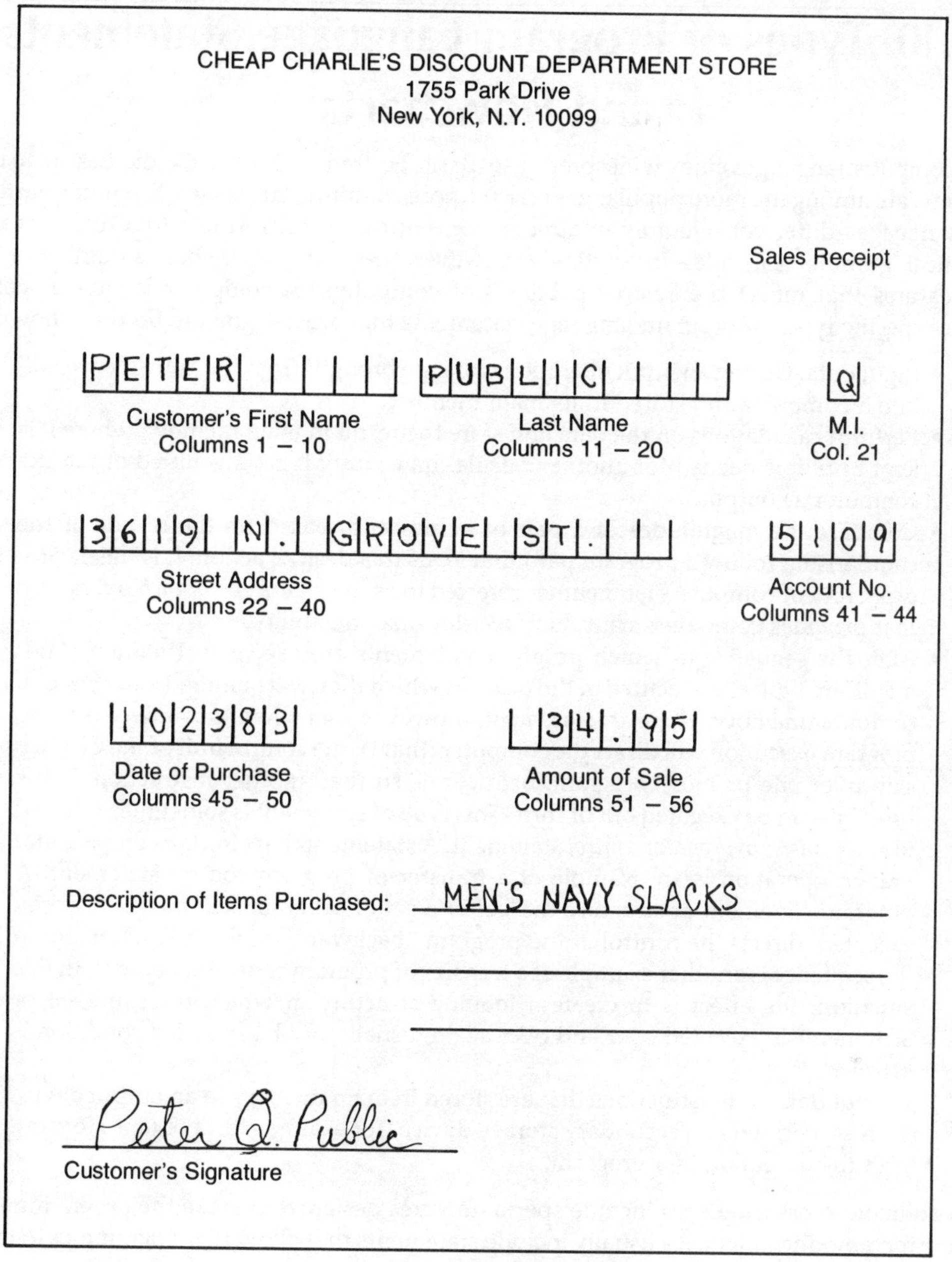

CHEAP CHARLIE'S DISCOUNT DEPARTMENT STORE
1755 Park Drive
New York, N.Y. 10099

Sales Receipt

| P | E | T | E | R | | | | | |

Customer's First Name
Columns 1 – 10

| P | U | B | L | I | C | | | | |

Last Name
Columns 11 – 20

| Q |

M.I.
Col. 21

| 3 | 6 | 1 | 9 | | N | . | | G | R | O | V | E | | S | T | . | | |

Street Address
Columns 22 – 40

| 5 | 1 | 0 | 9 |

Account No.
Columns 41 – 44

| 1 | 0 | 2 | 3 | 8 | 3 |

Date of Purchase
Columns 45 – 50

| 3 | 4 | . | 9 | 5 |

Amount of Sale
Columns 51 – 56

Description of Items Purchased: MEN'S NAVY SLACKS

Peter Q. Public
Customer's Signature

Figure 1.6

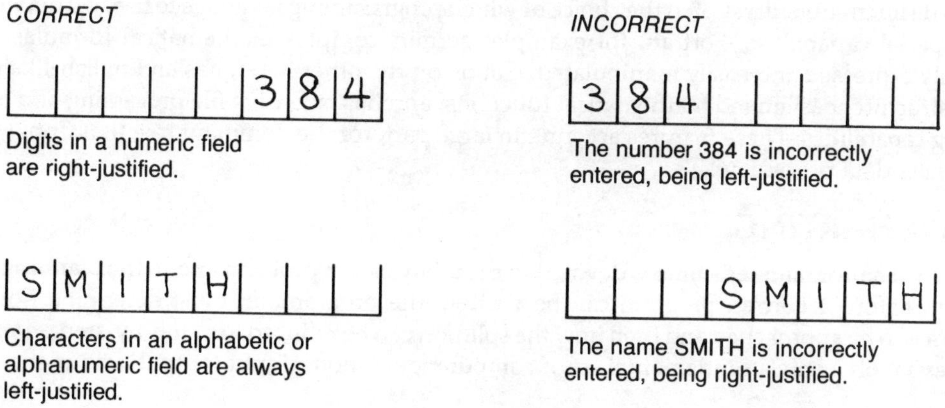

CORRECT

| | | | | | 3 | 8 | 4 |

Digits in a numeric field
are right-justified.

INCORRECT

| 3 | 8 | 4 | | | | | |

The number 384 is incorrectly
entered, being left-justified.

| S | M | I | T | H | | | |

Characters in an alphabetic or
alphanumeric field are always
left-justified.

| | | | S | M | I | T | H |

The name SMITH is incorrectly
entered, being right-justified.

Figure 1.7

1.10 Types of Program Language Statements and Flowcharts

Many computer languages enjoy widespread use. Basic, Fortran, Cobol, PL/1, and Pascal, to name just a few, are among the more popular general-purpose computer languages. Programs written in these languages differ considerably in appearance, with each conforming to a different set of syntactical (grammatical) rules. Interestingly, however, these languages share a number of common features that reflect the basic capabilities of computers. A computer language typically includes specific types of program language statements that are designed to do the following:

- Input data. During an input operation, data are brought from the "outside world" into a computer and stored in its main memory.
- Perform calculations on the data and store the result in main memory, where it is kept until it is needed for another calculation or until it is transmitted out of the computer as output.
- Compare the magnitudes of a pair of values and, based on the results of the comparison, follow a program path that leads to a desired action. It is this logical capability of computers (sometimes referred to as a *compare and branch* operation) that provides computers with their decision-making ability.
- Alter the sequence in which program statements are executed. Program statements are typically executed in the order in which they were entered and stored in computer memory. There are statements, however, that when encountered during program execution will direct the computer (that is, the control unit of the CPU) to skip over one or more program instructions so that another instruction in the program can be executed out of turn. This type of statement is sometimes referred to as a *transfer of program control* statement. A statement that effects a compare and branch operation is an example of a transfer of program control statement. A program statement or structure that, after a set of program statements has been executed, directs the control of the program "backward" to the first statement in the sequence is another example of a transfer of program control statement. In this situation, the effect is to create a looping structure in which the same set of statements is executed over and over again, usually until a specified condition is satisfied.
- Output data and instructions that are stored in main memory to an output device such as a printer or a secondary storage device (for example, disk or tape storage).
- Halt the execution of a program.

In addition, most languages include special features designed to make the programmer's job easier. Programming languages usually include statements that allow the programmer to tackle a complex program by subdividing it into smaller and more manageable component programs. More specialized programming features vary from language to language and help to give each language its own distinctive quality. Often the choice of which programming language to use will depend on these special capabilities. Fortran, for example, permits complex mathematical formulas to be concisely expressed and easily manipulated. Cobol, on the other hand, has an English-like paragraph structure, has limited mathematical functions, and has extensive file processing and report printing capabilities. These features account, in large part, for the dominant role that Cobol plays in business data processing.

FLOWCHARTING

Much of a programmer's time is devoted to the analysis of a problem and to the planning of its solution. Before a Fortran program can be written, the programmer must determine how the problem is to be approached and then how the solution can be reduced to a step-by-step procedure that may involve only a fundamental set of computer operations (input/output, arithmetic, com-

Program Flowchart Symbol	Explanation

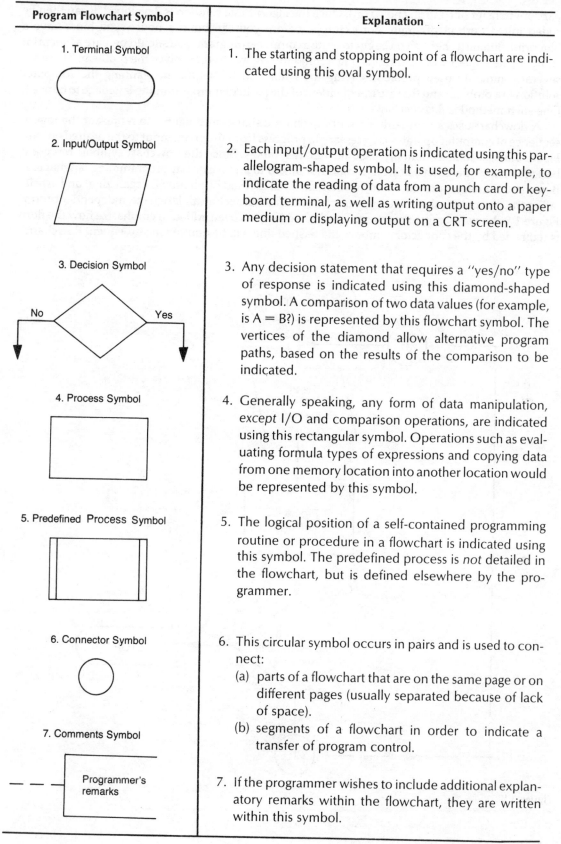	1. The starting and stopping point of a flowchart are indicated using this oval symbol.
	
	2. Each input/output operation is indicated using this parallelogram-shaped symbol. It is used, for example, to indicate the reading of data from a punch card or keyboard terminal, as well as writing output onto a paper medium or displaying output on a CRT screen.
	
	3. Any decision statement that requires a "yes/no" type of response is indicated using this diamond-shaped symbol. A comparison of two data values (for example, is A = B?) is represented by this flowchart symbol. The vertices of the diamond allow alternative program paths, based on the results of the comparison to be indicated.
	
	4. Generally speaking, any form of data manipulation, *except* I/O and comparison operations, are indicated using this rectangular symbol. Operations such as evaluating formula types of expressions and copying data from one memory location into another location would be represented by this symbol.
	
	5. The logical position of a self-contained programming routine or procedure in a flowchart is indicated using this symbol. The predefined process is *not* detailed in the flowchart, but is defined elsewhere by the programmer.
	
	6. This circular symbol occurs in pairs and is used to connect:
	  (a) parts of a flowchart that are on the same page or on different pages (usually separated because of lack of space).
	  (b) segments of a flowchart in order to indicate a transfer of program control.
	
	7. If the programmer wishes to include additional explanatory remarks within the flowchart, they are written within this symbol.

Figure 1.8

parison, transfer of control, and so on). Once the algorithmic solution is developed, it can then be coded into a Fortran program. For example, before you can build a house, you must have a blueprint. Similarly, before you begin to write a computer program, you should prepare a blueprint showing the sequence of operations that defines the algorithm that solves the problem. There are several commonly used problem solving tools that can be helpful in planning the computer solution to a problem and that are independent of the particular programming language to be used. One such method is *flowcharting*.

A flowchart uses a standardized set of geometric shapes and figures to represent the logical sequence of computer operations necessary to progress from the given input to the desired output. Figure 1.8 lists some commonly used flowchart symbols. Since the flowchart symbols represent basic *computer* operations, flowcharting is not linked to any particular programming language. A flowchart, therefore, provides a convenient pictorial method of planning, organizing, and articulating the computer solution to a given problem in a nontechnical, language-independent form. Figure 1.9 shows a sample flowchart. The dashed line has been added to emphasize how the flow is redirected by the connector symbols; the dashed line will be omitted in subsequent flowcharts.

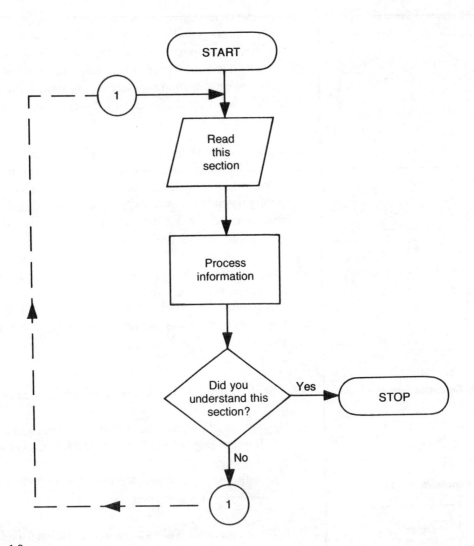

Figure 1.9

Program Documentation and Flowcharting

Program documentation refers to the collection of papers that explains how to use a program, what the program is supposed to accomplish, and proof that the program works. Preparing a *flowchart* serves at least two important functions:

- It encourages a programmer to plan the solution to a program before attempting to write the coded program.
- It provides an important article of program documentation, and is invaluable to a programmer who must change or improve a program that he or she wrote some time in the past or that was authored by another programmer.

Appreciation of flowcharting as a problem solving tool tends to increase as the required program logic becomes more complex. It is recommended that you make it a practice to prepare a flowchart before writing each Fortran program.

EXAMPLE 1.1 Explain the meaning of each of the following segments of a flowchart:

(a)

(b)

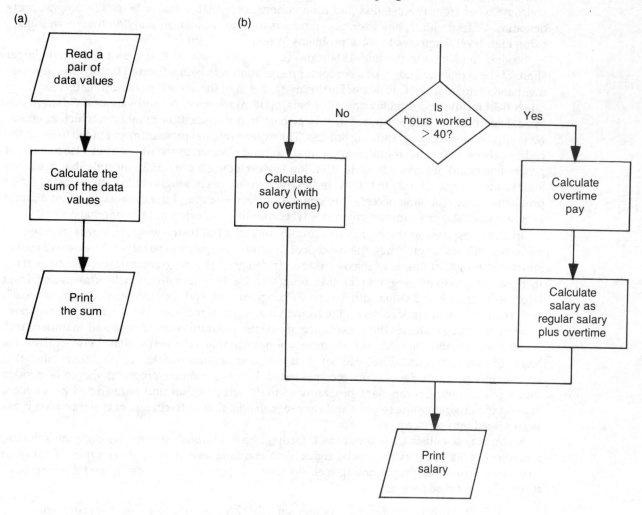

Solutions

(a) The flowchart symbols are executed in linear fashion: two data values, which must be externally supplied, are *inputted* (in a programming context, stored in computer memory); the sum of the two data values is calculated (and the sum is also stored in computer memory); the sum is displayed to the outside world as a result of executing the "Print" box.

(b) The number of HOURS worked is compared to the number 40. If HOURS is greater than (symbol: $>$) 40, then the program path labeled "Yes" is followed. In this example, the overtime pay is calculated and the gross SALARY is calculated next. The value of SALARY is then printed.

If the number of HOURS worked is *not* greater than 40 (that is, the value of HOURS is less than or equal to 40), then the program path labeled "No" is followed. This results in SALARY being computed by a straight-time calculation method (that is, no overtime); the calculated value of SALARY is then printed.

1.11 Structured Programming

In the late 1950s and 1960s programming languages such as Fortran and Cobol were introduced and warmly embraced by the programming community. These high-level languages provided a welcome relief from the detailed and monotonous logic that machine language programming demands. Unfortunately, however, programmers tend to wander off and "do their own thing," using high-level languages to solve problems in their own fashion.

Studies conducted in the mid-1960s and early 1970s revealed that a proportionately larger share of the economic budget of a computer installation was being directed toward the development and maintenance of software. Furthermore, much of the software was unreliable, requiring much field testing and modification after being put into service. A "software crisis" had developed. Experts in the field attributed it, in large part, to the unscientific manner in which programmers approached the programming process. The experts felt that programmers tended to begin the coding process before having adequately analyzed and planned the solution. They also noted that programmers did not give adequate attention to developing a programming style that made the logic of their programs easy to follow. Individual differences in programming style created major problems when it became necessary to change, correct, or expand the capabilities of an existing program since the programmer given this responsibility was often not the original author.

In direct response to these problems and to the lack of industry-wide standards in programming methods and approaches, the concept of *structured programming* evolved. The overall goal of structured programming is to maximize the efficiency of the programming process by placing increased emphasis on program planning, programming style, and program documentation. In an effort to overcome individual differences in programming style, a structured design approach imposes a strict set of guidelines on the form that a program may assume. A structured programming methodology stresses the importance of making programs easy to read and to understand. A program should include, for example, nonexecutable comments that help explain the logic of the program. The use of "cute" programming tricks or of short-cuts that compromise program clarity is not recommended. Large or complex programs should be divided into a related set of component programs so that each program unit is restricted in function, making the program more reliable and easy to *maintain*, that is, to change or enhance after it has been placed into service.

Computer scientists C. Bohm and G. Jacopini have established that any program solution, regardless of its complexity, can be reduced to combinations of only three types of program structures. Structured programming seeks to restrict a programmer to using the following three types of program sequences:

- A *simple sequence* of program statements that are executed as a unit, one statement following the other, in consecutive fashion. A simple sequence may not include any statements that alter the order in which program statements are executed. See Figure 1.10(a).

- A *selection sequence,* in which a logical comparison is made and one of two possible program paths is selected based on the results of the comparison. See Figure 1.10(b).
- A *repetition sequence,* in which the same set of statements is executed repeatedly within a looping structure, provided that a certain condition is true. See Figure 1.10(c).

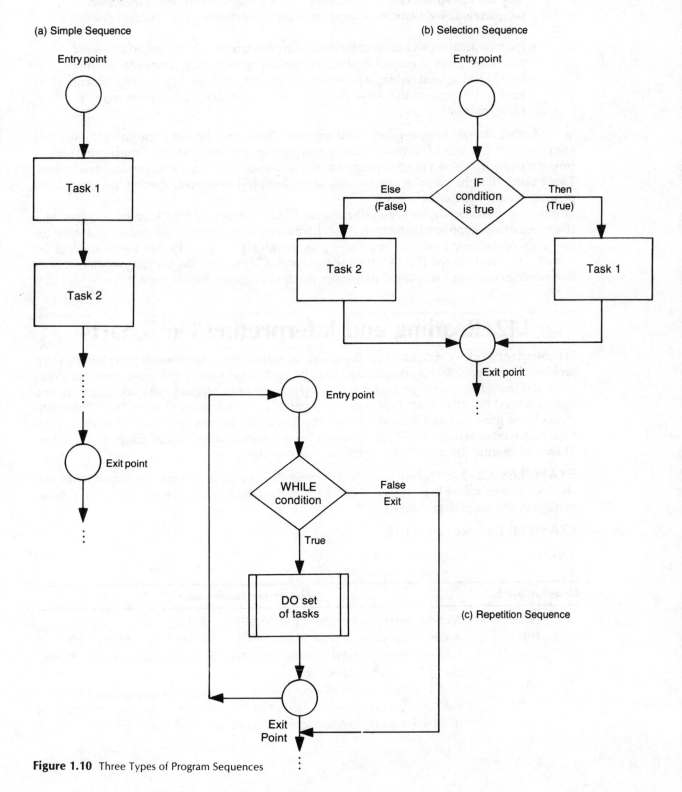

Figure 1.10 Three Types of Program Sequences

Limiting a programmer to the planned application of these three types of program *control structures* has at least two major advantages:

- *Program clarity* is enhanced. Structured programs are relatively easy to read, modify, and fix. Programs following a structured design approach tend to look alike, thereby simplifying the job of programmers who must revise programs that they did not write. As a result of the emphasis placed on the standardization of programming style, structured programming is sometimes referred to as "egoless" programming.
- *Program accuracy* is improved. Emphasis on program readability and on the use of only three types of control structures tends to prevent a programmer from using convoluted logic in writing a program. Algorithms produced in this environment tend to be more straightforward and well defined, leading to fewer errors in program logic.

To further increase program clarity and accuracy, there should be only one point of entry and one point of exit for each of the three fundamental program control structures. Transferring control from a statement outside a program sequence to a statement within the structure is not permitted. This ensures that the program can be read easily from top to bottom, making the logic of the program readily apparent.

Many of these principles are idealized goals. Some languages lend themselves more to a structured design approach than others. Pascal, for example, was specifically designed to allow for the unambiguous application of structured programming principles. Part of the motivation for updating Fortran IV to the 1977 ANSI standard (Fortran 77) was to offer the programmer features that would encourage a structured design approach to program development.

1.12 Reading and Interpreting Flowcharts

In subsequent work we will introduce flowcharts in order to help plan the computer solution to a problem. In addition, flowchart symbolism will be used to help illustrate Fortran program structures. It is important, therefore, that you develop confidence in working with flowcharts. In this section several flowcharts are displayed with sample data. Your job will be to "walk" the data through the flowchart and determine how the flowchart symbols manipulate the data. Each flowchart symbol (except the START symbol) has a corresponding Fortran program statement. These will be introduced gradually in the next several chapters.

EXAMPLES 1.2–1.5   For each of the following flowcharts, determine the output when the given set of data values is processed. (*Note:* Each of the flowcharts has been designed to process more than one set of data values.)

EXAMPLE 1.2   See Figure 1.11.

Solution

Flowchart Symbol	Interpretation/Significance
(a)	All flowcharts must begin with a START symbol.
(b)	A new data value is read from the data list supplied. The first time the symbol is encountered, the first data value in the list (10) is used for subsequent flowchart processing.
(c)	If, in attempting to read a data value in the preceding step, the data list is exhausted, then this symbol transfers control to the stop box. If the data list is not exhausted, then the flowchart continues in the branch labeled "No."

(d)   The value of F is calculated by multiplying the data value by 1.8 and then adding 32. The result will be that F will take on a value of 50 (18 + 32).

(e)   The values of the Celsius temperature and the equivalent Fahrenheit temperature are printed. This corresponds to the flowchart's output.

(f)   The connector symbol is used to transfer program control back to the input box so that the next data value (that is, Celsius temperature) can be processed. Each of the flowchart symbols is executed in the order in which it appears, provided that the data list has not been exhausted. A cyclic pattern results which is called *looping;* each complete cycle is called a *loop.*

Data list: 10, 0, 50

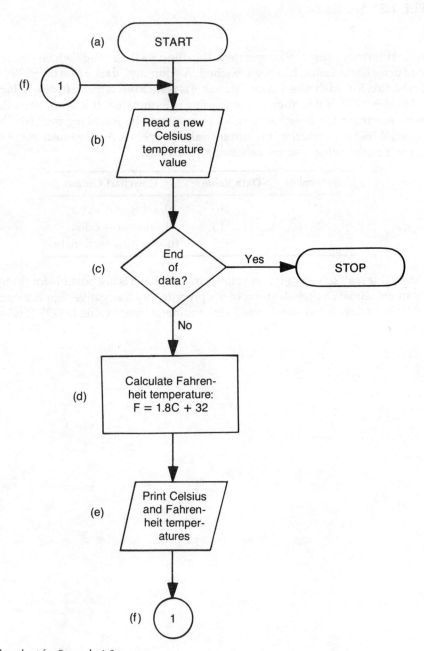

Figure 1.11 Flowchart for Example 1.2

Flowcharts may be traced using the table format illustrated below for Example 1.2:

Loop Number	Celsius Value	Fahrenheit Value	Flowchart Output	
1	10	50	Celsius = 10	Fahrenheit = 50
2	0	32	Celsius = 0	Fahrenheit = 32
3	50	122	Celsius = 50	Fahrenheit = 122
	None		Out of data	

Since three data values are provided for the Celsius temperatures, three *complete* loops are necessary to process the supplied data. Each complete loop is sometimes referred to as an *iteration*.

EXAMPLE 1.3   See Figure 1.12.

Solution

The flowchart illustrates how to incorporate within the data list a "flag" which signals that the end of the list of actual data values has been reached. A "dummy" data value of −9999 is inserted at the end of the data list. Each time a new data value is read, a test is made to determine whether the value read in is −9999. If it is, then the processing is terminated. If it is not, then the processing continues by executing the flowchart symbol encountered by following the "No" branch of the decision symbol that tests whether the current value is −9999. A value such as −9999 is usually referred to as a *trailer value, sentinel value,* or *program flag.*

Loop Number	Data Value	Flowchart Output
1	10	10, Integer is even
2	13	13, Integer is odd
	−9999	(processing terminates)

Remark: Any value may serve as a trailer value provided that it is not possible for the trailer value to appear as an actual data value. A string of 9's preceded by a negative sign is a commonly used numerical trailer value. A frequently used alphanumeric trailer value is EOF (End-Of-File).

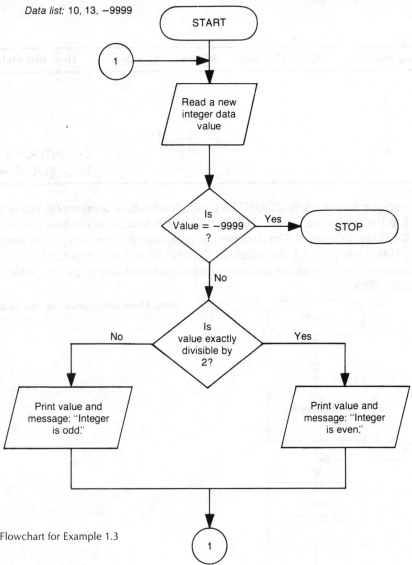

Data list: 10, 13, −9999

START

1

Read a new
integer data
value

Is
Value = −9999
?
Yes → STOP

No

Is
value exactly
divisible by
2?
No ← → Yes

Print value and
message: "Integer
is odd."

Print value and
message: "Integer
is even."

1

Figure 1.12 Flowchart for Example 1.3

EXAMPLE 1.4 See Figure 1.13.

Solution

Loop Number	COUNTER Value	RECIPROCAL Value	Flowchart Output
	0		
1	1	1	
2	2	0.5	
3	3	0.3333333	
4	4	0.25	COUNTER = 4
			RECIPROCAL = 0.25

Narrative description of flowchart: COUNTER is initialized to have a value of 0. The next assignment box adds 1 to the current value of COUNTER. In the next assignment box, the reciprocal of the COUNTER value is calculated. The decision box compares the current value of RECIPROCAL to 0.3. If the value is less than 0.3, the values of COUNTER and RECIPROCAL are printed and the program terminates; otherwise, program control is transferred back to the box, which adds 1 to the value of COUNTER.

Note: Flowchart generates its own data.

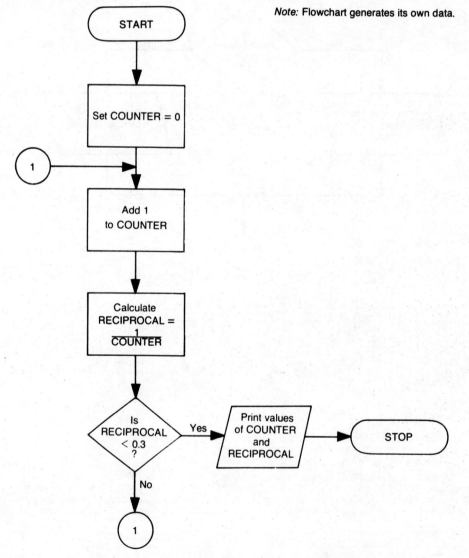

Figure 1.13 Flowchart for Example 1.4

EXAMPLE 1.5 See Figure 1.14.

Solution

Loop Number	Data Value	NEGCOUNT	POSCOUNT	Flowchart Output
1	−3	1		−3 value is negative
2	8		1	8 value is positive
3	7.1		2	7.1 value is positive
4	15		3	15 value is positive
5	−9.6	2		−9.6 value is negative
6	0			NEGCOUNT = 2 POSCOUNT = 3

Narrative description of flowchart: The values of NEGCOUNT and POSCOUNT are initialized to be 0. A data value is read and compared to 0. If it is equal to 0, then the current values of NEGCOUNT and POSCOUNT are printed and the program terminates; otherwise, the next decision box is executed. The data value is compared to 0. If it is greater than 0, then 1 is added to the current value of POSCOUNT (since the data value is positive) and the data value and indicated message are printed; otherwise, 1 is added to the current value of NEGCOUNT (since the value must be negative if it is not positive) and the data value and indicated message are printed. Program control is then transferred back to the input box so that another data value can be read.

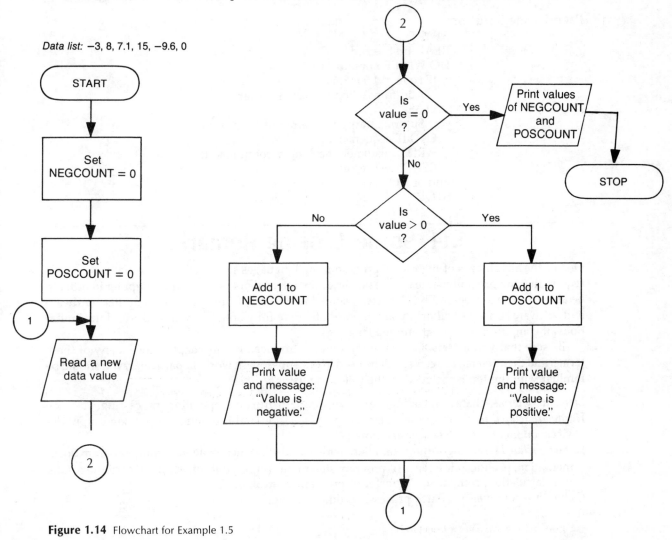

Figure 1.14 Flowchart for Example 1.5

1.13 Pseudocodes

To produce structured programs, a certain discipline of mind and habit is required. In planning a computer solution to a problem using a structured design methodology, programmers think exclusively in terms of the three control structures: a simple sequence, an IF/THEN/ELSE decision sequence, and a repetition sequence. In fact, programmers often frame a tentative solution to the problem using an English-like paragraph-form description that depends heavily on the phrases IF/THEN/ELSE and DO WHILE. This type of solution is called a *pseudocode,* since it is not an actual programming language. Since a pseudocode *resembles* a programming language, it can easily be coded into a computer program.

EXAMPLE 1.6   Read in a series of customer checking account transactions. A code number of 1 is used to indicate a deposit. If the code is 1, then the transaction amount should be added to the account balance; otherwise, it should be subtracted from the account balance. Print the updated customer checking account record. Assume that a trailer record with an EOF entry will terminate the processing. Develop a flowchart and a pseudocode solution to indicate the nature of the processing that is required.

Solution

The flowchart is shown in Figure 1.15. The pseudocode solution follows. Notice that paragraph indentation is used to improve the clarity of the solution and that Fortran keywords are capitalized.

Pseudocode Solution

```
START
READ first record
DO WHILE not end-of-file
   IF code = 1 THEN
       Add transaction amount to balance
   ELSE
       Subtract transaction amount from balance
   END IF sequence
   WRITE customer checking account record
   READ next record
End of DO WHILE loop
STOP
```

1.14 Some Closing Remarks

One of the advantages of high-level programming languages such as Fortran is that they do not require that the programmer learn the details of the internal operation of the computer in order to be able to write a program. Nevertheless, some knowledge of fundamental computer hardware and software concepts will help you to appreciate more fully both the capabilities and the limitations of computers and programming languages.

Be sure that you understand the terminology introduced in this chapter since many of these terms, and their related concepts, will be used in our subsequent work. In particular, you should be familiar with the terms included in the following list:

Elementary terms: character; coding; data; execution; instruction; operation; processing.
Hardware related terms: computer memory; data precision and E-notation; input and output devices; online; terminal; secondary storage.
Software related terms: algorithm; compiler; field-record-file concept; flowcharting; program documentation; pseudocodes; types of program statements (input/output, assignment of the results of a calculation, comparison, transfer of program control, halt).
Computing environments: batch processing; time-sharing.

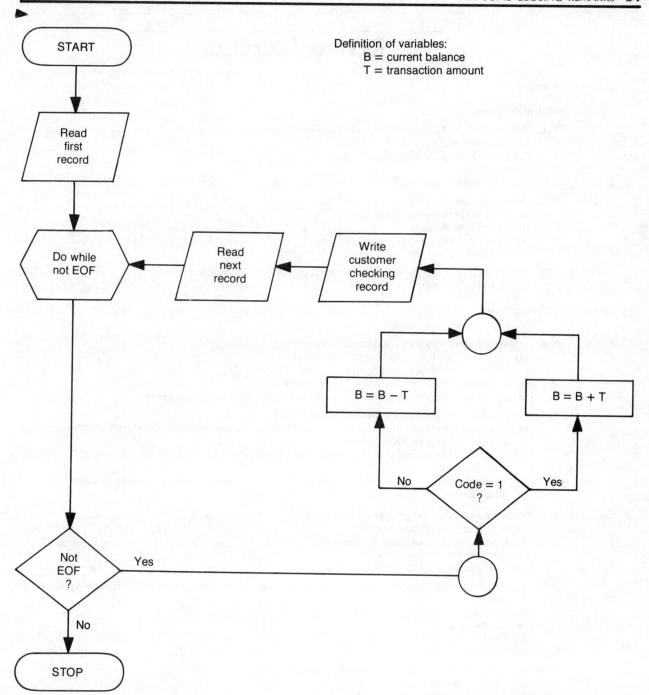

Figure 1.15

The concept of structured programming was also introduced. Throughout this presentation we will point out ways in which you can make your programs easier to read, debug, and change. To emphasize the importance of these principles, they will be captioned "STRUCTURED PROGRAMMING GUIDELINE."

Review Exercises

A star preceding the number of a problem indicates that a solution to that problem is given at the back of the book.

Multiple Choice

* **1.** Which of the following fields would contain alphanumeric data?
  (a) Zipcode field
  (b) Car-license-plate-identification field
  (c) Age field
  (d) Day-of-the-month field

* **2.** Computers are used to:
  (a) store and retrieve information
  (b) manipulate data
  (c) perform routine repetitive operations
  (d) do all of these

* **3.** In which type of storage can data be most quickly accessed (located)?
  (a) Main (semiconductor) memory
  (b) Disk
  (c) Tape
  (d) All are about the same.

* **4.** The major advantages of computers include:
  (a) accuracy, reliability, downtime, and speed
  (b) accuracy, reliability, speed, and a universal language
  (c) accuracy, declining cost, speed, and reliability
  (d) accuracy, reliability, speed, and ability to engage in heuristic processes

* **5.** Which of the following statements is true?
  (a) Data received from an on-line secondary storage device must first be stored in main memory before they can be operated on.
  (b) All data manipulations must be reduced to either copy (move), arithmetic, or "yes/no" comparison operations.
  (c) Records written in a tape file are read in the same order in which they were written.
  (d) All of these.

* **6.** Which is *not* a function of the control unit?
  (a) Fetching program instructions
  (b) Coordinating input/output operations
  (c) Decoding program instructions
  (d) Transmitting data to and from registers

* **7.** Which of the following flowchart symbol shapes represents an operation found in every selection sequence?
  (a) Rectangle
  (b) Parallelogram
  (c) Oval
  (d) Diamond

* **8.** Which of the following terms encompasses all of the other three?
  (a) File   (c) Record
  (b) Field   (d) Character

* **9.** During the compilation process, a(n) _____ program is converted into a(n) _____ program.
  (a) source; object
  (b) Basic; Fortran
  (c) object; source
  (d) machine language; assembled

* **10.** Which of the following statements is true?
  (a) During program execution, data and program instructions reside in main memory.
  (b) The same program written in a standardized version of Fortran will be translated into different machine language codes, depending on the computers the program is run on.
  (c) Assembly language is more powerful but less convenient to use than high-level languages.
  (d) All of these.

*11. Which of the following statements is false?
  (a) The control unit of the CPU directs the activities of the arithmetic logic unit.
  (b) Each program instruction written in a high-level language is translated into several machine language instructions.
  (c) Turnaround time tends to be greater in a time-sharing system than in a batch processing system.
  (d) Computer output may, at some later date, serve as computer input.

*12. Which of the following statements is true?
  (a) The choice of flowchart symbols depends on the particular programming language that is used.
  (b) Structured programming is concerned with how easily a program can be read by another programmer, as well as by a computer.
  (c) Compilers are hardware devices that are usually wired into the machine by the computer manufacturer.
  (d) The same compiler may be used to translate programs written in different high-level programming languages.

CHAPTER 2
Elements of Fortran

COMPUTER AXIOM

People solve problems; computers follow instructions.

COROLLARY

Before you begin to write a program, you must understand what the program is supposed to accomplish, what data are provided, and how the printed output is to look. If you don't know each of these things, you're not ready to write the program.

2.1 Computer Memory and Fortran Variables

In a computer program there are generally two categories of data: variable and constant. In a program designed to process a company payroll, for example, the FICA (social security) tax rate is known to the programmer at the time that he or she is preparing the program, being fixed by the federal government and the same for each employee. The FICA tax rate is an example of a *constant* data value. The number of hours worked and the hourly wage rate, on the other hand, will typically vary from employee to employee and are not usually known to the programmer when he or she is preparing the program. Each of these quantities must be represented by a symbol, called a *variable*.

The distinction between variables and constants is an important one. Program variables are quantities that may change in value as the program executes. They are therefore given symbolic names. The value of a constant is known, fixed in value, and does not change as a program executes. In the formula that converts Celsius temperatures (C) to Fahrenheit temperatures (F):

$$F = 1.8C + 32.0$$

the values 1.8 and 32.0 are constants. Regardless of the Celsius temperature, these numbers remain the same. The letters C and F are variables. The value of C may be *any* real number. The value of F is also unknown, being dependent on the choice of value for C. Variables may be thought of as placeholders for actual data values that are not currently known or that may change in value.

AN INSIDE LOOK AT COMPUTER MEMORY

As instructions and data are fed into a computer, they are neatly filed into individual storage compartments. In order to be able to write programs that manipulate data, the Fortran programmer needs a basic understanding of how computer memory is organized.

Walking into the lobby of a large apartment building, one notices an area reserved for several rows of consecutive mailboxes, one for each apartment. Essentially, we have just described what the computer's memory looks like. Instead of a postman placing letters in the boxes, data values (numbers and alphanumeric characters) are stored in a computer's mailboxes, which are sometimes referred to as *memory cells* or *storage locations*.

How does a postman know in which particular mailbox to place a letter that is addressed to a tenant? Simple—each mailbox is labeled with the apartment number, the person's name, or both. Similarly, each computer memory cell is labeled so that it can be distinguished from other memory cells. The label or "apartment number" of a memory cell is referred to as the *address* of a memory cell. The data value (that is, "postage letter") that is stored in a memory cell is referred to as the *contents* of that memory cell or storage location.

When a new tenant moves into an apartment building, a label bearing his or her name is usually affixed to the appropriate letterbox. Similarly, when a programmer introduces a variable into a program, a memory cell will be automatically labeled with the name of that variable. For example, suppose that in a certain program the variable BAL represents a person's savings account balance. Assume that the current balance is 487 dollars. In mathematical terms, we say that BAL equals 487 (that is, BAL = 487). In a programming context, however, the variable name BAL represents the address of a memory location, while 487 represents its stored contents. This is illustrated in Figure 2.1.

Throughout the execution of a program that processes the individual's savings and deposit transactions:

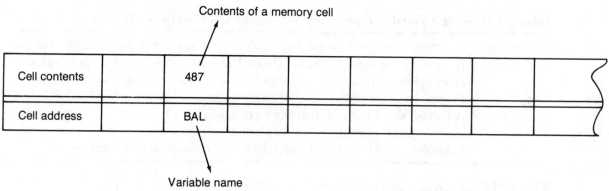

Figure 2.1

- The person's current balance is referred to by the symbol BAL rather than the actual value. In general, *a data value is referred to by its address in memory.*
- The memory cell remains labeled "BAL." The contents of memory cell BAL, however, may change during the execution of the program. If the individual has made three deposits, the processing of each deposit will result in a change in the stored contents of memory cell BAL. In general, *the address of a memory cell remains the same, although its contents may change.*

Although our mailbox analogy has been helpful, it fails in at least two important respects. A tenant's mailbox may at the same time hold a variety of unrelated mail items—a magazine, a postcard, a letter, and so on. A computer memory cell, however, may store only a single data item at a time. *When a data item is assigned to a memory cell, it automatically destroys the previous contents, if any, of that memory cell.*

A mailman may find it easier to reach one particular mailbox than another. For a computer, the physical location of a memory cell has nothing to do with the time or effort required to reach (that is, *access*) the contents of that memory cell. Each memory cell can be accessed with equal ease, regardless of its address in memory. We refer to this feature of computer memory by a special term—*random access memory.*

CHOOSING FORTRAN VARIABLE NAMES

Although the programmer normally selects the symbolic variable names to be used in a program, he or she is guided by the syntax of the particular programming language that is being used. For each programming language there are specific guidelines that must be strictly adhered to when selecting variable names. The rules for selecting a variable name in Fortran are presented in Table 2.1.

Table 2.1 Rules for Forming Fortran Variable Names

A Fortran variable name must:

- begin with an alphabetic letter (A – Z).
- contain one to six characters, consisting of combinations of letters (A – Z) and digits (0 – 9).
- *not* contain any special characters such as -, &, /, and #.

Fortran requires that its compiler be alerted as to whether a variable used in a program represents an integer or a real (floating-point) quantity. A programmer may declare a numeric variable type *implicitly* through the choice of variable names, using the guidelines presented in Table 2.2.

Table 2.2 Defining a Variable Type Implicitly (Implicit Data Declaration)

Integer type: A Fortran variable name that begins with I, J, K, L, M, or N defines a variable that represents an integer data value. (*Note:* The first two letters in the word "INteger" gives the range of letters, I through N, that defines an integer variable.)
Examples: ID, KOUNT, and NUM1 are examples of integer variables.

Real type: A Fortran variable name that does *not* begin with I, J, K, L, M, or N defines a variable that represents a real data value.
Examples: SUM, X12, and AMOUNT are examples of real variables.

EXAMPLE 2.1 Which of the following is a legal Fortran integer variable name?
(a) LAST-1   (b) 3ID   (c) ZIP   (d) MATH   (e) INTEREST

Solution

(d) MATH   *Note:* (a) LAST-1 is illegal since it includes a hyphen (-).
(b) 3ID is illegal since it begins with a digit.
(c) ZIP defines a real variable type.
(d) INTEREST is illegal since it exceeds six characters.

EXAMPLE 2.2 Which of the following is a legal Fortran real variable name?
(a) IQ   (b) L17   (c) TOTAL   (d) AMOUNTS   (e) $PRICE

Solution

(c) TOTAL   *Note:* (a) IQ defines an integer variable type.
(b) L17 defines an integer variable type.
(d) AMOUNTS is illegal since it exceeds six characters.
(e) $PRICE is illegal since it includes a special character symbol. (In WATFIV the dollar symbol may be included in variable names.)

ARITHMETIC OPERATOR SYMBOLS

As in mathematics, symbols are used in Fortran to represent the various arithmetic operations.

Operation	Fortran Symbol	Example
Addition	+	A + B
Subtraction	−	A − B
Multiplication	*	A * B
Division	/	A / B
Exponentiation (raising to a power)	**	A ** B

EXAMPLE 2.3   Evaluate: (a) $3.0 + 5.0$ (b) $2 * 16$ (c) $18.0 / 3.0$ (d) $3 ** 4$

Solutions

(a) 8.0   (b) 32   (c) 6.0   (d) 81 (since $3 ** 4 = 3 \times 3 \times 3 \times 3$)

The symbols $+, -, *, /$, and $**$ are examples of *operators*; the numbers or variables on which they act or operate are referred to as *operands*. In the expression $X - Y + M / 4$, the operators are the symbols $-, +$, and $/$; the operands are X, Y, M, and 4.

2.2 The Assignment Statement

A Fortran assignment statement is used to place a data value into a memory location. The value may be a constant, a variable, or the result of a calculation.

Example	Interpretation
1. ID = 2369	1. The constant integer value 2369 is assigned to (stored in location) ID.
2. VALUE = X	2. The variable value X is assigned to (stored in location) VALUE. After the statement is executed, the two variables represent (that is, store) the same value. The effect, therefore, is to *copy* the contents of memory cell X into memory cell VALUE.
3. N1 = A − B + 4.9	3. The right side is evaluated and the result is assigned to variable N1. The values of A and B must be previously assigned in the program.
4. A = A + B	4. Find the sum of the current values stored in memory locations A and B. Take this sum and make it the new value of A, thereby destroying the previous value stored in A.

The general form (syntax) of a Fortran assignment statement is as follows:

Fortran *variable* = *arithmetic* or *formula* expression

The execution of a Fortran assignment statement may be thought of as occurring in two distinct steps:

1. The expression that appears on the right side of the equal (=) symbol is evaluated.
2. The result of the evaluation is assigned to the Fortran variable named on the left side of the equal (=) symbol. Actually, the result is being stored in a computer memory location having the variable name as its symbolic memory address.

EXAMPLE 2.4   The current values of variables A and B are 2.0 and 7.6, respectively. What is the contents of each memory location after the assignment statement SUM = A + B is executed?

Solution

Before Execution			After Execution		
2.0	7.6		2.0	7.6	9.6
A	B		A	B	SUM

Note that the values (stored contents) of A and B are unaffected by the execution of the assignment statement SUM = A + B.

In Example 2.4 the value of A is written, not simply as 2, but rather as 2.0. The value 2.0 is consistent with the fact that variable A implicitly defines a real rather than an integer data value. In general, the programmer must be alert to whether a data value and the variable to which it is being assigned agree in type. For example, in the assignment statement INT = 9/4, the quotient of 9 divided by 4 is 2.25; but the variable to which it is being assigned may represent only integer values. In this instance, the fractional part of the value would be truncated and the value 2 would be assigned to the variable INT. A more detailed discussion of the effect of mixing data types will be postponed until Chapter 3.

EXAMPLE 2.5   The current values of integer variables K and L are 9 and 4, respectively. What is the contents of each memory cell after the assignment statement K = K − L is executed?

Solution

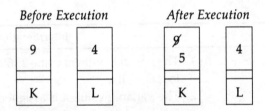

Example 2.5 illustrates the *destructive* nature of the assignment statement. Assigning the value of 5 (9 − 4) to K will wipe out its previously stored value of 9.

A common error is to use assignment statements and mathematical equations interchangeably. A very important difference exists between these two types of expressions. In a mathematical equation, algebraic expressions may appear on either side of the equal symbol. In a Fortran assignment statement, a Fortran variable must stand alone on the left side of the equal symbol. The right member of the assignment statement may contain a constant, an arithmetic expression, or an algebraic expression. This results from the fact that the computer always interprets the left member as the address of a computer memory cell and the right member as a quantity to be evaluated and assigned to ("deposited in") this memory cell.

EXAMPLE 2.6   State whether each of the following expressions represents a legal or an illegal assignment statement:

(a) PROD = 3.5 * TEN * 14.0   (b) A − 1 = B

Solutions

(a) Legal   (b) Illegal since A − 1 is not a valid Fortran variable name

EXAMPLE 2.7   Determine the value of the variable RESULT after the given set of statements is executed.

(a) JVAL = 3.9   (b) RESULT = 7.0
    KVAL = 2   A1 = 3.0
    RESULT = JVAL * KVAL   RESULT = 2.0 * A1

Solutions

(a) The integer variable JVAL may store only an integer value. Therefore, the decimal part of 3.9 is truncated and the integer value 3 is stored in (assigned to) JVAL. The product of the contents of JVAL and KVAL is 6; however, the real variable RESULT may store only a number having a decimal part. RESULT stores the real value 6.0.

(b) The effect of executing these statements in the order given can be summarized as follows:

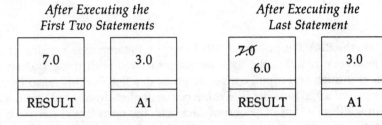

After Executing the First Two Statements		After Executing the Last Statement	
7.0	3.0	~~7.0~~ 6.0	3.0
RESULT	A1	RESULT	A1

Example 2.7(b) illustrates the destructive nature of the assignment statement. Assigning the value of 6.0 (2.0 * 3.0) to RESULT will wipe out its previous value of 7.0.

EXAMPLE 2.8 Determine the final value (storage contents) of A.

(a) A = 4.5   (b) A = 3.0
    A = 2 * A   A = A + 1.0

Solutions

In both parts, (a) and (b), the second assignment statement is a somewhat disturbing mathematical expression. Each assignment statement, however, is legal.

(a) The current value of A (4.5) is multiplied by 2.0, and the result (9.0) is stored back in A, destroying the previous value of A. The final value of A is 9.0.

(b) The sum of the initial value of A (3.0) is added to 1.0, and the result (4.0) is stored back in A, wiping out the previous value of A. The final value of A is 4.0. This type of assignment statement will prove to be especially useful in our subsequent work as it provides the basis for constructing a program structure that will allow a series of values to be accumulated.

STRUCTURED PROGRAMMING GUIDELINES

- Introduce meaningful variable names into your program. For example, in a program involving payroll, choose the variable name HOURS to represent the number of hours an employee works, rather than a variable such as H.
- Use blanks in Fortran statements to improve the readability of the program. You should insert a blank space on either side of an arithmetic operator symbol and on either side of an equal (=) symbol.

2.3 Some General Features of a Fortran Program

A nontrivial Fortran program will typically include provision for:

- an *input operation* in order to introduce and store variable data values that will be required for subsequent computer processing
- *data manipulation*, including performing arithmetic operations, comparing data values, and storing results of calculations
- an *output operation* in order to transmit processing results that are stored in main memory to an output device such as a printer or CRT display screen

Let's examine a simple Fortran program that includes an input and an output operation. Program 2.1 is designed to find the sum of any three real data values that are inputted.

```
READ *, A, B, C
SUM = A + B + C
PRINT *, SUM
STOP
END
```

Program 2.1.

The asterisk (*) in the READ (input) and PRINT (output) statements is a grammatical feature of the Fortran 77 language; it requires the data values associated with these I/0 statements to be supplied on input, or printed on output, consecutively as in a list. For this reason this type of I/0 statement is sometimes referred to as *list-directed*. Since under list-directed I/0 it is not necessary to specify the column width of an input or output data field, the term *format-free* is also used. With list-directed input, two consecutive data values entered on the same data record (for example, the same line of a CRT display), must be separated by a blank space or a comma. For example, Program 2.1 requires that three data values be supplied to the program during an input operation. The data values will typically be entered on the same line, with consecutive values separated by a single blank space. List-directed input/output is analogous to input/output statements used in the Basic programming language.

List-directed input and output is not available with most versions of Fortran IV. In WATFIV list-directed I/O statements are written without an asterisk. The corresponding READ statement in WATFIV for our present example would be

```
READ, A, B, C
```

The STOP and END statements are typically found in every Fortran program, although the STOP statement will not always immediately precede the END statement. The END statement is always the last statement in a Fortran program. The END statement serves an essential function *during the compilation process* when the Fortran source program is converted into the machine language object program. When the compiler encounters the END statement, it knows that the physical end of the source program has been reached. The END statement is our first example of a *nonexecutable* program statement. A nonexecutable program statement provides information to the computer during the compilation process and is not translated into machine language. The STOP statement, on the other hand, is an executable statement. It is converted into machine language. During program execution, it is the STOP statement that instructs the computer to halt processing.

If you're ready to type your program using a computer data entry device, begin typing your program statements in column 7. Columns 1–6 are reserved for other, related purposes (this will be discussed in Chapter 3). Actually, a Fortran program statement may be coded *anywhere* between columns 7 and 72. Columns 73–80 are not read by the Fortran compiler and may be used for identification, such as adding a number that gives the sequence number of the statement.

Notice that our sample Fortran program represents a *generalized* solution to a particular problem. In this instance, the problem is to determine the sum of three numbers. The programmer, *not* the computer, solves the problem by devising the list of program instructions that achieves the desired result. If there are no errors in syntax, the program is then stored in computer memory so that it can be executed. During program execution the computer follows the stored list of instructions and "solves" the problem for *particular* values of the program variables. See Figure 2.2.

The method used to enter programs and data will depend on the nature of the computer system. In a punch card system program statements and data are keypunched onto cards, usually 80 columns in width. The set of punch cards that contain program statements is called a *program deck*. A *data deck* consists of the group of cards that contain the set of data values to be processed by the program and is placed physically behind the program deck. Interspersing special control cards allows the computer to distinguish between program statements and data, as well as to reference the appropriate language compiler program. See Figure 2.3.

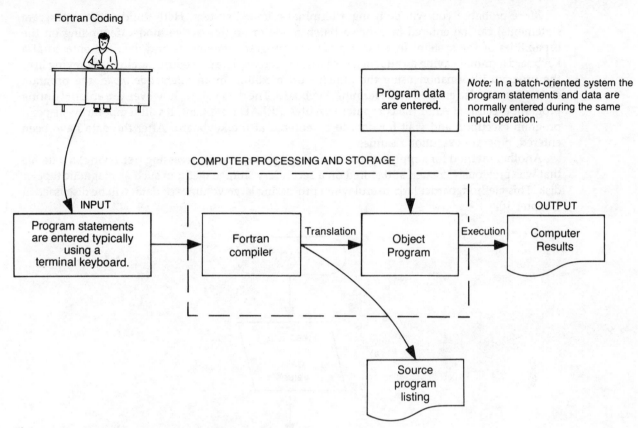

Figure 2.2 Program Preparation, Compilation, and Execution

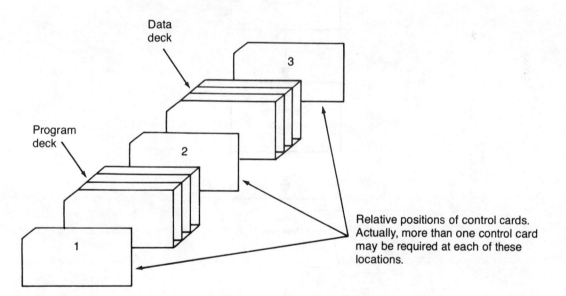

Figure 2.3 Organization of Control, Program, and Data Cards. Control cards are sometimes referred to (e.g. in an IBM environment) as Job Control Cards (JCL). Control cards use a machine dependent computer language which will vary from machine to machine. Their function, however, is the same regardless of the computer manufacturer. The control card(s) inserted at position 1 (see figure) serves to identify the programmer, program, and the specific compiler that is required; the control card(s) at position 2 signals the end of the program and/or the beginning of the data deck. The last control card is an end of job card. The format of the required control cards is normally available from the computer installation that will service your jobs.

More probably you will be using a terminal-oriented system. Here the data (and program statements) can be entered in either a batch mode or an interactive mode, depending on the capabilities of the system. In a *batch mode*, the program statements and data are entered at a keyboard terminal having an attached CRT display screen. The procedure parallels the keying in of the program information using the punch card medium. In an *interactive mode*, the program statements are also entered at the terminal keyboard. The data values, however, are entered during program execution. After the computer executes a READ statement, it will temporarily suspend program execution and wait for data to be entered at the keyboard. After the data have been entered, program execution resumes.

Another method for supplying data to a stored program is by accessing (retrieving) a data file that was previously created and stored on a secondary storage medium such as magnetic tape or disk. This method, particularly useful when processing large volumes of data, will be discussed in Chapter 10.

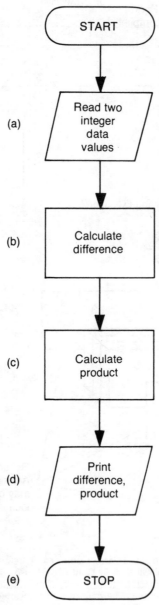

Figure 2.4 Flowchart for Example 2.9

EXAMPLE 2.9 Write a Fortran program that determines and prints the difference and the product of any given pair of integer values.

Solution

Figure 2.4 gives the flowchart solution to this problem. The coded program (see Program 2.2) may be directly translated from the flowchart (except that the END statement must be added as the last statement of every Fortran program).

```
(a) READ *, I, J
(b) KDIFF = I - J
(c) KPROD = I * J
(d) PRINT *, KDIFF, KPROD
(e) STOP
    END
```

Note: The letters (a), (b), (c), (d), and (e) have been inserted to emphasize the correspondence between the flowchart symbols and the Fortran program statements.

Program 2.2

Program 2.2 will display the difference and the product of the variables on the same horizontal line. If it was desirable to print each result on a separate line, the following program would be used:

```
READ *, I, J
KDIFF = I - J
KPROD = I * J
PRINT *, KDIFF
PRINT *, KPROD
STOP
END
```

2.4 List-Directed (Format-Free) Input and Output

The syntax of the list-directed input and output statements introduced in Section 2.3 is summarized in the display that follows. Keep in mind that not all versions of Fortran (for example, most implementation of Fortran IV) support format-free input and output.

Input: READ *, *variable₁*, *variable₂*, *variable₃*, . . .

Output: PRINT *, *variable₁*, *variable₂*, *variable₃*, . . .

Effect: When the READ statement is executed, the computer "requests" data from the input device, one value for each variable appearing in the list. The data values are then referred to by the variables to which they have been assigned.

The PRINT statement displays the current value of each variable that appears in its variable list.

The READ statement, like the assignment statement, is destructive in the sense that the value assigned to a variable via an input operation destroys the previous value, if any, of the variable. The PRINT statement, however, is nondestructive; the value of a variable may be printed any number of times without destroying the contents of the memory location to which the variable refers.

EXAMPLE 2.10 Determine the output if the data supplied to the following program are 5.9 and 8.6:

```
A = 3.0
B = 1.5
READ *, A, B
PRINT *, A
PRINT *, B
PRINT *, A, B
PRINT *, B, A
STOP
END
```

Solution

The result of executing the first three program statements is illustrated below:

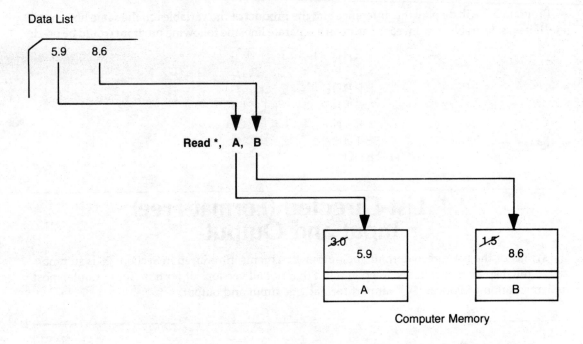

When a PRINT statement is executed, a *copy* of the contents of the memory cells that are referred to in the output variable list is written to an output medium such as the CRT screen (soft copy) or is printed on paper (hard copy).

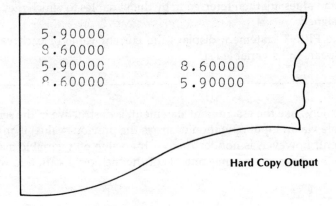

Hard Copy Output

The horizontal format (that is, spacing) of the output generated by a list-directed PRINT statement is determined by the nature of the particular computer system, rather than by the individual programmer. The advantage is that the programmer's job is simplified. The disadvantage is that the output may be difficult to read. A discussion of how to produce formatted output is given in Chapter 4.

In list-directed output, values are usually displayed in print fields, each having a preset field width. Arithmetic signs (+ and −) and decimal points occupy a field printing position. Although a field (column) position is reserved for a + sign, the printing of the + sign is normally suppressed by the computer. The actual number of column positions that the computer allocates to a print field is highly system dependent. An IBM 4341 mainframe with a WATFIV compiler, for example, will print integer values right-justified in a field having 12 column print positions. The same computer will print real values right-justified in a field having a width of 20 column positions. The first 12 columns are reserved for the integer part of the real value, while the last 7 columns are used for the decimal part of the number. Remember that a column is also required for the decimal point. As with most systems that use list-directed output, adjacent print fields are separated in this IBM computer by a single blank space.

Input and Output of Data

Data are entered in the same order as the variables to which they will be assigned appear in the input variable list. Consecutive data values on an input record are separated by a comma or a blank. When data are entered interactively, program execution halts and the screen display "freezes" until data are supplied to the program.

Output variable values are printed (using a list-directed PRINT statement) in fields having a predetermined width. Numerical values are printed right-justified, while alphanumeric data are printed left-justified. Adjacent print fields are separated by a blank. The length of a print field varies from machine to machine.

2.5 Data Declaration Statements

Numeric data types may be defined *implicitly*, relying on the first-letter convention when selecting variable names. Alternatively, variable types may be defined *explicitly*, using a special data declaration statement. Program 2.3 uses data declaration statements to "announce" to the compiler what types of data values the variables used in the program represent.

Data declaration statements →

```
REAL K, L, SUM
INTEGER A, B, PRODCT
READ *, A, B, K, L
SUM = K + L
PRODUCT = A * B
PRINT *, SUM, PRODCT
STOP
END
```

Program 2.3

The program declares the variables K, L, and SUM to be real variables. The variables A, B, and PRODCT are declared to be integer variables. A data declaration statement overrides the use of implicit data typing. For example, if the first data declaration statement was omitted, then variables K and L would be defined implicitly to be *integer* variables. Data declaration statements are *nonexecutable* program statements. During the compilation process they specify the nature of the variables used in the program. Data declaration statements must therefore appear in a program before all executable program statements.

STRUCTURED PROGRAMMING GUIDELINE

To eliminate any ambiguity, define your program variables explicitly using data declaration statements. In addition to variables named in input/output operations, remember to include variables used to store results of calculations in progress. If you forget to include a numeric variable in a data declaration statement, its type will be determined implicitly, based on the first letter of the variable name.

A character string is any sequence of alphanumeric characters and is written within apostrophes: 'string data item'. The number of characters contained in a string is referred to as the *length* of the string. Blanks and punctuation marks are counted as characters, as well as letters, digits, and other special characters. For example, the length of the string 'BOB T. SMITH' is 12 since there are 9 letters, 2 blank spaces, and 1 period enclosed by the pair of single apostrophes.

The character data item CAN'T is represented as a string by writing two single apostrophes between the letters N and T: 'CAN''T'. Its length is 5, which corresponds to the number of characters contained in the expression CAN'T. In general, when an apostrophe is itself a character within a string, it is represented by two consecutive apostrophes, but the additional apostrophe is not considered when determining the length of the string.

A variable that represents a character string is referred to as a *character* (or string) *variable*. A character variable must be defined by a data declaration statement having the following general form:

```
CHARACTER variable name * length
```

where the length refers to the maximum anticipated length of the character data item that the variable named will represent. Some examples are shown on page 47.

When one or more character variables have the same maximum length, the data declaration statement may take the form

```
CHARACTER * length variable 1, variable 2, . . .
```

The length given in the CHARACTER type statement refers to the *maximum* length of the corresponding character data string. The actual string assigned to the character variable may have fewer characters than the specified maximum, in which case the string data item is left-justified in the allocated memory cell and trailing blanks are added so that the length of the stored string is consistent with the length specified in the CHARACTER statement. If the length of the character data string exceeds the maximum length, the string is stored in truncated form, with the rightmost extra characters being deleted from the stored string.

Example of Data Declaration Statement	Interpretation
1. `CHARACTER ADDRSS * 24`	1. ADDRSS is defined as a character variable that may represent a string having a maximum length of 24 characters.
2. `CHARACTER A * 2, B * 8, C * 5`	2. Variables A, B, and C are defined to be character variables. Each may represent a character string having a different number of characters from the other strings. Variable A may represent a string having a maximum length of 2 characters, while variables B and C may represent strings having maximum lengths of 8 and 5 characters, respectively.
3. `CHARACTER * 7 BUS, CAR, TRAIN`	3. Variables BUS, CAR, and TRAIN are character variables *each* representing a string having a maximum of 7 characters.

EXAMPLE 2.11   Given this CHARACTER type statement:

$$CHARACTER\ STATE\ *\ 6$$

determine the contents of the memory cell whose address is STATE for each of the following data items:
(a) data: 'N.Y.'   (b) data: 'CALIFORNIA'

(a)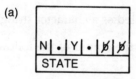

(b)

Note: b = blank space.

Solutions

EXAMPLE 2.12   Write a data declaration statement that satisfies each of the given conditions.
(a) Variables X, Y, and Z are integer variables.
(b) Variables MAX and MIN are real variables.
(c) Variables ITEM, VALUE, and QUANTY are character variables, each having a maximum length of 10 characters.
(d) TIME is a real variable, AGE is an integer variable, ORIGIN is a character variable having a maximum length of 9 characters, and LANG is a character variable having a maximum length of 12 characters.

Solutions

```
(a) INTEGER X, Y, Z
(b) REAL MAX, MIN
(c) CHARACTER * 10 ITEM, VALUE, QUANTY
(d) REAL TIME
    INTEGER AGE
    CHARACTER ORIGIN * 9, LANG * 12
```

If the length is omitted from the CHARACTER statement, it is assumed to be 1. The statements in the following pair are equivalent:

```
    CHARACTER * 1 A, B, C    and    CHARACTER A, B, C
```

EXAMPLE 2.13 Given the following data declaration statements:

```
        INTEGER IDNUM, SUM
        REAL MATH, TOTAL
        CHARACTER SIGMA * 5, NAME * 12
        CHARACTER SIGN
```

determine whether each of the following assignment or READ statements is legal:

```
(a) SUM = '4'          (f) READ *, IDNUM
(b) TOTAL = 108.9          (data: 4620)
(c) SIGN = 'NEG'       (g) NAME = 'HOLLERITH'
(d) SIGMA = 12345      (h) SIGN = '+'
(e) MATH = NINE        (i) READ *, SIGMA, MATH
                           (data: '987' 24.5)
```

Solutions

(a) Illegal since SUM is declared to be an integer variable
(b) Legal
(c) Illegal since the length of the string is a maximum of one character (Actually, the string will be stored in truncated form.)
(d) Illegal since SIGMA is declared to be a character variable.
(e) Illegal
(f) Legal
(g) Legal (The corresponding data string may have fewer characters than the declared length.)
(h) Legal
(i) Legal (Since 987 is enclosed in apostrophes, it is treated as a character string.)

EXAMPLE 2.14 Determine the column placement of the output of the following program:

```
        CHARACTER PERSON * 17
        PERSON = 'ADA LOVELACE'
        PRINT *, 'NAME IS', PERSON
        STOP
        END
```

Solution

This program illustrates that the length of a print field which displays the value of a character variable is defined by the CHARACTER data declaration statement, while the length of the field that displays a quoted character string is determined by the actual number of characters in the string.

$$\underline{|N|\,\underline{A}\,\underline{M}\,\underline{E}\,\underline{b}\,\underline{I}\,\underline{S}|\,\underline{b}|\,\underline{A}\,\underline{D}\,\underline{A}\,\underline{b}\,\underline{L}\,\underline{O}\,\underline{V}\,\underline{E}\,\underline{L}\,\underline{A}\,\underline{C}\,\underline{E}\,\underline{b}\,\underline{b}\,\underline{b}\,\underline{b}|}$$

Blank separates adjacent ————⌐
print fields
ⱕ = blank column space

Data Declaration Statements

Data declaration statements are nonexecutable program statements that must be placed in a program before the first executable program statement. When a data declaration statement is omitted for a numeric variable, the typing of the variable defaults to implicit typing so that the first letter of the variable defines the variable as either integer or real. If a data declaration statement is omitted for a character variable, an error results.

These statements have the following general forms:

REAL $variable_1$, $variable_2$, $variable_3$, . . .

INTEGER $variable_1$, $variable_2$, $variable_3$, . . .

CHARACTER $variable_1$ ✲ length, $variable_2$ ✲ length, . . .

When one or more character variables have the same maximum length, the data declaration statement may take the form

CHARACTER ✲ length $variable_1$, $variable_2$, . . .

STRUCTURED PROGRAMMING GUIDELINE

As a matter of good programming style, type numeric variables using data declaration statements.

2.6 Syntax versus Logic Errors

A computer is relentlessly accurate. It is also an extremely literal machine that is not capable of interpreting what the programmer had in mind when preparing a list of program instructions. In preparing input for a computer, therefore, extreme care must always be taken. Computers do not tolerate errors in spelling or punctuation, no matter how minor they may seem to the human observer. Any error that violates the grammatical principles of a programming language is referred to as a *syntax* error. A program that contains a syntax error cannot be successfully translated into machine language by the compiler, and therefore cannot be executed. Most compilers will "flag" or identify program statements that contain syntax errors in a computer generated program listing. It is the responsibility of the programmer to eliminate all syntax errors.

The output generated by a computer must also be scrupulously examined. Although a program may be free of syntax errors and produce printed results, the output may not reflect what the programmer intended. Invariably such erroneous results are due to some error in the logical planning and organization of the program. This type of error is referred to as an error in *program logic* and is usually more difficult to identify and correct than a syntax error. Any error in a program, syntax or logic, is referred to as a *bug*. The process of identifying and removing program bugs is called *debugging*. It is the fate of a programming student to spend much of his or her time debugging programs—do not become discouraged! The best way to avoid excessive debugging is to resist the temptation to hurriedly prepare a list of program instructions and then rush to submit it to the computer for execution. Thoughtful and patient program planning and coding will yield benefits in terms of reduced debugging time and a less frustrating interaction between you and the computer.

EXAMPLE 2.15 Each of the following unrelated program statements contains a syntax error. Rewrite the statement, removing the error.

(a) `END.`
(b) `READ *, A, B, C`
(c) `CONSTANT = -3`
(d) `A + B = SUM`
(e) `CHARACTER 8 * NAME`
(f) `PRINT *, J1, K2, L3,`

Solutions

(a) `END`
(b) `READ *, A, B, C`
(c) `CONSNT = -3`
(d) `A = SUM - B`
(e) `CHARACTER NAME * 8`
(f) `PRINT *, J1, K2, L3`

EXAMPLE 2.16 In each of the following programs, identify the error in program logic:

(a)
```
REAL X, CUBE
READ *, X
CUBE = X * X * X
STOP
END
```

(b)
```
REAL A, B, SUM
READ *, SUM
SUM = A + B
PRINT *, SUM
END
```

(c)
```
READ *, NAME, RATE, HOURS
REAL RATE, HOURS
WAGES = RATE * HOURS
PRINT *, NAME, WAGES
STOP
END
```

(d)
```
REAL VAL1, VAL2, PROD
READ *, VAL1, VAL2
PROD = VAL * VAL2
PRINT *, PROD
STOP
END
```

Solutions

(a) The PRINT statement `PRINT *, CUBE` should be added immediately before the STOP statement.
(b) The input variables are A and B. Therefore, the READ statement should list these variables: `READ *, A, B`
(c) The data declaration statement for the variable NAME has been omitted. Furthermore, all data declaration statements must precede the READ statement, which references these variables.
(d) The error is located in the assignment statement, in which the variable VAL rather than VAL1 has been written. This is *not* a syntax error. Since the variable VAL has not been explicitly declared, it will be typed following the first-letter convention. If a memory cell has not been assigned a value in the program, its value will be undefined.

2.7 Some Closing Remarks

Six basic types of program statements have been introduced in this chapter:

- data declaration
- READ
- assignment
- PRINT
- STOP
- END

Data declaration statements and the END statement are examples of nonexecutable program statements. During the compilation process they are not translated into machine language instructions, as are executable program statements such as the READ, assignment, PRINT, and STOP statements. Instead, they provide information required during the compilation process. Data declaration statements alert the compiler to the types of variables that will be referenced in the program, while the END statement advises the compiler that no additional Fortran program statements follow.

As a matter of good programming style, we suggested that numeric variables be typed explicitly, using data declaration statements. Character variables must be typed using data declaration statements. The use of meaningful variable names and the insertion of blanks were recommended as ways of further increasing program readability. Blanks may be freely inserted within any Fortran program statement, except, of course, within a character string enclosed by a pair of apostrophes. A Fortran program statement must be coded within columns 7 to 72.

Some differences between Fortran 77 and WATFIV are worthy of note. The list-directed READ and PRINT statements in Fortran 77 require an asterisk (*) before the first comma. In WATFIV, however, the asterisk is omitted, and a list of variables, separated by commas, follows the keywords READ and PRINT:

Fortran 77	WATFIV
`READ *, A, B`	`READ, A, B`
`PRINT *, A, B`	`PRINT, A, B`

Also, unlike Fortran 77, WATFIV permits the use of a dollar sign ($) in forming a variable name.

Some earlier versions of Fortran (for example, some implementations of Fortran IV) do not permit list-directed input and output statements. Chapter 4 will focus on I/O statements in which the programmer must completely specify the layout of an input and output record. This type of I/O statement is referred to as *format-directed* input/output. Fortran 77 supports both list-directed and format-directed I/O statements.

As the Fortran programs you write become more and more complex, the possibility increases that the program you submit for computer execution will not run successfully on the first attempt. Generally speaking, there are three types of program errors for which you should be alert:

1. *Compile-time errors.*

These are syntax errors that the Fortran compiler detects when attempting to translate a Fortran source program into an equivalent machine language program. The WATFIV statement

```
RAAD , A, B
```

would result in a compile-time (syntax) error since the keyword READ has been misspelled. All Fortran compilers flag syntax errors, typically annotating the offending line or expression with an error-diagnostic message when printing a listing of program statements, called a source program listing. (See Program 2.4.)

Keep in mind that programs containing compile-time errors do *not* execute since they are not translated successfully into machine language.

2. *Run-time errors.*

A program that is free of syntax errors can be executed. However, the execution of the program may end abruptly if there is an attempt to divide by zero or to perform another illegal action. This type of error will generate an error message during program execution. (See Program 2.5.)

3. *Program logic errors.*

A program may produce output, but the output may not be correct. For example, if the purpose of the program under consideration was to calculate the square of any number N, and the corresponding Fortran program statement was

```
        $JOB    WATFIV
        C THIS PROGRAM WAS RUN ON AN IBM COMPUTER USING WATFIV.
        C THE WORD 'READ' IS SPELLED INCORRECTLY,  CAUSING A SYNTAX ERROR.
     1          REAL A, B
     2          RAAD , A, B
***ERROR***  UNDECODEABLE STATEMENT
     3          PRINT , A, B
     4          STOP
     5          END

        $ENTRY

STATEMENTS EXECUTED=        0
```

Program 2.4.

```
        $JOB    WATFIV
        C THIS PROGRAM WAS RUN ON AN IBM COMPUTER USING WATFIV.
        C AN ATTEMPT IS MADE TO DIVIDE BY ZERO CAUSING A RUN TIME ERROR.
     1          REAL A, B
     2          A = .5
     3          B = 0
     4          C = A / B
     5          PRINT , A, B, C
     6          STOP
     7          END

        $ENTRY
***ERROR***  LIMIT EXCEEDED FOR FLOATING-POINT DIVISION BY ZERO
        PROGRAM WAS EXECUTING LINE     4 IN ROUTINE M/PROG WHEN TERMINATION OCCURRED
STATEMENTS EXECUTED=        3
```

Program 2.5

$$KSQR = N * 2$$

then incorrect results would be printed since the statement should have been coded as

$$KSQR = N ** 2$$

A run-time error may be considered to be a special type of program logic error.

It is also possible that the output may not be exactly what you expect, yet the program is correct. Program 2.6 illustrates the possibility that, depending on the data value and the computer system being used, round-off errors may be introduced. They result from the fact that a computer represents a number in its main memory in binary form. When some real numbers are first converted into binary and then converted back into decimal form, a decidedly small round-off error may creep in.

```
        $JOB    WATFIV
        C THIS PROGRAM WAS RUN ON AN IBM COMPUTER USING WATFIV.
     1          REAL A
     2          A = 7.2
     3          PRINT , A
     4          STOP
     5          END

        $ENTRY
        7.1999990
STATEMENTS EXECUTED=        2
```

Program 2.6

Review Exercises

A star preceding the number of a problem indicates that a solution to that problem is given at the end of the book.

Multiple Choice

* **1.** Each computer language typically includes specific program language statements designed to accomplish a number of functions with the possible exception of
  - **(a)** arithmetic calculations
  - **(b)** implicit data typing
  - **(c)** compare and branch
  - **(d)** unconditional jump

* **2.** Which of the following statements is FALSE?
  - **(a)** Fortran provides for both implicit and explicit typing of numeric data.
  - **(b)** The value of 3 ** 2 is 6.
  - **(c)** A data value may be allocated a storage location by either a READ or an assignment statement.
  - **(d)** If implicit data typing is assumed, and if ICOUNT = 5.8, then executing the statement
    ```
    PRINT *, ICOUNT
    ```
    will result in the number 5 being printed.

* **3.** Given
  ```
  A = 5
  A = A ** 2
  ```
  what is the final value of A?
  - **(a)** 5
  - **(b)** 10
  - **(c)** 25
  - **(d)** None of these

* **4.** Given the statement
  ```
  CHARACTER * 4 SUM, TOTAL
  ```
  what is the maximum string length allowed?
  - **(a)** 3
  - **(b)** 4
  - **(c)** 5
  - **(d)** None of these

5 and 6. Given the statements
```
INTEGER COUNT, ID
REAL MEAN
CHARACTER CURVE * 5
```

* **5.** Which of the following statements would result in a data value being stored in truncated form?
  - **(a)** `ID = 19.6`
  - **(b)** `MEAN = 105.4`
  - **(c)** `CURVE = 'NORMAL'`
  - **(d)** Choices (a) and (c)

* **6.** Which of the following statements is illegal?
  - **(a)** `CURVE = 'EXP'`
  - **(b)** `MEAN = 18.0`
  - **(c)** `COUNT = CURVE`
  - **(d)** `ID = 1987`

* **7.** Which of the following statements contains a syntax error?
  - **(a)** `READ * A,B`
  - **(b)** `PRINT *, X`
  - **(c)** `SUM = SUM + VAL`
  - **(d)** `CHARACTER J,K,L`

* **8.** What is the value of KSUM?
  ```
  INITAL = 5
  KSUM = 3 * INITAL + INITAL
  ```
  - **(a)** 15
  - **(b)** 20
  - **(c)** 8
  - **(d)** 30

* **9.** If implicit data typing is assumed, what is the value of KANS?
  ```
  INT = 9.99
  KANS = INT * 10
  ```
  - **(a)** 9.99
  - **(b)** 99.9
  - **(c)** 99.0
  - **(d)** 90
  - **(e)** 90.0

*10. Using this data list: 'CAR' 50.0 6.0, determine the output of the following program:

```
REAL RATE, TIME, DIST
CHARACTER VEHCLE * 8
READ *, VEHCLE,RATE,TIME
DIST = RATE * TIME
PRINT *, VEHCLE,DIST
STOP
END
```

(a) `CAR 50 6 300`   (c) `CAR 300`

(b) `CAR 50.0 6.0 300.0`   (d) `CAR 300.0`

*11. In a Fortran program three variables are used: ALPHA, BETA, and GAMMA. On the basis of the data to be supplied to the program for these three variables (see the table below), write an appropriate set of data declaration statements.

ALPHA	BETA	GAMMA
45.9	18	'DARTS'
1.6	109	'TENNIS'
0.8	9	'GOLF'
−189.3	8700	'ICE HOCKEY'
0.99	−7	'FOOTBALL'

12-17. Write a Fortran program for each of the following, using explicit data typing:

*12. Input the length of a side of a square. Print its area. (Area $= s^2$.)

13. A principal (sum of money) is invested for a certain time at a given rate of interest. Given the rate, time, and principal, print the amount of earned interest. ($I = P * R * T$.)

*14. Read in a purchased price. If the sales tax rate is 7%, print the dollar amount of the tax and the total purchase price.

*15. Input the radius of a circle and print its area. (Use area $= 3.14159 \times r^2$.)

*16. Read in a length expressed in inches, and print the equivalent length expressed in centimeters and in meters. (*Note:* 1 inch = 2.54 centimeters = 0.0254 meter.)

*17. Read in the list price of an item and its sale price. Print the list price, sale price, and percent of the discount.

CHAPTER 3
More on Input, Output, and Processing

COMPUTER AXIOM

Generally speaking, computers do not make mistakes; they merely follow instructions. Programmers, however, are prone to human error. Therefore, it is the fate of programmers to spend part of their workday debugging programs.

COROLLARY

As the amount of time devoted to program planning and program documentation increases, the amount of time required for debugging decreases.

3.1 Evaluating Fortran Expressions

What is the value of 3 + 2 * 4? This expression contains two different types of arithmetic operations. Depending on which operation is performed first, two different answers will be obtained:

Method 1	Method 2
3 + 2 * 4	3 + 2 * 4
5 * 4	3 + 8
20	11

To avoid any such ambiguity, let's agree on a certain "priority" of operations. For example, multiplication and division have a higher priority than addition or subtraction. Method 2, therefore, gives the correct result: 11.

Order of Operations

In evaluating arithmetic expressions, the order in which operations are performed is determined by their priority levels. Exponentiation has the highest priority and is performed first. Multiplication and division come next. Addition and subtraction are performed last.

	Priority	Operations	Symbols
Highest	1	Exponentiation	**
↓	2	Multiplication and division	* and /
Lowest	3	Addition and subtraction	+ and −

If an expression contains more than one operation at the same priority level, the operations are performed in order, going from left to right.

Exception: Consecutive exponentiations of the form A ✻ B ✻ C are performed from right to left:

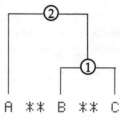

EXAMPLE 3.1   Evaluate: (a) 7 + 18 / 2 * 3   (b) 12 + 15 / 3 − 4 ** 2

Solutions

(a)   7 + 18 / 2 * 3

7 + 9 * 3

7 + 27

34

(b)   12 + 15 / 3 − 4 ** 2

12 + 15 / 3 − 16

12 + 5 − 16

17 − 16

1

EXAMPLE 3.2   Evaluate: (a) 2 ** 2 ** 3   (b) 4 ** 3 / 2 ** 5

Solutions

(a) This example represents the *exception* to the rule that operations at the same priority level are evaluated from left to right. Consecutive exponentiations are evaluated from right to left:

(b) Exponentiations are *not* consecutively written and are therefore performed from left to right:

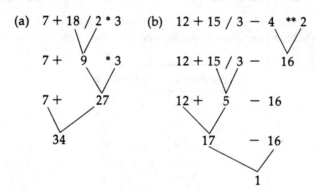

2 ** 2 ** 3

2 ** 8

256

4 ** 3 / 2 ** 5

64 / 2 ** 5

64 / 32

2

USING PARENTHESES

Sometimes it is necessary to override the assigned priority level of operations. For example, to find the average of two data values, say A and B, we must, *first*, add A to B, and, *second*, divide the sum by 2:

Incorrect	Correct
AVG = A + B / 2.0	AVG = (A + B) / 2.0

A *subexpression* is an expression that is part of a larger expression. In the above example the subexpression A + B, since it is enclosed within parentheses, is evaluated *before* the division operation is performed.

THE FIRST GOLDEN RULE OF PARENTHESES

Evaluate parenthesized expressions first. The subexpression that a set of parentheses encloses is evaluated before any other terms of the expression.

EXAMPLE 3.3 Evaluate: (a) 36 / (9 + 3)   (c) (2 ** 3) ** 3
(b) (12 − 6) / (2 + 1)   (d) 3 + (100 / 5) ** 2

Solutions

(a) 36 / (9 + 3)   (b) (12 − 6) / (2 + 1)   (c) (2 ** 3) ** 3   (d) 3 + (100 / 5) ** 2

    36 / 12   6   /   3   8 ** 3   3 +   20   ** 2

       3   2   512   3 +   400

                                                          403

EXAMPLE 3.4 If R = 2.0, S = 3.0, and T = 4.0, find the value that is assigned to variable W.
(a) W = R * S ** T
(b) W = S ** (T − R)
(c) W = (T * S) / (R + 1.0)

Solutions

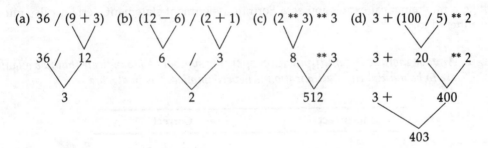

(a) W = R * S ** T
    W = 2.0 * 3.0 ** 4.0

       2.0 *   81.0

    W =   162.0

(b) W = S ** (T − R)
    W = 3.0 ** (4.0 − 2.0)

      3.0 **   2.0

    W =   9.0

(c) W = (T * S) / (R + 1.0)
    W = (4.0 * 3.0) / (2.0 + 1.0)

      12.0   / (2.0 + 1.0)

      12.0   /   3.0

    W =   4.0

The next sample illustrates how to evaluate expressions in which sets of parentheses are *nested* (that is, one or more sets of parenthesized expressions are enclosed by another set of parentheses).

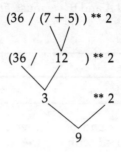

THE SECOND GOLDEN RULE OF PARENTHESES

Evaluate expressions containing nested parentheses by working inside out. The expression in the innermost parentheses is evaluated first. Since the parenthesis symbol must occur in pairs, be sure that the number of left parenthesis symbols equals the number of right parenthesis symbols.

3.2 Writing Fortran Expressions

In writing a mathematical expression as a Fortran assignment statement, certain rules must be strictly adhered to.

RULE 1. *Always include the multiplication operator symbol (∗) to indicate that two quantities are to be multiplied. Multiplication is never "implied," as in algebra.*

Incorrect	Correct
K = 3L	K = 3 ∗ L
M = 2(J − I)	M = 2 ∗ (J − I)

RULE 2. *Never write an expression containing two consecutively written operators.*

Incorrect	Correct
A ∗ − B	A ∗ (− B) *or* − B ∗ A

RULE 3. *Be sure that only a single Fortran variable name appears on the left side of the equal sign.*

Incorrect	Correct
A + B = C	C = A + B
3 = I	I = 3

RULE 4. *Avoid writing Fortran expressions that include both real and integer variable types. Be consistent in typing variables and constants in the same expression: use real constants with real variables and integer constants with integer variables. Although many versions of Fortran permit mixing data types (including Fortran 77, WATFOR, and WATFIV), in certain situations the practice may produce unexpected results (see Section 3.3).*

Mixed Expression	Preferred Expression	Type
`P = 4 * S`	`P = 4.0 * S`	Real
`KOUNT = KOUNT + 1.0`	`KOUNT = KOUNT + 1`	Integer
`INT = X + Y`	`RINT = X + Y`	Real

An important exception to Rule 4 occurs in exponentiation. Whenever possible, use an integer exponent regardless of whether the base is an integer or a real value. Most computers evaluate exponential expressions having an integer exponent by repeated multiplication. Thus `A ** 4` is evaluated as `A * A * A * A`. An exponential expression having a real exponent is typically evaluated by using logarithms. Thus `A ** 4.0` is evaluated using logarithms. Hence, the results of an exponentiation operation tend to be produced faster and more accurately when the exponent is expressed in integer rather than real form.

EXAMPLE 3.5   Identify the error in each of the following Fortran statements:
(a) `A = 3(B + C)`
(b) `X = Y / - C`
(c) `C ** 2 = A ** 2 + B ** 2`
(d) `SUM = SUM + 9,999`
(e) `X = ( (Y + Z) * T ** 2`
(f) `Q = A / 3`

Solutions

(a) An operator must be inserted between the number 3 and the left parenthesis.
(b) Two operators are written consecutively. Parentheses must be used.
(c) An arithmetic operation is being performed on the left side of the equal sign. A legal Fortran variable must stand alone on the left side of the equal symbol.
(d) The comma must be deleted.
(e) A right parenthesis has been omitted.
(f) Although this expression does not contain an error, it should be written with the real constant 3.0 instead of the integer constant.

Table 3.1 summarizes some frequently encountered algebraic forms and their Fortran equivalents. Sometimes, as in the following example, parentheses *must* be used in translating an algebraic expression into Fortran:

Algebraic Notation	Fortran Expression
$m = \dfrac{x2 - x1}{y2 - y1}$	`M = (X2 - X1) / (Y2 - Y1)`

Often the liberal use of parentheses in converting an algebraic expression into Fortran can simplify the translation process.

Algebraic Notation	Fortran Expression
$R = \dfrac{a}{b} + \dfrac{xy^3}{z^2}$	R = (A / B) + X * (Y ** 3) / (Z ** 2)
	or (with*out* parentheses)
	R = A / B + X * Y ** 3 / Z ** 2

THE THIRD GOLDEN RULE OF PARENTHESES

When in doubt, insert parentheses. The parentheses will then dictate the order of operations. Keep in mind that "extra" parentheses are *not* harmful. For example, the following expressions are equivalent:

(A ** B) + (C - D)   *and*   A ** B + C - D

Table 3.1 Some Algebraic Forms and Their Fortran Equivalents

Algebraic Form	Fortran Equivalent
1. abc	1. A * B * C
2. $a + bc$	2. A + B * C
3. $a(b + c)$	3. A * (B + C)
4. $\dfrac{a}{b} - c$	4. A / B - C
5. $\dfrac{a - c}{b}$	5. (A - C) / B
6. $\dfrac{a - c}{a + b}$	6. (A - C) / (A + B)
7. $\dfrac{ab}{c}$	7. A * B / C
8. $\dfrac{a}{bc}$	8. A / (B * C)
9. ab^c	9. A * B ** C
10. $(ab)^c$	10. (A * B) ** C
11. a^{bc}	11. A ** (B * C)
12. a^{b^c}	12. A ** (B ** C)
13. $\dfrac{a^c}{b}$	13. A ** C / B
14. $\left(\dfrac{a}{b}\right)^c$	14. (A / B) ** C

EXAMPLE 3.6   Express in Fortran:

(a) $x^2 + \dfrac{rs}{t + w}$ (b) $\dfrac{r^s}{cd} - \dfrac{e}{f + g}$

Solutions

(a) (X ** 2) + (R * S) / (T + W)
(b) (R ** S) / (C * D) - (E / (F + G))

TAKING ROOTS OF NUMBERS

In Fortran, roots of numbers are expressed in exponential form. In general, the *r*th root of a number may be expressed in exponential form as follows:

$$\sqrt[r]{A} = \text{A ** (1.0 / r)}$$

When convenient, the exponent should be expressed in decimal form.

Symbol	Interpretation	Fortran Expression
$\sqrt{A}$	Square root of A	A ** 0.5
$\sqrt[3]{A}$	Cube root of A	A ** 0.33333333
$\sqrt[4]{A}$	Fourth root of A	A ** 0.25
$\sqrt[5]{A}$	Fifth root of A	A ** 0.2

Caution: In each of the above expressions the value of variable A *must be positive.* In general, only a positive real value may be raised to a *real power.* The reason is based on the fact that the computer performs exponentiation involving real exponents by using logarithms. The logarithm of a negative number is undefined.

EXAMPLE 3.7 Evaluate: (a) 81.0 ** 0.5   (c) 8.0 ** (− 0.33333333)
(b) (− 8.0) ** 0.33333333   (d) − 36.0 ** 0.5

Answers

(a) 9.0
(b) Not defined. In attempting to evaluate such an expression the computer would generate an error message.
(c) The expression is evaluated as 8.0 raised to the *negative* one-third power. Since 8.0 raised to the positive one-third power is 2.0, 8.0 raised to the negative one-third power is the reciprocal of 2.0, or 0.5 (assuming that no round-off error creeps in).
(d) Following the order of operations, the expression would be evaluated as −(36.0 ** 0.5), which is −6.0.

The following table compares an algebraic statement with its Fortran representation.

Algebraic Expression	Fortran Assignment Statement
1. $z = \sqrt{xy}$	1. Z = (X * Y) ** 0.5
2. $r = \sqrt[3]{\dfrac{s}{t}}$	2. R = 3.0 * (S / T) ** 0.5
3. $d = \sqrt[3]{ax^5 + b}$	3. D = ((A * X ** 5) + B) ** 0.33333333
4. $b = \sqrt{\dfrac{a}{4} + \dfrac{1}{\sqrt{x}}}$	4. B = (A / 4.0 + (1.0 / X ** 0.5)) ** 0.5
5. $e = a^{2/7} + \dfrac{2}{7}a$	5. E = A ** (2.0 / 7.0) + (2.0 / 7.0 * A)
6. $z = x^{\sqrt{y}}$	6. Z = X ** (Y ** 0.5)
7. $s = \sqrt{\dfrac{(x-a)^2}{c} - b^2}$	7. S = ((X − A) ** 2 / C − (B ** 2)) ** 0.5

Note: Some of the Fortran assignment statements include more than the minimum number of sets of parentheses.

EXAMPLE 3.8 Which one of the following Fortran expressions has been translated *incorrectly* from the given algebraic expression?

Algebraic Expression	Fortran Expression
(a) $\dfrac{ab}{cd}$	(a) A * B / (C * D)
(b) $\left(\dfrac{x}{y-z}\right)^3$	(b) (X / (Y - Z)) ** 3
(c) $\left(\dfrac{a}{b}\right)^{c-2}$	(c) (A / B) ** C - 2
(d) $\dfrac{\sqrt{x+y}}{z}$	(d) (X + Y) ** 0.5 / Z

Solution (c). The correct Fortran expression is (A / B) ** (C - 2)

EXAMPLE 3.9

The Pythagorean theorem states that, in a right triangle, $c^2 = a^2 + b^2$, where a and b represent the lengths of the sides of the right triangle and c is the length of the hypotenuse. Write a program that reads in the lengths of the sides of a right triangle and calculates the length of the hypotenuse.

Solution

Program Analysis

Input: ASIDE, BSIDE (real variables)

Output: CHYP (real variable)

Processing: Since $c^2 = a^2 + b^2$, $c = \sqrt{a^2 + b^2}$.

In Fortran, CHYP = (ASIDE ** 2 + BSIDE ** 2) ** 0.5

See the program that follows.

```
* THIS PROGRAM IS RUN ON A PRIME COMPUTER USING A FORTRAN 77 COMPILER
      REAL ASIDE, BSIDE, CHYP
      READ *, ASIDE, BSIDE
      CHYP = (ASIDE * * 2 + BSIDE * * 2) ** 0.5
      PRINT *, ASIDE, BSIDE, CHYP
      STOP
      END
```

```
      3.0 4.0
          3.00000        4.00000        5.00000
      **** STOP
```

Data

3.3 Mixed-Mode Arithmetic

As a general principle, a variable and its stored data value must agree in type. If in executing an assignment statement a numeric variable and its assigned numeric value do *not* agree in type, then the data value is converted by the Fortran compiler so that it conforms to the variable type.

If implicit variable typing is assumed, and if K = VAL and VAL = 7.4, then the variable K will store the value 7. The decimal part of 7.4 will be truncated since K can store only an integer value.

Next, consider the statement `R = IVAL` where IVAL = 3. Since R can store only a real value, the data value 3.0 will be assigned to R.

EXAMPLE 3.10 Determine the output of the following program:

```
REAL A, P
INTEGER K, L
A = 13.9
K = 2
P = K
L = A
PRINT *, P, L
STOP
END
```

Solution

Output: 2.00000   13
        **** STOP

A *mixed* expression is one that involves both real and integer quantities. R = 2 + 6.99 is an example of a mixed expression since 2 is an integer constant while 6.99 is a real constant. In evaluating an assignment statement of the form

Fortran variable = *mixed expression*

the Fortran compiler converts the integer value(s) to real value(s) and then performs the required arithmetic operations (some older Fortrans do not permit mixed-mode arithmetic):

1. If the variable is typed as a real variable (either implicitly or explicitly), the calculated value will be assigned to the variable intact.
2. If the variable is typed as an integer variable, the decimal part of the calculated value will be truncated and the resulting integer will be assigned to the variable.

Mixed Expression	Stored Result	Comment
1. `R = 2 + 6.99`	8.99	When the statement is executed, 2 is converted to 2.0 and then added to 6.99.
2. `K = 1 + 3.16`	4	The number 4.16 cannot be assigned to an integer variable (we are assuming implicit variable typing). The decimal part is truncated so that the variable K stores the integer value 4.
3. `I = 3 + 9.0 / 4`	5	The number 4 is converted to 4.0 and the division is then performed, yielding 2.25. The value 3 is converted to 3.0 and added to 2.25. The sum is 5.25. Since I is an integer variable, the decimal part of the sum is truncated and 5 is assigned to I.

Expressions 2 and 3 on page 63 illustrate the necessity for the programmer to be alert to the possibility that an inappropriate choice of variable type may lead to truncation errors. Truncation also occurs when taking the quotient of two integer values in which there is a decimal remainder:

Expression	Stored Result	Comment
I = 5 / 4	1	The decimal part of the quotient (.25) is truncated.
R = 5 / 4	1.0	Since R is a real variable, it must store a real data value.
R = 5 / 4.0	1.25	No truncation error occurs. Since the expression is mixed, 5 is converted to real form. The division is performed, and the exact result of 1.25 is assigned to R.

EXAMPLE 3.11 Fill in the following table (assume implicit variable typing):

Expression		Stored Result
(a) K = 2 / 3	(a)	
(b) A = 2 * 5.4	(b)	
(c) B = 7 / 2	(c)	
(d) L = 9.0 / 5.0	(d)	
(e) Y = 12.0 / 8	(e)	
(f) S = 12 / 5 - 0.3	(f)	
(g) T = 12 / 5.0 - 0.3	(g)	
(h) R = 0.9 ** 2	(h)	

Solutions

(a) 0

(b) 10.8000

(c) 3.00000

(d) 1

(e) 1.50000

(f) 1.70000

(g) 2.10000

(h) 0.810000 (*Note:* A real expression raised to an integer power is not treated by the computer as a mixed expression. However, an integer expression raised to a real power is *evaluated* as a mixed expression.)

3.4 Explaining Computer Output

To ensure that computer output is correctly interpreted, it is recommended that a printed result be preceded by a descriptive comment or label. For example, instead of simply printing a value that represents the sum of two values, the answer should be preceded by the phrase SUM = .

(1)	(2)
Program with Annotated Output	**Program withOUT Annotated Output**
REAL A, B, S	REAL A, B, S
A = 15.8	A = 15.8
B = 10.1	B = 10.1
S = A + B	S = A + B
PRINT *, 'SUM =', S	PRINT *, S
STOP	STOP
END	END
Output:	*Output:*
SUM = 25.9000	25.9000

As program (1) illustrates, a character string may be printed simply by enclosing the string within apostrophes:

```
PRINT *, 'character string', . . .
```

The computer is very obedient — it will print the character string exactly as it appears within the apostrophes. For example, the result of executing the statement

```
PRINT *, '1 + 1 = 3'
```

would be 1 + 1 = 3.

STRUCTURED PROGRAMMING GUIDELINE

Always take steps to explain the meaning of printed results. This will make the output of your program easier to read and will decrease the possibility that the output values will be misinterpreted. When using an output statement of the form

```
PRINT *, 'descriptive label', program variable
```

keep in mind that the computer has no way of knowing whether the descriptive label corresponds to the variable that follows. That is the responsibility of the programmer.

3.5 The GOTO Statement

Each of the sample programs presented so far suffers from the same limitation — when executed, it processes only a single set of data values (that is, a single input data record consisting of one data value for each variable appearing in the input variable list).

Consider the following program, which calculates and prints the average of two real values:

```
REAL X, Y, AVG
READ *, X, Y
AVG = (X + Y) / 2.0
PRINT *, 'AVERAGE =', AVG
STOP
END
```

This program will process a single pair of data values and, after printing the average, will stop. Suppose that we wish to use this program to find the averages of *several* pairs of numbers, such as the following:

Data Set	X	Y
1	4.0	18.0
2	75.0	50.0
3	31.9	68.1

As the program now stands, after processing the first set of values (4.0 and 18.0), the computer will print the average (11.0) and then stop. In order to find the average of the second pair of data values (75.0 and 50.0), the user of the program has to initiate a set of commands or procedures that will restart the program. After processing the second pair of values, the program must again be restarted manually. The result is a good deal of wasted time.

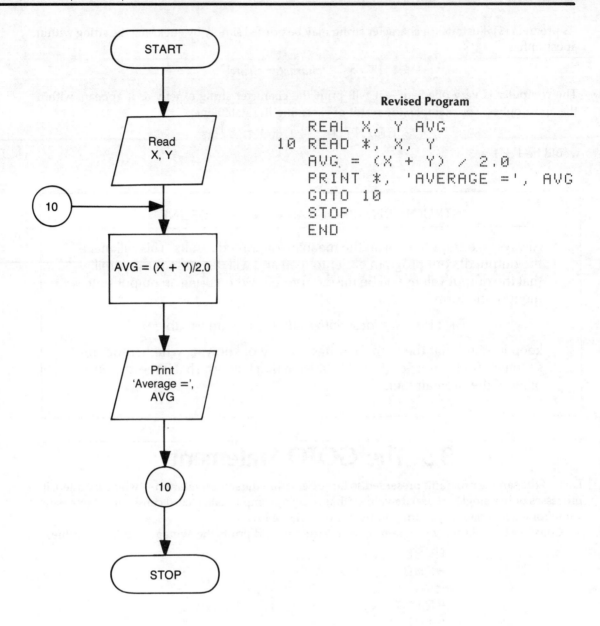

Revised Program

```
   REAL X, Y AVG
10 READ *, X, Y
   AVG = (X + Y) / 2.0
   PRINT *, 'AVERAGE =', AVG
   GOTO 10
   STOP
   END
```

Figure 3.1

One of the major advantages of using a computer is that it has the ability to execute the same set of tasks repeatedly, without the need for human intervention. In Fortran (as well as in a number of other high-level programming languages), the GOTO statement provides a means by which program control may be transferred automatically to a previously executed statement. This permits the same set of statements to be executed again. Figure 3.1 shows the revised Fortran program, which incorporates a GOTO statement, and the corresponding flowchart representation, in which the circular connector symbol corresponds to GOTO.

NOTE

Some programmers prefer to code GOTO as GO TO. Since Fortran ignores blanks, either form is acceptable.

THE STATEMENT LABEL

In our sample program, the READ statement is preceded by the number 10. The keyword GOTO is followed by the same number. When the GOTO statement is encountered during program execution, the flow of the program is redirected to the program statement that is preceded by the matching whole number. When the control of the program is transferred back to the READ statement, another input operation is performed, resulting in another data record being read. The *number* that precedes the statement to which program control is to be transferred (for example, 10) is called a *statement label* and

- must be a whole number between 1 and 99999, inclusive.
- must be coded in columns 1–5.
- is usually entered right-justified in its field. (Make certain that at least one column position separates a statement label and the first character of a Fortran statement.)

The GOTO Statement

Syntax: GOTO *statement label*

Effect: Fortran program statements are normally executed in the order in which they were written and stored in memory. When a GOTO statement is executed, the control of the program is transferred unconditionally (the computer has no choice) to the program statement that is preceded by the matching statement label. The GOTO statement may transfer program control to a statement that has already been executed ("backward" branching) or to a statement that comes after the GOTO ("forward" branching).

Caution: Always check to make certain that the GOTO statement and the statement to which control is to be transferred have matching statement labels.

In our sample program to find averages, the GOTO statement creates a cyclic pattern in which the same set of program statements is executed repeatedly, forming a *loop*. The program statement(s) that activates and controls a program loop is called a *looping structure*. A backward-branching GOTO statement represents the most elementary program looping structure.

STRUCTURED PROGRAMMING GUIDELINE

Keep the use of the GOTO statement to an absolute minimum. A program that includes several GOTO statements (forward and backward branching) will be difficult to read and unnecessarily prone to error.

As illustrated below, the statements that form the *body* (that is, are executed repeatedly) of a loop are indented. In a complex program this tends to make the program easier to read.

```
      REAL X, Y, AVG
   10 READ *, X, Y
         AVG = (X + Y) / 2.0
         PRINT *, 'AVERAGE = ', AVG
      GOTO 10
      STOP
      END
```

Note: The number of column spaces that are indented has been selected arbitrarily at 4.

By this time, you have probably noticed that our sample program has a glaring weakness — the STOP statement is never reached! How does the execution of the program stop? In a batch oriented system, the data values for each processing cycle are provided as separate input data records. In a card system, for example, each pair of data values would be punched on a separate data card and submitted with the program and appropriate control cards:

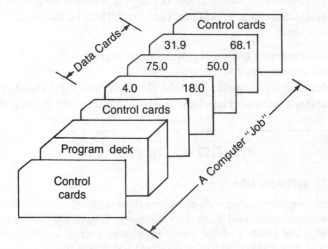

An analogous procedure is followed when the program is submitted for batch processing using a CRT terminal. During program execution each pair of data values is processed in turn. After the third pair of data values has been processed, the GOTO statement will transfer the control of the program back to the READ statement. The computer will attempt to perform another input operation. Instead of finding another data "card," however, the computer will encounter a control card. The program will then abruptly terminate with an ERROR message.

Some Fortran compilers will check whether the statement that follows an unconditional transfer of control statement can be reached. If it can't, a syntax error diagnostic is generated. This is illustrated in Program 3.1, which was run using an interactive Fortran 77 compiler on a PRIME 850 computer.

```
1    *PROGRAM CALCULATES THE AVERAGE OF TWO NUMBERS
2    *
3    *
4          REAL X, Y AVG
5    *
6    10 READ *, X, Y
7          AVG = (X + Y) / 2.0
8          PRINT *, 'AVERAGE =', AVG
9          GO TO 10
10         STOP
11         END
```

```
ERROR 294 SEVERITY 2 BEGINNING ON LINE 10
This statement cannot be reached due to an unconditional
transfer of control immediately preceding it.
```

Program 3.1

It is poor programming practice to terminate a program by allowing it to "run out of data" when attempting an input operation, or by overriding program execution by using an "escape/control" keystroke when working in an interactive Fortran environment. In Chapter 4 (see Section 4.5) the problem of how to incorporate an exiting mechanism into a Fortran program will be addressed.

VERTICAL LINE SPACING

To avoid having the outputs from successive runs bunched together, it is often helpful to "print" one or more blank lines between consecutive runs of the same program. The statement

```
PRINT *, ' '
```

"prints" a blank line that has the effect of skipping a line. In our sample program to find averages, in order to skip two consecutive lines between the outputs generated by successive executions of the program, two such PRINT statements must be written consecutively. This is illustrated in Program 3.2. Notice that, since this program is being run on the PRIME 850 interactive Fortran 77 system, a user prompt

```
'ENTER TWO DATA VALUES'
```

has been included. This helps to remind the user of the program that program execution has been temporarily suspended and will resume only after two data values have been keyed in by the user of the program. Also, the STOP statement has been omitted since on this system it would result in an error condition.

```
       REAL X, Y, AVG
   10  PRINT *, 'ENTER TWO DATA VALUES'
       READ *, X, Y
           AVG = (X + Y)/ 2.0
           PRINT *, 'AVERAGE =', AVG
           PRINT *, ' '
           PRINT *, ' '
       GO TO 10
       END

           ENTER TWO DATA VALUES
           4.0 18.0
            AVERAGE =       11.0000


           ENTER TWO DATA VALUES
           75.0 50.0
            AVERAGE =       62.5000


           ENTER TWO DATA VALUES
           31.0 68.1
            AVERAGE =       50.0000
```

Program 3.2

3.6 Some Additional Details on Coding Fortran Statements

After you write a Fortran program, it will probably be read by another person—an employer, another programmer, or perhaps a teacher. Moreover, you will probably have occasion to reexamine your own program, either during the debugging phase or sometime in the future when it may be necessary to modify the program. For these reasons, it is wise programming practice to incorporate nonexecutable, explanatory remarks into the text of your programs.

Figure 3.2 illustrates the inclusion of program comment lines, each identified by an asterisk in the first column of the statement. The program has been coded using a preprinted Fortran coding form, with each column corresponding to an 80-column input record. The first comment line explains the purpose of the program. This practice should be considered mandatory in every program that you write. Blank comment lines have been inserted to increase the readability of a computer generated listing of the program.

The rules that must be followed when coding a Fortran program are summarized in Table 3.2 on page 72.

FORTRAN Coding Form

PROGRAM | PUNCHING INSTRUCTIONS | GRAPHIC | PUNCH | PAGE OF | CARD ELECTRO

PROGRAMMER L. LEFF DATE 03-18-84

STATEMENT NUMBER | CONT. | FORTRAN STATEMENT

```
*PROGRAM CALCULATES THE AVERAGE OF TWO NUMBERS
*
*
      REAL X, Y, AVG
*
   1Ø READ *, X, Y
      AVG = (X + Y) / 2.Ø
      PRINT *, 'AVERAGE = ', AVG
      GOTO 1Ø
      STOP
      END
```

<u>NOTE:</u> 1) Zeros are slashed (Ø) in order to distinguish them from the letter O.

2) An asterisk (*) in column 1 denotes a comment line. Sometimes a blank comment line will be used in order to increase the readability of the program from the programmer's standpoint.

3) Keep in mind that column spaces within a FORTRAN statement are ignored, provided they are <u>not</u> within a character string that is enclosed within a pair of apostrophe marks.

Figure 3.2

EXAMPLE 3.12 Write a program that accepts as input three integer values and then prints the values that were read in, followed by a listing of the values in the reverse order in which they were entered (for example, if the data list is 3, 19, 65, then print 65, 19, 3). Include explanatory comments and provision to process more than one set of data values. Also, skip three blank lines between the outputs generated by successive runs of the program.

Solution

```
* PROGRAM PRINTS THREE DATA VALUES IN REVERSE
* ORDER
* PROGRAMMER:  L. LEFF        DATE:   JULY 4, 1984
*
*
      INTEGER J, K, L
   99 READ *, J, K, L
* . . . ECHO PRINT DATA VALUES
      PRINT *, 'DATA LIST:', J, K, L
      PRINT *, ' '
* . . . PRINT VALUES IN REVERSE ORDER
      PRINT *, L, K, J
* . . . SKIP MORE BLANK LINES
      PRINT *, ' '
      PRINT *, ' '
      PRINT *, ' '
      GOTO 99
      STOP
      END
```

Program Notes: Notice the use of comments to explain key parts of the program. Immediately after the data are read, they are printed. This technique, called *echo printing,* is used to verify that the data values that the programmer thinks were supplied to the computer during a READ operation were actually received by the machine and are being interpreted correctly.

Echo printing of data values is most appropriate in a batch processing system. If you are working with an interactive Fortran system, there is no need to echo-print data since data values that were entered during program execution via the keyboard console appear on the screen. Instead, you should provide a prompting message which alerts the user of the program that the computer is waiting for data values to be entered. The prompting message should *precede* the corresponding input statement. If the program written for Example 3.12 were being run on an interactive Fortran 77 system, the program would be coded as follows:

```
* PRIME 850 INTERACTIVE FORTRAN 77
      INTEGER J, K, L
      PRINT *, 'ENTER VALUES FOR J, K, AND L'
   99 READ *, J, K, L
      PRINT *, ' '
      PRINT *, L, K, J
      PRINT *, ' '
      PRINT *, ' '
      PRINT *, ' '
      GOTO 99
      END
```

Table 3.2 Rules for Coding a Fortran Program

Columns	Field Contents	Use
1	* or C	To indicate that a comment line follows. In Fortran 77 either an * or the letter "C" may be used. Most other Fortrans accept only "C" to denote a comment line. Comment lines may be inserted anywhere in a Fortran program. They appear in a source program listing, but are *not* executed since they are ignored by the Fortran compiler.
1–5	Statement label	To identify a Fortran statement that will be referenced by another statement in the program, such as a GOTO. The statement label must be some whole number between 1 and 99999, inclusive. To make for easy reading, a statement label is usually written right-justified in its field.
6	Any nonzero character other than a blank	To indicate that the Fortran expression that follows is a continuation of the Fortran statement coded on the preceding line. A single Fortran statement may be "wrapped around" or extended over a maximum of 19 lines.
7–72	Fortran statement	To represent program instructions that may be coded in any column between 7 and 72, inclusive.
73–80	Optional program identification	To help identify the program or to number statements sequentially (particularly in a card system). Any entry made in this field is ignored by the Fortran compiler, but appears on a source program listing. (*Note:* In a *data* record all 80 columns can be used to enter values for computer input.)

STRUCTURED PROGRAMMING GUIDELINE

If your programs are being run in a *batch* processing mode, make it a practice to echo-print data values supplied to a program via an input operation. This provides a convenient means for verifying that the correct data values were read and are being used by the program. In an interactive Fortran system, provide concise and meaningful user prompts in order to inform the user of the program what types of data the computer is waiting to receive.

STRUCTURED PROGRAMMING GUIDELINE

Make the text of your program easy to read. This is especially important when it becomes necessary to make changes in a program, either as a result of program debugging or because of the need to expand or modify features of the program. Comment statements can be used to improve the readability of your program as follows:

- Insert blank comment lines between the different logical units of the program. For example, use blank comment lines to separate data declaration statements and executable program statements.
- Use comment statements to describe key elements of the program. As a minimum, include comments that identify the purpose of the program, its author, and the date when it was written or last modified. In more complicated programs, comments should be used to introduce a set of statements that perform an essential processing task. Using comments to define the names of program variables is also a recommended practice.

3.7 Column Headings

To produce printed computer output that makes for easy reading, it is sometimes preferable to organize the output into columns, with each column having an appropriate heading. This is particularly useful in programs that are designed to generate tables of values or produce highly formatted types of hard-copy reports, especially in a batch mode of processing in which a group of input data records are processed. For example, a set of Celsius temperatures (C) can be converted to Fahrenheit temperatures (F) by using this formula:

$$F = 1.8 * C + 32.0.$$

The output can be conveniently displayed in table form as follows:

	CELSIUS	FAHRENHEIT
(sample data)	10.0000	50.0000

As Program 3.3 illustrates, column headings must be printed *before* any processing begins. If the column headings were included within the looping structure, the headings would be printed each time the loop was executed.

```
$JOB    WATFIV
C* * * * * PROGRAM INCLUDES COLUMN HEADINGS * * * * *
C*                                                    *
C* PROGRAMMER:  L. LEFF  DATE: MARCH 1, 1984          *
C* VARIABLE NAMES:                                    *
C*                                                    *
C*                  F = FAHRENHEIT TEMPERATURE        *
C*                  C = CELSIUS TEMPERATURE           *
C*                                                    *
C* THE PROGRAM WAS RUN USING WATFIV                   *
C*                                                    *
C* * * * * * * * * * * * * * * * * * * * * * * * * * *
C
C
```

```
   1              REAL C, F
   2              PRINT , '              CELSIUS       FAHRENHEIT'
   3              PRINT , '              -------       ----------'
   4              PRINT , ' '
   5          10 READ , C
   6              F = 1.8 * C + 32.0
   7              PRINT , C, F
   8              PRINT , ' '
   9              GOTO 10
  10              STOP
**WARNING**   UNNUMBERED EXECUTABLE STATEMENT FOLLOWS A
              TRANSFER
  11              END
        $ENTRY
              CELSIUS                FAHRENHEIT
              -------                ----------
          15.0000000              59.0000000
         100.0000000             212.0000000
           0.0000000              32.0000000
          54.0000000             129.1999000
```

Program 3.3

Program Notes:

1. Since this particular compiler recognizes that the STOP statement will never be executed, it prints this warning message:

   ```
   UNNUMBERED EXECUTABLE STATEMENT
         FOLLOWS A TRANSFER
   ```

2. Observe the use of the asterisk in forming a "banner" that highlights certain essential information. Each line in this section begins with an asterisk, which informs the Fortran compiler that the rest of the line should be ignored.

3. The column headings are included within the same pair of apostrophes. Assume that the programmer wishes the headings to be centered over the output values; he or she must then plan their placement within the apostrophe marks, based on knowledge of the predetermined width of a print field and the anticipated width of each data item. Since the width of a print field and the system's field spacing conventions vary among Fortran compilers, check with your instructor or computer facility. (A little experimentation may be necessary in order to understand fully how your computer will display list-directed output on a print line.)

Sometimes the nature of the list-directed output and the Fortran compiler being used make it difficult, if not impossible, to align a column heading with its associated output. In such cases it may be wise to abandon list-directed output statements in favor of *format-directed* output statements. Input/output statements that allow the programmer to exercise greater control over the precise column placement of input/output will be discussed in Chapter 4.

3.8 Planning a Fortran Program

A completed Fortran program represents the end product of human efforts to take a problem statement and design a set of instructions that a computer can follow and that achieves a desired outcome. Frequently, the program solution is not immediately apparent from the problem statement. In this section we offer a four-step approach that can be used to analyze a problem for which a computer solution is sought.

The following sequence of steps should be followed whenever you are asked to prepare a computer program:

Step 1: Understand the problem.
Read the problem carefully. Look for answers to the following questions: What is the *input*? What is the *output*? What *processing* is required?

Step 2: Devise a plan.
Select and define variable names. Develop the sequence of steps necessary in order to progress from the given input to the desired output. Describe the required algorithm by drawing a flowchart.

Step 3: Implement the plan.
Translate the flowchart into a coded set of Fortran program statements.

Step 4: Check your solution.
Are you certain that your program is correct? Choose convenient sample test data and run your program. Does the program produce correct results? If it doesn't, identify the source of error and make the appropriate corrections. If necessary, check your logic by returning to your flowchart. If the program runs successfully, can it be enhanced? For example, can the program text be clarified by using comments? Can the output be made more visually appealing? Can you think of a more efficient algorithm?

Example 3.13 illustrates this four-step approach.

EXAMPLE 3.13 It is a relatively simple matter to find the area of a *right* triangle, given the length of its base and its height (area $= \frac{1}{2} \times$ base $\times$ height). To find the area of *any* type of triangle, given the lengths of its three sides, we may use Heron's formula:

$$\text{AREA} = \sqrt{S \cdot (S - A) \cdot (S - B) \cdot (S - C)}$$

where A, B, and C represent the lengths of the sides of the triangle and S is the semiperimeter (one-half the sum of A, B, and C) of the triangle.

Write a Fortran program that reads values for variables A, B, and C, and calculates and prints the area of the triangle.

Solution

Step 1. Identify the input, the output, and the processing required.
Input: The lengths of the three sides of the triangle.
Processing: Calculate the semiperimeter and then the area, using Heron's formula.
Output: Print the lengths of the sides of the triangle and its area in table form:

SIDE A	SIDE B	SIDE C	AREA
XX.X	XX.X	XX.X	

Step 2. Assign variable names: Let A, B, and C represent the lengths of the three sides of the triangle; SEMI, the semiperimeter; and AREA, the area of the triangle.
The flowchart is displayed in Figure 3.3.

Step 3. Using the flowchart developed in Step 2 as a guide, write the Fortran coded program. See Program 3.4.

Step 4. Check your solution. Before submitting the program to the computer, using an appropriate input medium, you should perform a "desk check." The coded program should be scanned to detect any potential errors in spelling or punctuation, or any misuse of the rules of Fortran (for example, using a variable name that exceeds six characters). You should *not* be content after checking that a program is free of all such syntax errors. The program may still not work as intended. Choose convenient sample test data for which you can calculate the answer *manually*, such as:

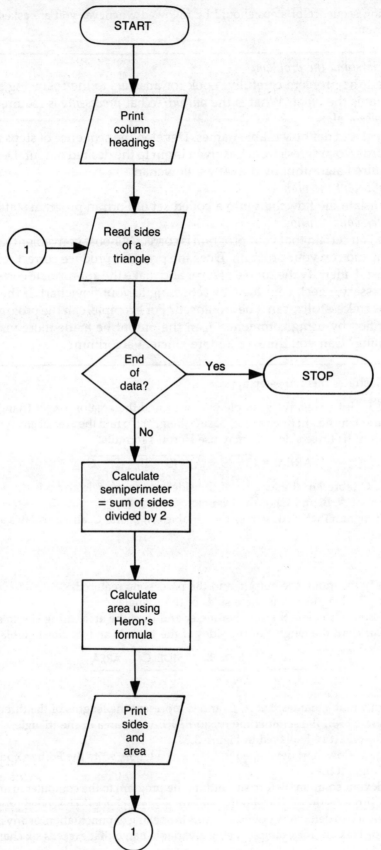

Figure 3.3 Flowchart for Example 3.13

	SIDE A	SIDE B	SIDE C	AREA
(sample data)	3.0	4.0	5.0	6.0

Next, obtain a computer run of your program and compare the computer-generated output with the results that were obtained by manually walking the data through the program (see the variable chart above). If necessary, make the appropriate corrections.

If the program yields the correct numerical output, concentrate next on the physical appearance of the output. Are the output data values aligned underneath the column headings? If not, make the appropriate adjustments in the spacing of the column headings.

```
$JOB    WATFIV
C*  *  *  *  *  * AREA OF A TRIANGLE USING HERON'S FORMULA  *  *  *  *  *
C*
C*   PROGRAMMER: L. LEFF             DATE:  MARCH 13, 1984
C*   COMPUTER: IBM
C*
C*   VARIABLE NAMES:
C*        A    = LENGTH OF SIDE A OF TRIANGLE ABC
C*        B    = LENGTH OF SIDE B OF TRIANGLE ABC
C*        C    = LENGTH OF SIDE C OF TRIANGLE ABC
C*        SEMI = SEMIPERIMETER OF TRIANGLE ABC
C*        AREA = AREA OF TRIANGLE ABC
C*
C*  *  *  *  *  *  *  *  *  *  *  *  *  *  *  *  *  *  *  *  *  *  *  *  *  *
1           REAL A, B, C, SEMI, AREA
C*
C* PRINT COLUMN HEADINGS
C*
2           PRINT ,'             SIDE A           SIDE B         SID
  -E C                  AREA'
3           PRINT ,'         ----------       ----------       -----
4           PRINT , ' '
C*
5     10 READ , A, B, C
6           SEMI = ( A + B + C ) / 2.0
7           AREA = ( SEMI * (SEMI - A) * (SEMI - B) * (SEMI - C) ) ** 0.5
8           PRINT , A, B, C, AREA
9           PRINT , ' '
10          GO TO 10
11          STOP
**WARNING** UNNUMBERED EXECUTABLE STATEMENT FOLLOWS A TRANSFER
12          END
```

```
$ENTRY
      SIDE A              SIDE B              SIDE C              AREA
   ----------          ----------          ----------          ----------
   4.000000            2.000000            3.000000            2.904737
   3.000000            2.199999            1.100000            0.9592655
   3.000000            4.000000            5.000000            5.999999
```

Program 3.4

If you are preparing a complex program, or if you find that computer time is a valuable commodity, you should subject your program to a "dry run" *before* submitting it for computer execution. Walk the sample test data through your program, statement by statement, while you play the role of the computer. Let your program statements direct your activities. If the desired output is obtained, then the program is ready to be prepared for computer input; if not, then the offending program statements must be identified and corrected.

The four-step method illustrated in this section can be used to advantage regardless of the complexity of the problem. Although we recommend that you rely heavily on this approach, and that you refer to it frequently, in order to conserve space we will not always use the exact format that has been shown here.

It would be misleading to imply that flowcharting is the only or the best method of devising a plan for the computer solution to a problem. In some situations problem solving tools such as pseudolanguage descriptions and structure charts may be used in addition to, or in place of, flowcharts. Some of these alternative approaches will be introduced later when their advantages can be more fully appreciated.

3.9 Some Closing Remarks

We began this chapter by focusing on how to write and evaluate formula types of expressions in Fortran. In evaluating an assignment statement of the form

$$variable = \text{Fortran } expression$$

an established hierarchy of operations must be observed. Subexpressions enclosed by parentheses receive the highest priority and must be evaluated first. Exponentiation is performed first, working from left to right, followed by multiplication and division; addition and subtraction are performed last.

Mixed-mode expressions should be avoided. When evaluating an expression that includes both real and integer data types, the expression is evaluated as a *real* expression, with all integer data values being converted to real form. The resulting value must agree in type with the variable that will store the value. If necessary, the calculated value is converted so that it is consistent with the variable to which it is being assigned. For example, if the calculated value is a real number and the variable that will store it is an integer variable, then the decimal portion of the calculated value will be truncated. Some older versions of Fortran do not permit mixed-mode arithmetic and will simply generate an error message whenever such an expression is encountered.

Throughout this chapter a number of suggestions were made regarding programming style. Some involved programming mechanics, while others were concerned with making program output more readable. Whenever appropriate:

- Be generous in using parentheses to help translate complex mathematical formulas into Fortran (when in doubt, parenthesize). Remember that a Fortran variable must stand alone on the left side of the equal symbol in an assignment statement.
- Express exponents in integer rather than real form.
- Make the output of your program "pretty" by:
  - skipping blank lines between consecutive lines of output;
  - explaining the output by preceding printed values with descriptive phrases;
  - using format-directed output statements (to be discussed in Chapter 4) to pinpoint the column placement of the output.
- Make the text of your program easy to read by:
  - using comment lines to identify what the program does, who authored the program, and when the program was written or last changed; complex programs can usually benefit by including additional comments that provide a concise narrative description of key elements of the program;
  - using blank comment lines to separate statements in a source program listing;
  - indenting program statements that form the body of a loop.

The debugging process begins when you code your *first* statement in a Fortran program. Attention to program clarity and Fortran grammatical rules at every stage of program development will help to minimize debugging time. Use a preprinted Fortran coding form to be certain that statements are entered in the correct columns. When completing a FORTRAN coding form:

- Use only capital letters.
- Distinguish between commonly confused character pairs.

Alpha	Numeric
O	0
Z	2
I	1
S	5

• Carefully scan the completed form for possible spelling and punctuation errors. Be sure that statement labels match. Also check that apostrophes and parentheses occur in pairs.

Check the logic of your program before you submit it for computer execution by choosing convenient sample test data and manually tracing the data through the program as a "desk check." When you are satisfied that the program is both syntactically and logically correct, you are ready to key in the program statements. Then run the program. Reconcile the output obtained by manually imitating computer execution with the actual computer generated output; they should agree (except, of course, if a computer round-off error has been introduced).

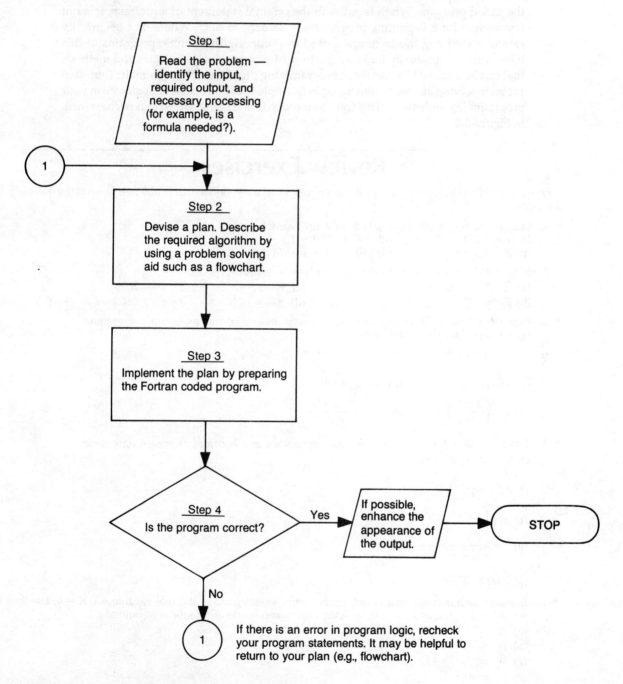

Figure 3.4

If the two sets of results do not agree, investigate. Make sure that the program is receiving correct data by echo printing the data values. It may also help to insert extra PRINT statements in order to check the values of variables as the execution of the program progresses. After you identify the source of the error, make the appropriate changes in the program and in the accompanying program documentation (for example, the flowchart), and rerun the program. Typically, several cycles of

$$\begin{bmatrix} \text{program} \\ \text{execution} \end{bmatrix} \Rightarrow \begin{bmatrix} \text{examining} \\ \text{output} \end{bmatrix} \Rightarrow \begin{bmatrix} \text{making} \\ \text{corrections} \end{bmatrix}$$

will be necessary before you are convinced that the program is correct.

All of the preceding comments assume that you are well under way in preparing the coded program. When faced with the original statement of a problem, it is not uncommon for a beginning programming student to ask, "Where do I begin?" By carefully studying the techniques used in preparing the sample programs in this book, you will gradually build a repertoire of programming strategies and methods that can be applied to a variety of programming problems. The systematic four-step problem solving approach illustrated in Example 3.13 will also serve you well in your programming endeavors. This four-step procedure is summarized in flowchart form in Figure 3.4.

Review Exercises

A star preceding the number of a problem indicates that a solution to that problem is given at the end of the book.

* **1.** Evaluate each of the following Fortran expressions:
  (a) $1 + 3 ** 2 - 12 / 3$ (c) $100 / 5 ** 2 - 1$
  (b) $2 * 18 / 6 + 3$ (d) $(10 - (27 - 15 / 5) / 4)$

* **2.** Identify the error in each of the following Fortran expressions:
  (a) $Z = 2.0 (X + Y)$ (c) $A + 1.0 = B ** 3 / C$
  (b) $R = D + E / - F * G$ (d) $X = (Y ** 2 + Z ** (A + B)$

* **3.** Express each of the following algebraic expressions as a Fortran assignment statement:
  (a) $y = ax^2 + bx + c$ (e) $a = e^{(1/2)qt^2}$

  (b) $a = \dfrac{x + 2y + 3z}{6}$ (f) $s = \dfrac{a(1 - r^n)}{1 - r}$

  (c) $b = p^k \cdot q^{n-k}$ (g) $x = wa^{(b+1)/c}$

  (d) $x = \left(\dfrac{a - b}{c + d}\right)^3$ (h) $b = \dfrac{xy^2 - x^2y}{3x + y}$

* **4.** Express each of the following algebraic expressions as a Fortran assignment statement:
  (a) $a = \sqrt{(x + z)^3 - xz}$

  (b) $c = \dfrac{x}{\sqrt{x^2 + y^2 + z^2}}$

  (c) $x = w^{\sqrt{y+z}}$

  (d) $r = \dfrac{s}{\sqrt{ax + b}} - \dfrac{s + t}{\sqrt{cx^2 + d}}$

  (e) $f = (\sqrt[3]{a + b})^{\sqrt{cx-d}}$

* **5.** Evaluate each expression and determine the value assigned to the real variable A if K = 4, L = 5, R = 18.0, S = 3.0, and T = 2.0. (Assume that mixed-mode arithmetic is permitted.)
  (a) $A = K * R / S + T$
  (b) $A = T * S ** K$
  (c) $A = S / K + R$
  (d) $A = (K / L) * R$
  (e) $A = ((L ** S) ** (L / K)) / (T * L)$

* **6.** Evaluate each expression and determine the value assigned to the integer variable M if K = 10, L = 5, N = 2, and X = 4.0.

   (a) M = (K / L) * L
   (b) M = (X * L) / K / N
   (c) M = (X + K) / N
   (d) M = (L + N) / X
   (e) M = (L / N) ** L / K

Problems 7–13. Write a Fortran program that satisfies the conditions of each problem. Choose your own sample test data. Label all output, and design the text of your program so that it is easy to read.

* **7.** The dimensions of a rectangular box are represented by l, w, and h. The volume of the box is given by the formula

$$V = l \times w \times h$$

   and the surface area by the relationship

$$\text{surface area} = 2(lw + lh + hw)$$

   Read values for the variables L, W, and H. Calculate and print the volume (V) and the surface area (SAREA).

8. If three resistors, R_1, R_2, and R_3, are connected in parallel, then the effective resistance of the three resistors is given by the relationship

$$\frac{R_1 \cdot R_2 \cdot R_3}{R_1 R_2 + R_1 R_3 + R_2 R_3}$$

   Read values for the variables R1, R2, and R3. Calculate and print the effective resistance.

* **9.** A Pythagorean triple is any set of three whole numbers, k, l, and m, such that $m^2 = l^2 + k^2$. If k is an odd integer greater than or equal to 3, then the set of numbers

$$k, \quad \frac{k^2 - 1}{2}, \quad \frac{k^2 + 1}{2}$$

   represents a Pythagorean triple. Read in an odd positive integer greater than or equal to 3, and print the corresponding Pythagorean triple.

10. In a coordinate plane the following relationships may be used to determine the length and the coordinates of the midpoint of the segment joining two points, $P_1(X_1, Y_1)$ and $P_2(X_2, Y_2)$:

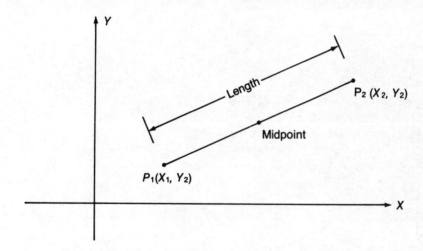

$$\text{length} = \sqrt{(X_2 - X_1)^2 + (Y_2 - Y_1)^2}$$

$$\text{midpoint of } X \text{ (XMIDPT)} = \frac{X_1 + X_2}{2}, \qquad \text{midpoint of } Y \text{ (YMIDPT)} = \frac{Y_1 + Y_2}{2}$$

Read values for the variables X1, Y1, X2, and Y2. Calculate and print LENGTH, XMIDPT, and YMIDPT.

*11. The compounded amount A of a principal P invested at an annual interest rate R is given by the formula

$$A = P\left(1 + \frac{R}{k}\right)^{Nk}$$

where $N =$ the number of years the principal is invested and $k =$ the number of times per year the amount is compounded. Read values for the variables P, N, R, and k. Calculate and print A.

12. The radius of gyration of a spherical shell revolving on its diameter is given by the relationship

$$r = 0.6325\sqrt{\frac{(r_1)^5 - (r_2)^5}{(r_1)^3 - (r_2)^3}}$$

where $r =$ radius of gyration, $r_1 =$ outer radius of shell, and $r_2 =$ inner radius of shell. Read values for the variables R1 and R2. Calculate and print R.

*13. Read a two-digit positive integer value. Print the number with the digits reversed. For example, if the original value is 75, then print 57.

CHAPTER 4

Controlling Input and Output

COMPUTER AXIOM

Computer programs and output are read by *people* as well as by machines.

COROLLARY

In designing a program, a wise programmer will assume that another person may be asked to read the output or the text of the program.

4.1 Format-directed Input/Output

List-directed (format-free) input and output statements are very convenient to use since the programmer is required only to list the variables that are involved in an input/output operation. For example, in the output statement

```
PRINT *, B, K, CHAR
```

the variable values to be printed and their order (B followed by K followed by CHAR) are specified, but the *computer* determines the horizontal column spacing of the printed values. This may lead to output that is difficult to read. Sometimes the programmer may wish to override the preset spacing feature of list-directed input/output statements and customize the format of printed output. Furthermore, some early versions of Fortran (Fortran IV), as well as some subsets of Fortran 77 that are available for desktop computers, do not support list-directed I/O statements. For these reasons we now turn our attention to I/O statements that specify the field layouts of input and output records.

AN OVERVIEW OF FORMATTED INPUT/OUTPUT

When using format-directed I/O statements, each I/O operation must be described using *two* statements: a statement that identifies the type of I/O operation (READ or WRITE) and a corresponding FORMAT statement that describes the column placement of variable values on an input or output *record*. An 80-column punch card with data keypunched on the card in reserved fields is an example of an input record. A line of data entered serially from a keyboard terminal, one value for each variable appearing in the input variable list, is another example of an input record. A line of printed results that includes the values of each variable listed in an output statement represents an output record. See Figure 4.1.

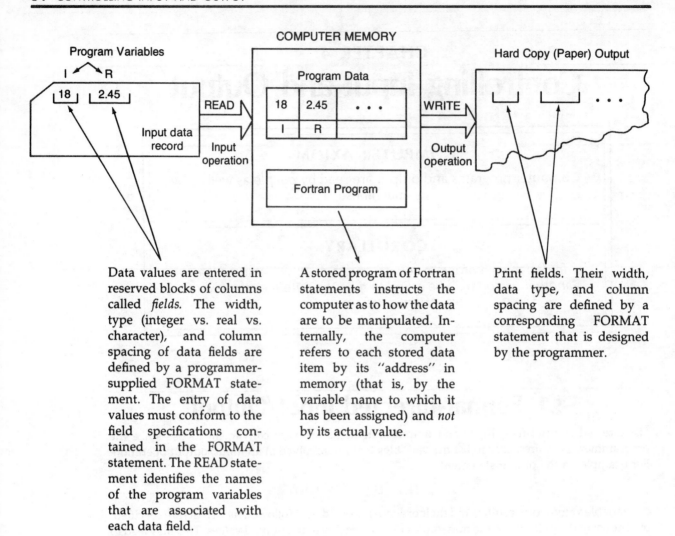

Data values are entered in reserved blocks of columns called *fields*. The width, type (integer vs. real vs. character), and column spacing of data fields are defined by a programmer-supplied FORMAT statement. The entry of data values must conform to the field specifications contained in the FORMAT statement. The READ statement identifies the names of the program variables that are associated with each data field.

A stored program of Fortran statements instructs the computer as to how the data are to be manipulated. Internally, the computer refers to each stored data item by its "address" in memory (that is, by the variable name to which it has been assigned) and *not* by its actual value.

Print fields. Their width, data type, and column spacing are defined by a corresponding FORMAT statement that is designed by the programmer.

Figure 4.1 An Overview of Using Formatted Input/Output

Larger computer systems generally accommodate a variety of input and output devices, including one or more card readers, CRT keyboard consoles, line printers, magnetic tape and disk drives, and card punch machines. Each device is referred to by a unit number which may vary from system to system. In an IBM computer system, the device number 5 refers to a card reader. In another computer system, a card reader may be assigned the unit number 1. Many desktop computers use an asterisk (*) to designate the keyboard console. To simplify matters, the unit number 5 will be used throughout our presentation to represent a "standard" input device such as a terminal keyboard, and the unit number 6 will designate a "standard" output device such as a line printer.

Incidentally, when using list-directed (format-free) I/O statements, it may be necessary to specify a particular I/O device. The following statements are equivalent:

```
READ (5, *) J, K, L
READ *, J, K, L
```

When a device number is specified in an output operation, the Fortran keyword WRITE is used instead of the keyword PRINT. The following statements are equivalent:

```
WRITE (6, *) A, B, C
PRINT *, A, B, C
```

Alternative Form of List-Directed Input/Output

`READ` (device number, *) *variable list*

`WRITE` (device number, *) *variable list*

A CLOSER LOOK AT FORMATTED INPUT/OUTPUT

The keyword READ is used to initiate an *input* operation under both format-free and format-directed input. The statement

`READ (5, 100) MONTH, JDAY, KYEAR`

directs the computer to "request" that the input device whose number is 5 transmit three data values which will be assigned in sequence to variables MONTH, JDAY, and KYEAR. In order for the computer to correctly interpret the stream of data that it receives, the programmer must inform the computer how the input data are arranged on the input record. This information is contained in a FORMAT statement, which is paired with the corresponding READ statement by using matching statement labels. The READ statement given above advises the computer that it should be guided by the statement having the label 100 when reading the input data record:

```
   ┌──────────────────────────────────────────────
   │         READ (5, 100) MONTH, JDAY, KYEAR
   │
   └──→ 100 FORMAT (description of data on input record)
```

Each field of the input data record is described within the parentheses of the FORMAT statement by specifying its width and the type of data value that it holds. Exactly how this is done will be explained shortly.

The format-directed *output* statement uses the keyword WRITE to initiate an output operation. The general form and purpose of the WRITE and its corresponding FORMAT statements are analogous to those for format-directed input. If values for ALPHA and BETA are currently stored in computer memory, the following statements may be used to print their values:

`WRITE (6, 200) ALPHA, BETA`
`200 FORMAT (description of print fields)`

Since FORMAT statements are nonexecutable (they specify the nature of data records to be read and written), they may be placed anywhere in a Fortran program. Good programming style suggests, however, that a FORMAT statement immediately follows the input/output statement which references it. (Since an input/output statement may reference the same FORMAT statement, this may not always be possible.)

Syntax of Format-Directed Input/Output Statements

`READ` (device number, FORMAT statement label) *variable list*

`WRITE` (device number, FORMAT statement label) *variable list*

Note: Keep in mind that in Fortrans which support list-directed input/output, if the FORMAT statement label is replaced by an asterisk, then the Fortran compiler will interpret these statements as format-free input/output. The statement

`READ (5, *) A, B, C`

does *not* require a corresponding FORMAT statement since it specifies that a list-directed input operation be performed using the input device having the number 5.

THE FORMAT STATEMENT

The FORMAT statement uses concise field descriptors to define the field type and its width for each variable that appears in the variable list of the corresponding input/output statement. See Figure 4.2.

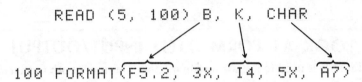

Figure 4.2 Some FORMAT Field Descriptors

The FORMAT specification for each variable, called an *edit descriptor* (or format code), is written in the same sequence as the variable it defines in the corresponding input/output statement. The X descriptor does *not* refer to a variable; it merely instructs the computer to skip a column before it reads or writes the next character. The edit descriptor 5X directs the computer to skip five column spaces.

Variable	Edit Descriptor	Interpretation
B	F5.2	The letter "F" defines the field as containing a real value. The variable B occupies a real field having a width of 5 columns, with 2 reserved column positions to the right of the decimal point. The decimal point occupies 1 column position. The maximum value of B is $\lfloor 9\rfloor 9 \rfloor . \lfloor 9\rfloor 9\rfloor$ width = 5 The minimum value of B is −9.99 since a negative sign must be allocated a column position.
	3X	Three column positions are skipped (ignored or left blank).
K	I4	The letter "I" identifies the field as containing an integer value. The variable K is stored in an integer field having a width of 4 columns. The maximum value of K is 9999, and the minimum value is −999.
	5X	Five column positions are skipped.
CHAR	A7	The letter "A" defines an alphanumeric field. The string variable CHAR occupies a field defined to be 7 column positions in width.

NUMERICAL EDIT DESCRIPTORS

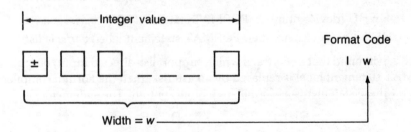

Figure 4.3. The Iw Descriptor

Integer Values

The edit descriptor Iw (Figure 4.3) defines a field w columns in width that will hold an integer value. If the value may be negative, the field width w must include provision for a negative sign. If an insufficient number of column positions are provided in the input (or output) format codes, then the value will not be accurately stored (or printed). If, on the other hand, the field width exceeds the actual width of the integer value being inputted, the value must be entered right-justified in its field. On output, this situation will result in the value being printed right-justified in its field, preceded by leading blanks in the unused field positions.

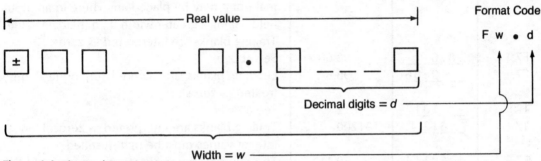

Figure 4.4 The Fw.d Descriptor

Real Values

The edit descriptor Fw.d (Figure 4.4) defines a field that is w columns in width and contains a real value with d decimal digits (that is, d digits appear to the right of the decimal point). On output, the field width w must provide for the printing of a decimal point and, if the value may be less than 0, an additional column position for a negative sign.

On input a real value may be entered on the data record with or without an actual decimal point. If the real value is entered in its field with an assumed ("imaginary") decimal point, then the decimal point is not written but is "understood" to be present. The Fw.d descriptor informs the compiler that, when the value is read, a decimal point is to be inserted between the d and $(d + 1)$th digits, counting from the rightmost field position and moving left. For example, if the value 26149 is entered in an input field described by the descriptor F5.3, it will be read and stored by the computer as 26.149.

Some programmers prefer to enter real values with an explicit decimal point. Since a decimal point occupies a column position, the corresponding edit descriptor must reflect this practice in its width specification. If the position of the entered decimal point is not consistent with its edit descriptor, the decimal point entered on the data record will override the edit descriptor. For example, if the value 2614.9 is entered in a field defined by the edit descriptor F6.3, the computer will store the value as written (2614.9) rather than as 26.149.

Example: If it is known that a real value has the form

$$+ XXXXXXX.XX$$

then the required edit descriptor is F11.2.

In the preceding example, the numbers 11 and 2 specify minimum values for the w and d components of the edit descriptor. Sometimes an edit descriptor will provide for more column positions than are required. Table 4.1 illustrates how real and integer values are interpreted by the computer under different column placements of the data value within its reserved input field. If too few column positions are provided on input, then the value will be stored in computer memory in truncated form. If this situation occurs on output, then an "overflow" condition results and the value will not be printed.

Table 4.1 Computer Interpretation of Numeric Data Values by Column Placement

Input Edit Descriptor	Input Data Value	Stored Value	Comments
F7.1	_98.6__	98.600	A real value that is entered with an explicit decimal point may be placed anywhere in an input field having a greater width than the data value. Trailing blanks are interpreted as zeros.
F7.1	98.6___	98.6000	See above.
F7.1	___9.86	98.6	Leading blanks are ignored (or, equivalently, treated as zeros).
17	___1812	1812	See above.
17	_1812__	181200	Trailing blanks are interpreted as zeros. Hence, integer values must be right-justified.
F7.3	__59114	59.114	The edit descriptor dictates the position of the decimal point when the value is read by the computer.
F7.3	_59114_	591.140	See above. This example suggests that a real value entered with an assumed decimal point must be right-justified in its field.

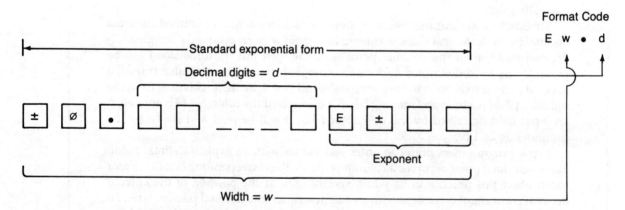

Figure 4.5 The Ew.d Descriptor

Numbers in Exponential Form

Very small and very large real values, as well as real values whose magnitudes are uncertain, may be concisely written on input or output in exponential form by describing the input/output field using the Ew.d edit descriptor (Figure 4.5), where w represents the number of columns occupied by a number expressed in exponential form and d corresponds to the number of decimal digits in the value. For example, the value 1,987,120.0 may be entered on an input record in standard exponential form as

$$0.198712E+07 \qquad (\textit{Note: } E+07 = 10^7)$$

with a corresponding edit descriptor of E12.6. The value 12 corresponds to the field width and includes provision for the decimal point, the number of decimal digits, the letter "E," the plus sign, and a two-digit exponent. The number 6 in E12.6 represents the number of significant decimal digits in the value $.198712E+07$.

To write a real number in standard exponential form, we adjust the exponent so that the real valued decimal part has an absolute value of less than 1. The following three values are numerically equal, but only the third value is expressed in standard exponential form:

(1) $70892E+00$
(2) $70.892E+03$
(3) $0.70892E+05$

Example: A value of the form $-0.00000XXXX$ can be expressed in standard exponential form on an input record as $-.XXXXE-05$ and would require an exponential edit descriptor of E10.4. Notice that the w component of the descriptor is 6 more than the d component. To provide for a possible negative sign, the decimal point, the letter "E," and the exponent, the width w of the Ew.d descriptor should always be at least 6 greater than the d component. To provide for a leading 0, as in $-0.XXXXE-05$, w should be at least 7 greater than d.

Example: The value stored in computer memory for a real variable is 247893.5. If the variable has the output edit descriptor E14.7, then the printed value will be $0.2478935E+06$. On output, a computer always prints a real value that has an Ew.d field descriptor in standard exponential form. Some computers may not print a leading zero to the left of the decimal point.

On input, a value described by an exponential edit descriptor need *not* be expressed in *standard* exponential form. Furthermore, the guidelines presented for the use of implied and explicit decimal points when entering data values described by a Fw.d descriptor apply also to the Ew.d descriptor, with the additional restriction that the *exponent* must be entered right-justified. Although there is some flexibility in representing and entering a data value in an *input* field described by an Ew.d descriptor, it is good practice to express values in standard exponential form and to enter each value right-justified in its field.

Here are some additional considerations to which you should be alert:

- The precision of the particular computer being used will impose a limit on the number of significant digits that the d component of the Fw.d and Ew.d descriptors can accurately represent. Every computer also places an upper and a lower limit on the range of exponent values.
- If the output edit descriptor of a numeric field provides for more column positions than are required, the numeric value will be printed right-justified in its field and the leftmost unfilled column positions will be padded with blanks. If, however, an insufficient number of columns is allocated by the edit descriptor, the value will

not be printed. When such an "overflow" condition occurs, most computers print asterisks in the output field, as shown below.

Output Descriptor	Value Stored in Memory	Print Field
I4	−9876	✳✳✳✳
F5.2	509.72	✳✳✳✳✳
E9.5	−.018356	✳✳✳✳✳✳✳✳✳

- On output, if the *d* component of the Fw.d or Ew.d descriptor falls short of the number of columns required to print the decimal part of the stored real value, the decimal part will be rounded off and the extra decimal digits truncated.

Output Descriptor	Value Stored in Memory	Print Field
F5.2	1.837	ⱷ1.84
E9.3	.00002613	0.261E−04

- As a general rule, on an input record numeric values should be entered right-justified in their designated fields. If an edit descriptor that defines an input field provides for too few column positions, or if the column placement of the data values is not consistent with the layout defined by the FORMAT statement, the computer will not accurately read and store the values entered on the input data record.

Example: The data record that has the following values entered consecutively in columns 1 to 12:

$$256789453198$$

is read using the input statements

```
READ (5, 100) A, J
100 FORMAT (F5.2, 3X, I2)
```

The following variable data assignments will occur:

```
A = 256.78
J = 31
```

Notice that the field which holds the value 945 is skipped over and that the last two digits on the data record have not been read.

- When an edit descriptor and the variable value that it describes do not agree in type, a run-time error occurs during the corresponding input/output operation. For example, an attempt to write a stored integer variable value to a print field defined by an Fw.d descriptor would abruptly stop the execution of the program.

REPETITION OF FORMAT CODES

Edit descriptors that appear consecutively within a FORMAT statement may be expressed in more compact form by writing the format code once and preceding it by the number of times it is repeated. For instance, the series F4.1, F4.1, F4.1 may be expressed as 3F4.1. The FORMAT statement

```
100 FORMAT (F8.3, F8.3, 10X, I4, I4, I4)
```

may be written as

```
100 FORMAT (2F8.3, 10X, 3I4)
```

A group of format codes may also be written using a repetition factor. The FORMAT statement

```
500 FORMAT (I3, 7X, F5.1, I3, 7X, F5.1, F12.4)
```

may be written as

```
500 FORMAT (2 (I3, 7X, F5.1), F12.4)
```

Sometimes the width of a field may be expanded slightly in order to take advantage of using a repetition factor. The FORMAT statement

```
900 FORMAT (I7, I6, I7)
```

may be written as

```
900 FORMAT (3I7)
```

EXAMPLE 4.1 Given a real number of the form AAAA.BB, print the number BB.AAAA, where the integer and decimal parts of the original number are reversed. For example, if the number 3027.64 is read, print the original number and the number 64.3027.

Solution

The program is based on the use of mixed-mode arithmetic. If INT is defined to be an integer value, then the assignment statement

```
INT = 3027.64
```

results in the value 3027 being assigned to INT. If DECMAL is defined to be a real value, then the decimal part of the original number may be "split off" using the assignment statement

```
DECMAL = 3027.64 - INT
```

Since INT = 3027, DECMAL = .64. By dividing and multiplying by appropriate powers of 10, these values may be converted to the integer and decimal parts of the new number. This is illustrated in Program 4.1, where the variable VALUE1 represents the original data value.

```
$JOB    WATFIV
C* * * * * * * * * * * * * * * * * * * * * * * * * * * * * *
C*                                                         *
C*    GIVEN A REAL NUMBER OF THE FORM AAAA.BB THIS PROGRAM *
C*    PRINTS A NUMBER OF THE FORM BB.AAAA WHERE THE INTEGER*
C*    AND REAL PARTS OF THE ORIGINAL NUMBER ARE REVERSED.  *
C*    IF A NUMBER 1234.56 IS READ, THEN THE REVERSE FORM OF*
C*    NUMBER IS 56.1234.                                   *
C*                                                         *
C*    PROGRAM VARIABLES                                    *
C*                                                         *
C*       VALUE1 = ORIGINAL NUMBER                          *
C*       VALUE2 = NEW REVERSED NUMBER                      *
C*       INT1   = INTEGER PORTION OF THE ORIGINAL NUMBER   *
C*       REAL1  = REAL PORTION OF THE ORIGINAL NUMBER      *
C*       INT2   = INTEGER PORTION OF THE NEW NUMBER        *
C*       REAL2  = REAL PORTION OF THE NEW NUMBER           *
C*                                                         *
C* * * * * * * * * * * * * * * * * * * * * * * * * * * * * *
 1          REAL VALUE1, VALUE2, REAL1, REAL2
 2          INTEGER INT1, INT2
 3          WRITE (6, 50)
 4    50    FORMAT (' ', 'ORIGINAL NUMBER', 5X, 'REVERSED NUMBER')
 5          WRITE (6, 60)
 6    60    FORMAT (' ')
 7    90    READ (5, 100, END = 300) VALUE1
 8    100       FORMAT (F7.2)
 9          INT1 = VALUE1
10          REAL1 = VALUE1 - INT1
11          INT2 = REAL1 * 100.0
12          REAL2 = INT1 / 10000.0
13          VALUE2 = INT2 + REAL2
14          WRITE (6, 200) VALUE1, VALUE2
15    200       FORMAT (' ',4X, F7.2, 13X, F7.4)
16          GOTO 90
17    300   STOP
18          END

        $ENTRY
ORIGINAL NUMBER        REVERSED NUMBER

     1234.56               56.1234
     1024.50               50.1024
```

Program 4.1

4.2 Controlling Vertical Line Spacing

In addition to using edit descriptors to control the horizontal spacing of printed output, the programmer may also exercise control over the vertical line spacing. For increased clarity, printed lines of output may be double rather than single spaced. When producing formatted reports, it may be desirable to begin printing on the top of a new page. When underlining or overprinting for increased emphasis on an expression already printed, it is necessary to return the print head mechanism to the beginning of the same line of print. The Fortran compiler interprets the *first entry* in a FORMAT statement that is referenced by a WRITE statement as a carriage control character. Special carriage control characters are generally associated with high-speed line printers, which typically offer 132 print positions per line and 66 lines per page. See Table 4.2.

Table 4.2 Some Special Carriage Control Characters

Control Character	Effect
' ' or 1X (blank)	Output is printed single spaced.
'0' (zero)	Output is printed double spaced.
'1'	The paper is advanced so that output begins printing on the first line of a new page.
'+'	Rather than moving to the next line, the print head returns to the beginning of the current line. (This is used when underlining or over-printing is required.)
Any other character	The character is interpreted as a blank so that output is single spaced.

Here are some examples (assume that the FORMAT statement given is associated with a WRITE statement).

Example: FORMAT (' ', F7.2)

Interpretation: The print head moves to the beginning of the next consecutive line and uses the edit descriptor F7.2 to print a real value.

Example: FORMAT ('0', I4)

Interpretation: The print head skips a line and then moves to the beginning of the next (second) line. The descriptor I4 is used to print an integer value.

Example: FORMAT (5X, F8.3)

Interpretation: The Fortran compiler reads the first character in the FORMAT statement and finds a blank. After single spacing, the print head skips four blank column positions. With the edit descriptor F8.3, a real value is printed in an eight-column field that begins in column 5.

Example: Assume that the edit descriptor in the following FORMAT statement refers to the integer value 72695:

FORMAT (I5)

Interpretation: Since the first character of a FORMAT statement is always used as a carriage control character, the computer reads the first digit of the value described by the edit descriptor, which is a 7. Since this is not one of the special carriage control characters, it is discarded and a blank is used instead. After single spacing, the next four characters of the stored integer value are printed. The number 2695 will appear in columns 1–4.

EXAMPLE 4.2 Assume that the stored value of an integer variable K is 123456. Describe how this value would be printed if its corresponding FORMAT statement was:

(a) FORMAT (I8)   (c) FORMAT (I6)

(b) FORMAT (3X, I6)   (d) FORMAT (1X, I5)

Solution

(a) A six-digit value has been allocated a field width of eight columns. Since no explicit carriage control character is provided, the first blank in the field is used for this purpose. Output is single spaced, and the contents of the print field would be ⌿123456.

(b) Output is single spaced; the first blank of the field defined by 3X is interpreted as a carriage control character. The contents of the print field would be ⌿⌿123456.

(c) The first digit of the data value is used as the carriage control character so that output is printed on the first line of a new page. The contents of the print field would be 23456.

(d) Output is single spaced. Since an overflow error occurs, the contents of the print field would be ⁕⁕⁕⁕⁕.

EXAMPLE 4.3   Assume that the stored value of a real variable R is 1111.88. Describe how this value would be printed if its corresponding FORMAT statement was:

(a) `FORMAT (F8.2)`   (c) `FORMAT (' ', E11.6)`
(b) `FORMAT (F8.1)`   (d) `FORMAT ('0', E11.5)`

Solution

(a) Output is single spaced; a blank carriage control character is embedded in the edit descriptor. The contents of the print field would be 1111.88.

(b) Output is single spaced; a blank carriage control character is embedded in the edit descriptor. Since there is provision for only one decimal digit, the machine rounds off and truncates the last decimal digit of the stored value. The contents of the print field would be ⌿1111.9.

(c) Output is single spaced. The contents of the print field would be .111188E+04.

(d) Output is double spaced. Since there is provision for only five decimal digits, the contents of the print field would be ⌿.11119E+04.

Examples 4.2 and 4.3 illustrate the possible dangers when a special carriage control character is not stated explicitly in the FORMAT statement and, instead, is embedded in the leading edit descriptor.

STRUCTURED PROGRAMMING GUIDELINE

To prevent unexpected results and to make the logic of your program more apparent, printer carriage control characters should be written explicitly within a FORMAT statement.

4.3 Some Additional Edit Descriptors

Literal expressions such as column headings and messages may be printed using the H (Hollerith) descriptor; this takes the form nH, where *n* represents the number of characters in the expression to be printed. The H descriptor immediately precedes the expression to be printed:

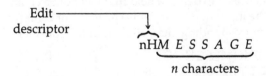

Example: `WRITE (6, 400) ANSWER`
       `400 FORMAT ('0', 14H THE`
            `RESULT IS, 2X, F5.1)`

Interpretation: The expression

```
                    THE RESULT IS
```

contains 14 characters (including the leading blank) so that the required H descriptor is 14H. After double spacing, this expression is printed (the first column is left blank so that the letter "T" is printed in column 2). Column print positions 15 and 16 are left blank, and in the next five-column print field the real value represented by the variable ANSWER is printed using the descriptor F5.1.

The H descriptor has the disadvantage that you must provide an exact count of the number of characters in the expression to be printed. In some versions of Fortran, including Fortran 77 and WATFIV, an apostrophe descriptor may be used instead of the H descriptor. The following FORMAT statement is equivalent to the one given in the example above:

```
400 FORMAT ('0', 'THE RESULT IS', 2X, F5.1)
```

Example:
```
        WRITE (6, 198)
    198 FORMAT ('1', 20X, 'NAME')
        WRITE (6, 199)
    199 FORMAT ('+', 20X, '_____')
```

Interpretation: The first pair of statements directs the printer to skip to the top of the next page, leave 20 blank columns, and then print NAME in columns 21–24. Rather than advancing to the next print line, the second pair of statements directs the print head back to the beginning of the *same* line. After skipping 20 column spaces, the character string '_____' is printed in the same column positions as NAME. The net effect is to have NAME appear underlined in columns 21–24.

EXAMPLE 4.4   Write a series of statements that will print the following column headings on the top of a new page:

<u>STUDENT ID NUMBER</u>   <u>GRADE AVERAGE</u>

The column headings are to be underlined. The first column should be printed beginning in column 30. Ten blanks spaces are to be left between the two column headings.

Solution

```
    WRITE (6, 200)
200 FORMAT ('1', 29X, 'STUDENT ID NUMBER',
        10X, 'GRADE AVERAGE')
    WRITE (6, 210)
210 FORMAT ('+', 29X, '_____',
        10X, '_____')
```

ALPHANUMERIC EDIT DESCRIPTORS

The Aw descriptor may be used to define a field that will hold a character variable value where *w* represents the width of the input or output field. The value of *w* may or may not be the same as the declared length of the corresponding character variable. Consider

```
        CHARACTER CITY * 8, STATE * 10
        WRITE (6, 100) CITY, STATE
    100 FORMAT(' ', A12, A5)
```

where the stored value of CITY is 'BOULDERbb', and the stored value of STATE is 'COLORADObb'. The output will be as follows:

A5 field

bbbbBOULDERbCOLOR

A12 field

Since the declared length of the variable CITY is less than the field width (8 < 12), the stored variable value of CITY ('BOULDERb') will be printed right-justified in a 12-column print field with the leftmost unused field positions filled with blanks. Notice that the declared length of the variable STATE is greater than the field width (10 > 5). In this situation, the stored variable value of STATE ('COLORADObb') will be printed in a field having a width of 5 columns; this means that only the first 5 characters of 'COLORADObb' will be printed, the remaining rightmost characters being deleted. The A descriptor provides more flexible format editing since the width of the print field will be adjusted by the computer to accommodate the exact number of characters in the stored character variable. The corresponding FORMAT statement would be

```
100 FORMAT(' ', A, A)
```

Let's now consider the other side of the coin and examine what happens when the declared length of a character variable and its field width on input do not agree. Consider these statements:

```
CHARACTER CITY * 8, STATE * 10
READ (5, 100) CITY, STATE
100 FORMAT (A12, A5)
```

where the data values are again CITY = 'BOULDER' and STATE = 'COLORADO'. Assume that the data are entered left-justified in their respective fields on the input data record. The computer reads the 12-column field from the data record, but assigns only the 8 (declared length) rightmost characters of the field to the variable CITY. The data value for CITY was entered as

B O U L D E R b b b b b

so that the value 'DERbbbbb' will be assigned in computer memory to the variable CITY. Since the descriptor for the variable STATE limits the width of the input field to 5, only the first (leftmost) 5 characters of the input data value are read and assigned to variable STATE. The character data declaration statement, however, provides 10 character storage positions for the variable STATE; the result is that the value 'COLORbbbbb' is assigned in computer memory to the variable STATE.

Once again, if the flexible A descriptor is used instead of the Aw format descriptor, the computer will be guided strictly by the declared length of the character variable in storing the value read during input.

The Aw Edit Descriptor

The Aw descriptor defines a field in either input or output that is w columns in width and will be assigned a character data value. If the w component of the edit descriptor is omitted, the field width will be automatically adjusted to reflect the declared length of the associated character variable. If w equals the declared length, then "what you see is exactly what you get." When the declared length l of the character variable is not equal to specified field width w, then there are two cases to consider.

INPUT

(1) If $l < w$, then
the l rightmost characters of the field will be read and assigned to the variable.
(2) If $l > w$, then
the variable will be assigned the w leftmost characters of the field with $l - w$ trailing blanks added to complete the variable's internal storage field in computer memory.

OUTPUT

(1) If $l < w$, then

the stored value will be printed right-justified in its field with $w - l$ leading blanks filling up the unused print positions.

(2) If $l > w$, then

the w leftmost characters of the stored value will be printed in its field.

(*Note*: With pre-Fortran 77 compilers (which generally do not feature the character data declaration statement), a single character variable can represent only a limited number of bytes (characters), the number depending on the design of the particular machine. For computers using these compilers typical maximum numbers are 4, 6, 8, and 10 characters.)

THE T DESCRIPTOR

The Tn edit descriptor affects the horizontal spacing in reading and writing characters in a way similar to that of the TAB key on a typewriter. When encountered in a FORMAT statement in an input operation, the descriptor Tn directs the computer to read the field that begins in the nth-column position on the input record.

Example:
```
      READ (5, 80) A, B
   80 FORMAT (T30, F9.2, T50, F6.3)
```

Interpretation: The T30 edit descriptor informs the computer to begin reading the value associated with variable A in a field that begins in column 30 and is defined by the descriptor F9.2. The T50 descriptor directs the computer to skip to column 50 on the input record and to read the value associated with variable B, using the edit descriptor F6.3.

Example: Rewrite the preceding FORMAT statement without using the T descriptor.

```
   80 FORMAT (29X, F9.2, 11X, F6.3)
```

On output, the T descriptor specifies the *absolute* position of the next character to be written to the output record. Since the first character in an output stream is always interpreted as a carriage control character, T1 corresponds to this character, while T2 represents the first *print* position on the output record. When the Tn descriptor is encountered in an output operation, it will direct the computer to write the next character in the field that begins in the $(n - 1)$th print position.

Example:
```
      WRITE (6, 90)
   90 FORMAT ('1', T54, 'EMPLOYEE WAGES
      FOR 1983-84')
```

Interpretation: The heading EMPLOYEE WAGES FOR 1983–84 is printed on the top of a new page, beginning in print position number 53 (*not* 54). If a print line of 132 positions is assumed, the heading will be centered on the print line. To center a heading, use the following relationship:

$$\text{initial column position} = \frac{132 - \text{length of message}}{2}$$

In our example, the heading has 26 characters so that

$$\text{initial column position} = \frac{132 - 26}{2} = \frac{106}{2} = 53$$

The use of the T descriptor makes it possible to read or write data in a sequence that does not conform to the order, in which the corresponding variables are listed in READ or WRITE statements.

Example: READ (5, 100) J, A, K
          100 FORMAT (T39, I7, T20, F5.3, T39, I7)

Interpretation: The T39 edit descriptor directs the computer to begin reading in the field that begins in column 39. The integer value appearing in columns 39 – 45 is assigned to variable J. The T20 descriptor informs the computer that the next field to be read on the input record begins in column 20. By means of the edit descriptor F5.3, the value appearing in this field is assigned to variable A. Notice that on the physical input record the value of A comes *before* the value of J. The T39 descriptor directs the computer to read the field that begins in column 39. The descriptor I7 is used in assigning the data value to K. Notice that the same value on the input record has been read twice. The first time it was assigned to variable J and the next time to variable K. On output, this technique can be used to print the same value more than once or to overwrite values written previously on the same line.

THE SLASH (/) DESCRIPTOR

When a slash is encountered in a FORMAT statement, the reading or writing of the current record is terminated. This permits the same FORMAT statement to describe more than one input or output record.

Example: READ (5, 600) K, W
          600 FORMAT (I3 / F6.2)

Interpretation: The slash will cause two input records to be read. The value of K will be read from the first data record using the descriptor I3. The current input record will then be discarded, regardless of whether it contains additional data values. The value of W is read from the next data record using the edit descriptor F6.2.

Example: WRITE (6, 700) K, W
          700 FORMAT (' ', I3 / ' ', F6.2)

Interpretation: After single spacing, the value of K is printed using the descriptor I3. The slash will cause printing on the current line to stop. The value of W is printed single spaced (on the next consecutive line) using the descriptor F6.2. Notice that for each new output record a carriage control character is included.

The appearance of k consecutive slashes at the beginning or end of a FORMAT statement results in k records being skipped on input and k blank lines being printed (skipped) on output.

Example: READ (5, 77) LAST
          77 FORMAT (//// I8)

Interpretation: Four input data records are skipped, and the fifth data record is read using the descriptor I8, the value being assigned to variable LAST.

Example: WRITE (6, 90)
          90 FORMAT (' ', 'PRINTING BLANK
          LINES' ///)

Interpretation: After printing the expression PRINTING BLANK LINES, three blank lines are printed (skipped).

Consecutive slashes may also appear anywhere within a FORMAT statement. When the first slash is encountered, the current input or output record will be terminated. The remaining slashes will cause succeeding input records (or print lines) to be skipped. In such a case, k consecutive slashes will result in $k - 1$ records being skipped. For example, on input, the statement

```
FORMAT (I7 //// F5.2)
```

will result in the first data record being read using I7. The first slash terminates the current data record. The following three slashes result in the next three data records being skipped. The next (fifth) data record is read using F5.2.

Example:
```
       WRITE (6, 40) AVERAGE, MEDIAN
    40 FORMAT ('1', 'AVERAGE = ', F6.2 ///
       ' ', 'MEDIAN = ', F4.1)
```

Interpretation: On the top of a new page the output would take the following form:

```
AVERAGE = nnn.nn
                   } two blank lines
MEDIAN = nn.n
```

Three slashes appear within the FORMAT statement. The first terminates the writing of the current print line. The next two slashes result in the printing of two blank lines. The computer then looks for a carriage control character and finds a blank (' ') so that MEDIAN and its value are printed on the next consecutive print line. Thus, two blank lines separate AVERAGE and MEDIAN.

To summarize:

- If a slash appears in the middle of a FORMAT statement, the reading (or writing) of the current record is terminated and a new record is readied for input (or output).
- If k consecutive slashes appear at the beginning or end of a FORMAT statement, k input records are skipped or k blank lines are printed.
- If k consecutive slashes appear in the middle of a FORMAT statement, the reading or writing of the current record is halted and $k - 1$ data records are skipped or $k - 1$ blank lines are printed.

THE Gw.d AND Dw.d DESCRIPTORS

When used to describe an input field, the Gw.d descriptor has the same effect as the Fw.d or Ew.d descriptor, depending on whether the data value has been entered in exponential form. On output, the Gw.d descriptor offers flexible editing. It is interpreted by the computer as either an Fw.d or an Ew.d descriptor, depending on the nature of the value to be printed. As usual, w represents the field width and d the number of significant digits. If the value can be printed in a field having a width of $w - 4$ column positions, the value will be printed using the corresponding Fw.d descriptor; if not, the value will be interpreted and printed using the corresponding Ew.d descriptor.

As discussed in Chapter 1, every computer is limited by its design in the number of significant digits it can store. Fortran provides a facility for effectively doubling the number of significant digits of a real value that can be represented accurately in memory. In describing an input/output field that contains a double-precision constant, the Dw.d descriptor must be used. The Dw.d descriptor is handled in exactly the same manner as the Ew.d descriptor except that the letter D replaces the letter E and a greater number of significant decimal digits can be accommodated.

A variable that represents a double-precision value must be declared in a data type statement. For example, if the variable EXTRA represents a double-precision value, it must be typed before any executable program statement, as follows:

```
DOUBLE PRECISION EXTRA
          .
          .
          .
      READ (5, 100) EXTRA
100 FORMAT (D21.16)
          .
          .
```

The FORMAT statement just shown assumes that the computer being used can accommodate a double-precision constant having 16 significant digits. Larger computers such as the Control Data 6000/7000 and Cyber series can handle 28 significant digits when operating in a double-precision mode. Since operations involving double-precision values take longer than those with single-precision values, this feature should be used only when extreme accuracy is required.

THE BN AND BZ EDIT DESCRIPTORS

The BN and BZ descriptors affect the way the Fortran compiler interprets blanks in an input/output field. The BN descriptor applies only to input. The FORMAT statement

```
FORMAT (BN, I7)
```

advises the Fortran compiler that, when it reads the field defined by format code I7, all blanks are to be ignored. The net effect is for the computer to automatically right-justify the entered data value in its field, with the number of leading blanks determined by the number of ignored blanks. For example, when this FORMAT statement is used, the following data records will be read so that the same value will be sent to the computer:

    (1) b̸b̸b̸b̸512
    (2) 512b̸b̸b̸b̸
    (3) b̸b̸b̸512b̸

In each case the field entry is interpreted as 512. If the FORMAT statement did not include the BN descriptor, the values entered on the three data records would be stored in memory as 512, 5120000, and 5120, respectively.

The BN descriptor will continue to be in effect when succeeding input fields are read. It will be "turned off," however, when a BZ edit descriptor is encountered. In our present example this can be accomplished by writing

```
FORMAT (BN, I7, BZ, . . .)
```

The BZ descriptor corresponds to the familiar way in which blanks are treated in input/output fields. On input, the BZ descriptor interprets all blanks in a field as zeros; on output, leading blanks are significant while trailing blanks are printed as zeros. The BZ descriptor is in effect by default as long as the BN descriptor is not "turned on."

REPRESENTING COMPLEX NUMBERS

In certain advanced mathematical applications, the need to represent complex numbers arises. A complex number consists of a real and an imaginary component and may be represented as follows:

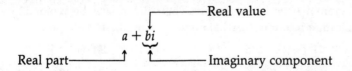

where i is the imaginary unit and is defined to be equal to $\sqrt{-1}$.

Fortran recognizes both complex *constants* and complex *variables*. A complex constant is represented as a parenthesized ordered pair of real numbers. Here are some examples:

Fortran Complex Constant	Mathematical Translation
(4.0, 1.5)	$4.0 + 1.5i$
(0.75E+03, −0.3E+02)	$750.0 − 30.0i$
(−8.9, 0.0)	$−8.9$
(0.0, 4.6)	$4.6i$

A Fortran variable that represents a complex value must be declared using a COMPLEX data declaration statement. The statement

```
COMPLEX X1, Z
```

specifies that variables X1 and Z are complex variables. Complex variable data values may be entered using a list-directed READ statement. The corresponding data values must be coded on the input data record as an ordered pair of complex constants; to record a complex data value, enter the real component followed by the real-valued coefficient of the imaginary part. To enter the complex data value $4.0 + 1.5i$, for example, the real values 4.0 and 1.5 would serve as input.

A complex variable may be given a value by using an assignment statement. The Fortran statement

```
Z = (4.0, 1.5)
```

assigns the complex value $4.0 + 1.5i$ to Z.

If A is a real variable, then the statement

```
Z = A + (4.0, 1.5)
```

is legal. In this case, the real variable A is converted to an equivalent complex Fortran constant of the form (a, 0.0), where a is the current stored value of A. The sum of the two complex constants is assigned to variable Z.

If format-directed input/output statements are used, the FORMAT statement uses two format codes to define each complex variable value. The first format code describes the a (real) component, while the second code specifies the b factor of the imaginary component. For example, if X1 and Z are declared to be complex variables, then the statements

```
    WRITE (6, 200) X1, Z
200 FORMAT ('1', 'X1 = ', F7.3, F5.0, 'Z = ', 2F6.1)
```

specify that the real component (a) of the complex variable X1 is printed using the format code F7.3, while the coefficient of its imaginary part (b) is written using the descriptor F5.0; since a repetition factor of 2 is indicated, each real valued item (a and b) of the complex variable Z are written on output into fields defined by the format code F6.1.

4.4 Testing for the End of a Data List

If an input operation is attempted and no data record is found, then some type of error condition results and the program may end prematurely. This situation can be avoided by incorporating an *END-of-data* specification into the READ statement. The READ statement

```
READ (5, 100, END = 300) B
```

may be interpreted as follows: Read a data record from input device number 5; if a data record is found, then assign the value to variable B according to the edit descriptor that may be found in the FORMAT statement having the statement label 100. If no data record is present, then execute the statement having the statement label 300. As Program 4.2 illustrates, this is particularly useful when a backward-branching GOTO statement is used to transfer program control back to the READ statement in order to process more than one set of data values.

If Program 4.2 is executed in a batch processing mode, then a special END-of-data control card is usually inserted after the last data card. When the computer encounters this card during an input operation, the END = *statement label* component of the READ statement is activated, with program control passing to the statement that has the same statement label. In our example, control would be transferred to the STOP statement, allowing the program to end "cleanly," without an error message being generated.

In some programs additional processing may be required after the last data value is read. In such cases, the END-of-data specification will be used to transfer control to a program statement other than the STOP statement. This will be illustrated in Section 4.6, where we show a program segment that determines the average of a list of data values in which the number of data values is not known in advance.

In a time-sharing system, the user of a program is typically required to type some special keyboard control keys in order to signal that the data set is exhausted. This will in turn trigger the END specification in the READ statement.

```
          SJOB    WATFIV
          C* THIS PROGRAM WAS RUN ON AN IBM COMPUTER USING WATFIV
          C* PROGRAM CALCULATES THE SQUARE OF INTEGER DATA VALUES
          C*
    1             INTEGER I, ISQR
    2       50 READ  (5, 100, END = 300) I
    3      100 FORMAT (I2)
    4             ISQR = I * I
    5             WRITE (6, 200) I, ISQR
    6      200    FORMAT ('0', 'I = ', I4, 6X, 'ISQR = ', I4)
    7             GOTO 50
    8      300 STOP
    9             END

          SENTRY

    I =    15       ISQR =  225

    I =    32       ISQR = 1024

    I =    25       ISQR =  625

    I =    34       ISQR = 1156
```

Program 4.2

The END-of-data specification may also be used with list-directed input/output, as illustrated in Program 4.3.

```
          SJOB    WATFIV
          C* THIS PROGRAM WAS RUN ON AN IBM COMPUTER USING WATFIV
          C* THE END SPECIFICATION IS USED WITH LIST DIRECTED I/O
          C* PROGRAM CALCULATES THE SQUARE OF INTEGER DATA VALUES
          C*
    1             INTEGER I, ISQR
    2       50 READ  (5, *, END = 300) I
    3             ISQR = I * I
    4             PRINT , 'I =', I, '      ISQR =', ISQR
    5             PRINT ,
    6             GOTO 50
    7      300 STOP
    8             END

          SENTRY
    I =       15      ISQR =        225
    I =       32      ISQR =       1024
    I =       25      ISQR =        625
    I =       34      ISQR =       1156
```

Program 4.3

END-of-data Specification

Syntax: Using format-*directed* input

  READ (device no., FORMAT *label*, END = *label*) variable list

Using format-*free* input

  READ (device no., *, END = *label*) variable list

Interpretation: When an attempt is made to read data but no data values are present, program control is transferred to the program statement having the statement label specified as follows:

$$END = label$$

Availability: The END-of-data specification is available in Fortran 77 and WATFIV but may not be available in subsets of Fortran 77 or with some earlier versions of Fortran.

4.5 Counting and Accumulating Totals

In processing a series of related records, it is often useful to know the number of records that have been processed or the sum of the values entered in one or more designated fields. Figure 4.6 provides a general description of this process.

The Fortran statement

```
KOUNT = KOUNT + 1
```

serves as a counter. Each time it is executed, the constant value 1 is added to the current value of KOUNT and the resulting value is made the new value of KOUNT.

The Fortran statement

```
SUM = SUM + FIELD
```

serves as a summer. Each time it is executed, the variable amount FIELD is added to the current value of SUM and the resulting value is made the new value of SUM.

The following program segment is designed to find the average of a series of values X, each value appearing on an individual data record. List-directed input/output is used.

```
100 READ (5, *, END = 200) X
        SUM = SUM + X
        KOUNT = KOUNT + 1
    GOTO 100
200 AVERGE = SUM / KOUNT
    PRINT *, 'AVERAGE =', AVERGE
    STOP
```

EXAMPLE 4.5 Write a program that accepts as input the initial odometer reading of a car at the beginning of a gas economy testing period that will span several weeks. Each subsequent data record contains the odometer reading and the number of gallons of gasoline consumed for a week. Print, in table form, the week number (data record number), the distance traveled during the week, the gallons of gas consumed during the week, and the mileage per gallon (MPG). Use an END-of-data specification label. Print the following summary totals:

1. the number of weeks in the test period
2. the total distance traveled
3. the total number of gallons of gas used
4. the average mileage per gallon for the test period

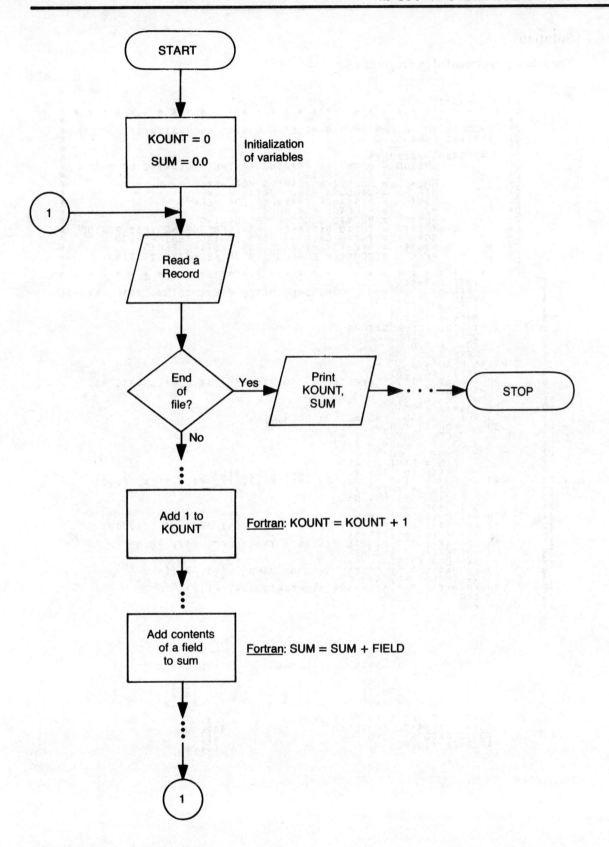

Figure 4.6 KOUNT and SUM Processes

Solution

The solution is presented in Program 4.4.

```
$JOB    WATFIV
C* * * * * * * * * * * * * * * * * * * * * * * * * * * * * * * *
C*                                                              *
C*    PROGRAM TO DETERMINE GAS MILEAGE DURING AN ARBITRARY      *
C*    TESTING PERIOD.                                           *
C*                                                              *
C*    PROGRAM VARIABLES                                         *
C*            INITOD = ODOMETER READING AT THE BEGINNING OF THE *
C*                     TEST PERIOD                              *
C*            ODOM   = ODOMETER READING FOR WEEK                *
C*            GAL    = GALLONS USED DURING WEEK                 *
C*            DIST   = DISTANCE TRAVELED FOR WEEK               *
C*            MIL    = MILEAGE FOR WEEK                         *
C*            PREV   = PREVIOUS ODOMETER READING                *
C*            TDIST  = TOTAL DISTANCE TRAVELED DURING TEST PERIOD *
C*            TGAL   = TOTAL GALLONS USED DURING TEST PERIOD    *
C*            AVGMIL = AVERAGE MILEAGE FOR TESTING PERIOD       *
C*            WEEK   = COUNTER FOR NUMBER OF WEEKS IN TESTING   *
C*                     PERIOD                                   *
C* * * * * * * * * * * * * * * * * * * * * * * * * * * * * * * *
1            INTEGER WEEK
2            REAL MIL, INITOD, ODOM, GAL, DIST, PREV, TDIST, TGAL, AVGMIL
3            READ (5, 10) INITOD
4        10 FORMAT (F8.2)
5            PREV = INITOD
   C INITIALIZE ACCUMULATORS
6            TDIST = 0.0
7            TGAL = 0.0
8            WEEK = 0
   C WRITE HEADINGS
9            WRITE (6, 20)
10       20 FORMAT ('1', ' WEEK', 7X, 'DISTANCE', 4X, 'GALLONS', 9X,
           -' MILEAGE')
11           WRITE (6, 21)
12       21 FORMAT (' ')
13      100 READ (5, 30, END = 200) ODOM, GAL
14       30    FORMAT (F8.2, F5.1)
15           WEEK = WEEK + 1
16           DIST = ODOM - PREV
17           PREV = ODOM
18           MIL = DIST / GAL
19           WRITE (6, 40) WEEK, DIST, GAL, MIL
20       40    FORMAT (' ', 2X, I2, 8X, F7.2, 7X, F4.1, 11X, F6.2)
21           TDIST = TDIST + DIST
22           TGAL = TGAL + GAL
23           GOTO 100
24      200 WRITE (6, 50) WEEK
25       50 FORMAT ('0', 'NUMBER OF WEEKS IN TEST PERIOD', 9X, I2)
26           WRITE (6, 60) TDIST
27       60 FORMAT (' ', 'TOTAL DISTANCE TRAVELED', 13X, F8.2)
28           WRITE (6, 70) TGAL
29           AVMIL = TDIST / TGAL
30       70 FORMAT (' ', 'TOTAL GALLONS USED', 19X, F6.1)
31           WRITE (6, 80) AVMIL
32       80 FORMAT (' ', 'AVERAGE MILEAGE', 22X, F7.2)
33           STOP
34           END
```

WEEK	DISTANCE	GALLONS	MILEAGE
1	100.00	8.1	12.35
2	200.00	15.1	13.25
3	242.00	16.3	13.22

```
NUMBER OF WEEKS IN TEST PERIOD          3
TOTAL DISTANCE TRAVELED            542.00
TOTAL GALLONS USED                  41.5
AVERAGE MILEAGE                     13.06
```

Program 4.4

Counters and Summers

Assignment statements are used to construct mechanisms that, when executed, count by a constant amount or accumulate a variable amount. The general forms of these statements are as follows:

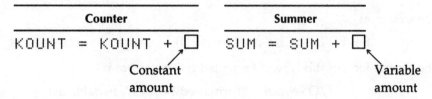

Counter	Summer
KOUNT = KOUNT + ☐	SUM = SUM + ☐

Constant amount   Variable amount

The names of the variables that are used to maintain a count or a running total are immaterial, provided that they appear on both sides of the equal symbol and are consistent with the type of data (real or integer) that are being accumulated. If a counter is being increased by a constant integer amount (1 or 2 or 3 . . .), an integer variable is used to represent the count.

4.6 Some Closing Remarks

The READ/FORMAT and WRITE/FORMAT statement combinations may be used to define layouts of input and output records in all implementations of Fortran, including Fortran 77. In addition, Fortran 77 gives the programmer the option of using the PRINT statement in formatting output. For example, the statement

```
WRITE (6, 200) B, K
```

may be written as

```
PRINT 200, B, K
```

where the number 200 refers to the FORMAT statement label. A similar form may be used on input.

In general, we may write formatted I/O statements as follows:

I/O *keyword* FORMAT *label, variable* list

Fortran 77 also permits the FORMAT specification to be incorporated within the input and output statement by enclosing the FORMAT codes within a pair of apostrophes. The single statement

```
READ '(F6.2, 8X, I3)', A, I
```

is equivalent to the pair of statements

```
READ 100, A, I
100 FORMAT (F6.2, 8X, I3)
```

The statements

```
PRINT 200, B, K
200 FORMAT ('1', F8.3, 9X, I4), B, K
```

may be consolidated and written as

```
PRINT '(''1'', F8.3, 9X, I4)', B, K
```

Notice that the carriage control character has been enclosed in two consecutive single apostrophes since it represents an embedded string. Anytime a literal expression is used in the format specification using this form, it must be delimited using two consecutive single apostrophes.

As another illustration, the statements

```
          PRINT 800, N
      800 FORMAT (1X, 'ANSWER = ', I5)
```

may be written as

```
      PRINT '(1X, ''ANSWER = '', I5)', N
```

The general form of this type of formatted I/O statement is

I/O *keyword*, '(format edit codes)', *variable* list

Keep the following points in mind when using this form:

- The keyword for an output operation is PRINT.
- An asterisk (*) does *not* follow the keyword READ or PRINT.
- Quoted character strings that appear within the parenthesized format specification must be delimited by two consecutive single apostrophes.

Why use formatted I/O statements? Here are several reasons.

- List-directed input/output may not be available with the Fortran compiler that you are using.
- With list-directed output, the design of the particular compiler dictates the column placement of the output; this often results in output that is difficult to read. Using formatted output statements allows the programmer to exercise greater control over the appearance of the output — a feature that is particularly important when it is necessary to create highly structured, table-like reports.
- The handling of special types of values, such as very large or very small numbers, can often be facilitated by using edit descriptors to describe the input/output fields.
- In format-free input, input data fields must be separated by commas or blanks. When processing large volumes of data, the addition of these "extra" characters can consume valuable storage space on the input medium. In format-directed input, the use of edit descriptors makes it unnecessary to use a character such as a blank to separate adjacent data fields.

If your computer supports format-free I/O, then check the logic of your program by first using list-directed I/O. Debug your program and, if required, substitute formatted I/O statements. Once again, run and, if necessary, correct your program.

Review Exercises

A star preceding the number of a problem indicates that a solution for that problem is given at the back of the book.

* **1.** Give the format edit descriptors of data values that take the following forms:
  (a) $\pm$ N N N   (c) $ $ $ $ $ $ (character data)
  (b) $\pm$ X X X X . X X X   (d) $\pm$. X X X X X X E $\pm$ X X

* **2.** The input data value 8193 is entered in a seven-column field as follows:

$$\llcorner \_8193 \lrcorner$$

Determine the stored data value if the corresponding edit descriptor is
(a) I7   (b) I5   (c) F5.2   (d) F6.1   (e) F4.1

* **3.** Given the input data record shown below and the corresponding input statement,

```
      READ (5, 100) L, X, K,
```

determine the values that are assigned to variables L, X, and K for each of the following FORMAT statements:

(a) `100 FORMAT (I7, 5X, F5.2, I5)`
(b) `100 FORMAT (3X, I4, 5X, F5.3, I3)`
(c) `100 FORMAT (F7.2, 4X, I5, 2X, F3.1)`

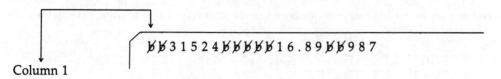

Column 1   ⌀⌀31524⌀⌀⌀⌀⌀16.89⌀⌀⌀987

* **4.** Fill in the following table by determining, in each case, the value of the corresponding output variable:

	Output Format	Data Value Stored in Memory	Printed Value
(a)	I8	7134	
(b)	I3	−819	
(c)	I4	16.8	
(d)	F7.1	185.7	
(e)	F6.2	185.7	
(f)	F4.1	185.7	
(g)	F5.2	51.438	
(h)	E12.7	9873.2	
(i)	E12.5	9873.2	
(j)	E10.4	9873.2	

* **5.** Assume that the stored value of an integer variable L is 97503 and the associated output statement is `WRITE (6, 200) L`. Describe the output if the corresponding FORMAT statement is as follows:

(a) `200 FORMAT (' ', I5)`
(b) `200 FORMAT ('1', I4)`
(c) `200 FORMAT (I9)`
(d) `200 FORMAT (I5)`
(e) `200 FORMAT (3X, I5)`

* **6.** Assume that the stored value of a real variable Z is 1876.125 and that the associated output statement is `WRITE (6, 200) Z`. Describe the output if the corresponding FORMAT statement is as follows:

(a) `200 FORMAT (F8.3)`
(b) `200 FORMAT ('0', F9.4)`
(c) `200 FORMAT (' RESULT =', F10.3)`
(d) `200 FORMAT (F8.2)`
(e) `200 FORMAT ('1', F7.3)`
(f) `200 FORMAT (F11.5)`

* **7.** The column headings of the output of a program are as follows:

STUDENT ID	MIDTERM	FINAL	EXAM AVERAGE
XXXXX	XX	XX	XX.XX

Write the corresponding set of WRITE and FORMAT statements that would print these column headings. Leave a margin of 19 blank columns to the left of the first column heading and to the right of the last column heading. Leave the same number of blank columns between each two column headings. Assume that a line of print contains 132 column positions.

* 8. Given the following data record:

```
8 6 3 5 0 7 4 1 3 2 9 8 6 5
```

in which the data are entered in 14 consecutive columns beginning in column 1, determine the values that are passed to the computer when the data record is read using each of the following FORMAT statements:

(a) FORMAT (I3, F4.1, I7)
(b) FORMAT (T2, F5.2, 4X, I5)
(c) FORMAT (I3,T8, F6.2)
(d) FORMAT (F8.3 / I6)
(e) FORMAT (// F3.1, 5X, F6.3)
(f) FORMAT (I5, T13, I3, T6, F7.2)

* 9. Suppose that BEGIN, MIDDLE, and END are three character variables whose stored string values are as follows:

```
BEGIN = 'LIST-DIRECTED OUTPUT'
MIDDLE = 'IS EASIER TO USE'
   END = 'BUT HARDER TO READ'
```

Given these statements:

```
CHARACTER BEGIN * 20, MIDDLE * 18, END * 15
WRITE (6, 199) BEGIN, MIDDLE, END
```

describe the output and its column placement if the corresponding FORMAT statement is as follows:

(a) 199 FORMAT (' ', A20, 2X, A16, 2X, A18)
(b) 199 FORMAT (' ', A20, T26, A16, T57, A18)
(c) 199 FORMAT (' ', A20 / ' ', A16 // ' ', A18 ///)
(d) 199 FORMAT ('1', //T11, A20, T31, A16, T48, A18)

*10. Given the following input data record:

178.0E−03	216.32ᵇᵇE+4	34E−06	4.396E+08	

write the corresponding E descriptor (assume that the data values are written in consecutive columns beginning with column 1). Also express each input value in decimal form (that is, without using an exponent).

*11. Suppose that the stored decimal values for variables R, S, and T are as follows: R = 0.000001834, S = 186,000,000.0, and T = −7208.09. Given the statement

```
WRITE (6, 808) R, S, T
```

describe the output for each of the following FORMAT statements:

(a) 808 FORMAT (' ', E10.4 / ' ', E9.3 / ' ', E12.6)
(b) 808 FORMAT ('0', E11.4, T20, E9.3, T30, E12.5 //)
(c) 808 FORMAT ('1', E13.7 // T20, E9.3, 3X, E16.8)

12. The following formula may be used to estimate the resistance of a hollow cylinder to collapse:

$$p = C \frac{H^{2.19}}{LD}$$

where p = pressure in pounds/square inch
  H = thickness of cylinder in inches
  D = diameter of cylinder in inches
  L = length of cylinder in inches
  C = a constant having the value 9,675,000

Write a program that reads values for H, D, and L and prints, in table form,

THICKNESS   DIAMETER   LENGTH   PRESSURE

*13. An input data record contains the following information:

Column Numbers	Data Item	Data Type
1–5	Auto part number	Integer
6–10	Blank	
11–16	Unit cost	Real
17–22	Blank	
23–25	Quantity ordered	Integer
26–80	Blank	

Write a program that calculates the cost of each auto part that is ordered. Print in table form:

PART NUMBER   **UNIT COST**   **QUANTITY ORDERED**   **TOTAL COST**

Your program should be designed to process a series of input records. In addition, print the sum of all entries appearing in the Total Cost column and the total number of records processed. Design your program and its output for easy reading.

14. The average (sometimes called *mean*) of this set of data values: 77, 75, 74, 76, and 73, is 75. The mean of the set of data values 107, 88, 50, 90, and 40 is also 75. The individual data values in the first group are closely grouped around the mean. In the second data set, the individual data values are widely scattered about the mean. The *standard deviation* is a statistical measure that indicates how closely the individual data values of a set of data are centered about the mean. For example, if the standard deviation for a set of data is a relatively large number, then the individual data values are scattered widely about the mean.

The following formula may be used to calculate the standard deviation of a data set that contains N values:

$$SDEV = \sqrt{\frac{N\Sigma X^2 - (\Sigma X)^2}{N(N-1)}}$$

where the notation Σ means to find the sum of the variable that follows. The notation ΣX^2 means that we accumulate the sum of the squares of the data values X, while the notation $(\Sigma X)^2$ means that we accumulate the sum of the data values X and, after the last data value X is processed, we calculate the square of the final sum.

Write a program that reads a list of data values using the END-of-data specification to signal the end of the list. As the individual data values are read, your program must accumulate the two required sums and maintain a count of the number of data values. The final output should look as follows:

NUMBER OF DATA VALUES	SUM OF THE SQUARES OF X	SUM OF X SQUARED	STANDARD DEVIATION

*15. Given a "scattered" collection of pairs of sample data points (X, Y), can we find the equation of the straight line that most closely fits the sample points?

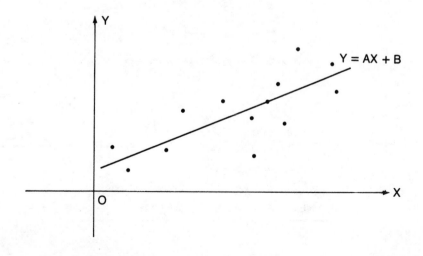

By "the straight line that most closely fits" we mean the straight line such that the sum of the distances of the sample points from the desired line is a minimum. The method of least squares (that is, simple linear regression) is a statistical technique that can be used to determine the coefficients A and B of the line $Y = AX + B$ that gives the best fit with respect to the given set of points. The following relationship may be used to estimate the coefficients A and B:

$$B = \frac{N(\Sigma XY) - (\Sigma X)(\Sigma Y)}{N(\Sigma X^2) - (\Sigma X)^2}$$

$$A = \frac{\Sigma Y - B(\Sigma X)}{N}$$

Write a program that reads in pairs of data values X and Y and calculates and prints the values of the regression coefficients A and B. (Use either list- or format-directed input/output statements.) Test your program using the following sample test data:

X	Y
4.7	9.6
3.2	6.0
4.1	7.8
3.8	7.2
4.6	6.7
3.9	8.8
6.1	10.8
5.3	13.2
4.0	9.5
6.5	13.0

CHAPTER 5
Decision Structures

COMPUTER AXIOM

A computer cannot make *qualitative* comparisons; it cannot decide whether something is pretty or unattractive, interesting or boring, and so on. A computer can make only *quantitative* comparisons; it can decide, for example, whether one value is larger than another value, equal to another value, or less than another value.

COROLLARY

If you want the computer to make a decision, you must express the decision in terms of a comparison of the magnitudes of data values.

5.1 Making Decisions: the Block IF

Consider the problem of preparing a program that reads in two unequal data values and prints the larger of the two data values, A and B. The flowchart solution is given in Figure 5.1. At first glance, it may appear that we could immediately write the corresponding Fortran program. A problem arises, however, in attempting to translate into a Fortran statement the decision box that compares the values of A and B. Our next concern, therefore, is to learn how to program the computer to "decide" whether value A is greater than value B, or less than value B, or equal to value B.

In algebra we express comparisons using special inequality and equality symbols. Fortran also uses special notation to represent possible combinations of inequality and equality relations. These operators are summarized in Table 5.1.

Table 5.1. Relational Operators

Algebra	Meaning	Fortran
<	is less than	.LT.
≤	is less than or equal to	.LE.
=	is equal to	.EQ.
≠	is not equal to (is unequal to)	.NE.
>	is greater than	.GT.
≥	is greater than or equal to	.GE.

EXAMPLE 5.1 If A = 5.0, B = 4.0, and C = 20.0, determine whether each of the following relations is true or false:

(a) `A .GT. B`   (d) `C / B .LT. C / A`

(b) `B .LE. C`   (e) `(B + 2.0) .GE. (C / B + 1.0)`

(c) `A * B .EQ. C`   (f) `C ** 2 .NE. B * 100.0`

111

Solutions

(a) True since 5.0 is greater than 4.0
(b) True since 4.0 is less than or equal to 20.0
(c) True since 20.0 (4.0 * 5.0) is equal to 20.0
(d) False since 5.0 (20.0 / 4.0) is *greater* than 4.0 (20.0 / 5.0)
(e) True since 6.0 (4.0 + 2.0) is greater than or equal to 6.0 (20.0 / 4.0 + 1.0)
(f) False since 20.0 ** 2 (400.0) is *equal to* 4.0 * 100 (400.0).

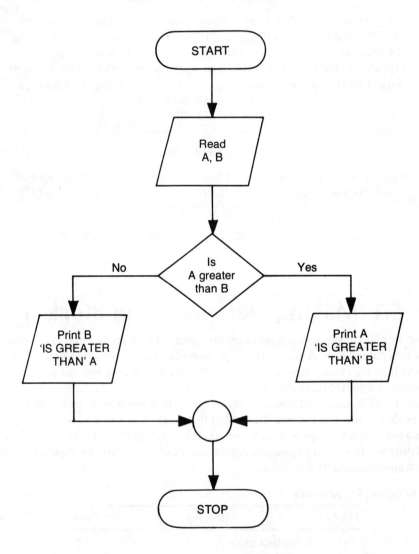

Figure 5.1

We are now in a position to develop the tools necessary to allow us to program the computer to compare two data values. The decision flowchart symbol shown in Figure 5.1 may be equivalently expressed as shown on page 112.

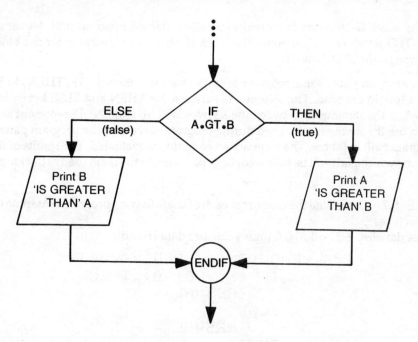

The segment of the Fortran program that can be used to translate the decision symbol and the two alternative operations is based on the IF/THEN/ELSE program sequence:

```
READ *, A, B
IF (A .GT. B) THEN
    PRINT *, A, 'IS LARGER THAN', B
ELSE
    PRINT *, B, 'IS LARGER THAN', A
ENDIF
STOP
END
```

Block IF
Structure

The set of statements that has been bracketed illustrates one of the most powerful and widely used Fortran structures: the *block IF* decision (or selection) structure. Note the following:

- The block IF begins with the keyword IF and terminates with the keyword ENDIF (which may be written as END IF).
- The set of statements bounded by the IF and ENDIF keywords is interpreted as follows: If the condition written inside the parentheses is true (that is, A *is* greater than B), then all statements that follow are executed until the ELSE keyword is reached; program control is then transferred to the statement that immediately follows the ENDIF keyword. If, on the other hand, the condition is *not* true (that is, A is *not* greater than B), then all statements sandwiched between the keywords THEN and ELSE are skipped; all statements that are between the keywords ELSE and ENDIF are executed. When the ENDIF statement is reached, program control automatically passes to the program statement that immediately follows it.
- The comparison condition is always enclosed by parentheses.
- The statements that follow the keywords THEN and ELSE are indented to increase program readability. The Fortran compiler does *not* require that these statements be indented.

• The block IF structure is treated as a self-contained program unit. Never use a GOTO statement to penetrate the block IF structure. Always enter the block IF through the IF statement.

If you regard the path that a program follows as a road, then the IF/THEN/ELSE structure represents a fork in the road. The statements between the THEN and ELSE keywords represent one path, while the statements between the keywords ELSE and ENDIF represent an alternative path. When the IF statement is reached during program execution, the program pauses to decide which program path to follow. The comparison condition is evaluated. The results of the comparison determine which path will be followed. Both paths rejoin the main road at the juncture labeled ENDIF.

EXAMPLE 5.2 Determine the output for each of the following programs. Assume implicit data typing in each case.
(a) Use this data list: 8.5, −3.6, 0.0 (one value per data record).

```
100 READ (5, *, END = 200) X
       IF (X .GE. 0) THEN
           ABSVAL = X
       ELSE
           ABSVAL = - X
       ENDIF
       PRINT *, X, ABSVAL
    GOTO 100
200 STOP
    END
```

(b) Use this data list: 8.0, −14.0, 0.0, 9.4 (one value per data record).

```
100 READ *, X
       IF (X .NE. 0.0) THEN
           X = 2.0 * X
           PRINT *, X
       ELSE
           STOP
       ENDIF
    GOTO 100
    END
```

(c) Use this data list: 4.0, 19.0, 11.0, 7.0, 14.0 (one value per data record).

```
    KOUNT = 1
    SUM = 0.0
100 READ *, X
    SUM = SUM + X
    IF (KOUNT .EQ. 5) THEN
        XMEAN = SUM / KOUNT
        PRINT *, 'MEAN =', XMEAN
        STOP
    ELSE
        KOUNT = KOUNT + 1
    ENDIF
    GOTO 100
    END
```

Solutions

(a)

X	ABSVAL	Output	
8.5	8.5	8.500000	8.500000
−3.6	3.6	−3.600000	3.600000
0.0	0.0	0.000000	0.000000

Program Note: The program is designed to determine the absolute value of the data value that is entered.

(b)

X (Input)	X (after Processing)	Output
8.0	16.0	16.00000
−14.0	−28.0	−28.00000
0.0		Program terminates

Program Notes: The data value 9.4 is never processed since the program is designed to terminate as soon as it encounters the value 0.0. This program illustrates how a particular data value can be used to control a looping mechanism. The program continues to loop back to the READ statement and checks that the value is not equal to zero. If it is equal to zero, the program stops. More will be said about this technique in Section 5.4.

(c)

X	KOUNT	SUM	Output
4.0	1	4.0	
19.0	2	23.0	
11.0	3	34.0	
7.0	4	41.0	
14.0	5	55.0	MEAN = 11.00000

Program Notes: This program illustrates how a counter can be used to control the number of times a loop is executed. After a data value is read and processed (SUM = SUM + X), the current value of the counter is compared with the exit value (5). If the current value is equal to 5, some summary type of processing is performed (the average is calculated), and the program terminates. Otherwise, the counter is increased by 1 and program control passes to the GOTO statement, which transfers program control back to the READ statement. More will be said about this technique in Section 5.4.

EXAMPLE 5.3 Write a program that calculates the real roots of a quadratic equation of the form $AX^2 + BX + C = 0$. Read in values for the coefficients A, B, and C, and use the following formula to calculate the two real roots:

$$ROOT1 = \frac{-B + \sqrt{B^2 - 4AC}}{2A} \qquad ROOT2 = \frac{-B + \sqrt{B^2 - 4AC}}{2A}$$

provided that A is not equal to zero. In writing your program you may assume that the value entered for A is not equal to zero. You must, however, test for the possibility that the discriminant, $B^2 - 4AC$, is less than zero; if it is less than zero, then print the message

```
ROOTS ARE IMAGINARY
```

Solution

We will use this example as a means for reviewing the four-step problem solving approach previously developed. Instead of devising a program flowchart, we will take this opportunity to illustrate an alternative problem solving tool that is based on using Fortran keywords to develop an English-like, paragraph description of the solution algorithm, called a *pseudocode*.

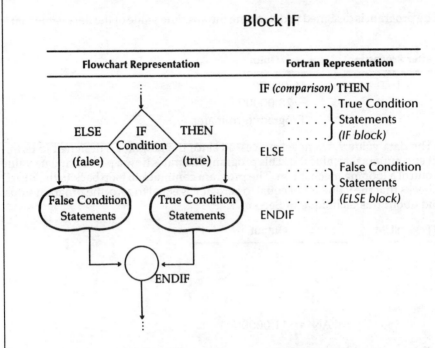

Block IF

Flowchart Representation	Fortran Representation

Notes: 1. The general form of the *comparison* within the IF statement is

$$(\text{expression}_1 \; .\textit{relational operator.} \; \text{expression}_2)$$

All of the following are examples of valid Fortran statements:

```
IF (A + B .GT. C) THEN
IF (A ** 2 + B ** C .EQ. C ** 2) THEN
IF ( (X + Y) / 2.0 .LE. (X*Y) ** 0.5) THEN
```

2. The block IF structure is available in Fortran 77 and WATFIV but is *not* supported by many implementations of Fortran IV.

Step 1. *Input variables:* A, B, and C
Processing: Calculate ROOT1 and ROOT2 using the quadratic formula, *provided that* the DISCriminant ($= B^2 - 4AC$) is not less than zero.
Output:

	A	B	C	ROOT1	ROOT2
(sample data)	2.0	1.0	−15.0	−3.0	2.5
	16.0	−40.0	25.0	1.25	1.25
	3.0	7.0	5.0	ROOTS ARE IMAGINARY	

Step 2. Our plan may be summarized by the following pseudocode description of the processing steps required:

Pseudocode Solution

```
READ coefficients A, B, C
    Calculate the discriminant
    IF discriminant < 0 THEN
        PRINT 'ROOTS ARE IMAGINARY'
    ELSE
        Calculate ROOT1
        Calculate ROOT2
        PRINT ROOT1, ROOT2
    ENDIF
    GOTO READ
    STOP
```

Step 3. With the pseudocode solution used as a guide, the actual Fortran program can be coded easily. (See Program 5.1.)

Step 4. Trace the sample data values through the program, and verify that a manual simulation of the program yields the correct output. Next obtain a computer run, and compare the computer generated output with the sample output obtained by manually walking the data through the program. Keep in mind that, since the calculations involve powers and roots, it is possible that for certain sets of data values a computer round-off error may creep into the results.

```
$JOB    WATFIV
C* * * * * *SOLVING A QUADRATIC EQUATION* * * * * *
C*
C*      PROGRAMMER L. LEFF           DATE:   MARCH 26,1984 *
C*      COMPUTER: IBM MAINFRAME                            *
C*                                                         *
C*      PROGRAM VARIABLES:                                 *
C*                                                         *
C*          A,B,C = COEFFICIENTS OF THE EQUATION           *
C*          DISC = DISCRIMINANT                            *
C*          ROOT1 = ONE REAL ROOT                          *
C*          ROOT2 = SECOND REAL ROOT                       *
C*                                                         *
C* * * * * * * * * * * * * * * * * * * * * * * * * *
C*
C
     1          REAL A, B, C, DISC, ROOT1, ROOT2
     2      100 READ (5, *, END = 200) A, B, C
        C . . . . .REMEMBER, IT MAY BE HELPFUL  TO ECHO PRINT DATA VALUES
     3          PRINT , '    A =', A, '        B =', B, '        C =', C
     4          DISC = B * B - 4.0 * A * C
     5          IF (DISC .LT. 0) THEN
     6              PRINT , 'ROOTS ARE IMAGINARY'
     7          ELSE
     8              ROOT1 = (-B + DISC ** 0.5) / 2.0 * A
     9              ROOT2 = (-B - DISC ** 0.5) / 2.0 * A
    10              PRINT , 'ROOT1 =', ROOT1, '      ROOT2 =', ROOT2
    11          ENDIF
    12          PRINT, ' '
    13          PRINT, ' '
    14          GOTO 100
    15      200 STOP
    16          END

        $ENTRY
    A =          2.0000000        B =          2.0000000    C =        1.0000000
ROOTS ARE IMAGINARY

    A =          1.0000000        B =          3.0000000    C =        1.0000000
ROOT1 =         -0.3819661        ROOT2 =     -2.6180330
```

Program 5.1

5.2 Single-Choice Decision Structures

In Section 5.1 we focused on situations in which there were *two* alternative courses of action, depending on the evaluation of a comparison condition. Some problems involve only a *single* set of

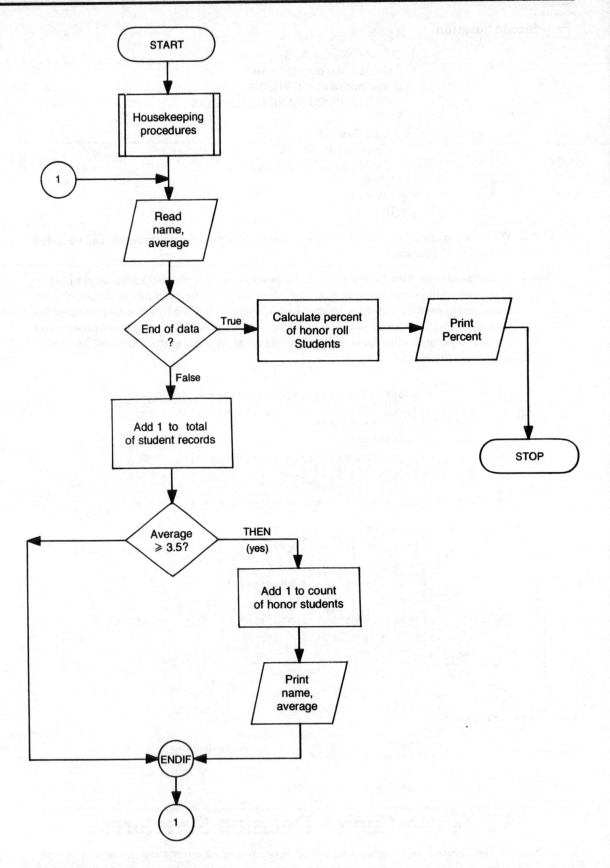

Figure 5.2 Flowchart for Example 5.4

tasks to be performed if the comparison condition is true. If the comparison is false, the decision structure is skipped over. In this situation we may still use the block IF structure. Since there are no statements to be executed if the condition evaluates as false, the keyword ELSE is omitted. This is illustrated in the sample program that follows.

EXAMPLE 5.4   Write a program that reads in a list consisting of a student's name followed by his or her grade point average. The program is to produce an honor roll listing consisting of the names and averages of all students whose grade point averages are greater than or equal to 3.5 (a grade of A = 4.0). In addition, calculate what percent of the total number of students processed qualify for the honor roll.

Solution

Figure 5.2 shows the flowchart solution. Note that the percent of honor roll students can be calculated using this relationship:

$$\text{percent} = \frac{\text{count of honor roll students}}{\text{count of total students}} \times 100.0$$

The Fortran program is displayed in Program 5.2. Provision has been made to include the column headings HONOR STUDENTS and AVERAGE.

The two counters (COUNT and TOTAL) have been defined as real variables since they will be used in a calculation that involves taking their quotient.

```
     $JOB    WATFIV
     C* * * * * * * * * *HONOR ROLL LISTING* *  * * * * * * * * * * * * *
     C*                                                                 *
     C* THIS PROGRAM WAS RUN ON AN IBM COMPUTER USING WATFIV           *
     C*                                                                 *
     C*      PROGRAM VARIABLES:                                         *
     C*                                                                 *
     C*              NAME = STUDENT NAME                                *
     C*              AVG = STUDENT'S GRADE POINT AVERAGE               *
     C*              TOTAL = TOTAL NUMBER OF STUDENT RECORDS            *
     C*              COUNT = COUNT OF THE NUMBER OF HONOR ROLL STUDENTS *
     C*              PERCNT = PER CENT OF TOTAL STUDENTS THAT APPEAR     *
     C*                       ON THE HONOR ROLL                         *
     C*                                                                 *
     C* * * * * * * * * * * * * * * * * * * * * * * * * * * * * * * * * *
     C
     C HOUSEKEEPING ROUTINES FOLLOW
     C
1           REAL AVG, TOTAL, COUNT, PERCNT
2           CHARACTER NAME * 20
     C
3           TOTAL = 0.0
4           COUNT = 0.0
     C PRINT COLUMN HEADINGS
5           PRINT , 'HONOR STUDENTS                  AVERAGE'
6           PRINT , ' '
     C MAIN ROUTINE FOLLOWS
     C
7     100   READ (5, *, END = 200) NAME, AVG
8               TOTAL = TOTAL + 1.0
9               IF (AVG .GE. 3.5) THEN
10                  COUNT = COUNT + 1.0
11                  PRINT , NAME, AVG
12              ENDIF
13          GOTO 100
14    200   PERCNT = (COUNT / TOTAL) * 100.0
15          PRINT , ' '
16          PRINT , ' '
17          PRINT , 'PER CENT ON HONOR ROLL =', PERCNT, '%'
18          STOP
19          END

        $ENTRY
HONOR STUDENTS                  AVERAGE

PETERSON TOM                    3.5000000
SANDERS SUE                     3.8000000

PER CENT ON HONOR ROLL =        66.6666500 %
```

Program 5.2

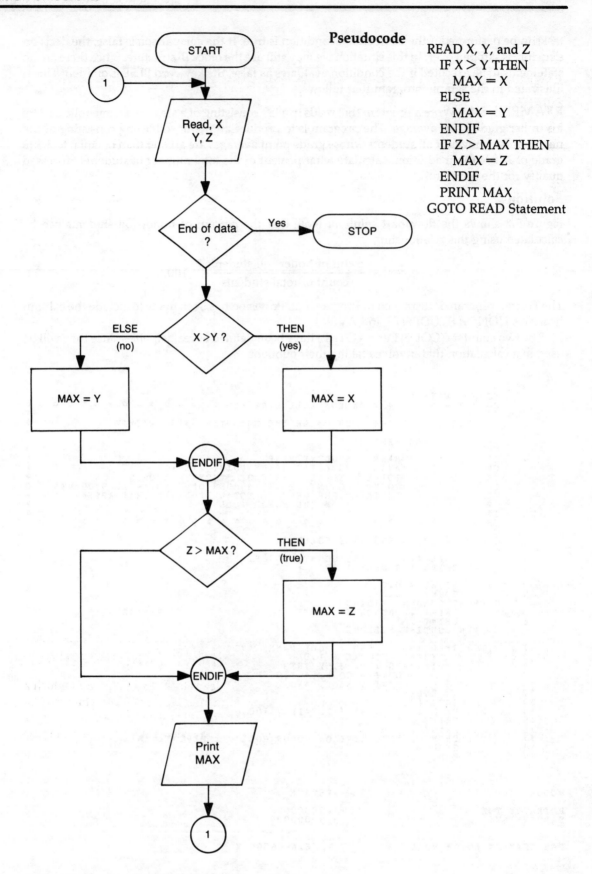

Pseudocode

```
READ X, Y, and Z
  IF X > Y THEN
    MAX = X
  ELSE
    MAX = Y
  ENDIF
  IF Z > MAX THEN
    MAX = Z
  ENDIF
  PRINT MAX
GOTO READ Statement
```

Figure 5.3 Flowchart for Example 5.5

The next sample program illustrates the fact that a program may include more than one decision structure.

EXAMPLE 5.5   Read in three unequal real numbers, and print the largest of the three.

Solution

The most efficient algorithm is based on comparing the first two data values and storing the larger of the two in a temporary storage location, say MAX. The third data value is compared with the contents of MAX. If it is larger than MAX, then MAX is assigned its value. The value of MAX is printed. The solution algorithm is summarized in Figure 5.3. See Program 5.3.

```
      $JOB     WATFIV
      C* * * * * *DETERMINING THE LARGEST OF THREE NUMBERS* * * * *    *
      C*                                                               *
      C*          PROGRAM VARIABLES:                                   *
      C*                                                               *
      C*              X ,Y, Z = THREE NUMBERS                          *
      C*              MAX = LARGEST OF THE THREE NUMBERS               *
      C*                                                               *
      C* * * * * * * * * * *  * * * * * * * * * * * * * * *
      C
  1            REAL X, Y, Z, MAX
  2       100  READ (5, *, END = 200) X, Y, Z
      C . . . .ECHO PRINT DATA VALUES
  3            PRINT . '           X =', X, '       Y=', Y, '        Z =', Z
  4            IF (X. GT. Y) THEN
  5                MAX = X
  6            ELSE
  7                MAX = Y
  8            ENDIF
  9            IF (Z. GT. MAX) THEN
 10                MAX = Z
 11            ENDIF
 12            PRINT , ' '
 13            PRINT , ' MAXIMUM VALUE =', MAX
 14            PRINT , ' '
 15            PRINT , ' '
 16            GO TO 100
 17       200  STOP
 18            END
```

```
      $ENTRY
            X =           8.0000000       Y=        3.0000000       Z =       11.0000000
MAXIMUM VALUE =         11.0000000

            X =           7.0000000       Y=       10.0000000       Z =        6.0000000
MAXIMUM VALUE =         10.0000000
```

Program 5.3

5.3 The Logical and Arithmetic IF Statements

When a single-choice decision (that is, no ELSE component) leads to a program path in which a single statement must be executed if the condition evaluated is true, the block IF structure may be simplified. The *logical IF* statement allows the programmer to consolidate the decision structure by writing the comparison condition and the corresponding action statement on the same line, as follows:

Block IF	Logical IF
| ```
IF (AVG .GE. 3.5) THEN
    PRINT *, NAME, AVG
ENDIF
``` | ```
IF (AVG .GE. 3.5) PRINT *, NAME, AVG
``` |

Notice that when the logical IF is used the keyword THEN is omitted.

The *arithmetic IF* represents another form of decision structure and is supported by all versions of Fortran. The arithmetic IF statement accomplishes a compare and branch operation by evaluating an arithmetic Fortran expression and then comparing the numerical result with zero. One of three program statements will be branched to, depending on whether the result is less than zero, equal to zero, or greater than zero. For example, the arithmetic IF statement

$$IF \ (expression) \ 100, \ 200, \ 300$$

may be interpreted as follows:

- Evaluate the *expression,* obtaining a numerical result.
- Compare the result with zero.
- If the result is less than zero, then transfer program control to the program statement that has the statement label 100. If the result is equal to zero, then transfer program control to the program statement that has the statement label 200. If result is greater than zero, then transfer control to the statement having the label 300.

Example	Interpretation
1. ```IF (B*B - 4.0 * A * C) 210, 220, 230```	1. If the expression B*B − 4.0 * A * C is less than zero (that is, B*B is less than 4.0 * A * C), then program control is transferred to statement 210. If the expression is equal to zero, (that is, B*B is equal to 4.0 * A * C), then control is passed to statement 220. If the expression is greater than zero (that is, B*B is greater than 4.0 * A * C), then the next statement that is executed has the statement label 230.
2. ```IF (X - Y) 150, 200, 200```	2. If X is less than Y, then statement 150 is executed. If X is greater than or equal to Y, then control is transferred to statement 200.

The use of the arithmetic IF tends to produce more careless errors than are made with the block IF or logical IF. Therefore, since it is always possible to use combinations of the logical IF instead of the arithmetic IF, the arithmetic IF statement will *not* be used here.

SUMMARY

We have presented three forms of decision sequences:

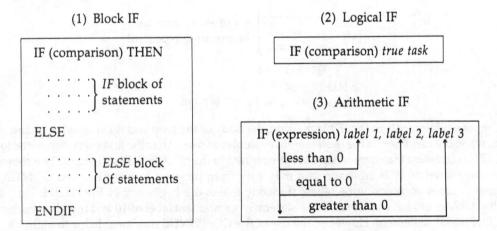

(1) Block IF

```
IF (comparison) THEN

. . . . .  ⎤  IF block of
. . . . .  ⎬  statements
. . . . .  ⎦

ELSE

. . . . .  ⎤  ELSE block
. . . . .  ⎬  of statements

ENDIF
```

(2) Logical IF

```
IF (comparison) true task
```

(3) Arithmetic IF

```
IF (expression) label 1, label 2, label 3
            less than 0
            equal to 0
            greater than 0
```

Since the block IF structure tends to produce highly readable and error-free code, this form will be stressed. The logical IF will be used to represent a single-alternative decision statement that requires a single operation to be performed if the condition is evaluated as true. In our subsequent work, no reference will be made to the arithmetic IF statement.

5.4 Using Decision Structures to Control Loops

At the heart of many computer solutions to problems is the ability to get the computer to repeat the same set of instructions over and over again. A mechanism for identifying a group of statements that are to be executed repeatedly, and for controlling the number of times this body of statements is executed, is referred to as a *looping* or *repetition* structure.

WHILE . . . DO STRUCTURE

Often it is desired that a set of statements be executed again and again while a certain condition is true. This is referred to as a *WHILE . . . DO* loop and takes this general form:

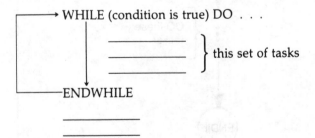

```
WHILE (condition is true) DO . . .

    _____  ⎫
    _____  ⎬ this set of tasks
    _____  ⎭

ENDWHILE

    _____
    _____
```

If the condition is true, then the set of tasks bounded by the WHILE and ENDWHILE statements is executed. If the condition evaluates as false, then program control is transferred to the statement that comes after the ENDWHILE. Regrettably, Fortran IV and the Fortran 77 standard do not recognize the WHILE . . . DO statement. In Fortran 77 the block IF may be used to create a WHILE . . . DO loop, as follows:

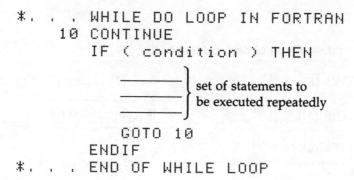

```
*. . . WHILE DO LOOP IN FORTRAN
    10 CONTINUE
       IF ( condition ) THEN
       _____
       _____   } set of statements to
       _____   }   be executed repeatedly

          GOTO 10
       ENDIF
*. . . END OF WHILE LOOP
```

The set of statements in the IF block forms the body of the loop and is executed over and over again, while the condition in the IF statement evaluates as true. After the first execution of the loop, the GOTO statement transfers control of the program to the CONTINUE statement. The choice of a statement label of 10 is arbitrary, and may vary from program to program. The CONTINUE statement causes no action to be taken; it merely marks the beginning of the WHILE . . . DO construct. We could have assigned the IF statement a statement label of 10 and thereby eliminated the CONTINUE statement. However, the use of the CONTINUE statement helps to highlight the WHILE . . . DO loop that follows. When the condition in the IF statement evaluates as false, the body of the loop is skipped over and program control passes to the first executable instruction after the ENDIF. See Figure 5.4 for the flowchart representation of the WHILE . . . DO loop.

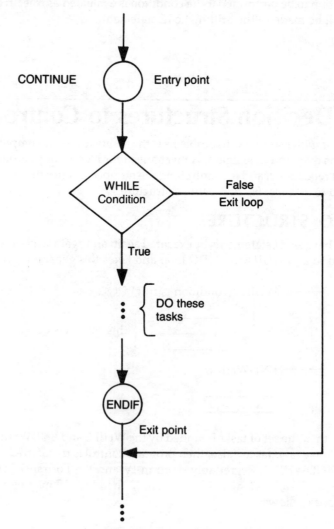

Figure 5.4

As an illustration of the use of the WHILE . . . DO loop, consider a simple application in which a series of data records, each containing a single integer value, is to be read and each value echo printed. There is a complication. It is not known how many data records will be processed, and we will assume that the END-of-data specification feature is not available. Suppose that there are 100 data records. After processing the 99th record, the program must loop back in order to read and process the 100th data value; and after reading and processing the 100th record, the program will automatically try to read another data record. Anticipating this looping mechanism, the programmer can "outsmart" the computer by providing a 101st data record that is used to signal that all the actual data records have already been processed.

A data record used for this purpose is referred to by a variety of names, including *trailer* record, *dummy* record, *sentinel* record, and *end-of-file* record. The technique is to enter on this trailer record a data value, known to the programmer, that cannot represent an actual data value. This trailer value frequently consists of a series of 9's. The string 'EOF' (End of File) is frequently used as a trailer value when alphanumeric data are being read. After each data record is read, a test is performed to determine whether the trailer value has been read. If it has, then the last data record has been read and processed; otherwise, the normal processing of the data continues. This situation may be represented in flowchart form as shown in Figure 5.5.

In Program 5.4 the test for the trailer record is used to control the number of times the WHILE . . . DO loop is executed. While JDATA is not equal to the trailer value of −999, the WHILE loop is performed; otherwise, the loop is exited. In addition, the program maintains a KOUNT of the number of records processed.

In WATFIV, the WHILE . . . DO structure may be coded directly, with the WHILE . . . DO WATFIV statement replacing the IF statement and the corresponding ENDWHILE WATFIV

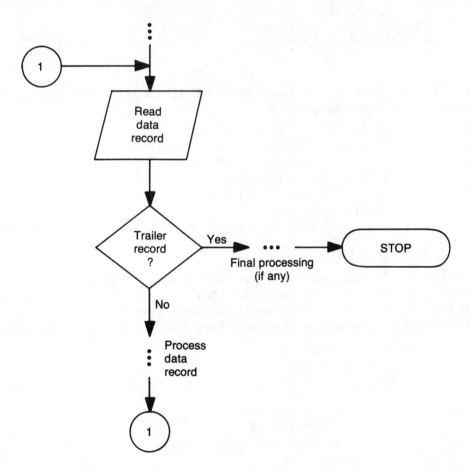

Figure 5.5

```
       *  JUST ECHO PRINTING
       *  THE LAST DATA RECORD CONTAINS A TRAILER VALUE OF -999
       *
  1            INTEGER KOUNT, JDATA
  2            KOUNT = 0
  3            READ * , JDATA
       *       BEGIN WHILE DO LOOP
  4     10     CONTINUE
  5            IF ( JDATA .NE. -999 ) THEN
  6               KOUNT = KOUNT + 1
  7               PRINT * , JDATA
  8               READ * , JDATA
  9               GOTO 10
 10            ENDIF
       *       END OF WHILE LOOP
       *       TRAILER RECORD MUST HAVE BEEN ENCOUNTERED
 11            PRINT * , ' '
 12            PRINT * , ' '
 13            PRINT * , 'RECORDS PROCESSED = ', KOUNT
 14            STOP
 15            END

                         15
                         18
                     300000
                        456
       RECORDS PROCESSED =                  4
```

Program 5.4

statement eliminating the need for the GOTO and ENDIF. Here is the WATFIV implementation of the WHILE . . . DO loop of Program 5.4:

```
  *  .  .  .  WHILE  .  .  .  DO LOOP IN WATFIV
             WHILE ( JDATA .NE. -999 ) DO
                  KOUNT = KOUNT + 1
                  PRINT, JDATA
                  READ, JDATA
             ENDWHILE
  *  .  .  .  END OF THE WATFIV WHILE  .  .  .  DO LOOP
```

DO . . . UNTIL STRUCTURE

The WHILE . . . DO structure executes a set of statements *many* times or *no* times, depending on whether a condition evaluates as true or false. The *DO . . . UNTIL* repetition structure executes the body of a loop at least one time. The set of statements is then executed over and over again until the condition evaluates as false. The general form of this looping structure is as follows:

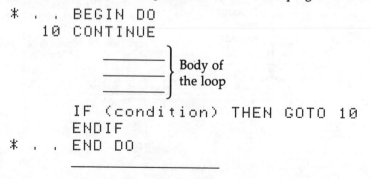

```
  *  .  .  BEGIN DO
     10 CONTINUE

     _____  } Body of
     _____  }  the loop

          IF (condition) THEN GOTO 10
          ENDIF
  *  .  .  END DO
     _____

          .  .  .  .  .
```

If the condition initially evaluates as false, then the body of the loop will have been executed exactly once before program control passes to the statement following the ENDIF. If the condition evaluates as true, then the backward-branching GOTO effects another repetition of the body of the loop.

LOOPING BY MAINTAINING A COUNTER

The WHILE . . . DO and DO . . . UNTIL structures use a test condition to control the number of times a loop is executed. Sometimes the number of data records to be processed is known when the program is prepared. The programmer can capitalize on this information by maintaining a running count of the number of data records that are read and using the counter value to control the number of times the loop is executed. The loop is executed provided that the current value of the counter does not exceed the number of records to be processed.

Consider the problem of writing a program designed to read in exactly 10 data records. Each data record contains two real values whose average is to be calculated and then printed. The pseudocode solution to Program 5.5 shows that a counting loop consists of three major components: *initialization, testing,* and *incrementation*.

PSUEDOCODE SOLUTION

```
Initialize KOUNT at 1
CONTINUE statement
IF KOUNT less than or equal to 10 THEN
    READ A and B
    Find average of A and B
    PRINT A, B, and average
Add 1 to KOUNT
    GOTO CONTINUE statement
ENDIF
END
```

→ Incrementation step
→ Exit test step
→ Initialization step

```
*  PROGRAM USES A COUNTER CONTROLLED LOOP
*
        REAL A, B, AVG
        INTEGER KOUNT
        KOUNT = 1
*
    10 CONTINUE
        IF ( KOUNT .LE. 10 ) THEN
            READ *, A, B
            AVG = (A + B) / 2.0
            PRINT *, A, B, AVG
            KOUNT = KOUNT + 1
            GOTO 10
        ENDIF
        STOP
        END
```

Program 5.5

The general form of a counter-controlled counting loop is given in flowchart form in Figure 5.6.

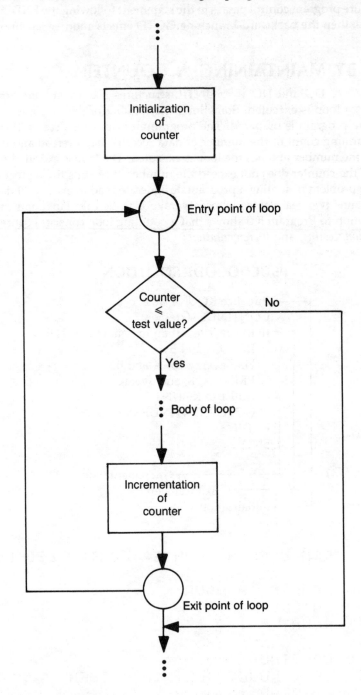

Figure 5.6

A counter may also be used to internally generate "data" values from within a program. Program 5.6 creates a table of values consisting of Celsius and Fahrenheit temperatures, for Celsius temperatures from 0 to 100 degrees in steps of 10 degrees. The pseudocode solution and Program 5.6 follow.

Pseudocode Solution

Initialize Celsius at 0.0
PRINT column headings
CONTINUE statement
IF Celsius is less than or equal to 100.0 THEN
    Calculate Fahrenheit temperature
    PRINT Celsius and Fahrenheit
    Add 10.0 to Celsius
    GOTO CONTINUE statement
ENDIF
END

```
     $JOB    WATFIV
     C* * * * * * * * * * * * * * * * * * * * * * * * * * * * * * *  *
     C* THIS PROGRAM DOES NOT INCLUDE A READ STATEMENT              *
     C*   A COUNTER IS USED TO GENERATE DATA VALUES                 *
     C*                                                             *
     C* PROGRAM VARIABLES:                                          *
     C*         C = CELSIUS TEMPERATURE                             *
     C*         F = FAHRENHEIT TEMPERATURE                          *
     C*                                                             *
     C* THE PROGRAM WAS RUN ON AN IBM COMPUTER USING WATFIV         *
     C* * * * * * * * * * * * * * * * * * * * * * * * * * * * * * *  *
     C
     C
     C OUTPUT COLUMN HEADINGS FOLLOW
 1         PRINT, '              CELSIUS            FAHRENHEIT'
 2         PRINT, ' '
     C
     C
 3         C = 0.0
 4     100 CONTINUE
 5         IF (C .LE. 100) THEN
 6           F = 1.8 * C + 32
 7           PRINT , C, F
 8           PRINT , ' '
 9           C = C + 10.0
10           GOTO 100
11         ENDIF
12         STOP
13         END
     $ENTRY
         CELSIUS            FAHRENHEIT
        0.0000000           32.0000000
       10.0000000           50.0000000
       20.0000000           68.0000000
       30.0000000           86.0000000
       40.0000000          104.0000000
       50.0000000          122.0000000
       60.0000000          140.0000000
       70.0000000          158.0000000
       80.0000000          176.0000000
       90.0000000          194.0000000
      100.0000000          212.0000000
```

Program 5.6

Some Programming Tips

Selecting Trailer Values

Any value that cannot represent an actual data value may be used as a trailer value; otherwise, a data value other than the trailer value may cause the premature termination of a program. A numerical trailer value consisting of a sequence of 9's is commonly used. The value -999.9 will be used as a trailer value in all programs that require a real-valued numerical trailer value. In some programs it may be necessary to choose some character string as a trailer value. In these programs, the value 'EOF' will be used as a trailer value. (As stated previously, EOF is a standard acronym for End of File.) For example, in processing a list of names (variable name: NAME), the trailer value 'EOF' may be used. The test for the trailer value would take the form

```
IF (NAME .EQ. 'EOF') . . .
```

Constructing a Counting Loop

In constructing a loop that is controlled by a counter, three components must be included:

- an *initialization* statement, which establishes the starting value of the counter
- an *exit step*, which tests the current value of the counter in order to determine whether the control of the program should be transferred out of the counting loop
- an *incrementation* statement, which specifies the amount by which the counter is to be increased in each execution of the loop

5.5 Nested Decision Structures

The solutions to a wide variety of programming problems involve a sequence of decisions in which the evaluation of a comparison condition will require that one or more additional decision statements be executed before the original decision structure can be exited. For example, in a program designed to process customer checking account transactions, a decision structure will be needed that will test whether a check amount is greater than or equal to the customer's current account balance. If the condition evaluates as true, then another test must be performed to determine whether the customer has a credit reserve. If the customer does have a credit reserve, then another test must be performed to determine whether the check amount is less than or equal to the sum of the current account balance and the available credit reserve amount; if it is, the check can be processed.

Figure 5.7 illustrates this pattern of decisions. The decision box labeled (3) is said to be *nested* within the decision structure created by decision box (2); similarly, decision box (2) is nested within the decision structure created by decision box (1). Program 5.7 reads in the customer account number, amount of check, checking account balance, and reserve amount, if any. The processing is based on our discussion.

EXAMPLE 5.6 A survey is taken at a "singles" social dance, and the following data are recorded for each individual:

(a) sex code (M or F)   (b) age

A program is required that will determine and print:

1. the total numbers of males and females
2. the number of males over 30 years of age
3. the number of females over 30 years of age

In addition, the program is to provide for the possibility that a letter other than "M" or "F" may have been inadvertently entered for the sex code.

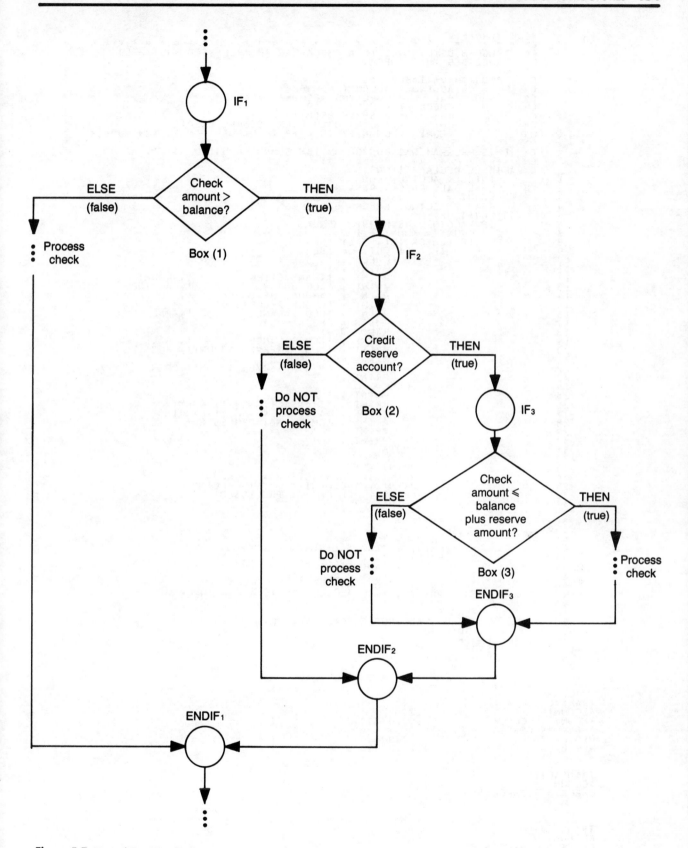

Figure 5.7 Nested Decision Structure

```
      $JOB   WATFIV
C* * * * * * * * * * * * * * * * * * * * * * * * * * * * * * * * * *
C*   PROGRAM DETERMINES IF A CHECK CAN BE PROCESSED AND IF SO
C*   PROCESSES THAT CHECK.
C*
C*     PROGRAM VARIABLES :
C*           ACCTNO = ACCOUNT NUMBER
C*           BAL    = CHECKING ACCOUNT BALANCE
C*           CHECK  = AMOUNT OF CHECK
C*           RES    = RESERVE CREDIT
C*           RUSED  = AMOUNT USED FROM RESERVE CREDIT
C*           KOUNT  = COUNTER TO KEEP TRACK OF TRANSACTION NUMBER
C*
C*   THIS PROGRAM WAS RUN ON AN IBM COMPUTER USING WATFIV
C* * * * * * * * * * * * * * * * * * * * * * * * * * * * * * * * * *
      C VARIABLE DECLARATIONS
  1         INTEGER ACCTNO, KOUNT
  2         REAL BAL, CHECK, RES, RUSED
  3         KOUNT = 0
  4         READ , ACCTNO, CHECK, BAL, RES
  5     100 CONTINUE
  6         IF (ACCTNO .NE. 999) THEN
  7           KOUNT = KOUNT + 1
  8           IF (CHECK .GT. BAL) THEN
  9             IF (RES .GT. 0) THEN
 10               IF (CHECK .LE. BAL + RES ) THEN
 11                 PRINT , ' '
 12                 PRINT , 'TRANSACTION #        ', KOUNT
 13                 PRINT , 'ACCOUNT #            ', ACCTNO
 14                 PRINT , 'AMOUNT OF CHECK      ', CHECK
 15                 PRINT , 'CHECK PROCESSED'
 16                 PRINT , 'OLD BALANCE          ', BAL
 17                 RUSED = CHECK - BAL
 18                 BAL = 0.0
 19                 PRINT , 'NEW BALANCE          ', BAL
 20                 PRINT , 'OLD RESERVED AMOUNT', RES
 21                 RES = RES - RUSED
 22                 PRINT , 'NEW RESERVED AMOUNT', RES
 23                 PRINT , ' '
 24               ELSE
 25                 PRINT , ' '
 26                 PRINT , 'TRANSACTION # ', KOUNT
 27                 PRINT , 'ACCOUNT #     ', ACCTNO
 28                 PRINT , 'CHECK NOT PROCESSED'
 29                 PRINT , ' '
 30                 PRINT , ' '
 31               ENDIF
 32             ELSE
 33               PRINT , ' '
 34               PRINT , 'TRANSACTION # ', KOUNT
 35               PRINT , 'ACCOUNT #     ', ACCTNO
 36               PRINT , 'CHECK NOT PROCESSED'
 37               PRINT , ' '
 38               PRINT , ' '
 39             ENDIF
 40           ELSE
 41             PRINT , ' '
 42             PRINT , 'TRANSACTION # ', KOUNT
 43             PRINT , 'ACCOUNT #     ', ACCTNO
 44             PRINT , 'AMOUNT OF CHECK', CHECK
 45             PRINT , 'CHECK PROCESSED'
 46             PRINT , 'OLD BALANCE      ', BAL
 47             PRINT , 'NEW BALANCE      ', BAL - CHECK
 48             PRINT , ' '
 49           ENDIF
 50           READ , ACCTNO, CHECK, BAL, RES
 51           GOTO 100
 52         ENDIF
 53         STOP
 54         END

      $ENTRY

TRANSACTION #            1
ACCOUNT #              123
AMOUNT OF CHECK       300.0000000
CHECK PROCESSED
OLD BALANCE           400.0000000
NEW BALANCE           100.0000000


TRANSACTION #            2
ACCOUNT #              345
CHECK NOT PROCESSED


TRANSACTION #            3
ACCOUNT #              468
CHECK NOT PROCESSED
```

```
TRANSACTION #               4
ACCOUNT #                   769
AMOUNT OF CHECK             700.0000000
CHECK PROCESSED
OLD BALANCE                 300.0000000
NEW BALANCE                   0.0000000
OLD RESERVED AMOUNT         900.0000000
NEW RESERVED AMOUNT         500.0000000
```

Program 5.7.

Solution

The required pattern of decisions is shown in Figure 5.8. The Fortran solution appears as Program 5.8.

```
       $JOB   WATFIV
       C* * * * * * * * * * * * * * * * * * * * * * * * * * * * * * * * * * *
       C* PROGRAM GIVES A BREAKDOWN OF PEOPLE ATTENDING A SINGLE'S PARTY  *
       C*  A TRAILER VALUE OF 'EOF' IS ENTERED IN THE SEX CODE FIELD      *
       C*                                                                 *
       C*     PROGRAM VARIABLES :                                         *
       C*           SEX = SEX (M OR F) OR 'EOF'                           *
       C*           AGE = AGE OF MEN OR WOMEN                             *
       C*           MTOTAL = TOTAL NUMBER OF MEN                          *
       C*           WTOTAL = TOTAL NUMBER OF WOMEN                        *
       C*           MCOUNT = NUMBER OF MEN OVER 30 YEARS OLD              *
       C*           WCOUNT = NUMBER OF WOMEN OVER 30 YEARS OLD            *
       C*                                                                 *
       C*  THIS PROGRAM WAS RUN ON AN IBM COMPUTER USING WATFIV . . . . . *
       C* * * * * * * * * * * * * * * * * * * * * * * * * * * * * * * * * * *
       C VARIABLE DECLARATIIONS
   1          CHARACTER SEX * 3
   2          INTEGER AGE, MTOTAL, WTOTAL, MCOUNT, WCOUNT
       C INTIALIZATION OF COUNTERS
   3          MTOTAL = 0
   4          WTOTAL = 0
   5          MCOUNT = 0
   6          WCOUNT = 0
       C PRINT HEADING
   7          PRINT , 'SEX              AGE'
   8          PRINT , ' '
   9          READ , SEX, AGE
  10      100 CONTINUE
  11          IF (SEX .NE. 'EOF') THEN
  12             IF (SEX .EQ. 'M') THEN
  13                MTOTAL = MTOTAL + 1
  14                PRINT , SEX, AGE
  15                IF (AGE. GT. 30) THEN
  16                   MCOUNT = MCOUNT + 1
  17                ENDIF
  18             ELSE IF (SEX .EQ. 'F') THEN
  19                WTOTAL = WTOTAL + 1
  20                PRINT , SEX, AGE
  21                IF (AGE. GT. 30) THEN
  22                   WCOUNT = WCOUNT + 1
  23                ENDIF
  24             ELSE
  25                PRINT , SEX, AGE ,'  ERROR IN ENTRY OF SEX CODE'
  26             ENDIF
  27             READ , SEX, AGE
  28             GO TO 100
  29          ENDIF
       C PRINT FINAL TOTALS
  30          PRINT , ' '
  31          PRINT , ' '
  32          PRINT , 'NUMBER OF MEN =          ', MTOTAL
  33          PRINT , 'NUMBER OF MEN OVER 30 =  ', MCOUNT
  34          PRINT , ' '
  35          PRINT , 'NUMBER OF WOMEN =        ', WTOTAL
  36          PRINT , 'NUMBER OF WOMEN OVER 30 = ', WCOUNT
  37          STOP
  38      END

       $ENTRY
```

Output:

```
       SEX              AGE

       M                41
       M                28
       F                27
       K                31       ERROR IN ENTRY OF SEX CODE
       F                36
       M                30


       NUMBER OF MEN =                          3
       NUMBER OF MEN OVER 30 =                  1

       NUMBER OF WOMEN =                        2
       NUMBER OF WOMEN OVER 30 =                1
```

Program 5.8

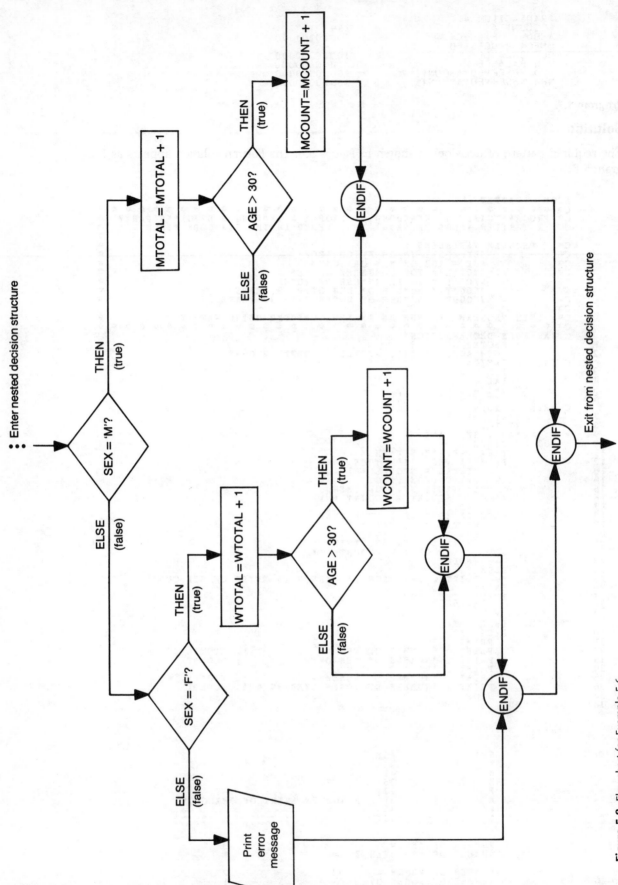

Figure 5.8 Flowchart for Example 5.6

Program Notes: Observe that sample data have been selected so that each possible decision structure and program path is executed at least once. This is necessary in order to be sure that the program is correct. In testing program correctness, always include sample data so that, before the program completes execution, each possible program path is tested.

Nested Decision Structures

In making comparisons it is permissible, and frequently necessary, to *nest* or embed one decision structure within another, *provided* that the decision structures are self-contained and do not overlap.

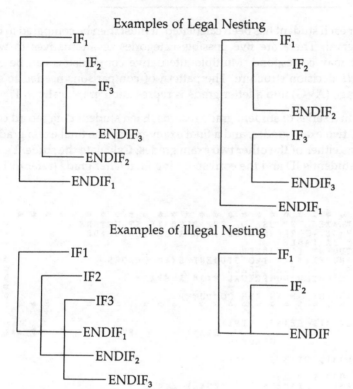

Examples of Legal Nesting

Examples of Illegal Nesting

To ensure program readability and reduce the possibility of introducing errors in program logic, you should *not* attempt to nest more than two decision structures within another block IF structure.

5.6 Multiple-Alternative Decision Structures

Quite frequently problems arise which require that a successive series of comparison tests be performed until a condition is satisfied. When this occurs, program control may be transferred out of the decision structure once the associated set of true tasks has been performed. Problems that involve classifying a variable data item according to some given set of criteria typically require this type of *multiple-alternative* decision testing in order to determine the category into which the variable data item falls.

ELSE IF STRUCTURE

As an example, suppose that during a semester a college instructor gives three exams, which are graded numerically. At the end of the semester the instructor averages these exam grades and must then convert the average score into a letter grade. The letter grade is to be assigned according to Table 5.2.

Table 5.2 Assignment of Letter Grades

Category	Term Average	Letter Grade
(1)	90 – 100	A
(2)	80 – 89	B
(3)	70 – 79	C
(4)	60 – 69	D
(5)	Below 60	F

After the term average for each student has been calculated, it must then be compared to the cutoff value of each grade interval. There are five possible categories or alternatives to which the numerical average grade may correspond. Multiple-alternative comparisons can be efficiently handled using the *ELSE IF* decision structure. The pattern of comparisons needed to convert a student's numerical average (AVG) into a letter grade is represented graphically in Figure 5.9.

EXAMPLE 5.7 Read in a series of student grade records. Each student data record consists of the student's ID number, two exam grades, and a final exam grade. The final exam grade is to be weighted twice as much as either of the other two exam grades. Calculate the student's weighted exam average. Print the student's ID and the corresponding final *letter* grade (refer to Table 5.2).

```
$JOB    WATFIV
C* * * * * * * * * * * * * * * * * * * * * * * * * * * * * *
C*   PROGRAM DEMONSTRATES THE USE OF THE ELSE IF STRUCTURE           *
C*   A WEIGHTED AVERAGE IS TRANSLATED INTO A LETTER GRADE            *
C*             PROGRAM VARIABLES                                     *
C*             ID = STUDENT ID NUMBER                                *
C*             EXAM1 AND EXAM2 = TWO STUDENT EXAM GRADES             *
C*             FINAL = FINAL EXAM GRADE                              *
C*             AVG = WEIGHTED NUMERICAL EXAM AVERAGE                 *
C*                                                                   *
C*   THIS PROGRAM WAS RUN ON AN IBM COMPUTER                         *
C* * * * * * * * * * * * * * * * * * * * * * * * * * * * * *
1          REAL AVG
2          INTEGER ID, EXAM1, EXAM2, FINAL
3          PRINT , '     ID          EXAM1        EXAM2          FINAL
          -        AVG          GRADE'
4          PRINT , ' '
5          READ , ID, EXAM1, EXAM2, FINAL
6     100 CONTINUE
7          IF (ID .NE. -9999) THEN
8             AVG = (EXAM1 + EXAM2 + 2 * FINAL) / 4.0
9             IF (AVG .GE. 90.0) THEN
10               PRINT, ID, EXAM1, EXAM2, FINAL, AVG, '          A'
11            ELSE IF (AVG .GE. 90.0) THEN
12               PRINT, ID, EXAM1, EXAM2, FINAL, AVG, '          B'
13            ELSE IF (AVG .GE. 70.0) THEN
14               PRINT, ID, EXAM1, EXAM2, FINAL, AVG, '          C'
15            ELSE IF (AVG .GE. 60.0) THEN
16               PRINT, ID, EXAM1, EXAM2, FINAL, AVG, '          D'
C THE ONLY REMANING POSSIBILITY IS  GRADE = F
17            ELSE
18               PRINT, ID, EXAM1, EXAM2, FINAL, AVG, '          F'
19            ENDIF
20            READ , ID, EXAM1, EXAM2, FINAL
21            GOTO 100
22         ENDIF
23         STOP
24         END
```

ID	EXAM1	EXAM2	FINAL	AVG	GRADE
11111	90	80	70	77.5000000	C
22222	95	65	35	57.5000000	F
33333	95	96	100	97.7500000	A
44444	72	80	70	73.0000000	C
55555	40	40	22	31.0000000	F
66666	80	80	80	80.0000000	B

$ENTRY

Program 5.9

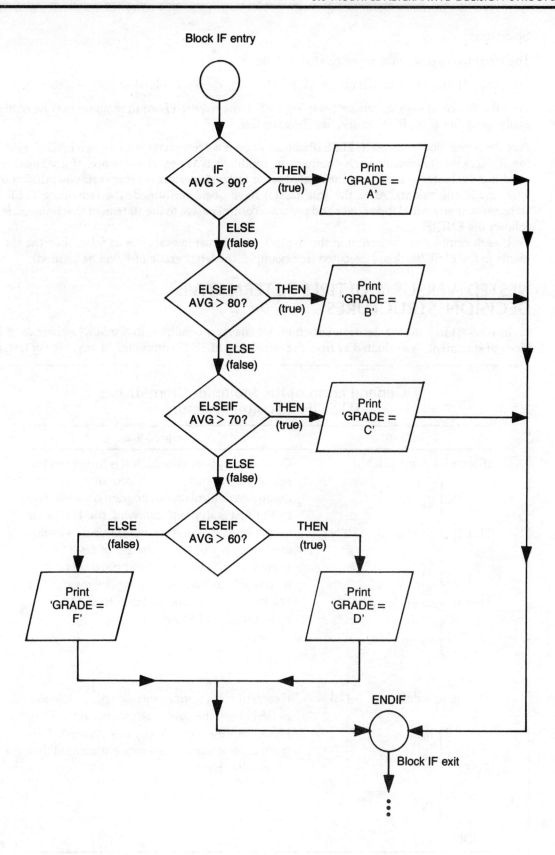

Figure 5.9 Flowchart for Example 5.7

Solution

The weighted average may be calculated as follows:

```
AVG = (EXAM1 + EXAM2 + 2 * FINAL) / 4.0
```

With the flowchart segment presented in Figure 5.9, the required Fortran program may be written easily using the ELSE IF structure. See Program 5.9.

Program Notes: Notice that each ELSE IF statement does *not* terminate with its own ENDIF. Within the IF block of statements, each comparison condition is tested in sequence. If a comparison condition evaluates as true, then the related set of task(s) is performed (for example, printing the letter grade equivalent). After the true task(s) have been performed, the remaining ELSE IF statements, if any, are skipped over and program control passes to the statement that immediately follows the ENDIF.

If each comparison condition in the IF block of statements evaluates as false, then the statements in the ELSE block are executed (for example, the letter grade of F will be printed).

NESTED VERSUS MULTIPLE-ALTERNATIVE DECISION STRUCTURES

In contrast to a nested decision structure, whenever a condition in a multiple-alternative IF block of statements is evaluated as true, the remaining ELSE IF conditions, if any, are *not* tested.

General Form of the Multiple-Alternative (ELSE IF) Decision Structure

Fortran	Interpretation
IF (condition p_1) THEN $\left.\begin{array}{l}\cdots\cdots\\\cdots\cdots\end{array}\right\} q_1$ ELSE IF (condition p_2) THEN $\left.\begin{array}{l}\cdots\cdots\\\cdots\cdots\end{array}\right\} q_2$ ELSE IF (condition p_3) THEN $\left.\begin{array}{l}\cdots\cdots\\\cdots\cdots\end{array}\right\} q_3$ $\vdots$	Condition p_1 is evaluated. If it is true, then the set of statements represented by q_1 is executed and control of the program is transferred to the first statement following the ENDIF. If condition p_1 is false, then condition p_2 is evaluated. If p_2 is true, then the set of tasks represented by q_2 is executed and program control is passed to the statement following the ENDIF. If p_2 evaluates as false, then condition p_3 is tested, and so on.

ELSE IF (condition p_{n-1}) THEN
 	
$\left.\begin{array}{l}\cdots\cdots\\\cdots\cdots\end{array}\right\} q_{n-1}$
 	
ELSE
 	
$\left.\begin{array}{l}\cdots\cdots\\\cdots\cdots\end{array}\right\} q_n$
 	
ENDIF
	If each of conditions p_1 through p_{n-1} evaluates as false, then the set of statements in the ELSE block, represented by q_n, is executed. Program control then passes to the statement that follows the ENDIF.

After executing the related set of true tasks, any remaining ELSE IF conditions are skipped over, with program control passing to the first statement that follows the multiple-alternative ENDIF keyword. Although a decision condition within a nested decision structure may evaluate as true, it still may be necessary to test the logical comparison conditions of more deeply embedded decision statements before the nested block IF structure is exited.

Some additional remarks:

1. If q_n does not consist of any statements, the ELSE block may be omitted. This is *not* recommended (see the next remark).
2. Consider what would happen in Example 5.7 if the condition corresponding to a letter grade of D was omitted from the IF block. If AVG was between 60 and 70, then, since each condition in the IF block would evaluate as false, control would pass to the statement in the ELSE block, resulting in a letter grade of F being printed. To avoid such erroneous output, it is suggested that *each* of the conditions to be tested be explicitly listed in the IF block. In the preceding example, rather than having the letter grade of F assigned as a default condition, the grade of F should be tested for in the IF block. The ELSE block can then be reserved for the printing of an appropriate diagnostic message such as

```
EACH CONDITION IN THE IF BLOCK EVALUATED AS FALSE
```

3. The condition that has the greatest chance of being evaluated as true should be placed first, provided that this does not compromise program clarity or readability.

5.7 The CASE and Computed GOTO Structures

WATFIV offers a special decision structure, the DO CASE, which can be used when a program path must be selected based on the value of a single integer variable. For example, consider the following program segment, where DAY is an integer variable:

```
          ┌──DO CASE DAY
          │  CASE
          │     PRINT, 'SUNDAY'
          │  CASE
          │     PRINT, 'MONDAY'
   Case   │  CASE
Structure │     PRINT, 'TUESDAY'
          │  CASE
          │     .
          │     .
          │     .
          │  CASE
          │     PRINT, 'SATURDAY'
          └──ENDCASE
```

The statements DO CASE and ENDCASE frame the *CASE* structure. If the integer variable DAY has a value of 1, then the *first* CASE statement is executed. After SUNDAY is printed, control of the program passes to the statement that follows ENDCASE. If DAY has a value of 2, then control is transferred to the *second* CASE statement and MONDAY is printed; program control then passes to the statement that follows ENDCASE. In general, if DAY has an integer value of i ($1 \leq i \leq 7$), the statement in the ith CASE statement is executed, with program control then passing to the statement that comes after ENDCASE. If DAY has a value outside this range, the CASE structure is ignored and program control passes to the first statement after ENDCASE.

The Fortran 77 standard does *not* include the CASE structure. The *computed GOTO* (available in all Fortrans) may be used to imitate the WATFIV case structure. The general form of the computed GOTO is as follows:

$$GOTO \ (label_1, \ label_2, \ . \ . \ . \ , \ label_n) \ integer \ variable$$

If the value of the variable is 1, then control of the program is transferred to the statement having $label_1$; if the value of the variable is 2, then the program branches to the statement having $label_2$; and so on. As an illustration, our program segment that prints the day of the week may be coded using a computed GOTO statement as follows:

```
          GOTO (15, 25, 35, 45, 55, 65, 75) DAY
*         CASE 1
    15 PRINT *, 'SUNDAY'
          GOTO 99
*         CASE 2
    25 PRINT *, 'MONDAY'
          GOTO 99
*         CASE 3
    35 PRINT *, 'TUESDAY'
          GOTO 99
              .
              .
*         CASE 7
    75 PRINT *, 'SATURDAY'
          GOTO 99
*         ENDCASE
              . . .
              . . .
    99 . . .
```

Note the use of comments in identifying the different CASE statements. An unconditional GOTO (GOTO 99) must be inserted to prevent control of the program from automatically passing in linear fashion to the next CASE statement. In forming a computed GOTO statement, an integer *variable* must be used if you are using a Fortran IV or WATFIV compiler. The full Fortran 77 standard permits the use of either an integer variable or an integer valued *expression*.

The CASE structure is another way of expressing a multiple-alternative decision. Our day of the week example could have been coded using the ELSE IF structure as follows:

```
IF (DAY .EQ. 1) THEN
     PRINT *, 'SUNDAY'
ELSE IF (DAY .EQ. 2) THEN
     PRINT *, 'MONDAY'
ELSE IF (DAY .EQ. 3) THEN
     PRINT *, 'TUESDAY'
ELSE IF (DAY .EQ. 4) THEN
     .    .    .    .    .
     .    .    .    .    .
     .    .    .    .    .
ELSE IF (DAY .EQ. 7) THEN
     PRINT *, 'SATURDAY'
ELSE
     PRINT *, 'INVALID DAY NUMBER = ', DAY
ENDIF
```

EXAMPLE 5.8   In a certain municipal job, employees are paid according to their salary steps. Suppose that there are five salary steps:

Step	Yearly Salary
1	$16,000
2	17,000
3	18,000
4	19,000
5	20,000

Read in a series of employee records. For simplicity assume that each record contains the employee's name, followed by his or her step number. Print the employee's name and yearly salary. Also print a count of the number of employees who are being paid at each salary step. In addition, print the total yearly payroll. (Use a trailer record that has 'EOF' entered in the employee name field.)

Solution

Program 5.10 illustrates how the computed GOTO implements the CASE structure to achieve a straightforward solution to this problem.

```
$JOB    WATFIV
C* * * * * * * * * * * * * * * * * * * * * * * * * * * * * * * * *
C* THIS PROGRAM ILLUSTRATES THE USE OF THE COMPUTED GOTO         *
C* STATEMENT.  WORKERS OF THE XYZ CORPORATION ARE PAID BASED     *
C* ON 5 SALARY STEPS. EACH WORKER'S NAME AND YEARLY SALARY IS    *
C* LISTED. IN ADDITION TOTALS ARE GENERATED FOR EACH SALARY      *
C* STEP AND FOR THE COMPANY AS A WHOLE.                          *
C*                                                               *
C*   PROGRAM VARIABLES                                           *
C*      NAME  = EMPLOYEE NAME                                    *
C*      SALARY= YEARLY SALARY FOR EACH EMPLOYEE                  *
C*      STEP  = SALARY STEP FOR EACH EMPLOYEE                    *
C*      STEP1 = PAYROLL ACCUMULATOR FOR STEP1 EMPLOYEES          *
C*      STEP2 = PAYROLL ACCUMULATOR FOR STEP2 EMPLOYEES          *
C*      STEP3 = PAYROLL ACCUMULATOR FOR STEP3 EMPLOYEES          *
C*      STEP4 = PAYROLL ACCUMULATOR FOR STEP4 EMPLOYEES          *
C*      STEP5 = PAYROLL ACCUMULATOR FOR STEP5 EMPLOYEES          *
C*      TSAL  = ACCUMULATOR FOR TOTAL COMPANY PAYROLL            *
C*      COUNT1= COUNTER FOR STEP1 EMPLOYEES                      *
C*      COUNT2= COUNTER FOR STEP2 EMPLOYEES                      *
C*      COUNT3= COUNTER FOR STEP3 EMPLOYEES                      *
C*      COUNT4= COUNTER FOR STEP4 EMPLOYEES                      *
C*      COUNT5= COUNTER FOR STEP5 EMPLOYEES                      *
C*      TCOUNT= COUNTER FOR TOTAL NUMBER OF EMPLOYEES            *
C*  THIS PROGRAM WAS RUN ON AN IBM COMPUTER USING WATFIV         *
C* * * * * * * * * * * * * * * * * * * * * * * * * * * * * * * * *
C
C DATA DECLARATIONS FOLLOW
1           REAL STEP1, STEP2, STEP3, STEP4, STEP5, TSAL, SALARY
2           INTEGER COUNT1, COUNT2, COUNT3, COUNT4, COUNT5, TCOUNT, STEP
3           CHARACTER NAME*15
C INITIALIZATION OF VARIABLES FOLLOW
4           STEP1 = 0.0
5           STEP2 = 0.0
6           STEP3 = 0.0
7           STEP4 = 0.0
8           STEP5 = 0.0
9           TSAL  = 0.0
10          COUNT1 = 0
11          COUNT2 = 0
12          COUNT3 = 0
13          COUNT4 = 0
14          COUNT5 = 0
15          TCOUNT = 0
16          READ (5, 100) NAME, STEP
17      100 FORMAT (A15, I1)
C WRITE HEADINGS
18          WRITE (6, 200)
19      200 FORMAT ('1', 'EMPLOYEE NAME', 13X, 'SALARY')
20          WRITE (6, 300)
21      300 FORMAT (' ')
22      400 CONTINUE
23          IF (NAME .NE. 'EOF') THEN
24              GOTO (500, 600, 700, 800, 900), STEP
C
25      500     SALARY = 16000.00
26              STEP1 = STEP1 + SALARY
27              COUNT1 = COUNT1 + 1
28              GOTO 1000
C
```

```
29     600    SALARY = 17000.00
30            STEP2 = STEP2 + SALARY
31            COUNT2 = COUNT2 + 1
32            GOTO 1000
       C
33     700    SALARY = 18000.00
34            STEP3 = STEP3 + SALARY
35            COUNT3 = COUNT3 + 1
36            GOTO 1000
       C
37     800    SALARY = 19000.00
38            STEP4 = STEP4 + SALARY
39            COUNT4 = COUNT4 + 1
40            GOTO 1000
       C
41     900    SALARY = 20000.00
42            STEP5 = STEP5 + SALARY
43            COUNT5 = COUNT5 + 1
       C
       C
44     1000   WRITE (6, 1100) NAME, SALARY
45     1100   FORMAT (1X, A15, 10X, F8.2)
46            TSAL = TSAL + SALARY
47            TCOUNT = TCOUNT + 1
48            READ (5, 1200) NAME, STEP
49     1200   FORMAT (A15, I1)
50            GOTO 400
51            ENDIF
       C
       C
       C PRINT FINAL TOTALS
52            WRITE (6, 1300)
53     1300   FORMAT ('0', ' ')
54            WRITE (6, 1310)
55     1310   FORMAT (' ', '*********************************')
56            WRITE (6, 1320)
57     1320   FORMAT ('0', ' ')
58            WRITE (6, 1330)
59     1330   FORMAT (' ', 'NUMBER OF EMPLOYEES')
60            WRITE (6, 1340) COUNT1
61     1340   FORMAT ('0', ' '            STEP 1', '- - - - - - - - - -', I3)
62            WRITE (6, 1350) COUNT2
63     1350   FORMAT (' ', ' '            STEP 2', '- - - - - - - - - -', I3)
64            WRITE (6, 1360) COUNT3
65     1360   FORMAT (' ', ' '            STEP 3', '- - - - - - - - - -', I3)
66            WRITE (6, 1370) COUNT4
67     1370   FORMAT (' ', ' '            STEP 4', '- - - - - - - - - -', I3)
68            WRITE (6, 1380) COUNT5
69     1380   FORMAT (' ', ' '            STEP 5', '- - - - - - - - - -', I3)
70            WRITE (6, 1390) TCOUNT
71     1390   FORMAT ('0', ' '            TOTAL ', '- - - - - - - - - -', I3)
72            WRITE (6, 1400)
73     1400   FORMAT ('0', ' '*********************************')
74            WRITE (6, 1410)
75     1410   FORMAT ('0', ' ')
76            WRITE (6, 1420)
77     1420   FORMAT (' ', 'YEARLY PAYROLL')
78            WRITE (6, 1430) STEP1
79     1430   FORMAT ('0', ' '            STEP 1', ' - - - - -', F10.2)
80            WRITE (6, 1440) STEP2
81     1440   FORMAT (' ', ' '            STEP 2', ' - - - - -', F10.2)
82            WRITE (6, 1450) STEP3
83     1450   FORMAT (' ', ' '            STEP 3', ' - - - - -', F10.2)
84            WRITE (6, 1460) STEP4
85     1460   FORMAT (' ', ' '            STEP 4', ' - - - - -', F10.2)
86            WRITE (6, 1470) STEP5
87     1470   FORMAT (' ', ' '            STEP 5', ' - - - - -', F10.2)
88            WRITE (6, 1480) TSAL
89     1480   FORMAT ('0', ' '            TOTAL ', ' - - - - -', F10.2)
90            STOP
91            END
```

Output:

```
EMPLOYEE NAME              SALARY

JONES MIKE              17000.00
PETERSON BILL           19000.00
DANIELS SALLY           18000.00
BROWN MICHAEL           20000.00
SMITH JOHN              16000.00
MICHAELS TOM            18000.00
SILBER SUE              17000.00
MILLER MARY             19000.00
STEVENS JEFF            18000.00
JEFFRIES STEVEN         16000.00


*************************************
```

```
NUMBER OF EMPLOYEES
        STEP 1- - - - - - - - -    2
        STEP 2- - - - - - - - -    2
        STEP 3- - - - - - - - -    3
        STEP 4- - - - - - - - -    2
        STEP 5- - - - - - - - -    1

        TOTAL - - - - - - - - -   10

    *******************************

YEARLY PAYROLL
        STEP 1 - - - - -   32000.00
        STEP 2 - - - - -   34000.00
        STEP 3 - - - - -   54000.00
        STEP 4 - - - - -   38000.00
        STEP 5 - - - - -   20000.00

        TOTAL  - - - - -  173000.00
```

Program 5.10

STRUCTURED PROGRAMMING GUIDELINE

Always enter a program control structure (for example, block IF, WHILE/ DO, or CASE) through the topmost statement of the structure. Do not transfer program control to a statement within the structure from a statement in the exterior of the structure. Also, do not transfer control from one alternative of a multiple-alternative ELSE IF or DO CASE structure to another alternative within the structure.

5.8 The Logical .AND. and .OR.

If John earns more than an 80 average in his high school courses *and* if he passes his driver's license exam, his father will buy him a car. If John has less than an 80 average but passes his driver's license exam, his father will *not* buy him a car. If John has an average greater than 80 but does not pass his driver's exam, his father will *not* buy him a car.

Two conditions that are linked together with the word *and* must both be true at the same time in order for the statement to be true (and, in this case, for John to get his own car).

Sometimes the pattern of comparisons that evolves in designing a solution to a problem can be simplified by including a pair of conditions in a decision statement and linking them by using a logical operator such as .AND. or .OR. Table 5.3 summarizes the meaning of the following block IF, which uses the logical .AND. operator:

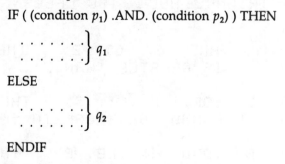

IF ((condition p_1) .AND. (condition p_2)) THEN

$$\left. \begin{array}{c} \cdots \cdots \cdots \\ \cdots \cdots \cdots \end{array} \right\} q_1$$

ELSE

$$\left. \begin{array}{c} \cdots \cdots \cdots \\ \cdots \cdots \cdots \end{array} \right\} q_2$$

ENDIF

Table 5.3 Interpretation of Block IF with .AND. Operator

Condition p_1	Condition p_2	Set of Statements Executed
True	True	q_1
True	False	q_2
False	True	q_2
False	False	q_2

Table 5.4 summarizes the meaning of the following block IF, which uses the logical .OR. operator:

IF ((condition p_1) .OR. (condition p_2)) THEN

$$\left.\begin{array}{c} \cdots\cdots\cdots \\ \cdots\cdots\cdots \end{array}\right\} q_1$$

ELSE

$$\left.\begin{array}{c} \cdots\cdots\cdots \\ \cdots\cdots\cdots \end{array}\right\} q_2$$

ENDIF

Table 5.4 Interpretation of Block IF with .OR. Operator

Condition p_1	Condition p_2	Set of Statements Executed
True	True	q_1
True	False	q_1
False	True	q_1
False	False	q_2

EXAMPLE 5.9 Write a block IF structure that satisfies each of the following conditions:

(a) If X is greater than Y, and Y is greater than Z, then print

'X IS GREATER THAN Z'

(b) If K is greater than 5 or is less than 5, then print

'K CANNOT BE EQUAL TO 5'

(c) If X is between values A and B (A < B), then print

'X IS A VALID DATA VALUE'

(d) If A equals B or B equals C or A equals C, then print

'TRIANGLE ABC IS ISOSCELES'

Solutions

(a)
```
IF ( (X .GT. Y) .AND. (Y .GT. Z) ) THEN
     PRINT *, 'X IS GREATER THAN Z'
ENDIF
```

(b)
```
IF ( (K .GT. 5) .OR. (K .LT. 5) ) THEN
     PRINT *, 'K CANNOT BE EQUAL TO 5'
ENDIF
```

(c)
```
IF ( (X .GE. A) .AND. (X .LE. B) ) THEN
     PRINT *, 'X IS A VALID DATA VALUE'
ENDIF
```

```
(d) IF ( (A .EQ. B) .OR. (B .EQ. C) .OR.
       (A .EQ. C) ) THEN
       PRINT *, 'TRIANGLE ABC IS ISOSCELES'
    ENDIF
```

As Example 5.9(d) illustrates, a decision statement may include more than one logical operator. For the sake of completeness we will mention that there is a third logical operator, .NOT., which serves to negate the condition that follows. Unlike the .AND. and .OR. operators, the .NOT. operator is associated with a single relation. Table 5.5 summarizes the meaning of the following block IF, which uses the logical .NOT. operator:

$$\text{IF (.NOT. (condition } p) \text{) THEN}$$

$$\left.\begin{array}{c} \cdots\cdots\cdots \\ \cdots\cdots\cdots \end{array}\right\} q_1$$

$$\text{ELSE}$$

$$\left.\begin{array}{c} \cdots\cdots\cdots \\ \cdots\cdots\cdots \end{array}\right\} q_2$$

$$\text{ENDIF}$$

Table 5.5 Interpretation of Block IF with .NOT. Operator

Condition p	.NOT. (condition p)	Set of Statements Executed
True	False	q_2
False	True	q_1

5.9 Validating Input Data

A potential source of error is the use of inconsistent or illegal data. You should take steps to ensure that valid data are supplied to your programs. One method of validating input data has already been discussed. *Echo-printing* input data values allows the programmer to visually inspect the data used by the program.

Another method is to include program statements that screen input data *before* the data are manipulated by the program. For example, in designing a program that calculates the quotient of two numbers, a statement should be included which tests for the possibility that the second value (divisor) is equal to zero. If it is, the pair of values should not be processed; an appropriate error message must be printed. To illustrate, consider the following program segment, where A and B are the pair of input data values:

```
IF (B .EQ. 0.0) THEN
    PRINT *, 'B = 0. DIVISION BY ZERO IS ILLEGAL.'
ELSE
    Q = A / B
    PRINT *, 'QUOTIENT = ', Q
ENDIF
```

EXAMPLE 5.10 Write a segment of a program that validates the input data. The desired program reads in an employee's social security number, number of hours worked, and the employee's hourly wage rate. An employee cannot work less than 0 hours or more than 70 hours. In addition, each employee earns at least $3.75 per hour.

Solution

```
* * * * * * * * INPUT VALIDATION ROUTINE * * * * * * * * * *
      IF ( (HOURS .LE. 0.0) .OR. (HOURS .GT. 70.0) THEN
          PRINT *, '*****ERROR IN HOURS.  HOURS = ', HOURS
      ENDIF
      IF ( RATE.LT. 3.75) THEN
          PRINT *, '*****ERROR IN RATE. RATE = ', RATE
      ENDIF
* * * * * * * * * * * * * * * * * * * * * * * * * * * * * * *
```

HANDLING DATA TYPE ERRORS

An input validation routine typically checks to make sure that data fall within a specified range, which is imposed by the nature of the problem. When formatted input is used, a potential error arises when a data value does not agree in type with its corresponding edit descriptor. For example, suppose that a real value having an explicit decimal point is inadvertently entered into a field that is defined by an integer edit descriptor. When an attempt is made to read this data record, the program will terminate abruptly, with the computer system printing an error message.

To avoid cancellation of the program when such an error is encountered (there may be additional data that can be processed), an ERRor specification label may be incorporated into the READ statement. The READ statement

```
READ (5, 200, END = 500, ERR = 999) IVALUE, XDATA
```

may be interpreted as follows: Read a data record from input device number 5; interpret the data record by using FORMAT statement 200, assigning the data value in the first field to integer variable IVALUE and the data value in the next field to real variable XDATA. If an attempt is made to perform a read operation when no more data records are present, program control is transferred to the statement labeled 500. *If an error condition results in attempting to interpret a particular data record, then transfer program control to the statement labeled 999.*

Typically, the statement labeled 999 should initiate an error routine in which an error message of the programmer's design is printed, and a GOTO statement is executed that transfers control back to the READ statement so that the next data record can be processed:

```
100 READ (5, 200, END = 500, ERR = 999) IVALUE, XDATA
200 FORMAT (I6, 5X, F6.1)
```

```
    _____ ⎫
    _____ ⎬ Body of program
    ........................ ⎪
    _____ ⎭
999 _____ ⎫ Print error
    _____ ⎬ message
    GOTO 100
```

5.10 Some Built-in Fortran Functions

Frequently, a programmer will need to calculate the square root of an expression, take the absolute value of a number, convert data types within a program, and evaluate trigonometric, logarithmic, and exponential functions. As a convenience, Fortran features a library of built-in programming routines (called *functions*), which eliminates the need for the programmer to write a set of statements that accomplish these and other frequently needed tasks. Each function is identified by a mnemonic name. For example, the name of the square root function is SQRT, and the name of the absolute value function is ABS. The expression that a function is to operate on is written inside parentheses and immediately follows the function. The assignment statement

Read ERRor Specification

Syntax:

READ   (device, FORMAT, END = *j*, ERR = *k*) input variable list
        number label *i*

Interpretation: If a data type error is encountered during an input operation, program control passes to the program statement having label number *k*. Provision should be made to print an error message and, if appropriate, to return to the READ statement so that normal program execution may be resumed.

Availability: Although the ERR input specification is available in Fortran 77 and WATFIV, it may not be available with some earlier versions of Fortran.

$$C = SQRT (A + B)$$

illustrates the use of the square root function to calculate the square root of an expression. The expression that is being operated on is called the *argument* of the function. In the previous assignment statement, the argument of the square root function is A + B.

In general, all Fortran functions take the form

function *name* (argument)

and have the following effect:

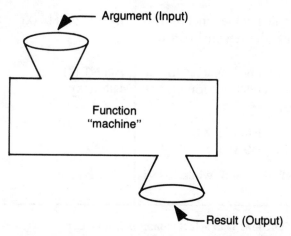

A listing of selected Fortran 77 functions is displayed in Table 5.6. Each function has a *generic* name, as well as a *specific* name. The generic name indicates the effect of the function. The specific name defines the data type of the argument, as well as the data type of the value that is returned by the function. Earlier versions of Fortran (for example, Fortran IV) require the use of a function's specific name. Fortran 77 permits the use of either the generic name or the specific name. When the generic name is used, the Fortran 77 compiler determines the argument's data type and then automatically converts the generic name into the appropriate specific function name.

EXAMPLE 5.11 In each of the following statements determine the value that is assigned to variable X or L:

```
(a) X = SQRT (ABS (-49.0) )
(b) L = MOD ( 13,7 )
(c) L = NINT ( - 4.9 )
(d) X = SQRT ( REAL (INT (81.7) ) )
```

Solutions

(a) X = 7.0 (the absolute value function is evaluated *before* the square root function)

(b) L = 6 since 13 divided by 7 is equal to 1 and a *remainder* of 6

(c) L = −5 since NINT *rounds off* the argument in returning an integer result

(d) X = 9.0 since INT truncates the decimal part of the argument in returning an integer result; REAL converts the integer result (81) to real form (81.0). The SQRT function evaluates 81.0 as 9.0. (*Note:* In Fortran 77 it is not necessary to include the REAL function in evaluating this expression.)

Table 5.6 A Partial Listing of Fortran 77 Library Functions

Fortran 77 Generic Name	Explanation	Fortran IV Specific Name (Argument)	Type of: Argument	Type of: Result
SQRT	Returns the square root of a nonnegative argument.	SQRT (X)	Real	Real
ABS	Returns the absolute value of the function's argument.	ABS (X)	Real	Real
		IABS (J)	Integer	Integer
MOD	Returns the remainder when the first argument is divided by the second argument. For example, MOD (5, 3) returns the value 2.	AMOD (X, Y)	Real	Real
		MOD (J, K)	Integer	Integer

Functions That Convert Data Types

REAL	Returns the real value of the function's argument.	REAL (J) or FLOAT (J)	Integer	Real
INT	Returns the integer value of the function's argument by truncating the decimal part of a real argument.	INT (X) or IFIX (X)	Real	Integer
NINT	Returns the whole number nearest to the functions argument. Function rounds off rather than truncates: $$NINT = \begin{cases} INT\ (X + 0.5),\ \text{if } X \ge 0 \\ INT\ (X - 0.5),\ \text{if } X < 0 \end{cases}$$ For example, NINT (7.8) = 8 while NINT (−3.4) = −3.	ANINT (X) NINT (X)	Real Real	Real Integer

Functions That Select Numbers from a List

MAX	Returns the argument that has the largest value from a list consisting of at least two arguments. Arguments must be of the same data type. For example, MAX (8, 15, 11) = 15.	MAXO (I, J, K, . . .) AMAX1 (X, Y, Z, . . .)	Integer Real	Integer Real
MIN	Returns the argument that has the smallest value from a list consisting of at least two arguments. Arguments must be of the same data type. For example, MIN (8, 15, 11) = 8.	MINO (I, J, K, . . .) AMIN1 (X, Y, Z, . . .)	Integer Real	Integer Real

EXAMPLE 5.12 Express each of the following algebraic formulas in Fortran using one or more Fortran library functions. Assume implicit data typing of variables.

(a) $C = \sqrt{A^2 + B^2}$ (c) $Q = \dfrac{K}{L}$

(b) $X = \sqrt{|A - 1| + B}$ (d) $I = MAX(K^2, L/2, M)$

Solutions

(a) `C = SQRT (A ** 2 + B ** 2)`
(b) `X = SQRT ( ABS(A - 1) + B )`
(c) `Q = REAL (K) / REAL(L)`
(d) `I = MAXO (K ** 2, L / 2, M)`

EXAMPLE 5.13   A set of experimental statistics is used as data. Write a program which determines the number of data values that fall within 0.01 of the real value 2.0.

Solution

The program must count only values that are in the interval 1.99 to 2.01, since any value in this interval is 0.01 or less away from 2.0:

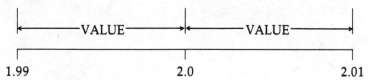

Any value that satisfies the relationship

$$\text{ABS (VALUE} - 2.0) \le 0.01$$

will fall within the desired range. A number such as 0.0 that helps to define the acceptable range of values is sometimes referred to as a *tolerance factor*. The absolute value function is used in order to provide for the possibility that VALUE may be greater than *or* less than the number 2.0 by an amount less than or equal to the tolerance factor, 0.01. See Program 5.11.

```
      $JOB    WATFIV
  1           REAL VALUE
  2           INTEGER KOUNT
  3           KOUNT = 0
  4           READ , VALUE
  5     100 CONTINUE
  6           IF (VALUE .NE. -999.9) THEN
  7             IF ( ABS (VALUE - 2.0) .LE. 0.01 ) THEN
  8               KOUNT = KOUNT + 1
  9               PRINT , 'VALUE=', VALUE, ' VALUE IN DESIRED RANGE'
 10             ELSE
 11               PRINT , 'VALUE=', VALUE, ' VALUE NOT IN DESIRED RANGE'
 12             ENDIF
 13             READ , VALUE
 14             GOTO 100
 15           ENDIF
 16           PRINT , ' '
 17           PRINT , ' '
 18           PRINT , 'TOTAL NUMBER OF VALUES IN THE DESIRED RANGE', KOUNT
 19           STOP
 20           END


      $ENTRY
VALUE=          1.9989090    VALUE IN DESIRED RANGE
VALUE=          3.0000000    VALUE NOT IN DESIRED RANGE
VALUE=          2.0000890    VALUE IN DESIRED RANGE
VALUE=          3.5000000    VALUE NOT IN DESIRED RANGE

TOTAL NUMBER OF VALUES IN THE DESIRED RANGE                2
```

Program 5.11

ROUNDING OFF

The INT function may be used to round off a real value to any desired decimal place. If X represents a positive real value, the following relationships illustrate how X can be rounded off, depending on the desired accuracy.

Position to the Right of the Decimal Point	Decimal Accuracy	Round-off Expression
One	Tenths	X = INT (X * 10.0 + 0.5) / 10.0
Two	Hundredths	X = INT (X * 100.0 + 0.5) / 100.0
Three	Thousandths	X = INT (X * 1000.0 + 0.5) / 1000.0
.	.	.
.	.	.
.	.	.
N		X = INT (X * 10.0 ** N + 0.5) / 10.0 ** N

For example, suppose that X = 21.463. To round off to the nearest tenth:

```
X = INT (21.463 * 10.0 + 0.5) / 10.0
X = INT (214.63 + 0.5) / 10.0
X = INT (215.13) / 10.0
X = 215 / 10.0
X = 21.5
```

To round off a real value in the position N digits to the *left* of the decimal point, we may use this relationship:

```
X = INT (X / 10.0 ** N + 0.5) * 10.0 ** N
```

For example, suppose that X = 21.463. To round off the value X to the nearest units digit (that is, one place to the left of the decimal point):

```
X = INT (21.463 / 10.0 + 0.5) * 10.0
X = INT (2.1463 + 0.5) * 10.0
X = INT (2.6463) * 10.0
X = 2 * 10.0
X = 20.0
```

TESTING FOR DIVISIBILITY

The MOD function may be used to test for the divisibility of two numbers. If value X is divisible evenly by value Y, the remainder obtained when X is divided by Y must be zero.

Test for Divisibility

If MOD (X, Y) equals zero, then X is divisible by Y.

Alternatively, if INT (X/Y) * Y is equal to X, then X is divisible by Y. For example, if X = 12.0 and Y = 3.0 (that is, X is divisible by Y), then

```
INT ( 12.0/3.0 ) * 3.0 = INT ( 4.0 ) * 3.0
        = 4 * 3.0 = 12.0 = X
```

On the other hand, if X = 12.0 and Y = 5.0 (that is, X is *not* divisible by Y), then

```
INT ( 12.0/5.0) * 5.0 = INT ( 2.4) * 5.0
        = 2 * 5.0 = 10.0 ≠ X
```

TESTING FOR EQUALITY

Consider the following program and try to predict the output:

```
REAL X
READ *, X
IF ( ( SQRT (X) ) ** 2 .EQ. X) THEN
    PRINT *, 'TRUE'
ELSE
    PRINT *, 'FALSE'
ENDIF
STOP
END
```

Regardless of the value of X (provided that X is greater than or equal to zero), the expected output is 'TRUE' since, if the square root of a number is squared, the result should be the original number. Algebraically,

$$(\sqrt{X})^2 = X \qquad \text{for all } X \geq 0$$

For some values of X, some computers will yield the output 'FALSE' since taking the square root of an irrational number results in a small round-off error that is compounded when the value is squared.

There is a variety of situations in which testing for the equality of two calculated expressions may produce erroneous results because of a very small round-off error. With most computers, calculated values that are being compared in a decision statement may be considered to be equal if they differ by an amount less than or equal to 0.000001. The revised decision statement of the program that compares the square of the square root of a value to the original value is

```
IF ( ABS ( (SQRT(X)) ** 2 - X ) .LE. 0.000001 )
```

Notice that the *absolute value* of the difference of the two expressions is taken. This allows for the possibility that the first expression is slightly greater or slightly smaller than the second expression.

Testing for Equality

In decision statements that test for the equality of two calculated real expressions, introduce a tolerance factor of 0.000001.

Rather than writing

```
IF ( expression 1 .EQ. expression 2),
```

use the statement

```
IF (ABS (expression 1 - expression 2) .LE. 0.000001 )
```

5.11 Some Closing Remarks

In this chapter we focused on developing program structures that compared Fortran expressions and, based on the results of the comparison, selected the corresponding program path. During program execution, these structures direct the computer's decision-making activities.

Several patterns of decision sequences were illustrated, including the *block IF* [IF/THEN/ELSE], the *logical IF* [IF (comparison) *perform a single true task*], and the *arithmetic IF* (which performs a compare and branch operation based on whether an expression evaluates as negative, zero, or positive).

The block IF has several variations, including the following:

- *Single-alternative* block IF, in which a single group of tasks are performed if the condition evaluates as true. If the condition evaluates as false, program control is passed to the first statement after ENDIF. The keyword ELSE may therefore be omitted.

- *Double-alternative* block IF, in which one of two alternative sets of tasks is performed, depending on the result of the comparison. If the condition evaluates as true, then the statements grouped between the keywords THEN and ELSE are executed. Program control then passes to the next statement after ENDIF. If the condition evaluates as false, then the previous group of statements are skipped over, and the set of statements located between the keywords ELSE and ENDIF is executed.

- *Multiple-alternative* block IF, in which more than two alternative sets of tasks may be specified. Each set of tasks corresponds to a comparison condition. A set of tasks in the IF block is executed only if the related comparison condition evaluates as true.

  The comparison conditions are listed sequentially using the ELSE IF form. If a condition evaluates as true, then the corresponding set of tasks is performed and program control is transferred to the first statement after ENDIF; any remaining tests are ignored. If each comparison condition evaluates as false, then the set of tasks in the ELSE block is executed. The ELSE block should never be omitted. It was suggested that all comparison testing be performed in the IF block, and a diagnostic message, for example,

```
ALL COMPARISON CONDITIONS EVALUATED AS FALSE
```

  be placed in the ELSE block.

Complex programs typically involve combinations of these decision structures, as well as nested decision sequences.

Trailer values and counters may be used in conjunction with decision statements to provide a looping escape mechanism. In choosing a trailer value, be careful not to select a value that may be encountered in processing the actual data set. In constructing a counter controlled looping structure, be sure to provide for the initialization of the counter, an exit step, and the incrementation of the counter. Trace sample data through the program to ensure that these critical components have been properly set.

As a convenience to the programmer, Fortran offers a library of built-in (sometimes called *intrinsic*) functions. Only a sampling of these library functions has been offered in this chapter. Some additional, more mathematically oriented functions will be presented in Chapter 9. If you are using a Fortran 77 compiler, you may use the function's generic name or its specific name. To maximize the portability of your program, it is a good idea to use the function's specific name. If you do use the specific name, be certain that the argument is of the correct type.

Another multiple-alternative decision structure, the CASE structure, also was introduced. WATFIV offers a DO CASE statement that permits its direct translation into program code. In other versions of Fortran, the computed GOTO statement may be used to implement this form. In both cases, the value of an integer variable is used to select a program branch, after which control is transferred out of the structure.

DEBUGGING AIDS

To help minimize a source of potential error, it was suggested that you validate the input data. Echo-printing the values assigned to an input variable list allows for visual inspection of data in a batch processing mode. Sometimes it is not obvious from visual examination of the data what types or range of values is illegal or is inconsistent with the requirements or logic of the program. You can prevent bad data from contaminating the program's output by including program statements designed to screen the data according to some given criteria. Sometimes the use of logical operators is helpful in constructing decision statements that can filter out illegal data. When using formatted input, it may be helpful to include an ERR = *label* specification within the READ statement, where the *label* references an error handling routine. This will eliminate the aborting of a program if a data type error occurs when a particular data record is read in a file.

When testing programs that include one or more decision statements, it is essential that you choose sample data which activate and test the logic of each possible program path. Some programs may appear to be correct only because some of the program branches have not been tested. In a payroll program, for example, use data in which the salary is calculated with*out* overtime and provide data in which the salary is computed *with* overtime. In testing a program that calculates the roots of a quadratic equation of the form $AX^2 + BX + C = 0$, include data values for A, B, and C that lead to real and unequal roots ($B^2 - 4AC > 0$), real and equal roots ($B^2 - 4AC = 0$), and complex roots ($B^2 - 4AC < 0$). In addition, you must remember to "protect" your program by providing for the possibility that the value entered for variable A may be zero.

In examining the output of a program, be alert to round-off errors. In a decision statement *never* test for the equality of two *calculated* real expressions. Always introduce a tolerance factor. The magnitude of the tolerance factor will vary from computer to computer, depending on the precision of the machine. With most computers, if two calculated expressions differ in absolute value by an amount less than 0.000001, they may be assumed to be equal.

Review Exercises

A star preceding the number of a problem indicates that a solution to that problem is given at the back of the book.

Problems 1–7. Code each of the following statements or program fragments using a block IF structure.

* **1.** If A divided by B equals C divided by D, then print

  > A, B, C AND D ARE IN PROPORTION.

* **2.** If A is less than or equal to B, then add 1 to KOUNT1; if A is greater than B, then add 1 to KOUNT2.

* **3.** If C is less than the square root of $A^2 + B^2$, then print

  TRIANGLE ABC IS ACUTE

  If C is equal to the square root of $A^2 + B^2$, then print

  TRIANGLE ABC IS RIGHT

  If C is greater than the square root of $A^2 + B^2$, then print

  TRIANGLE ABC IS OBTUSE.

* **4.** If K is between 100 and 200, inclusive, then calculate $L = 3 * K$ and print L.

* **5.** If X equals Y or is greater than 12, then print AVALUE; if X is less than Y or equal to 13, then print BVALUE; otherwise, print CVALUE.

* **6.** If ANGLE is less than zero or greater than 180, then the measure of ANGLE is invalid.

* **7.** If SALES is less than or equal to 100 units, then SALARY equals 300 dollars. If SALES is greater than 100 units and less than or equal to 200 units, then SALARY equals 300 plus 5 percent × unit PRICE × number of UNITS in excess of 100. If SALES is greater than 200 units, then add a 50 dollar bonus to SALARY.

* **8.** A program is designed to input three data values, A, B, and C, and then to process them in some fashion. In preparing the program, the programmer has assumed that the largest of the three data values is entered first. Write a block IF structure that serves to validate the input data.

* **9.** The SIGNUM function is defined as follows:

  $$\text{SIGNUM}(X) = \begin{cases} -1 & \text{if } X < 0 \\ 0 & \text{if } X = 0 \\ 1 & \text{if } X > 0 \end{cases}$$

  Code a multiple-alternative block IF structure so that, for any argument X, the correct value of the SIGNUM function is printed.

* **10.** Read in a whole number N (N > 1). Find the sum of all integer values between 1 and N, inclusive.

*11. The mathematician Stanislav Ulam proposed that any positive integer would always reduce to 1 if the following algorithm was repeated a sufficient number of times:

    1. If the number is even, divide it by 2.
    2. If the number is odd, multiply it by 3 and then add 1.

For example, if the original number is 13, then the algorithm would generate the following sequence of numbers:

$$13\ 40\ 20\ 10\ 5\ 16\ 8\ 4\ 2\ 1$$

Write a Fortran program which inputs a positive integer greater than 1 and uses a DO . . . UNTIL structure to display the sequence of numbers that are produced by applying Ulam's algorithm. Also print the number of terms in Ulam's sequence.

*12. Read a series of student records containing the student's last name and three exam scores: EXAM1, EXAM2, and FINAL. In calculating the students' averages, EXAM2 is to be weighted twice as much as EXAM1; the FINAL exam is to be weighted three times as much as EXAM1. Print each student's name and average. In addition, print the name and average of the student who has the highest average.

13. The formula to convert degrees Fahrenheit (F) to degrees Celsius (C) is $C = 5/9\ (F - 32)$. Read exactly seven Fahrenheit temperatures that correspond to the average temperatures for the seven days during a certain week in January. Print the equivalent Celsius temperatures (C). In addition, print the number of days the average temperature was below freezing (C < 0), equal to freezing (C = 0), and above freezing (C > 0).

14. Find the smallest integer value of N such that the sum of the terms in the following series exceeds 4:

$$1 + \frac{1}{2} + \frac{1}{3} + \frac{1}{4} + \cdots + \frac{1}{N}$$

15. Read in three data values: the number of the month, the number of the day in the month, and the year. Print the date in the following form:

name of month ⌀ day of month, year

For example, if a data record consists of the data 05, 31, 1984, then print MAY 31, 1984. (Use the computed GOTO and formatted input and output.)

16. Read a real number and print the number of digits in the integer part of the number. For example, if a number has the form XXX.XX, the output should be:

NUMBER	**INTEGER DIGITS**
XXX.XX	3

17. Read a positive integer and determine whether it is a perfect square. (*Hint:* Make use of the INT function.)

*18. Read a series of employee payroll records. Each record consists of the employee's last name, hourly wage rate, and the number of hours worked. An employee is entitled to overtime pay at the rate of 1.5 times ("time and a half") his or her regular hourly wage rate for each hour worked in excess of 35 hours. Print the employee's name, gross pay, and overtime pay (if any). If the amount of overtime pay exceeds the employee's regular salary, print 10 asterisks (*) following the printed amount of overtime pay. In addition, print the total amounts of regular salary and overtime pay.

19. The Newton-Raphson algorithm provides a means for approximating the square root of a positive number. The algorithm may be stated as follows:

Step 1. Make an initial estimate of $\sqrt{X}$.
Step 2. Calculate the average of the estimate and the quotient of the number and the estimate:

$$\sqrt{X} \approx \frac{\text{ESTIMATE} + X/\text{ESTIMATE}}{2}$$

Step 3. For a closer approximation use the result obtained in Step 2 as a refined estimate of the value of $\sqrt{X}$.
Step 4. Go to step 2.

Each time the process is repeated, the estimate of the square root of the number becomes more accurate. For example, suppose we wished to evaluate the square root of 28.

Step 1. Make an initial estimate of $\sqrt{28}$, say 5.

Step 2.

$$\sqrt{28} \approx \frac{5 + 28/5}{2} = \frac{5 + 5.6}{2} = 5.3$$

Step 3. Let 5.3 be the new estimate.
Step 4.

$$\sqrt{28} \approx \frac{5.3 + 28/5.3}{2} \approx \frac{5.3 + 5.28}{2} = 5.29$$

The new estimate would be 5.29, and so on. By repeating Steps 2, 3, and 4 a sufficient number of times, a value of the square root of a number can be obtained that is as close as we wish to the value returned by the square root function SQRT.

Read in a positive number and calculate its square root using this algorithm. Stop when the value obtained with this method is within 0.001 of the value returned by the SQRT function. Print both of these values and the number of times the algorithm must be repeatedly executed in order to achieve the desired accuracy. (Use one-third of the original number as the initial guess.)

*20. Three positive numbers may represent the sides of a triangle only if *each* number is less than the sum of the other two numbers. Read in three positive numbers, and determine whether they can represent the sides of a triangle. If they can, classify the triangle as equilateral (all sides are equal), isosceles (two sides are equal), or scalene (no sides are equal). Check your program using the following sample test data:

ASIDE	BSIDE	CSIDE	Sample Output
9.0	40.0	41.0	SCALENE TRIANGLE
7.0	11.0	4.0	NO TRIANGLE CAN BE FORMED
5.0	3.0	5.0	ISOSCELES TRIANGLE
1.1	1.1	1.1	EQUILATERAL TRIANGLE
6.0	6.0	13.0	NO TRIANGLE CAN BE FORMED

*21. The *range* of a list of numbers is defined as the difference between the largest and smallest values contained in the list. Read a list of positive numbers that terminates with a trailer value of −999.9. Determine the range of the list. (*Hint:* Create temporary storage locations, say SMALL and LARGE. Initialize LARGE at zero and assign the first data to SMALL. As data values are read, compare them with the current contents of these variables and make any appropriate assignments.)

*22. A certain municipal government levies income tax on its residents according to the following schedule:

Adjusted Income		Amount of Tax
Above	But Less than	
$ 1,000	$ 4,000	$ 21 plus 1.8% of excess over $ 1,000
4,000	7,000	75 plus 2.2% of excess over 4,000
7,000	10,000	141 plus 2.5% of excess over 7,000
10,000	13,000	216 plus 2.9% of excess over 10,000
13,000	16,000	303 plus 3.4% of excess over 13,000
16,000	20,000	405 plus 4.0% of excess over 16,000
20,000	25,000	565 plus 4.4% of excess over 20,000
25,000	. . .	785 plus 4.5% of excess over 25,000

Read an individual's social security number and adjusted income. Print the social security number, the adjusted income, and the required amount of tax. Design your program so that it processes exactly 10 sample records.

*23. Write an inventory control program that reads first the current inventory balance of a particular product and then a series of product order data records. Each data record contains the following entries:

1. customer account number
2. quantity ordered
3. a code number of −1, 0, or 1

The code number −1 is used to designate the trailer record.

For each customer record, compare the quantity ordered with the current inventory. If the quantity ordered is less than the current inventory, then print

```
CUSTOMER ACCOUNT NUMBER:....
QUANTITY SHIPPED:....
```

Deduct the quantity shipped from the inventory balance. If the quantity ordered is greater than the current inventory on hand, check the code number. If the code is 0, then the customer will accept only a complete shipment of his or her order. If the code is 1, then the customer will accept a partial shipment equivalent to one-fourth of the total amount ordered, provided that sufficient inventory is on hand. In either case, print

```
CUSTOMER ACCOUNT NUMBER:....
NUMBER OF UNITS SHIPPED:....
NUMBER OF UNITS BACKORDERED:....
```

After updating the inventory balance, read the next customer data record. At the end of the processing, print the updated inventory balance, the total number of units shipped, and the total number of units backordered, if any. Your program should include provision for validating the code number that appears on each input data record. Use the following sample test data:

Initial inventory balance = 1000 units

Code	Account Number	Units Ordered
1	4896	300
0	5503	100
0	7721	200
1	3496	800
3	1299	500
0	1168	250
1	8124	500
0	6537	180
−1	0	0

CHAPTER 6
Do Loops

COMPUTER AXIOM

Computers never become tired from repeatedly executing the same set of program statements.

COROLLARY

In designing a counting loop, you must tell the computer what number to start at, how much to count by, and what number to stop at.

6.1 The Anatomy of a DO Loop

We saw in Chapter 5 that a counter may be used to control a loop. The following set of statements, for example, will be executed exactly seven times:

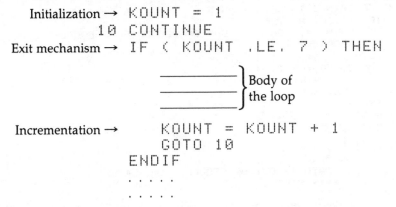

```
Initialization →   KOUNT = 1
                10 CONTINUE
Exit mechanism → IF ( KOUNT .LE. 7 ) THEN
                   _____ } Body of
                   _____ } the loop
Incrementation →   KOUNT = KOUNT + 1
                   GOTO 10
                ENDIF
                . . . . .
                . . . . .
```

Fortran provides a very convenient statement that establishes a counter-controlled loop. The following Fortran DO loop is equivalent to the preceding program segment:

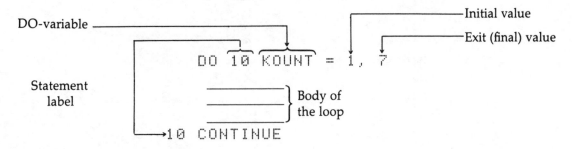

```
DO-variable
                                   Initial value
                                   Exit (final) value
       DO 10 KOUNT = 1, 7
Statement          _____ } Body of
label              _____ } the loop
    →10 CONTINUE
```

The body of the DO loop is defined by the set of statements up to and including the statement that has the same statement label as is found in the DO statement. It is common programming practice to use a CONTINUE statement to mark the physical end of a DO loop. When this structure is first encountered during program execution, the *index* (or *DO-variable*) KOUNT is initialized at 1. The body of the DO loop (also called the *range* of the DO loop) is executed. After the statement having the label 10 is reached (that is, the CONTINUE statement), program control is transferred automatically back to the DO statement.

When the DO statement is executed, two actions are taken. The current value of KOUNT is increased by 1, and the new value of KOUNT is then compared to the exit value (7 in our example). Since the current value of KOUNT does not exceed 7, the group of statements enclosed by the DO and CONTINUE statements are again executed, with program control transferring back to the DO statement. The value of KOUNT is again incremented by 1 and compared to the exit value, and so on. This pattern repeats until the value of KOUNT exceeds 7. When this occurs, program control is transferred to the statement that immediately follows the CONTINUE statement.

The DO statement may increase the DO-variable by amounts other than 1. For example, the statement

```
DO 10 KOUNT = 1, 7, 3
```

specifies that the variable KOUNT is to be incremented in steps of 3 so that KOUNT will take on the values 1, 4, and 7.

EXAMPLE 6.1   Read in two integer values I and N, where I is less than N. Print all integer values between I and N, including I and N.

```
* THIS PROGRAM USES VARIABLES AND DO PARAMETERS
* THIS PROGRAM WAS RUN ON A PRIME 850 COMPUTER SYSTEM USING
* A FORTRAN 77 COMPILER.
      INTEGER I, N, X
      READ *, I, N
* MAKE CERTAIN I IS LESS THAN N
      IF (I .GE. N) THEN
          PRINT *, 'DATA IS OUT OF SEQUENCE OR EQUAL'
          STOP
      ELSE
          DO 50 X = I, N
              PRINT *, X
   50     CONTINUE
      ENDIF
      STOP
      END
```

```
      15 15
       DATA IS OUT OF SEQUENCE OR EQUAL
      **** STOP

      15 3
       DATA IS OUT OF SEQUENCE OR EQUAL
      **** STOP

         3 15
                    3
                    4
                    5
                    6
                    7
                    8
                    9
                   10
                   11
                   12
                   13
                   14
                   15
```

Program 6.1   **** STOP

Solution

See Program 6.1. Notice that, in the DO statement in the ELSE block, variables appear as the initial and final parameter values. This is legal provided that these variables are assigned values *before* the first execution of the DO statement.

An input validation routine has been included to make certain that the data values in the pair are entered in the correct order. The sample data illustrate what happens if the two input data values are equal (for example, 15 and 15) or if the first value (15) is larger than the second value (3). When the first value (3) is less than the second data value (15), all integer values between these (3, 4, 5, . . . , 15) are printed.

EXAMPLE 6.2   Using implicit data typing, write a program that prints

```
5
4
3
2
1
BOOM!
```

Solution

We may use a DO loop to generate the numbers 5, 4, 3, 2, and 1, provided that a step value of −1 is used. In WATFIV and Fortran IV the initial, final, and increment values must each have a *positive* integer value. See Program 6.2.

```
* THIS PROGRAM WAS RUN ON A PRIME 850 COMPUTER SYSTEM USING
* A FORTRAN 77 COMPILER.
      DO 99 N = 5, 1, -1
         PRINT *, N
 99   CONTINUE
      PRINT *, '          BOOM!'
      STOP
      END
```

Program 6.2

```
5
4
3
2
1
BOOM!
```

The DO Loop

DO *statement label* index variable = initial, exit, increment

$$\left.\begin{array}{l} \cdot \\ \cdot \\ \cdot \end{array}\right\} \text{Body or } range \text{ of the DO loop}$$

   label CONTINUE

A DO statement initiates a counter-controlled loop and includes the following components:

- The *index* or *DO-variable*, which maintains a running count. This variable is sometimes referred to as the loop control variable (lcv).
- The *initial* value of the DO-variable, its *exit* (that is, final) value, and the *incrementation* (step) value. These quantities are sometimes referred to as the *parameters* of the DO statement.

STRUCTURED PROGRAMMING GUIDELINE

In order to make your programs "more structured," make sure that every repetition sequence takes one of the following forms:

- WHILE . . . DO
- DO . . . UNTIL
- DO loop

In working with DO loops, keep in mind that:

- In Fortran IV and WATFIV, the initial, final, and increment values must be *positive integer* constants or *positive integer* valued variables (expressions are *not* permitted). Fortran 77 offers greater flexibility, permitting the use of integer and real valued constants, variables, and expressions as loop parameters.
- Although it is recommended that the last statement in the range of a DO loop be a CONTINUE statement, this *need not* be the case. The statement label that appears in the DO statement may be paired with any executable statement, *except* statements that can transfer program control.
- When the step value is omitted, it is assumed to be 1.
- Each execution of a DO loop (or any controlled looping mechanism) is referred to as a loop *iteration*.

EXAMPLE 6.3   Determine the number of times the loops controlled by the given DO statement are executed if $I = 2$, $J = 4$, and $K = 5$.

(a) `DO 75 L = 1, 7, I`
(b) `DO 50 N = 3, J + K`
(c) `DO 99 M = 11, 1, -2`
(d) `DO 40 L = K, K, 2`
(e) `DO 70 M = 3, 4.5, I / J`

Solutions

(a) 4
(b) 7 in Fortran 77. The statement is illegal in WATFIV and Fortran IV since it contains an expression $(J + K)$ as one of the loop parameters.
(c) 6 in Fortran 77
(d) 1
(e) Since the step value is 0.5, the loop will be executed 4 times in Fortran 77. In WATFIV and Fortran IV the statement is illegal for two reasons: a loop parameter is an expression and a loop parameter has a real value.

6.2 Using the DO Loop in Fortran Programs

The DO loop provides a convenient means by which a program can generate its own data. For example, Program 6.3 is designed to calculate the sum of all *odd* integers between 3 and 147, inclusive. Note that, in order to restrict the range of the DO-variable to odd integers, the increment value is 2.

As another example, suppose that we wish to produce a square root table for all integers between 10 and 50, inclusive. Program 6.4 includes column headings. The argument of the square root function is converted to a real value before the function is evaluated. Implicit data typing is assumed.

```
      $JOB    WATFIV
      C CALCULATE SUM OF ODD INTEGERS BETWEEN 3 AND 147
 1            INTEGER I, KSUM
 2            KSUM = 0
 3            DO 100 I = 3, 147, 2
 4                KSUM = KSUM + I
 5        100 CONTINUE
 6            PRINT , 'SUM =', KSUM
 7            STOP
 8            END

      $ENTRY
SUM =           5475
```

Program 6.3

```
 *  THIS PROGRAM IS RUN ON A PRIME 850 COMPUTER SYSTEM USING
 *  A FORTRAN 77 COMPILER.
         PRINT *, '          NUMBER   SQUARE ROOT'
         PRINT *, ' '
         DO 100 N = 10, 50
             SQROOT = SQRT ( REAL(N) )
             PRINT *, N, SQROOT
     100 CONTINUE
         STOP
         END

         OK, SEG SQROOT

         OK, SEG SQROOT
               NUMBER   SQUARE ROOT

                 10     3.16228
                 11     3.31662
                 12     3.46410
                 13     3.60555
                 14     3.74166
                 15     3.87298
                 16     4.00000
                 17     4.12311
                 18     4.24264
                 19     4.35890
                 20     4.47214
                 21     4.58257
                 22     4.69042
                 23     4.79583
                 24     4.89898
                 25     5.00000
                 26     5.09902
                 27     5.19615
                 28     5.29150
                 29     5.38516
                 30     5.47723
                 31     5.56776
                 32     5.65685
                 33     5.74456
                 34     5.83095
                 35     5.91608
                 36     6.00000
                 37     6.08276
                 38     6.16441
                 39     6.24500
                 40     6.32455
                 41     6.40312
                 42     6.48074
                 43     6.55744
                 44     6.63325
                 45     6.70820
                 46     6.78233
                 47     6.85565
                 48     6.92820
                 49     7.00000
                 50     7.07107
```

Program 6.4   **** STOP

The DO loop may also be used expressly to control the number of times a loop is executed. For instance, suppose that we wish to calculate the tuition payments of a group of students attending a certain college. Each student record contains the student's ID number and the number of credits the student has registered for. Instead of using a trailer record to signal the end of the series of student payment records, a *header* record is inserted in *front* of the data records. The exact number of data records that follow is entered on the header record. If 1200 student payment records are to be processed, the number 1200 will appear on the first data record.

Program 6.5 calculates the tuition payments due based on the following tuition charge schedule:

Number of Credits	Payment Due
Less than 15	$175 per credit plus a $60 library and student activity fee
15 or more	A flat fee of $2500

```
$JOB   WATFIV
C PROGRAM CALCULATES TUITION DUE GIVEN THE COURSE CREDITS TAKEN
C
C      PROGRAM VARIABLES
C            HEADER = NUMBER OF STUDENT PAYMENT RECORDS TO BE PROCESSED
C            ID     = STUDENT ID NUMBER
C            CREDIT = NUMBER OF CREDITS TAKEN
C            FEE    = TUITION PAYMENT DUE
C
1            INTEGER HEADER, ID
2            REAL CREDIT, FEE
C PRINT COLUMN HEADINGS
3            PRINT , '        ID            CREDIT            FEE'
4            PRINT , ' '
5            READ , HEADER
6            DO 50 I = 1, HEADER
7               READ , ID, CREDIT
8               IF (CREDIT .LT. 15) THEN
9                  FEE = CREDIT * 175 + 60
10              ELSE
11                 FEE = 2500
12              ENDIF
13              PRINT , ID, CREDIT, FEE
14       50 CONTINUE
15          STOP
16          END
```

```
$ENTRY
ID                 CREDIT              FEE

193872          10.0000000       1810.0000000
240096          16.0000000       2500.0000000
```

Program 6.5

EXAMPLE 6.4 N! is read as "N factorial" and is defined for positive integer values of N (N > 0) as follows:

$$N! = 1 \times 2 \times 3 \times 4 \times \cdots \times (N-1) \times N$$

By definition, 0! = 1. For example, 5! = $1 \times 2 \times 3 \times 4 \times 5 = 120$. Write a program that calculates N! for any given nonnegative value of N.

Solution

The program is based on this calculation: NFACT = NFACT * I, where I is the DO-variable, which ranges in value from 1 to N. NFACT will be the variable that stores the value of N!. We must remember to initialize the value of NFACT at 1; otherwise, the calculated value of NFACT will be zero. In addition, before the DO loop is entered, we must test for the possibility that N equals zero. The flowchart and pseudocode solutions are given in Figure 6.1.

The required Fortran program is shown as Program 6.6.

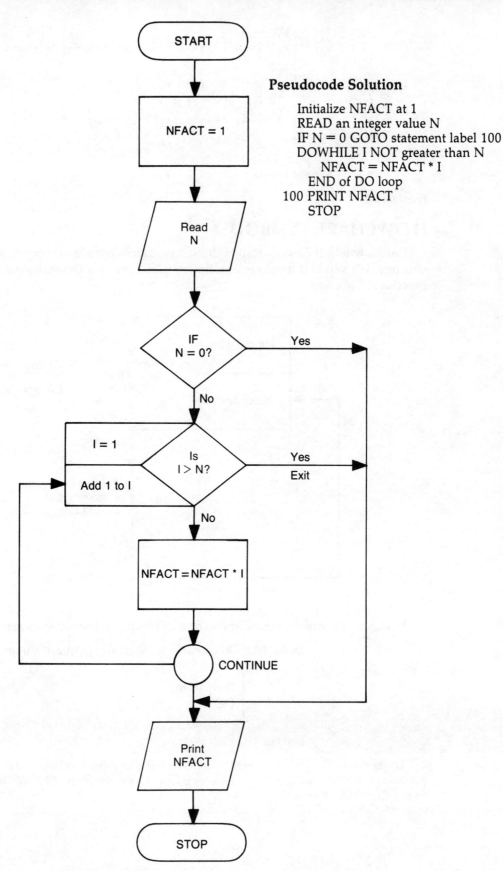

Pseudocode Solution

Initialize NFACT at 1
READ an integer value N
IF N = 0 GOTO statement label 100
DOWHILE I NOT greater than N
     NFACT = NFACT * I
END of DO loop
100 PRINT NFACT
STOP

Figure 6.1   Flowchart and Pseudocode Solution for Example 6.4

```
$JOB    WATFIV
C PROGRAM CALCULATES N FACTORIAL!
C THIS PROGRAM WAS RUN ON AN IBM COMPUTER USING WATFIV
 1          INTEGER N, NFACT
 2          NFACT = 1
 3          READ , N
 4          IF (N .EQ. 0) GOTO 100
 5          DO 50 I = 1, N
 6              NFACT = NFACT * I
 7      50 CONTINUE
 8     100 PRINT , N, 'FACTORIAL =', NFACT
 9          STOP
10          END

$ENTRY
   6 FACTORIAL =            720
```

Program 6.6

FLOWCHART SYMBOLISM

Unfortunately, there is no standardized flowchart or pseudocode representation of a DO loop structure. We will find it convenient, however, to express a DO statement using the following flowchart symbolism:

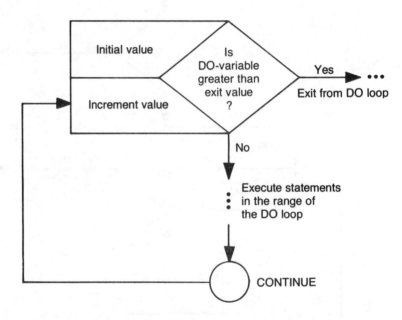

In writing a pseudocode description of a DO loop, the following format will be used:

DOWHILE *DO-variable* NOT greater than *exit value*

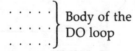

Body of the
DO loop

END of DO loop

The keyword DOWHILE is used to indicate that a looping structure is to be executed repeatedly provided that the condition which follows is true. The expression "END of DO loop" corresponds to the CONTINUE statement.

EXAMPLE 6.5 Determine the number of integer values in the interval 139 to 497, inclusive, that are evenly divisible by 7. (Use the MOD function.)

Solution

The flowchart and pseudocode solution are given in Figure 6.2. See Program 6.7.

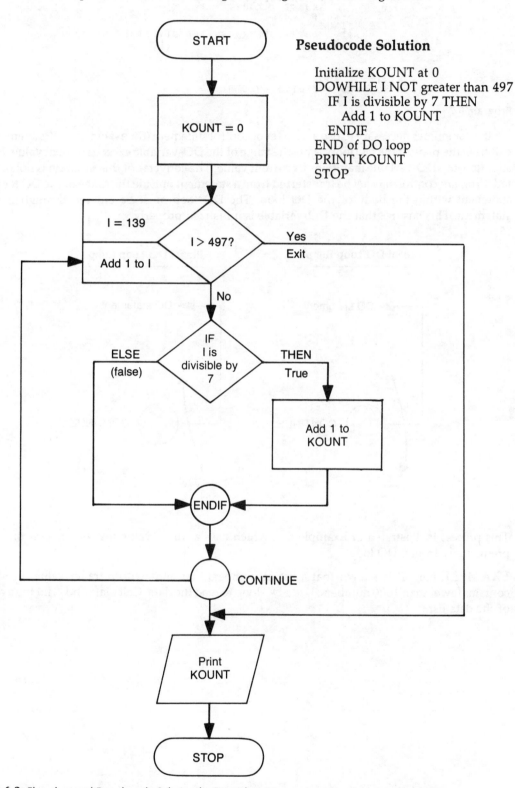

Pseudocode Solution

Initialize KOUNT at 0
DOWHILE I NOT greater than 497
   IF I is divisible by 7 THEN
     Add 1 to KOUNT
   ENDIF
END of DO loop
PRINT KOUNT
STOP

Figure 6.2 Flowchart and Pseudocode Solution for Example 6.5

```
$JOB    WATFIV
C PROGRAM DETERMINES NUMBERS DIVISIBLE BY 7
C       INTERVAL TESTED IS:  139 TO 497
C THIS PROGRAM WAS RUN ON AN IBM COMPUTER USING WATFIV
C
1          INTEGER I, KOUNT
2          KOUNT = 0
3          DO 50 I = 139, 497
4             IF ( MOD (I, 7) .EQ. 0 ) THEN
5                KOUNT = KOUNT + 1
6             ENDIF
7       50 CONTINUE
8          PRINT , KOUNT, 'NUMBERS ARE DIVISIBLE BY 7'
9          STOP
10         END

   $ENTRY
      52 NUMBERS ARE DIVISIBLE BY 7
```

Program 6.7

It is sometimes necessary to use a transfer of control statement (for example, an IF statement) to exit from the body of the DO loop *before* the value of the DO-variable exceeds the exit value. In this situation, the DO-variable maintains its current value. The converse of this situation is not permitted. Program control may *not* be transferred from a statement outside the range of the DO loop to a statement within the body of the DO loop. The DO loop must be entered through the DO statement. This ensures that the DO-variable is initialized properly.

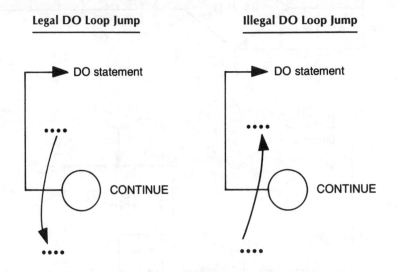

This process is illustrated in Example 6.6, which uses a trailer value test as a means of exiting prematurely from a DO loop.

EXAMPLE 6.6   It is known that a list of numbers that ends with a trailer value of −999.9 contains fewer than 1000 numbers. Use a DO loop to read the data. Calculate and print the average of the data list.

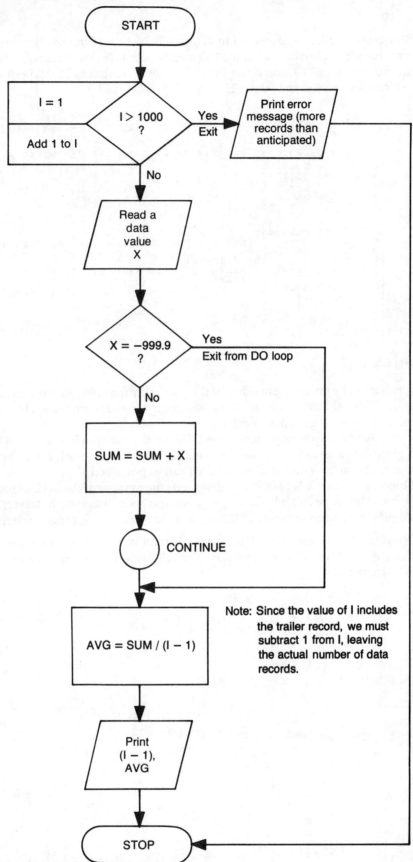

Figure 6.3 Flowchart for Example 6.6

Solution

The flowchart solution is presented in Figure 6.3. Note that the solution uses the value of the DO-variable for a calculation after the DO loop is exited. This is permissible only when control is transferred out of the DO loop *before* the DO-variable exceeds its normal exit value. See Program 6.8, which uses these sample data: 15.0, 6.0, 3.0, and −999.9.

```
$JOB    WATFIV
C CALCULATING THE AVERAGE OF A LIST OF NUMBERS ENDING WITH A
C TRAILER VALUE
C
C THIS PROGRAM WAS RUN ON AN IBM COMPUTER USING WATFIV
C
1          INTEGER I
2          REAL X, SUM, AVG
3          SUM = 0.0
4          DO 50 I = 1, 1000
5              READ , X
6              IF (X .EQ. -999.9) GOTO 100
7              SUM = SUM + X
8       50 CONTINUE
9          PRINT , 'ERROR : MORE RECORDS PRESENT THAN ANTICIPATED'
10         GO TO 200
11     100 AVG = SUM / (I - 1)
12         PRINT , 'NUMBER OF DATA VALUES = ', I - 1
13         PRINT , 'AVERAGE =                 ', AVG
14     200 STOP
15         END


        $ENTRY
NUMBER OF DATA VALUES =              3
AVERAGE =                           8.0000000
```

Program 6.8

Program Notes: The program provides for the possibility that 1000 or more numbers are contained in the list. If this should occur, the DO loop is exited in the normal way, but an error message is printed and the average is not calculated.

If the trailer value is encountered, the DO loop is prematurely exited and the average calculated. Since the value of the DO-variable I includes the trailer record, 1 must be subtracted from it in order to obtain the number of actual data values processed.

Observe that the PRINT statement that prints the number of data values performs the calculation I − 1. This is permitted. Good programming style suggests, however, that only "minor calculations" be performed within PRINT statements; otherwise, program clarity may be reduced.

The availability of the block IF in Fortran 77 (and WATFIV) permits Program 6.8 to be coded following a structured design approach. The following version of Program 6.8 eliminates the GOTO statements:

```
* REVISED PROGRAM SOLUTION FOR EXAMPLE 6.6
      INTEGER I
      REAL X, SUM, AVG
      SUM = 0.0
      DO 50 I = 1, 1000
         READ *, X
         IF ( X .EQ. -999) THEN
            AVG = SUM / (I - 1)
            PRINT *, 'NUMBER OF DATA
            VALUES = ', I - 1
            PRINT *, 'AVERAGE = ', AVG
            STOP
         ELSE
            SUM = SUM + X
      ENDIF
```

```
   50 CONTINUE
      PRINT *, 'ERROR? MORE RECORDS PRESENT
      THAN ANTICIPATED'
      STOP
      END
```

Some DO Loop Don'ts

- Do *not* enter the body of a DO loop via a transfer of control statement. Always enter a DO loop through the DO statement.
- Do *not* use real constants or real variables in a DO statement if you are using a Fortran compiler other than Fortran 77; WATFIV and Fortran IV compilers require that DO parameters be positive valued integer constants or variables, not expressions.
- Do *not* include any program statements within the body of the DO loop that adjust the value of a parameter of the DO loop. DO loop variable parameters, however, may be used in calculations within the DO loop (that is, they may appear on the right side of the equal sign in an assignment statement).
- Do *not* use variables as initial, exit, or increment parameters unless they have been assigned values by the program *before* the DO statement is executed.
- Do *not* use the DO loop control (index) variable after the DO loop is exited in the normal way by the DO-variable's running through its range of values. When a DO loop is exited prematurely through a transfer of control statement, the DO-variable is available for calculations outside the DO loop. With most Fortran compilers, when the DO loop is exited as a result of the DO-variable's exceeding its final value, the DO-variable leaves the loop having an undefined or unpredictable value.

EXAMPLE 6.7 Identify the error in each of the following program segments:

(a)
```
      DO I 50 = 1, 10
         PRINT *, I
   50 CONTINUE
```
(b)
```
      DO 75 K = 3, 17, 2
         PRINT *, K
         K = K + 2
   75 CONTINUE
```
(c)
```
      DO 50 L = 1, 10
         READ *, X
         SUM = SUM + X
   50 CONTINUE
      AVG = SUM / REAL (L)
      PRINT *, AVG
      STOP
```
(d)
```
      READ *, X
      IF (X .GT. 0.0) GOTO 40
      STOP
   40 DO 50 N = X, Y
         Q = X / Y
         PRINT *, Q
   50 CONTINUE
      STOP
      END
```

Solutions

(a) The DO statement should read as follows: `DO 50 I = 1, 10`

(b) The value of the DO-variable is altered in the range of the DO loop by the statement K = K + 2.

(c) After a *normal* exit from the DO loop, the DO-variable is used in a calculation. Since the value of the DO-variable is unpredictable, its use in a calculation may produce an incorrect result.

(d) If it is assumed that this is a complete program, the value of one of the DO parameters, namely Y, is undefined.

6.3 The Prime Number Problem

Searching for prime numbers is one of the best known problems in mathematics. A *prime number* is a positive integer greater than 1 that is divisible only by itself and 1. The numbers 11, 13, and 17 are examples of prime numbers. The number 21 is *not* a prime number since 21 is divisible by numbers other than itself and 1, namely, 3 and 7. A number that divides evenly into another number is said to be a *factor* of the number. Each of the numbers 1, 3, 7, and 21 is a factor of 21.

Let us prepare a program that reads in a positive integer and prints whether it is prime. By definition the number 2 is a prime number and the number 1 is not a prime number. To simplify matters, we will assume that the data value is an integer greater than 2. A "brute force" method will be used, which is based on using a DO loop to generate and test, as possible factors of the number, all integers between 2 and 1 less than the data value. If the set of all possible factors that is defined by the initial and exit values of the DO-variable is exhausted without a factor being found, the DO loop is exited and a message is printed which advises us that the number is prime. If, on the other hand, a factor is encountered, an appropriate message is printed, and the program terminates. Figure 6.4 outlines the algorithm just described in flowchart form and gives the corresponding Fortran program.

Although this program satisfies the requirements of the problem, it is not an *efficient* program solution. We have stressed a number of factors relating to program design, with particular emphasis on the features that make programs easy to read and debug. We now add another consideration—computers should not be asked to do unnecessary work. Programs should be written using the most efficient algorithm, provided that program clarity is not unduly compromised by doing so.

In revising our prime number computer program, we take the following factors into consideration:

1. If the number being tested is even, it cannot be prime. We will therefore discard all even numbers and test only odd numbers as candidates for being prime.
2. If the number is odd, it cannot be divisible by an even number. We will therefore initialize the DO-variable (which represents potential divisors) at 3 and increment it in steps of 2.
3. As a result, the number will be tested for divisibility by 3, 5, 7, . . . , and so on. What should be the final value that is tested as a possible factor of the number? Let's pause to consider the factors of 36.

<u>Fortran Program</u>

```
READ NUMBR
DO 50 I = 2, NUMBR - 1
    IF ( MOD(NUMBR, I) .EQ. 0) THEN
        PRINT *, NUMBR, 'IS NOT PRIME'
        STOP
    ENDIF
50 CONTINUE
PRINT *, NUMBR, 'IS PRIME'
STOP
END
```

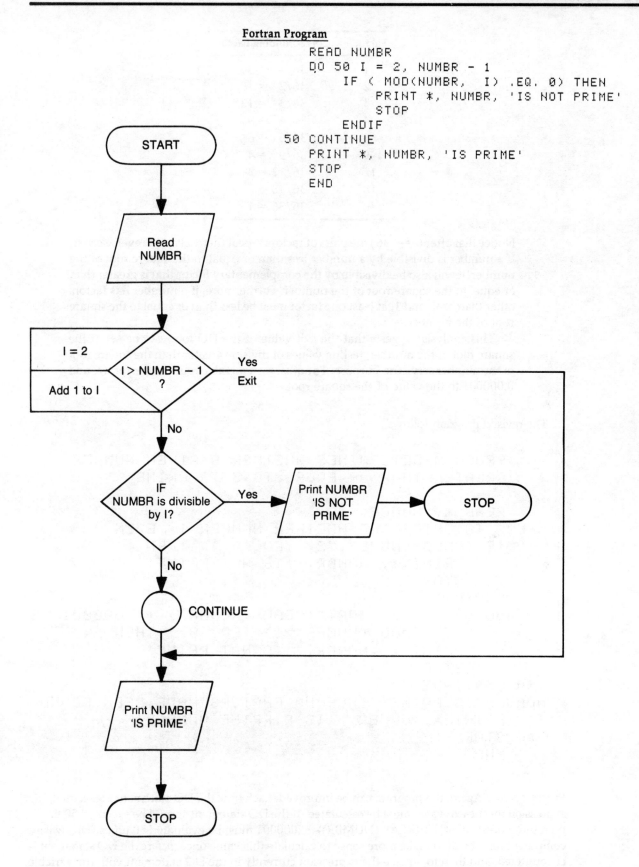

Figure 6.4

Factor	Corresponding Factor
1	36/1 = 36
2	36/2 = 18
3	36/3 = 12
4	36/4 = 9
6	36/6 = 6
9	36/9 = 4
12	36/12 = 3
18	36/18 = 2
36	36/36 = 1

Notice that after 6 ($=\sqrt{36}$) the pairs of factors repeat themselves in reverse order. If a number is divisible by a number less than or equal to the square root of the number, it will also be divisible by the complementary factor that is greater than or equal to the square.root of the number. Furthermore, if a number has factors other than itself and 1, at least one factor must be less than or equal to the square root of the number.

This analysis suggests that the exit value of the DO loop can be set at the square root of the number; testing values of divisors greater than the square root of the number serves no purpose. To adjust for a possible round-off error, we add 0.000001 to the value of the square root.

The revised program follows.

```
*      PROGRAM DETERMINES WHETHER A GIVEN NUMBER
*      GREATER THAN OR EQUAL TO 3 IS PRIME
*
       READ *, NUMBR
* CHECK TO DETERMINE WHETHER NUMBER IS EVEN
       IF ( MOD (NUMBR, 2) .EQ. 0 )   THEN
            PRINT *, NUMBR, 'IS NOT PRIME'
            STOP
       ENDIF
       DO 50 I = 3, SQRT (REAL (NUMBR)) + .000001, 2
            IF ( MOD (NUMBR, I) .EQ. 0 ) THEN
            PRINT *, NUMBR, 'IS NOT PRIME'
            STOP
   50 CONTINUE
* NUMBER IS PRIME SINCE NO FACTORS HAVE BEEN FOUND
       PRINT *, NUMBR, 'IS A PRIME NUMBER'
       STOP
       END
```

Program Notes: Again, the program can be improved. Each time the DO statement is executed, the expression for the exit value must be calculated. If the DO statement should be executed 50 times, then the expression SQRT (REAL (NUMBR)) + .000001 must be evaluated 50 times. This wastes computer time. It would make more sense to calculate this value once, *before* the DO statement is encountered, and then to replace the expression currently in the DO statement with the variable that is storing the calculated constant. For example:

```
EXIT = SQRT (REAL (NUMBR)) + .000001
DO 50 I = 3, EXIT, 2
        .   .   .   .
        .   .   .   .
```

Program 6.9 shows the WATFIV version of the enhanced prime number program. The FLOAT function is used instead of the REAL function. Since each of the parameters of a DO statement in WATFIV must be a positive integer, the IFIX function is used to convert the calculated exit value into an integer value. To allow for truncation errors, 1 is added to the resulting value.

```
    $JOB     WATFIV
    C PROGRAM DETERMINES WHETHER A GIVEN NUMBER GREATER THAN
    C          OR EQUAL TO 3 IS PRIME
    C
    C THIS PROGRAM WAS RUN ON AN IBM COMPUTER USING WATFIV
    C IN THIS VERSION OF FORTRAN, ONLY INTEGERS MAY BE USED
    C AS CONSTANTS OR VARIABLES IN A DO STATEMENT. THE
    C IFIX FUNCTION IS THEREFORE USED TO CONVERT A REAL VALUE TO
    C AN INTEGER VALUE.
    C
 1          READ , NUMBR
    C CHECK TO DETERMINE WHETHER NUMBER IS EVEN
 2          IF ( MOD (NUMBR, 2) .EQ. 0) THEN
 3              PRINT , NUMBR, 'IS NOT PRIME'
 4              STOP
 5          ENDIF
 6          EXIT = SQRT ( FLOAT (NUMBR) )
 7          IEXIT = IFIX (EXIT) + 1
 8          DO 50 I = 3, IEXIT, 2
 9              IF (MOD (NUMBR, I) .EQ. 0 ) THEN
10                  PRINT , NUMBR, 'IS NOT PRIME'
11                  STOP
12              ENDIF
13       50 CONTINUE
    C NUMBER IS PRIME SINCE NO FACTORS HAVE BEEN FOUND
14          PRINT , NUMBR, 'IS A PRIME NUMBER'
15          STOP
16          END

    $ENTRY
     30 IS NOT PRIME
```

Program 6.9

EXAMPLE 6.8   Read in a positive integer. Then print its factors in pairs. Print an appropriate message if the number is prime.

Solution

The problem solution (see Program 6.10) is similar to the approach taken in the prime number problem. In the DO loop we will print the factors of the number and maintain a count of the number of factors found. Upon exiting the DO loop, the value of the counter will be compared to zero. If it is equal to zero (that is, no factors were found), then the number is prime. Since every number is divisible by itself and 1, these factors will be printed before the DO loop is entered (this is an example of improving program efficiency).

```
    * PROGRAM VARIABLES:
    *       EXIT = CALCULATED EXIT VALUE
    *       KOUNT = A COUNT OF THE NUMBER OF FACTORS FOUND
    *                   OTHER THAN THE NUMBER ITSELF
    *       NUMBER = DATA VALUE
    *
    * THIS PROGRAM WAS RUN ON A PRIME 850 COMPUTER USING FORTRAN 77
    *
    *
            REAL EXIT
            INTEGER KOUNT, NUMBR
            KOUNT = 0
            READ *, NUMBR
            PRINT *, '         FACTORS OF ', NUMBR
            PRINT *, ' '
            EXIT = SQRT ( REAL(NUMBR) ) + .000001
            I = 1
```

```
        PRINT *, I, NUMBR
        DO 50 I = 2, EXIT
            IF ( MOD (NUMBR, I) .EQ. 0 ) THEN
                KOUNT = KOUNT + 1
                PRINT *, I, NUMBR / I
* . . . . NOTE THAT PREVIOUS PRINT STATEMENT INCLUDED A
* . . . . CALCULATION (NUMBR/I). THIS IS PERMITTED.
            ENDIF
   50 CONTINUE
* NUMBER IS PRIME IF KOUNT = 0
        IF ( KOUNT .EQ. 0 ) THEN
                PRINT *, 'NUMBER IS PRIME'
        ENDIF
        STOP
        END




    23
                FACTORS OF              23

                    1           23
        NUMBER IS PRIME
 **** STOP




    36
                FACTORS OF              36

                    1           36
                    2           18
                    3           12
                    4            9
                    6            6
 **** STOP
```

Program 6.10

6.4 DO Loops Within DO Loops

Let's have some fun with printing numbers. First, let us decide on the best way to print the integers 1 through 10 with 12 blank lines skipped between each two consecutive printed values. The numbers can be generated using a DO loop. It would be silly to write 12 PRINT statements, with each designed to skip a line. Instead, we can place the statement PRINT *, ' ' in the body of another DO loop, which executes 12 times. Since this second DO loop must be executed *after* the first DO loop generates an integer to be printed, the second DO loop is placed inside the first DO loop:

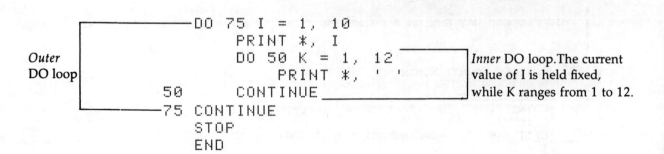

Outer DO loop

```
        DO 75 I = 1, 10
            PRINT *, I
            DO 50 K = 1, 12
                PRINT *, ' '
   50       CONTINUE
   75 CONTINUE
        STOP
        END
```

Inner DO loop. The current value of I is held fixed, while K ranges from 1 to 12.

We say that the inner DO loop is *nested* in the outer DO loop.

As another illustration of nested DO loops, suppose that we wish to print each integer value in the interval 1 to 10 the same number of times as the value of the number. The output should look like this:

```
1
2
2
3
3
3
 .
 .
 .
```

An outer DO loop will be used to generate the number, while a nested DO loop will print the value the required number of times:

```
      DO 75 I = 1, 10
          DO 50 K = 1,  I ⎱ prints the value of I,
              PRINT *,  I ⎰ I times
  50          CONTINUE
  75 CONTINUE
      STOP
      END
```

You should verify that, when the program executes, the outer loop is activated first and begins by setting I equal to 1. The inner DO loop is then executed. In this case, since the initial value and the exit value of the inner DO loop are equal, the loop is executed only once, which is exactly what we want. Control then passes back to the outer DO loop, and the value of I becomes 2. The inner DO loop now is executed two times, printing the current value of I (2) each time, and so on.

There are three rules that must be followed in constructing nested DO loops:

- The ranges of the nested DO loops may not overlap. The inner loop must be completely enclosed by the outer loop.

Correct:

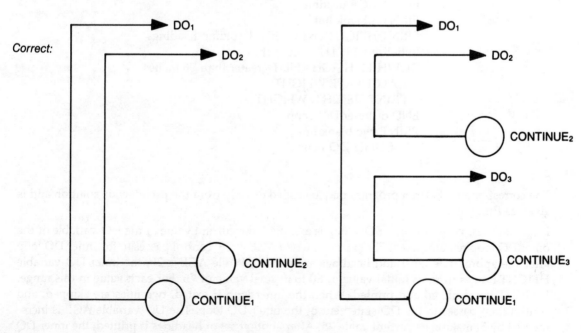

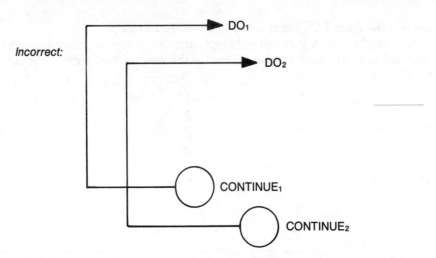

Incorrect:

- DO loops may not share the same loop control variable.
- More than two DO loops should not be nested inside another DO loop as this tends to severely compromise program readability and increases the likelihood of error. Furthermore, some Fortran compilers impose an explicit restriction on the depth of the nesting.

EXAMPLE 6.9 Assume that the following formula gives an approximation of a person's average body weight, given his or her height in inches and age:

```
WEIGHT = 5.0 * (HEIGHT - 38.0) + .3 * (AGE - 21)
```

Produce a height and weight table for each of the following age groups: 20, 25, 30, 35, 40, 45, and 50. The heights should range from 5'0" to 6'4".

Solution

The pseudocode solution may be stated as follows:

Pseudocode Solution

> Initialize AGE at 20
> DOWHILE AGE NOT greater than 50 in STEPS of 5
>   PRINT AGE heading
>   PRINT a blank line
>   PRINT HEIGHT and WEIGHT column headings
>   Initialize HEIGHT at 60 inches
>   DOWHILE HEIGHT NOT greater than 76 inches
>   CALCULATE WEIGHT
>   PRINT HEIGHT, WEIGHT
>   END of Inner DO Loop
>   PRINT two blank lines
> END of Outer DO Loop
> STOP

The corresponding Fortran program may be coded directly from the pseudocode solution and is given as Program 6.11.

Program Notes: When the inner DO loop is executed, the current value of the DO-variable of the outer DO loop remains fixed. For example, when AGE = 20, control passes to the inner DO loop after the appropriate label and headings are printed. While AGE = 20, the inner DO-variable HEIGHT ranges from its initial value of 60 to its final value of 76. For each value in this range, WEIGHT is calculated and printed. When the inner loop is exited, two lines are skipped, and control then passes to the DO statement of the outer DO loop. The DO-variable AGE is incremented by 5, making its current value 25. After another set of headings is printed, the inner DO loop is executed for each value of HEIGHT, from 60 to 76, and so on.

```
        $JOB    WATFIV
        C PROGRAM GENERATES A HEIGHT/WEIGHT TABLE FOR GIVEN AGES
   1            INTEGER AGE, HEIGHT
   2            DO 75  AGE = 20, 50, 5
   3                PRINT , '        AGE =', AGE
   4                PRINT , ' '
   5                PRINT , '        HEIGHT            WEIGHT'
   6                PRINT , ' '
        C INNER DO LOOP CALCULATES WEIGHT FOR EACH HEIGHT
        C BETWEEN 60 AND 76 INCHES WHILE AGE REMAINS CONSTANT
   7                DO 50 HEIGHT = 60, 76
   8                    WEIGHT = 5.0 * (HEIGHT -38.0) + .3 * (AGE - 21)
   9                    PRINT , HEIGHT, WEIGHT
  10        50      CONTINUE
  11                PRINT , ' '
  12                PRINT , '*********************************************'
  13                PRINT , ' '
  14                PRINT , ' '
  15        75 CONTINUE
  16            STOP
  17            END
```

```
        $ENTRY
        AGE =            20

        HEIGHT           WEIGHT

            60       109.6999000
            61       114.6999000
            62       119.6999000
            63       124.6999000
            64       129.6999000
            65       134.6999000
            66       139.6999000
            67       144.6999000
            68       149.6999000
            69       154.6999000
            70       159.6999000
            71       164.6999000
            72       169.6999000
            73       174.6999000
            74       179.6999000
            75       184.6999000
            76       189.6999000

*********************************************

        AGE =            25

        HEIGHT           WEIGHT

            60       111.1999000
            61       116.1999000
            62       121.1999000
            63       126.1999000
            64       131.1999000
            65       136.1999000
            66       141.1999000
            67       146.1999000
            68       151.1999000
            69       156.1999000
            70       161.1999000
            71       166.1999000
            72       171.1999000
            73       176.1999000
            74       181.1999000
            75       186.1999000
            76       191.1999000

*********************************************

        AGE =            30

        HEIGHT           WEIGHT

            60       112.6999000
            61       117.6999000
            62       122.6999000
            63       127.6999000
            64       132.6999000
            65       137.6999000
            66       142.6999000
            67       147.6999000
            68       152.6999000
            69       157.6999000
            70       162.6999000
            71       167.6999000
            72       172.6999000
            73       177.6999000
            74       182.6999000
            75       187.6999000
            76       192.6999000

*********************************************
```

```
                  AGE =              35

                  HEIGHT              WEIGHT

                    60          114.1999000
                    61          119.1999000
                    62          124.1999000
                    63          129.1999000
                    64          134.1999000
                    65          139.1999000
                    66          144.1999000
                    67          149.1999000
                    68          154.1999000
                    69          159.1999000
                    70          164.1999000
                    71          169.1999000
                    72          174.1999000
                    73          179.1999000
                    74          184.1999000
                    75          189.1999000
                    76          194.1999000

     *****************************************************

                  AGE =              40

                  HEIGHT              WEIGHT

                    60          115.6999000
                    61          120.6999000
                    62          125.6999000
                    63          130.6999000
                    64          135.6999000
                    65          140.6999000
                    66          145.6999000
                    67          150.6999000
                    68          155.6999000
                    69          160.6999000
                    70          165.6999000
                    71          170.6999000
                    72          175.6999000
                    73          180.6999000
                    74          185.6999000
                    75          190.6999000
                    76          195.6999000

     *****************************************************

                  AGE =              45

                  HEIGHT              WEIGHT

                    60          117.1999000
                    61          122.1999000
                    62          127.1999000
                    63          132.1999000
                    64          137.1999000
                    65          142.1999000
                    66          147.1999000
                    67          152.1999000
                    68          157.1999000
                    69          162.1999000
                    70          167.1999000
                    71          172.1999000
                    72          177.1999000
                    73          182.1999000
                    74          187.1999000
                    75          192.1999000
                    76          197.1999000

     *****************************************************

                  AGE =              50

                  HEIGHT              WEIGHT

                    60          118.6999000
                    61          123.6999000
                    62          128.6999000
                    63          133.6999000
                    64          138.6999000
                    65          143.6999000
                    66          148.6999000
                    67          153.6999000
                    68          158.6999000
                    69          163.6999000
                    70          168.6999000
                    71          173.6999000
                    72          178.6999000
                    73          183.6999000
                    74          188.6999000
                    75          193.6999000
                    76          198.6999000
```

Program 6.11   ***

6.5 Some Closing Remarks

It should be mentioned again that in most older versions of Fortran, including Fortran IV and WATFIV, only integer constants and variables having a value greater than zero may be used as loop parameters in the DO statement. Another important difference between Fortran 77 and these older compilers involves the interpretation of a DO statement in which the initial value of the DO-variable exceeds the exit value, while the increment value is positive. In Fortran 77, the comparison between the value of the DO-variable and the exit value is made at the *beginning* of each loop iteration. In this situation, *no* loop iterations are performed since the first comparison test reveals that the current value of the DO-variable exceeds the final exit value. The net effect is for the DO loop to be ignored. With a typical Fortran IV or WATFIV compiler, however, the comparison between these values is made at the *end* of each loop iteration. This implies that these compilers must execute at least once each DO loop that has valid loop parameters.

In general, the number of DO loop iterations performed by a Fortran 77 compiler may be determined using the following relationship:

$$\text{iterations} = \text{INT}[(\text{exit value} - \text{initial value} + \text{step value}) / \text{step value}]$$

If this relationship evaluates to zero, the DO loop is ignored. This will occur whenever a DO loop is first encountered *and*

- the initial value exceeds the exit value while the step value is positive; *or*
- the initial value is less than the exit value while the step value is negative.

Fortran Implementations of the DO Loop

Fortran IV and WATFIV place the same restrictions on the DO statement. The loop parameters must be integer constants or integer variables that have positive values. The initial value should be less than the exit value; if it is not, then the DO loop will be executed exactly once.

Fortran 77 permits the use of both integer and real constants, variables, and expressions in establishing the parameters of the DO loop. A DO loop will *not* be executed if

(1) the initial value exceeds the exit value and the increment value is positive; *or*
(2) the initial value is less than the exit value and the increment value is negative.

EXAMPLE 6.10 Assuming a Fortran 77 compiler, determine the number of loop iterations in each of the following:

(a) `DO 40 K = 23, 87, 4`   (c) `DO 60 M = 17, 99, 3`
(b) `DO 30 L = 9, -6`   (d) `DO 50 I = -7, 10, -2`

Solutions

(a) Number of iterations = INT (87 − 23 + 4) / 4
$\qquad\qquad\qquad\qquad$ = INT (68 / 4)
$\qquad\qquad\qquad\qquad$ = INT (17)
Number of iterations = 17

(b) Since the initial value exceeds the exit value, with a positive increment, the number of iterations is 0.

(c) Number of iterations = INT (99 − 17 + 3) / 3
$\qquad\qquad\qquad\qquad$ = INT (82 + 3) / 3
$\qquad\qquad\qquad\qquad$ = INT (85 / 3)
$\qquad\qquad\qquad\qquad$ = INT (28.3333 . . .)
Number of iterations = 28

(d) Since the initial value is less than the exit value, with a negative increment, the number of iterations is 0.

Suppose that you are working with a Fortran IV compiler and want to prepare a program that generates a table which converts inches to centimeters in *increments of 0.5* inch, from 1 inch to 36 inches. The immediate problem is to fashion a solution that does not involve a fractional increment. Program 6.12 illustrates one possible approach.

```
       $JOB   WATFIV
       C STATEMENTS WHICH BEGIN WITH THE LETTER C ARE COMMENTS
       C TO CONVERT FROM INCHES TO CENTIMETERS IN STEPS OF 0.5 INCH
       C          NOTE: 1 INCH = 2.54 CENTIMETERS
       C
       C WRITE HEADINGS
  1          WRITE (6, 10)
  2       10 FORMAT ( '1', 'INCHES      CENTIMETERS')
  3          WRITE (6, 15)
  4       15 FORMAT ( ' ' )
       C MULTIPLY DO STATEMENT PARAMETERS (1, 36, 5) BY 10
       C
  5          DO 50 I = 10, 360, 5
  6             XINCH = FLOAT (I) / 10.0
  7             CENTMR = 2.54 * XINCH
  8             WRITE (6, 20) XINCH, CENTMR
  9       20    FORMAT (' ', F4.1, 11X, F5.2)
 10       50 CONTINUE
 11          STOP
 12          END
```

Program 6.12

Take a look at Program 6.13. Can you explain why the output is 0.9999878? Since 0.001 is being added to itself 1000 times, the output should have the value of 1.0000000 (= 0.001 * 1000). The explanation is quite simple. The value 0.001 does not have an exact binary representation. Each time it is added to the variable SUM, a very, very small round-off error is introduced. The error is magnified because the statement that is accumulating the sum is executed 1000 times.

The moral of this example is that you should be alert to round-off errors. Remember that, in testing for the equality of two calculated expressions, you should introduce an appropriate tolerance factor.

```
       $JOB   WATFIV
  1          SUM = 0.0
  2          DO 50 I = 1, 1000
  3             SUM = SUM + .001
  4       50 CONTINUE
  5          PRINT , SUM
  6          STOP
  7          END

       $ENTRY
          0.9999878
```

Program 6.13

PROGRAM DESIGN CONSIDERATIONS

There are three elements that are fundamental to the design of a computer program: program *correctness*, program *readability*, and program *efficiency*.

To be of value to its user, a program must correctly perform its intended functions. After writing a program, you must verify that it works by testing it with all conceivable types of input data. Use large data values, small data values, and invalid data values in order to make certain that your program remains well behaved. Remember to select sample data that test each program path.

The text of the program, as well as its output, should be easy to read and to understand. Use comments to add a self-documenting quality to your programs. This will help during the debugging phase of program development. It will also be of invaluable assistance whenever it becomes necessary for you or another programmer to reexamine the logic of the program. Make the output of your program as visually attractive as possible by annotating answers with descriptive labels or by printing column headings.

Programs submitted in a batch processing environment should echo-print input data values, while programs executed in an interactive mode should include messages that prompt the user to enter the appropriate data.

The term *program efficiency* refers to the speed at which a program executes on a given computer system. Increased attention to program efficiency is required when designing programs that involve repetition structures. Any slip in the design of a looping structure that leads to a loss in program efficiency is magnified by the number of loop repetitions. In constructing DO loops, therefore, verify that the parameters of the DO-variable are properly set. If the initial value is lower than is required, or the exit value is larger than is necessary, extra loop repetitions will be performed. These not only result in a loss of program efficiency, but also may lead to erroneous output. Perhaps the most common error in working with looping structures is to include inside the loop calculations that can (or should) be performed outside the loop.

Also carefully review all program statements that have been assigned statement labels. Verify that program control is being transferred to the correct statement. Avoid the use of the GOTO statement in creating loops (except when simulating the WHILE . . . DO loop). Strive to frame all repetition sequences using one of the three forms presented in Chapter 5 and in this chapter (WHILE . . . DO, DO . . . UNTIL, and DO loop). This will tend to produce more highly readable and error-free program code.

Program Efficiency Versus Program Clarity

Sometimes it is possible to achieve program efficiency only at the expense of program readability. There are no hard and fast guidelines in this situation. Keep in mind, however, that the expense of computer time is declining at the same time that computer speed is increasing. On the other hand, the cost of developing and maintaining software continues to represent a significant economic burden. This would seem to suggest that changes which improve the efficiency of a program should be made only if the readability of the program is not significantly impaired. Needless to say, the application area of the program may influence the decision as to whether program efficiency should override considerations of program clarity. For example, if the response time of a computer is critical, as in a hospital patient-care monitoring system, then program efficiency (speed) is the more important of the two factors.

Review Exercises

A star preceding the number of a problem indicates that a solution to that problem is given at the back of the book.

Problems 1–12. Write a Fortran program that satisfies the requirements of each problem. Whenever appropriate, make up your own sample test data.

* **1.** A list of numbers is preceded by a header label which gives the number of values that follow. Use a DO loop to read in the values. Print the number and the cube of the number in table form.

* **2.** Read in two unequal positive integer values. After determining the larger of the two numbers, find the sum of the squares of all whole numbers between the two values, inclusive.

* **3.** Multiplication can be accomplished through repeated additions. For example, $5 \times 3 = 5 + 5 + 5$. Read in two positive integer values, and print their product using repeated additions.

* **4.** Generate a two-column table that converts feet to meters. The number of feet should range from 1 to 25. After every 5 feet, skip three blank lines in order to increase the clarity of the output. (*Note:* 1 foot = 0.3048 meter.)

5. Euclid's relationship among the numbers that form a Pythagorean triple can be expressed as follows:

$$r^2 - s^2, \quad 2rs, \quad r^2 + s^2$$

where r and s are positive integers and r is greater than s. Generate Pythagorean triples for all values of r less than or equal to 6.

6. The area under the curve $y = f(x)$ from $x = a$ to $x = b$ may be approximated by subdividing this region into n trapezoids, each having a height (altitude) equal to $(b - a)/n$. This may be pictured as follows:

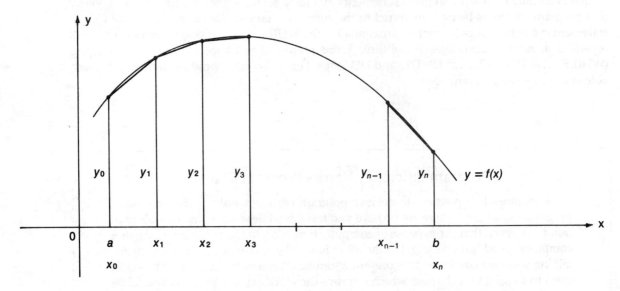

$$\text{where height} = x_i - x_{i-1} = \frac{b - a}{n}$$

The area of each trapezoid is given by the formula

$$\text{area} = \tfrac{1}{2} \text{ height(sum of bases)}$$

An approximation for the area under the curve $y = f(x)$ is merely the sum of the n trapezoids into which the region under the curve from $x = a$ to $x = b$ is subdivided:

$$\text{area under curve} \approx \frac{b - a}{2n} (y_0 + 2y_1 + 2y_2 + \cdots + 2y_{n-1} + y_n)$$

As n increases, the approximation becomes increasingly accurate.

(a) Approximate the area under the curve whose equation is $y = 3x^2 + 1$ from $x = 1$ to $x = 6$, for $n = 10$.

Note: Since

$$\frac{b - a}{n} = \frac{6 - 1}{10} = 0.5,$$

$x_0 = 1$, $x_1 = 1.5$, $x_2 = 2$, $x_3 = 2.5$, . . . , $x_9 = 5.5$, and $x_{10} = 6$.

(b) For the function $y = 3x^2 + 1$, the area can be calculated using the definite integral

$$\int_1^6 (3x^2 + 1)\, dx = 220$$

Determine the value of n such that the trapezoid rule gives an approximation of the area within 0.025 of the actual answer.

* **7.** Leibniz, who is best known for his contributions to the development of calculus, discovered that the series

$$4\left(1 - \frac{1}{3} + \frac{1}{5} - \frac{1}{7} + \frac{1}{9} - \cdots\right)$$

offers an approximation for the value of pi (π) as the number of terms in the series becomes large. Determine and print approximations of pi using this series, after calculating the series sum for 10 terms, 20 terms, 30 terms, . . . , 100 terms.

* **8.** The straight-line method for calculating the yearly amount of depreciation of an asset is based on depreciating equal amounts of money each year. The following formula may be used when applying this method:

$$\text{DEPRECIATION} = \frac{\text{COST} - \text{SCRAP}}{\text{YEARS}}$$

where COST = original cost of the asset, SCRAP = estimated worth of the asset after the last year of depreciation, and YEARS = number of years over which the asset is being depreciated.

A second method, called the "sum of the years' digits" method, is based on taking a declining fraction of the difference between the COST and SCRAP values. To illustrate, suppose that a piece of machinery costs $5400 and has a life of 4 years, at the end of which time it can be sold for scrap metal for $400. The yearly amount of depreciation may be calculated, using this second method, as follows:

Step 1. Calculate the sum of the digits from 1 to the number of years over which the asset is being depreciated:

$$\text{SUM} = 1 + 2 + 3 + 4 = 10$$

Step 2. Calculate the amount of depreciation for each year using this relationship:

$$\text{DEPRECIATION} = \frac{\text{years remaining} + 1}{\text{SUM of years' digits}} \times (\text{COST} - \text{SCRAP})$$

In our example:

After Year	Years Remaining + 1	Depreciation Amount
1	3 + 1 = 4	$\frac{4}{10} \times 5,000 = 2,000$
2	2 + 1 = 3	$\frac{3}{10} \times 5,000 = 1,500$
3	1 + 1 = 2	$\frac{2}{10} \times 5,000 = 1,000$
4	0 + 1 = 1	$\frac{1}{10} \times 5,000 = 500$

Write a program that reads in the cost of an asset, its scrap value, and the number of years over which it will be depreciated. Compare in table form the amount of depreciation at the end of each year using the straight-line method and the sum of the years' digits method.

Note: The sum of all digits from 1 to N may be calculated using the formula

$$\text{SUM} = \frac{N(N + 1)}{2}$$

9. Suppose that the current population of Greentown is 1,250,000, and the current population of Bluetown is 1,900,000. It is know that the population of Greentown is growing at a constant annual rate of 3.5% and that the annual growth rate of Bluetown is 1.7%. Assume that in each town the number of deaths balances the number of births, and the number of people who move into the town offsets the number of people who move out of the town. If these growth rates remain constant, calculate the number of years it will take the population of Greentown to exceed the population of Bluetown.

10. Credit institutions base their customer loan repayment schedules on the following formula:

$$A = \frac{L \cdot r/12 \cdot (1 + r/12)^N}{(1 + r/12)^N - 1}$$

where A = amount of each *monthly* loan repayment, L = amount of loan, N = number of monthly payments, and r = annual interest rate expressed as a decimal fraction. Read in values for L and N. Calculate the amount of the monthly loan repayment (A) for each annual interest rate from 10% to 20%, in steps of 1.25%. The output should take the following form:

```
LOAN AMOUNT = $ XXXXXX.XX
NUMBER OF MONTHLY PAYMENTS = XXX

INTEREST          AMOUNT OF
  RATE          MONTHLY PAYMENT
 _____        _____

  0.08               XXXX.XX
  0.0925
  0.150
    .
    .
    .
```

In addition, print the total amount of interest that is paid on the loan.

11. Modify the program written in Problem 10 so that values for L, N, and the interest rate (r) are entered as data. Print:

```
LOAN AMOUNT = $ XXXXXX.XX
ANNUAL INTEREST RATE = XX %
NUMBER OF MONTHLY PAYMENTS = XXX
AMOUNT OF EACH LOAN REPAYMENT = $ XXXX.XX
PAYMENT   MONTHLY INTEREST   AMOUNT REPAID   UNPAID
NUMBER         CHARGE         ON PRINCIPAL   BALANCE
_____    _____   _____  _____

   1
   2
   3
   .
   .
   .
```

The *monthly interest charge* is calculated by multiplying the previous month's balance (which appears in the UNPAID BALANCE column) by the monthly interest rate. The loan amount should appear as the initial entry in the UNPAID BALANCE column. The *amount repaid on principal* is simply the difference between the amount of each loan repayment and the monthly interest charge.

*12. If you compared each student's grade on an exam with the number of hours the student studied for the exam, you would expect to find some *correlation* between these two statistics. A *correlation coefficient* is a statistical measure that indicates whether two variables are related. The calculation of the correlation coefficient is such that the coefficient may vary between −1 and +1. If it has a value close to 0, then we may assume that virtually no relationship exists between the two groups of statistics. If it has a value close to +1, then there exists a close connection between the two variables. If it has a value close to −1, then there exists a close *inverse* relationship (for example, the *higher* the test grade, the *fewer* number of hours the student studied).

Use a DO loop to input a series of pairs of data values represented by the variables X and Y. The first value in the list is a header label which gives the number N of data pairs that follow. Calculate the correlation coefficient between the two variables using the following relationship:

$$r = \frac{N(\Sigma XY) - (\Sigma X)(\Sigma Y)}{\sqrt{N(\Sigma X^2) - (\Sigma X)^2} \cdot \sqrt{N(\Sigma Y^2) - (\Sigma Y)^2}}$$

If the calculated value of the coefficient r is betwen 0.75 and 1, print the message "X AND Y ARE CLOSELY RELATED." If the coefficient r is between 0.25 and 0.74, print the message "X AND Y MAY BE RELATED." If the coefficient r is between −0.24 and +0.24, print the message "X AND Y ARE NOT STRONGLY RELATED." If the coefficient r is between −1 and −0.25, print the message "X AND Y ARE INVERSELY RELATED."

Use the following two sample data sets:

Sample Data Set 1

X	83	52	61	93	89	43	76	81	89	71
Y	12	7	11	17	15	4	9	10	23	8

Sample Data Set 2

X	119	80	49	131	76	100	65	98	53	86
Y	21	75	93	28	159	181	81	91	110	99

Problems 13-15. Use Fortran's built-in MOD function in designing a program solution to each of the following problems:

*13. Print all positive integers less than 250 that leave a remainder of 2 when divided by 3 *and* a remainder of 1 when divided by 5.

14. Determine and print all prime numbers found in the interval 701–799.

*15. The lowest common multiple (LCM) of a pair of whole numbers is the smallest whole number that each number is a factor of. Read in two whole numbers, and print their LCM. The output should take the following form:

NUMBER 1	NUMBER 2	LCM
10	15	30
4	8	8
17	3	51

CHAPTER 7
Subscripted Variables

COMPUTER AXIOM

It is better to use a *single variable* name to refer to a list of 100 related data items than to use 100 distinct variable names to refer to 100 individual data items in a single list.

COROLLARY

In mathematics it is sometimes convenient to use subscripted variables to refer to a collection of related numbers: x_1, x_2, x_3, x_4, . . . , x_N. In Fortran we borrow this approach and write X(1), X(2), X(3), X(4), . . . , X(N).

7.1 Storing a Data List as an Array

The following program segment finds the average of 100 data values:

```
DO 50 K = 1, 100
    READ *, X
    SUM = SUM + X
50 CONTINUE
AVG = SUM / 100.0
```

It might be useful to know how many of the original data values are less than the average and how many are greater than the average. This presents a bit of a problem since the computer currently stores in its memory only the last (that is, the hundredth) data value. One possible solution would be to read the data list a second time, but this would be inefficient. Another possible approach would be to use 100 different variable names, say X1, X2, X3, . . . , X100, and read in the list of 100 data values during the same input operation:

```
READ *, X1, X2, X3, . . . , X100
```

Imagine having to write the entire input and corresponding assignment statements!

The preferred approach is based on using a single variable name to refer to the entire list of data values and then identifying individual members of the list by their position numbers. Let us temporarily leave the problem at hand and consider how this is accomplished in Fortran.

The variable X will be used to refer to the entire list of data values. In order to be able to distinguish individual members of the list, X will be followed by a number enclosed in parentheses that gives the position number of the particular data value in the list. The first value in the list will be called X(1), the second member of the list is X(2), the data value occupying the third position is X(3), and so forth. The number enclosed in parentheses is called a *subscript*, and a variable such as X(1) is called a *subscripted variable*.

The entire set of subscripted variables that refers to a single list is called an *array*. The variable X, without a subscript, is the name of the array. Figure 7.1 illustrates how the data list consisting of the

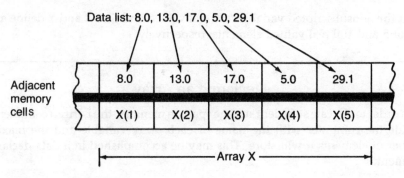

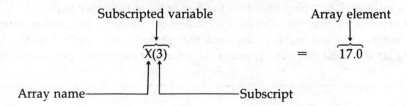

Figure 7.1 Storage of Data List as an Array

numbers 8.0, 13.0, 17.0, 5.0, and 29.1 would be stored in computer memory as an array. Notice that the array name X refers to a block of adjacent memory cells. The computer preserves the ordering of the numbers in the data list by labeling each memory cell in the array with the appropriate subscripted variable and then filling the memory cells sequentially with the individual data items. The contents of each memory cell (the value of each subscripted variable) are referred to as an *element* of the array.

To summarize some of this terminology, consider the third element of array X:

Subscripted variable   Array element

$$X(3) \quad = \quad 17.0$$

Array name ——————— Subscript

The rules for naming arrays are the same as those for naming nonsubscripted variables. The fact that an array that stores numeric data may be typed as real or integer implies that the elements of a given array must agree in type; they must be either all integer valued or all real valued. As we shall see in Chapter 8, an array may also be declared to contain character data.

The maximum number of elements that an array may represent is called the *size* or *dimension* of the array. In order to provide sufficient storage in computer memory, the Fortran compiler must receive information from the programmer regarding the size of the array and the type of data it will store. The pair of statements

```
REAL X
DIMENSION X(5)
```

may be used to declare an array. The data declaration statement establishes that each element of the array will be a real value. The DIMENSION statement is a nonexecutable program statement that declares the maximum size of the array. It specifies the upper limit of a subscript value of array X to be 5. The lower limit is defined implicitly to be 1. These statements allow the computer to anticipate storage requirements and to set aside a sufficient number of adjacent memory cells [five in our example, corresponding to X(1), X(2), X(3), X(4), and X(5)].

In many implementations of Fortran, including Fortran 77 and WATFIV, an array may be defined with a single statement as follows:

```
REAL X(5)
```

This form of the data declaration statement announces at once that X is the name of an array and that it will include a maximum of five real valued elements.

It is also correct to include both subscripted and nonsubscripted variables in the same data declaration statement. As an illustration,

```
REAL A, X(5), Y(100)
```

declares that the nonsubscripted variable A is real valued and that X and Y define arrays having maximums of 5 and 100 real valued elements, respectively.

Declaring an Array

In order to allocate sufficient storage space in memory, the Fortran compiler must provide the computer with the name of each array variable and the maximum number of elements it will store. This may be accomplished in a data declaration statement:

data type keyword array$_1$(size$_1$), array$_2$(size$_2$), . . .

The array size corresponds to the maximum value of a subscript. The minimum value is assumed to be 1.

Alternatively, a DIMENSION statement may be used to declare an array:

DIMENSION array$_1$(size$_1$), array$_2$(size$_2$), . . .

If a DIMENSION statement is used, the data type of an array may be established in a data declaration statement that lists the array name but without a subscript. If a data declaration statement is not used, the data type of each array element is defined using implicit data typing based on the first letter of the array name.

Keep in mind that the DIMENSION statement, like data declaration statements, is a nonexecutable program statement that provides information to the Fortran compiler and must therefore appear before the first executable program statement.

INPUT/OUTPUT OF ARRAYS

The following set of statements may be used to read five data values (one data value entered per data record) into array SAMPLE:

```
READ *, SAMPLE(1)
READ *, SAMPLE(2)
READ *, SAMPLE(3)
READ *, SAMPLE(4)
READ *, SAMPLE(5)
```

This approach is somewhat tedious, particularly when there are a large number of values to be stored in an array. DO loops are generally used to assign data values to an array and to manipulate the elements of a stored array. The following program segment is equivalent to the preceding set of five READ statements:

```
DO 50 I = 1, 5
    READ *, SAMPLE(I)
50 CONTINUE
```

Notice that in this input routine integer variable I is used as a temporary placeholder for the subscript. This is permitted since I is assigned a value before a reference is made to the associated subscripted variable contained in the READ statement.

A DO loop may also be used to manipulate selected elements of an array. The following program segment replaces *alternate* elements of array SAMPLE, beginning with the first element, by ten times their original values:

```
DO 75 I = 1, 5, 2
    SAMPLE(I) = 10 * SAMPLE(I)
75 CONTINUE
```

In order to see the current contents of array SAMPLE we could use a DO loop to control the printing of each subscripted variable in the array:

```
    DO 99 I = 1, 5
        PRINT *, SAMPLE(I)
 99 CONTINUE
```

This output routine prints the current contents of array SAMPLE with the value of each subscripted variable appearing on a separate print line, one underneath the other.

Here is the consolidated program, which creates a five-element array having the name SAMPLE, replaces alternate elements by ten times their original values, and then prints the stored contents of the array:

```
        INTEGER SAMPLE(5)
*  .  . CREATE AN ARRAY SAMPLE
        DO 50 I = 1, 5
            READ *, SAMPLE(I)
     50 CONTINUE
*  .  . MANIPULATE ALTERNATE ELEMENTS
        DO 75 I = 1, 5, 2
            SAMPLE(I) = 10 * SAMPLE(I)
     75 CONTINUE
*  .  . PRINT CONTENTS OF ARRAY SAMPLE
        DO 99 I = 1, 5
            PRINT *, SAMPLE(I)
     99 CONTINUE
        STOP
        END
```

If the values 5, 71, 32, 14, and 19 were used as data (one per data record), then, after each major phase of the program executed, the contents of the array would be as follows:

Input	Processing	Output
SAMPLE(1) = 5	SAMPLE(1) = 50	SAMPLE(1) = 50
SAMPLE(2) = 71	------------------------------>	SAMPLE(2) = 71
SAMPLE(3) = 32	SAMPLE(3) = 320	SAMPLE(3) = 320
SAMPLE(4) = 14	------------------------------>	SAMPLE(4) = 14
SAMPLE(5) = 19	SAMPLE(5) = 190	SAMPLE(5) = 190

EXAMPLE 7.1   A data list consists of 12 real values arranged in ascending (increasing) numerical order. Write a program that stores the list as an array and then prints the list in descending (decreasing) numerical order.

Solution

See Program 7.1.

```
    * THIS PROGRAM WAS RUN ON A PRIME 850 COMPUTER USING WATFIV
        REAL A(12)
        DO 50 I = 1, 12
            READ *, A(I)
     50 CONTINUE
    * PRINT NUMBERS IN REVERSE ORDER STEP = -1
        DO 75 I = 12, 1, -1
            PRINT *, A(I)
     75 CONTINUE
        STOP
        END
```

Output:

```
OK, SEG REVERSE
2.0
3.0
3.2
3.3
4.5
4.9
6.9
10.0
12.5
14.0
15.9
18.0
              18.0000
              15.9000
              14.0000
              12.5000
              10.0000
              6.90000
              4.90000
              4.50000
              3.30000
              3.20000
              3.00000
              2.00000
**** STOP
```

Program 7.1

EXAMPLE 7.2 The problem that first motivated our discussion of subscripted variables may be restated as follows: Input a list of 100 real data values. Determine the average of the list and the number of values that are less than the average and the number of values that are greater than or equal to the average.

Solution

See Program 7.2.

```
* THIS PROGRAM WAS RUN ON A PRIME 850 COMPUTER USING A FORTRAN 77
* COMPILER
*           PROGRAM VARIABLES
*               X = ARRAY OF DATA VALUES
*             SUM = SUM OF DATA VALUES
*             AVG = AVERAGE OF DATA VALUES
*           JHIGH = NUMBER OF ELEMENTS GREATER
*                   THAN OR EQUAL TO AVERAGE
*            JLOW = NUMBER OF ELEMENTS LESS THAN
*                   AVERAGE
*
      REAL X(100), SUM, AVG
      INTEGER JHIGH, JLOW
      SUM = 0.0
      JHIGH = 0
      JLOW = 0
      DO 50 I = 1, 100
          READ *, X(I)
          SUM = SUM + X(I)
   50 CONTINUE
      AVG = SUM / 100.0
      DO 75 I = 1, 100
          IF ( X(I) .LT. AVG ) THEN
              JLOW = JLOW + 1
          ELSE
              JHIGH = JHIGH + 1
          ENDIF
   75 CONTINUE
      PRINT *, 'AVERAGE =              ', AVG
      PRINT *, 'BELOW AVERAGE:         ', JLOW
      PRINT *, 'GREATER OR = AVERAGE: ', JHIGH
      STOP
      END
```

Program 7.2

LEGAL SUBSCRIPTS

Different versions of Fortran place different restrictions on the types of expressions that may appear as subscripts. In Fortran 77 an array subscript (sometimes called an *index*) must be an integer constant or an expression that evaluates to an integer value. A real valued subscript will produce an error in Fortran 77, but will be tolerated by a WATFIV compiler. In WATFIV, real valued subscripts are converted automatically into integer valued subscripts by truncation. Although negative integer valued subscripts may be used in Fortran 77, the same is not true for WATFIV and Fortran IV compilers. Fortran 77 also permits a subscripted variable to serve as a subscript for another subscripted variable. For example, an expression such as $B(3*A(5) + 1)$ would be legal in Fortran 77 provided that $A(5)$ is an integer value and the evaluated subscript expression falls within the dimensional value of array B.

Fortran IV limits subscript expressions to the following forms, where c and d represent integer constants and K represents an integer variable:

Subscript	Example
c	ALPHA(19)
K	BETA(K)
c * K	GAMMA(3 * K)
K ± c	MAT(IYEAR − 7)
c * K ± d	X(8 * JAGE + 14)

Table 7.1 gives examples of legal and illegal subscripted variables.

Table 7.1 Examples of Legal and Illegal Subscripted Variables

Subscripted Variable	Subscript	Legal in Fortran 77?	Comments
AGE(K + 2)	K + 2	Yes	Legal in all Fortrans.
XAM(5 ** 3)	5 ** 3	Yes	Exponentiation in a subscript expression is not legal in Fortran IV.
C(3 * L − 2)	3 * L − 2	Yes	Legal in all Fortrans.
TIME(−8)	−8	Yes	Illegal in Fortran IV and WATFIV. In these Fortrans the lowest subscript value is 1.
D(J(9))	J(9)	Yes	Illegal in some implementations of Fortran, including Fortran IV.
BETA(1.3 * A)	1.3 * A	No	Real subscript expressions are illegal in Fortran 77. In WATFIV and some other Fortran extensions, real subscripts are permitted. However, these Fortran compilers will convert the real expression into an integer value by truncation.

EXAMPLE 7.3   Assume that an array K is declared using the statement INTEGER K(8) and that its current contents are as follows:

K(1)	K(2)	K(3)	K(4)	K(5)	K(6)	K(7)	K(8)
25	17	10	8	14	−13	89	42

Find the value of each of the following expressions:

(a) `2 * K(3)`

(b) `K(2 * 3)`

(c) `(K(3) + K(4)) / 2`

(d) `K(K(4) - 1)`

(e) `K(2 ** 3 - 1)`

(f) `K(5 * J)`, where the current value of J is 2

Solutions

(a) `2 * K(3) = 2 * 10 = 20`

(b) `K(2 * 3) = K(6) = -13`

(c) `( K(3) + K(4) ) / 2 = (10 + 8) / 2 = 18 / 2 = 9`

(d) `K(K(4) - 1) = K(8 - 1) = K(7) = 89`

(e) `K( 2 ** 3 - 1) = K(8 - 1) = K(7) = 89.`

(f) `K(5 * J) = K(10)`, which would generate an error since the subscript 10 exceeds the declared size of the array

Note: The subscript expressions in parts (d) and (e) are legal in Fortran 77 but are not permitted in older Fortrans, including Fortran IV.

To provide for negative valued subscripts, the size of an array in Fortran 77 may be expressed as a range having the form

$$array\ name(I : J)$$

where I is the lower subscript bound and J is the upper subscript bound. For example, an array H defined as follows:

```
REAL H(-3 : 2)
```

would consist of the subscripted variables $H(-3)$, $H(-2)$, $H(-1)$, $H(0)$, $H(1)$, and $H(2)$. There are seven elements in array H, as can be determined by taking the difference between the upper and lower bounds and then adding 1. In general,

$$array\ size = upper\ bound - lower\ bound + 1$$

EXAMPLE 7.4 The population of Metro City for 6 years is given in the following table:

Year	Population
1978	58,123
1979	65,098
1980	74,446
1981	80,649
1982	83,704
1983	88,045

Write a program segment which stores the population figures in an array YEAR such that the year serves as a subscript value for the corresponding population figure.

Solution

```
      INTEGER YEAR(1978 : 1983), POP K
      DO 50 K = 1978, 1983
         READ *, YEAR(K)
   50 CONTINUE
```

Program Note: Alternatively, the array YEAR could be declared without upper and lower bounds as INTEGER YEAR(1983). This would be an inefficient use of computer memory, however, since 1977 locations would be reserved needlessly.

The following errors represent common programming pitfalls; with care and attention they can be avoided:

- Failing to declare the size of an array.
- Attempting to assign an element that does not agree in data type with the array. For example, assigning an integer value to an array that has been declared to be real will produce an error.
- Using an illegal subscript value or expression.
- Attempting to reference a subscripted variable having a subscript value that falls outside the declared size or range of the array. When this happens, a run-time error occurs during program execution. See Program 7.3.

```
       $JOB   WATFIV
   C IS PROGRAM ILLUSTRATES A RUN TIME ERROR. AN ATTEMPT WAS MADE
   C TO READ OUTSIDE THE BOUNDARIES OF AN ARRAY
 1            REAL X(5)
 2            SUM = 0.0
 3            DO 50 I = 1, 10
 4            READ , X(I)
 5            SUM = SUM + X(I)
 6         50 CONTINUE
 7            AVG = SUM /10.0
 8            PRINT , 'AVERAGE =          ', AVG
 9            STOP
10            END
       $ENTRY
***ERROR***  SUBSCRIPT NUMBER 1 OF X       HAS THE VALUE          6
       PROGRAM WAS EXECUTING LINE      4 IN ROUTINE M/PROG WHEN TERMINATION OCCURRED
```

Program 7.3

Estimating the Size of an Array

If the exact number of elements that will be assigned to an array is not known to the programmer, it is better to slightly overestimate the declared size of the array than to underestimate its size. The only disadvantage in overestimating the size of an array is that more memory space is reserved than may actually be needed. This can be a significant disadvantage, however, in situations in which the amount of available computer memory is limited.

EXAMPLE 7.5 Determine the error, if any, in each of the following program segments:

(a)
```
    INTEGER X
    READ *, N
    DO 50 I = 1, N
       READ *, X(I)
 50 CONTINUE
```

(b)
```
    REAL X(5)
    DO 50 I = 1, 5
       READ *, X(I)
 50 CONTINUE
    DO 75 K = 1, 5
       PRINT *, X(2 * K - 1)
 75 CONTINUE
    STOP
```

```
(c)       INTEGER X
          READ *, N
          DIMENSION X(N)
          DO 50 I = 1, N
              READ *, X(I)
      50 CONTINUE
(d)       INTEGER X(5)
          DO 50 I = -2, 2
              READ X(I)
      50 CONTINUE
(e)       INTEGER A(6)
          DO 50 J = 1, 4
              A(J) = 2 * J
      50 CONTINUE
```

Solutions

(a) The size of array X has not been declared.

(b) When the current value of K is 4, the subscript expression $2 * K - 1$ evaluates to 7, which falls outside the subscript bounds of array X.

(c) A variable appears as the dimensioned size of array X. The Fortran compiler must be advised of the size of array X before *program* execution. The DIMENSION statement must be placed before the READ statement and must declare the size of the array, using an appropriate constant.

(d) $X(-2)$ is an illegal subscripted variable since the array is defined for subscript values between 1 and 5, inclusive. Declaring the array as follows:

$$\text{INTEGER X(-2 : 2)}$$

would resolve the problem. Keep in mind that defining the size of an array by using upper and lower limits is legal only in Fortran 77.

(e) No error is present. The variable assignments would be made as follows:

		←————— Array A —————————→				
2 * J	2	4	6	8		
A(J)	A(1)	A(2)	A(3)	A(4)	A(5)	A(6)

The contents of A(5) and A(6) would be undefined. If the stored contents of A(5) and A(6) were printed, the machine would display some symbol such as ''U'' or an asterisk to indicate that values had not been assigned to these subscripted variables.

7.2 Manipulating the Elements of an Array

The advantage of storing a list of related data values as an array is that it allows a programmer to process the list of values efficiently as a group, or to manipulate individual elements of the array while maintaining the entire list in computer memory. In this section, various techniques for manipulating the elements of an array are presented through a series of examples.

Example 7.6 illustrates how to input an array when the exact number of values that the array will store is not specified.

EXAMPLE 7.6 A list of integer values ends with a trailer value of -999. Write a program that stores the list as an array and then prints the array. Assume that the list contains a maximum of 50 data values. Include an input data validation routine that prevents an attempt to store more than 50 data values in the array.

Solution

The program segment that follows uses a WHILE . . . DO type of construction to control the input of data. A counter (called KOUNT) is used to maintain a running count of the data values that are read and also serves as the subscript of the array variable X.

The logic of the program is based on reading a value and first assigning it to a nonsubscripted integer variable, say A. If the value of A is not equal to -999, then the value of KOUNT is increased by 1 and the current value of A is assigned to the subscripted variable X(KOUNT), provided that the value of KOUNT is not greater than 50.

```
      $JOB    WATFIV
      C THIS PROGRAM WAS RUN ON AN IBM COMPUTER USING WATFIV
      C STORING A DATA LIST ENDING WITH A TRAILER VALUE
 1            INTEGER X(50), KOUNT, A
 2            KOUNT = 0
 3            READ , A
      C WHILE TRAILER IS NOT FOUND PLACE DATA INTO THE ARRAY
 4        10 CONTINUE
 5            IF ( A .NE. -999) THEN
 6               KOUNT = KOUNT + 1
      C . . . .CHECK FOR TOO MANY DATA VALUES
 7               IF ( KOUNT .GT. 50) THEN
 8                  PRINT , 'LIST EXCEEDS 50 VALUES'
 9                  STOP
10               ELSE
11                  X(KOUNT) = A
12                  READ , A
13               ENDIF
14               GOTO 10
15            ENDIF
16            PRINT , 'KOUNT =', KOUNT
17            DO 75 I = 1, KOUNT
18               PRINT , X(I)
19        75 CONTINUE
20            STOP
21            END
      $ENTRY
KOUNT =               6
          95
          83
         100
         101
          90
          65
```

EXAMPLE 7.7 Assume that an array X(I) can store a maximum of 50 elements. For any given integer value of N less than 50, write a program that reads values into the first N elements of array X, and then reads another value (say, YNEW) and makes this new value the *first* element of the array by "bumping" each of the original elements into the next highest valued subscripted variable. For example, if N = 5, move the original elements X(1), X(2), X(3), X(4), and X(5) so that X(6) stores the original contents of X(5), X(5) stores the original contents of X(4), . . . , and X(1) stores the value YNEW. Print the original array, the new element to be inserted (YNEW), and the new array.

Solution

See Program 7.4.

EXAMPLE 7.8 Assume that array A has already been stored in computer memory. Write a program segment that switches the contents of the subscripted variable A(3) with the contents of the subscripted variable A(19).

Solution

Imagine that the two subscripted variables are glasses, one filled with water and the other with milk. How can we switch their contents? We must have a third container that temporarily holds the contents of one of the original glasses:

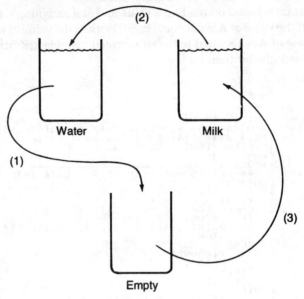

```
* THIS PROGRAM WAS RUN ON A PRIME 850 COMPUTER USING A FORTRAN 77 COMPILER
      INTEGER X(50), YNEW
      N = 5
* INITIALIZE ARRAY X TO ALL ZEROES
      DO 40 K = 1, 50
          X(K) = 0
   40 CONTINUE
*
* READ VALUES INTO THE FIRST N ELEMENTS OF ARRAY X
      DO 50 K = 1, N
          READ *, X(K)
   50 CONTINUE
*
* PRINT THE CONTENTS OF THE FIRST N ELEMENTS OF ARRAY X
      PRINT *, 'THE ORIGINAL ARRAY'
      PRINT *, ' '
      DO 55 K = 1, N
          PRINT *, X(K)
   55 CONTINUE
      PRINT *, ' '
*
* FIRST MOVE EACH ELEMENT TO THE NEXT HIGHEST SUBSCRIPTED VARIABLE, STARTING
* WITH X(N) AND WORKING BACKWARDS
      DO 60 K = N, 1, -1
          X(K+1) = X(K)
   60 CONTINUE
*
* NEXT READ THE NEW VALUE AND ASSIGN IT TO X(1)
      READ *, YNEW
      X(1) = YNEW
      PRINT *, 'YNEW'
      PRINT *, YNEW
*
* NOW PRINT THE NEW ARRAY
      PRINT *, ' '
      PRINT *, ' '
      PRINT *, 'THE NEW ARRAY'
      DO 70 K = 1, N + 1
          PRINT *, X(K)
   70 CONTINUE
      STOP
      END
```

Output:

```
OK, SEG BUMP
14
3
6
7
9
      THE ORIGINAL ARRAY

                     14
                      3
                      6
                      7
                      9

           5
          YNEW
                      5


         THE NEW ARRAY
                      5
                     14
                      3
                      6
                      7
                      9
**** STOP
```

Program 7.4

Similarly, to switch the contents of memory cells we must introduce a third variable that will temporarily store a copy of the contents of one of the cells while that cell is "filled" with the contents of the other cell:

$$\text{(1) } TEMP = A(3)$$
$$\text{(2) } A(3) = A(19)$$
$$\text{(3) } A(19) = TEMP$$

Notice that *three* assignment statements are necessary to accomplish the switch. After step (1) is executed, the variable TEMP will store the same value as A(3). After step 2 is executed, the value of A(19) will be stored in A(3), thereby wiping out the original contents of A(3). Fortunately, we have saved the original contents of A(3) in TEMP. After step 3 is executed, A(19) will store the original value of A(3). This technique will be used extensively when we discuss how to sort a data list.

Exchanging Array Data Elements

To switch the contents of two subscripted variables, say X(I) and X(K), a TEMPorary storage location must be introduced. The following set of program statements accomplishes the switch:

$$TEMP = X(I)$$
$$X(I) = X(K)$$
$$X(K) = TEMP$$

Example 7.9 illustrates how subscripting variables can be used to advantage in maintaining a sum or a count, where the subscript identifies the item being totaled.

EXAMPLE 7.9 A company has eight salespersons, each identified by an integer from 1 to 8. A series of sales records is to be processed in order to determine the amount of commission to be paid to the salesperson for a particular sale. Each record contains the following information:

(1) the number of the salesperson
(2) the amount of the sale
(3) the rate of commission

Calculate and print:

    (a) the total number of sales records processed for each salesperson

    (b) the total amount of commission paid to each salesperson

Assume that the data records are preceded by a header record which gives the number of data records that follow.

Solution

The key to this problem is to use a subscripted variable to represent the number of sales records processed for each salesperson and another subscripted variable to sum the amount of commission paid to each salesperson. The subscript in each case is the salesperson's identification number. The desired Fortran program is shown as Program 7.5.

```
$JOB     WATFIV
C PROGRAM USES SUBSCRIPTED VARIABLES AS COUNTERS AND SUMMERS
C THIS PROGRAM WAS RUN ON AN IBM COMPUTER USING WATFIV
C
C          UNSUBSCRIPTED PROGRAM VARIABLE NAMES:
C
C                ID = SALESPERSON'S NUMBER
C              SALE = AMOUNT OF THE SALE
C              RATE = COMMISSION RATE EXPRESSED AS A DECIMAL NUMBER
C                 N = TOTAL NUMBER OF SALES RECORDS TO BE PROCESSED
C
C          SUBSCRIPTED PROGRAM VARIABLES NAMES:
C
C                      TOTAL(ID) = TOTAL NUMBER OF SALES RECORDS FOR
C                                  SALESPERSON HAVING NUMBER ID
C                      SUMCOM(ID) = SUM OF THE COMMISSION AMOUNTS TO
C                                   BE PAID TO SALESPERSON HAVING
C                                   NUMBER ID
C
1             INTEGER ID, N, TOTAL(8)
2             REAL SALE, RATE, SUMCOM(8)
C INITIALIZE VALUE OF COUNTER AND SUMMER
3             DO 25 ID = 1, 8
4                TOTAL(ID) = 0
5                SUMCOM(ID) = 0.0
6          25 CONTINUE
C
C READ HEADER RECORD
C
7             READ , N
C
8             DO 50 I = 1, N
9                READ , ID, SALE, RATE
10               TOTAL(ID) = TOTAL(ID) + 1
11               SUMCOM(ID) = SUMCOM(ID) + SALE * RATE
12         50 CONTINUE
C PRINT COLUMN HEADINGS
13            PRINT , '      SALESPERSON       TOTAL          TOTAL'
14            PRINT , '        NUMBER         RECORDS       COMMISSION'
15            PRINT , ' '
16            PRINT , ' '
17            DO 75 ID = 1, 8
18               PRINT , ID, TOTAL(ID), SUMCOM(ID)
19         75 CONTINUE
20            STOP
21            END
```

Program 7.5

Program Notes: Notice that the first DO loop is used to initialize the value of each element of the arrays TOTAL and SUMCOM. The next DO loop performs the actual processing. The amount of the commission is calculated in the statement that accumulates its sum. The next DO loop prints the required output in table form.

    Consider how the program would have to be modified if subscripted variables were not used. In one alternative approach, a CASE structure could provide a transfer of control to an appropriate block of program statements, based on the value of the salesperson's ID. This method would increase considerably the amount of program code needed in the solution.

Using these data:

ID	Sale	Rate
8	500.00	.10
6	4000.00	.05
7	300.00	.07
3	500.00	.10
2	400.00	.20
8	3000.00	.07
1	400.00	.06
2	500.00	.05
4	5.00	.20
3	78.00	.09
6	9000.00	.10
6	50000.00	.09
7	3000.00	.08
5	300.00	.09
4	200.00	.08

the following output was obtained:

```
   SALESPERSON       TOTAL            TOTAL
      NUMBER         RECORDS        COMMISSION

         1              1             23.9999800
         2              2            104.9999000
         3              2             57.0199800
         4              2             16.9999800
         5              1             26.9999800
         6              3           5599.9960000
         7              2            260.9997000
         8              2            259.9997000
```

7.3 Sorting a List of Numbers

Imagine trying to locate on a computer-printed list a particular credit account number if the numbers were randomly arranged on the page. Some sort of order is essential. Similarly, in printing a student honor roll list, it is necessary to organize the students' grade averages from the highest average to the lowest qualifying average, or in the reverse order. In many other data processing applications also, it is frequently necessary to arrange lists so that the individual members of the list appear in either ascending (lowest to highest) or descending (highest to lowest) order. The process of arranging items in a list according to some given condition is called *sorting*. Alphabetizing a list of names is another example of sorting and will be discussed in Chapter 8.

A number of different algorithms can be used to sort a list of numbers into either ascending or descending numerical order. Some are more efficient than others, and they vary also in ease of understanding. In this section we describe the exchange sort method, which uses a straightforward algorithm. The algorithm will be developed so that at the completion of the sort a list of numbers is arranged in ascending numerical order. If, for example, there are five numbers in array X, then, at the completion of the sort, X(1) (the "topmost" array variable) will store the smallest value in the list, X(2) will hold the next smallest value, and so on, so that X(5) (the "bottommost" array variable) is assigned the largest value in the array.

To accomplish this, the bottommost element of the unsorted array is systematically compared with each of the remaining elements of the array. An exchange is made whenever an element of

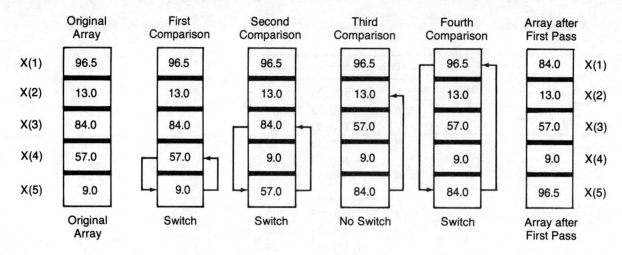

Figure 7.2 Comparison/Switches in the First Pass of an Exchange Sort

the array is greater than the element that is currently occupying the bottommost position of the unsorted array. This is illustrated in Figure 7.2. Notice that, since the array contains 5 elements, 5 − 1 or 4 comparisons are made in order to ensure that the largest element of the array is placed in X(5).

A set of comparisons in which one subscripted variable is compared with each of the remaining subscripted variables of an array is called a *pass*. The exchange sort algorithm is based on making successive passes through the array. In each pass the bottommost element X(J) of the unsorted array is compared with each element X(I) having a lower valued subscript. If X(I) is greater than X(J), an exchange is made using the technique developed in Example 7.8.

For example, in a second pass through the array illustrated in Figure 7.2, X(4) becomes the new bottommost array element. X(3), X(2), and X(1) are compared in turn with the current contents of X(4). An exchange is made if X(3) is greater than X(4), or if X(2) is greater than X(4), or if X(1) is greater than X(4). In a third pass through the array, X(3) would become the bottommost array element with X(2) and X(1) being compared with X(3). In the fourth and final pass, X(1) would be compared with X(2).

The Fortran 77 representation for a single pass follows:

```
      DO 50 I = J - 1, 1, -1
         IF ( X(I) .GT. X(J) ) THEN
*. . . . .MAKE EXCHANGE
            TEMP = X(J)
            X(J) = X(I)
            X(I) = TEMP
         ENDIF
   50 CONTINUE
```

Although this program segment will assign the largest element of the first J elements of the array to X(J), the remaining elements of the array will not necessarily be sorted. An outer DO loop is needed to generate the subscript of the succeeding "bottom" elements of the array, which are to be compared with elements on "top." This will in turn control the number of passes required to produce a sorted list. The value of the outer DO variable will need to range from J = N to J = 2, where N represents the number of elements in the array.

Program 7.6 shows the complete exchange sort algorithm. A data list that is preceded by a header value N (N < 50) is stored in array X and then printed. After array X is sorted, it is printed.

```
* * * * * * * * * * * EXCHANGE SORT ROUTINE* * * * * * * * * * * *
*                                                                 *
*               X = ARRAY NAME (N ELEMENTS)                       *
*                                                                 *
* THIS PROGRAM WAS RUN ON A PRIME 850 COMPUTER USING FORTRAN 77   *
*
      REAL X(50)
      READ *, N
*
* READ N ELEMENTS INTO ARRAY X
      DO 40 J = 1, N
         READ *, X(J)
   40 CONTINUE
*
* PRINT CONTENTS OF ARRAY X BEFORE THE SORT
      PRINT *, 'THE ORIGINAL ARRAY'
      PRINT *, ' '
      DO 45 K = 1, N
         PRINT *, X(K)
   45 CONTINUE
*
*
* THE SORT ROUTINE BEGINS
*
* OUTER DO SETS VALUE OF THE SUBSCRIPT OF BOTTOMMOST ELEMENT
*
      DO 75 J = N, 2, -1
*
* INNER DO MAKES COMPARISONS BETWEEN X(J) AND REMAINING ELEMENTS
         DO 50 I = J - 1, 1, -1
            IF ( X(I) .GT. X(J) ) THEN
* . . . . . . . . . MAKE EXCHANGE
               TEMP = X(J)
               X(J) = X(I)
               X(I) = TEMP
            ENDIF
   50    CONTINUE
* RETURN TO OUTER DO TO INITIATE NEXT PASS
*
   75 CONTINUE
* PRINT CONTENTS OF ARRAY AFTER SORT
      PRINT *, ' '
      PRINT *, ' '
      PRINT *, 'THE SORTED ARRAY'
      PRINT *, ' '
      DO 90 I = 1, N
         PRINT *, X(I)
   90 CONTINUE
      STOP
      END
```

Program 7.6

Some additional remarks on the exchange sort:

1. An array can be sorted into descending order simply by reversing the sense of the inequality (change .GT. to .LT.) when comparing elements of the array.

2. The number of comparisons performed in an exchange sort is given by the relationship

$$(1/2) * (N - 1) * N$$

This follows from the fact that in the first pass $N - 1$ comparisons are necessary and in each succeeding pass 1 less comparison is made, so that

$$(N - 1) + (N - 2) + (N - 3) + \cdots + 2 + 1 = (1/2) * (N - 1) * N$$

3. In sorting large arrays that require a good deal of arrangement, the exchange sort is relatively inefficient. More advanced textbooks on programming should be consulted if you need to use a more efficient sorting program.
4. Problem 8 at the end of this chapter discusses another sorting algorithm.

EXAMPLE 7.10   The exchange sort program that appears as Program 7.6 was written for a Fortran 77 compiler. Revise the exchange sort algorithm so that this program will run on a Fortran compiler that does not permit computations within a DO statement or negative step values.

Solution

The revised program is based on having the top element of the array store the smallest value of the array. Comparisons are made between this element and each element having a higher subscript value. An exchange is made when the top element is greater than the element with which it is being compared. See Program 7.7.

```
*         THE REVISED EXCHANGE SORT ALGORITHM
          L = N - 1
          DO 75 J = 1, L
*         INNER DO MAKES COMPARISONS
             K = J + 1
             DO 50 I = K, N
                IF ( X(J) .GT. X(I) ) THEN
*     . . . . . .    MAKE EXCHANGE
                   TEMP = X(J)
                   X(J) = X(I)
                   X(I) = TEMP
                ENDIF
   50        CONTINUE
   75 CONTINUE
```

Program 7.7

EXAMPLE 7.11   In a certain sports league, there are 12 teams. Each team is identified by an integer from 1 to 12. Read in 12 data records (not necessarily arranged in team order), each of which contains the following data items: team number, number of wins, number of losses.

Calculate the winning percentage for each team. Print the teams in order of their winning percentages, so that the team having the highest winning percentage is printed first.

Solution

In order to be able to keep track of a given team and its winning percentage, we will construct *two* arrays. The first array will contain the team number, and the second array will store the calculated winning percentage of the team. In performing the sort on the array that stores the team's winning percentages, each time a switch is made between a pair of elements of this array, a switch must also be made between the corresponding elements of the array that stores the team numbers. This second switch is necessary in order to ensure that the elements occupying the same number position of each array always correspond.

Before presenting the coded Fortran program, let's look at the pseudocode solution.

Pseudocode Solution

```
        DOWHILE I is not greater than 12
           READ team data record
           TEAM(I) = team number
           PERCNT(I) = wins / (wins + losses)
        END of DO
    *
    * USE EXCHANGE SORT TO ARRANGE ELEMENTS OF PERCNT(I)
    * IN DESCENDING ORDER
    *
        DOWHILE NOT last pass
           DOWHILE NOT last comparison made in a given pass
              IF any element is less than the bottom array element THEN
                 Switch elements of PERCNT array
                 Switch corresponding elements of TEAM array
           END of inner DO
        END of outer DO
    * PRINT SORTED ARRAY
        DOWHILE I is not greater than 12
           PRINT TEAM(I), PERCNT(I)
        END of DO
        STOP
```

The Fortran program solution is given in Program 7.8. Keep in mind that we are applying the exchange sort algorithm and are sorting the elements of the PERCNT array in *descending* order. Since the variables WINS and LOSSES are involved in calculations in which a real valued result is desired, these variables have been declared as REAL.

```
* * * * * * * * * * BUBBLE SORT ROUTINE* * * * * * * * * * * * * *
*                                                                *
*            X = ARRAY NAME (N ELEMENTS)                         *
*                                                                *
* THIS PROGRAM WAS RUN ON A PRIME 850 COMPUTER USING FORTRAN 77  *
*
      REAL X(50)
      READ *, N
* READ N ELEMENTS INTO ARRAY X
      DO 40 J = 1, N
         READ *,  X(J)
   40 CONTINUE
* PRINT CONTENTS OF ARRAY X BEFORE THE SORT
      PRINT *, 'THE ORIGINAL ARRAY'
      PRINT *, ' '
      DO 45 K = 1, N
         PRINT *, X(K)
   45 CONTINUE
* THE SORT ROUTINE BEGINS
      DO 75 K = 1, N - 1
*
         DO 50 I = 1, N - K
            IF ( X(I) .GT. X(I + 1) ) THEN
* . . . . . . . . . MAKE SWITCH
                  TEMP = X(I)
                  X(I) = X(I + 1)
                  X(I + 1) = TEMP
            ENDIF
   50    CONTINUE
* RETURN TO OUTER DO LOOP
   75 CONTINUE
```

```
* PRINT CONTENTS OF ARRAY AFTER SORT
      PRINT *, ' '
      PRINT *, ' '
      PRINT *, 'THE SORTED ARRAY'
      PRINT *, ' '
      DO 90 I = 1, N
          PRINT *, X(I)
  90 CONTINUE
      STOP
      END
```

Program 7.8

For these data:

TEAM NO	WINS	LOSSES
11	6.0	3.0
2	5.0	4.0
9	4.0	5.0
4	7.0	2.0
8	2.0	7.0
5	1.0	8.0
1	8.0	1.0
6	8.0	1.0
3	0.0	9.0
7	3.0	6.0
10	5.0	4.0
12	7.0	2.0

the output is as follows:

```
TEAM    WINNING
NO      PERCENT

 1      0.888889
 6      0.888889
12      0.777778
 4      0.777778
11      0.666667
 2      0.555555
10      0.555555
 9      0.444444
 7      0.333333
 8      0.222222
 5      0.111111
 3      0.000000
```

7.4 Searching an Array for a Particular Element

Sometimes it is necessary to examine the elements of a stored data list in order to identify which subscripted variable, if any, has been assigned a particular data value. For example, if an array stores a list of student ID numbers, the array would have to be scanned in some systematic fashion to locate the subscripted variable which stores a *particular* student ID number that is specified before the search begins.

There are two cases to be considered. If the array is *not* sorted, then a *linear (sequential) search* may be performed. In a linear search, the value being sought is compared with each element of the array, beginning with the first element. For example, if A is an unsorted array having 50 elements which have already been read into computer memory, and the element being searched for has a value of X, the following program segment locates the value of the subscripted variable, if any, that holds the value X:

```
*           LINEAR SEARCH ALGORITHM
            DO 75 I = 1, 50
                IF ( X .EQ. A(I) ) THEN
*     . . . . . . X HAS BEEN FOUND
                    PRINT *, 'SUBSCRIPT VALUE IS', I
                    STOP
                ENDIF
        75 CONTINUE
            PRINT *, X, 'HAS NOT BEEN FOUND'
            STOP
            END
```

A linear search may also be performed if the array is sorted. If the array contains a large number of elements, however, a linear search can be a relatively inefficient process.

A *binary* search, on the other hand, capitalizes on the fact that the array is sorted. Consider the problem of determining which subscripted variable of array A, if any, has been assigned the value of X. Rather than initiating a pattern of comparisons that compares X with array elements beginning with A(1), we begin a binary search by splitting the array in half. The value X is then compared with the middle value of the array, A(MID). If X equals A(MID), then our work is finished. If X is less than A(MID), then (since the array is sorted) we are guaranteed that the value X cannot be assigned to a subscripted variable in the bottom half of the array, so that this set of elements may be eliminated from consideration. Similarly, if X is greater than A(MID), then the top half of the array may be discarded. By systematically repeating this halving process on the remaining part of the array, the value of X will be found (or it will be determined that the array does not contain this value).

Before further detailing the specifics of the binary search algorithm, it will be helpful to introduce the following terminology:

JLOW = the lowest valued subscript of the part of the array that is being searched
JHIGH = the highest valued subscript of the part of the array that is being searched
  MID = the value of the subscript of the "middle" value of the array that is being searched:

$$MID = (JHIGH + JLOW) / 2$$

SUB = the value of the subscript of the array variable which stores the element X that is being searched for

The binary search algorithm may be stated as follows:

Step 1. Initialize JLOW = 1 and JHIGH = N.
Step 2. Determine whether JHIGH − JLOW = 1, that is, determine whether JLOW and JHIGH are consecutively numbered subscripts. If they are, test whether X = A(JLOW). IF true, THEN set SUB = JLOW and GOTO Step 6. Otherwise, test whether X = A(JHIGH). IF true, THEN set SUB = JHIGH and GOTO Step 6; ELSE, X is not an element of the array.
Step 3. If JHIGH − JLOW is not equal to 1, then determine the "center" of the array, that is, calculate

$$MID = (JLOW + JHIGH) / 2$$

Step 4. If X = A(MID), THEN set SUB = MID and GOTO Step 6.

Step 5. If X is not equal to A(MID), THEN discard the half of the array that is not needed. This can be determined by comparing X with A(MID). If X is less than A(MID), THEN X must be contained in the lower half of the array; by letting JHIGH = MID, we restrict the array to the elements A(JLOW) to A(JHIGH), where JHIGH has been assigned the value MID. ELSE (that is, X is *not* less than A(MID)), X must be contained in the bottom half of the array; by letting JLOW = MID, we restrict the array to the elements A(JLOW) to A(JHIGH), where JLOW has been assigned the value MID. Next, GOTO Step 2.

Step 6. Print SUB.

Step 7. Stop.

The flowchart for the algorithm just presented is shown in Figure 7.3. The flowchart does *not* show the reading of the data into array A or the sorting of the elements of array A. The variable X in the flowchart refers to the value that is being searched for. Problem 10 at the end of this chapter asks you to prepare the corresponding Fortran program.

7.5 The Implied DO Loop

Consider the following program segment, which reads ten data values into an array X using a DO loop:

```
DO 50 I = 1, 10
      READ *, X(I)
50 CONTINUE
```

Each time the DO loop is executed, a value is read from a *new* data record (line) and then stored in array X.

It is sometimes preferable to read values into an array by incorporating the parameters of a DO statement *within* the READ statement. The following single program statement serves the same function as the preceding DO loop:

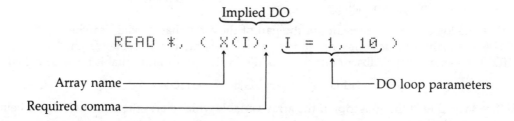

When this statement is executed, a DO loop is initiated. Values will be read consecutively across a given data record and stored in array X. The individual data values are entered on the same physical data record (provided that there is enough room). Adjacent data values are separated by a comma or blank space. If, for example, seven data values are stored on the first physical data record and the remaining three data values are stored on a second data record, then, after reading and assigning the seventh data value to X(7), the next physical data record will be read.

The READ statement that has been illustrated is said to include an *implied* DO loop, and is equivalent to the following statement:

```
READ *, X(1), X(2), X(3), X(4), X(5), X(6),
        X(7), X(8), X(9), X(10)
```

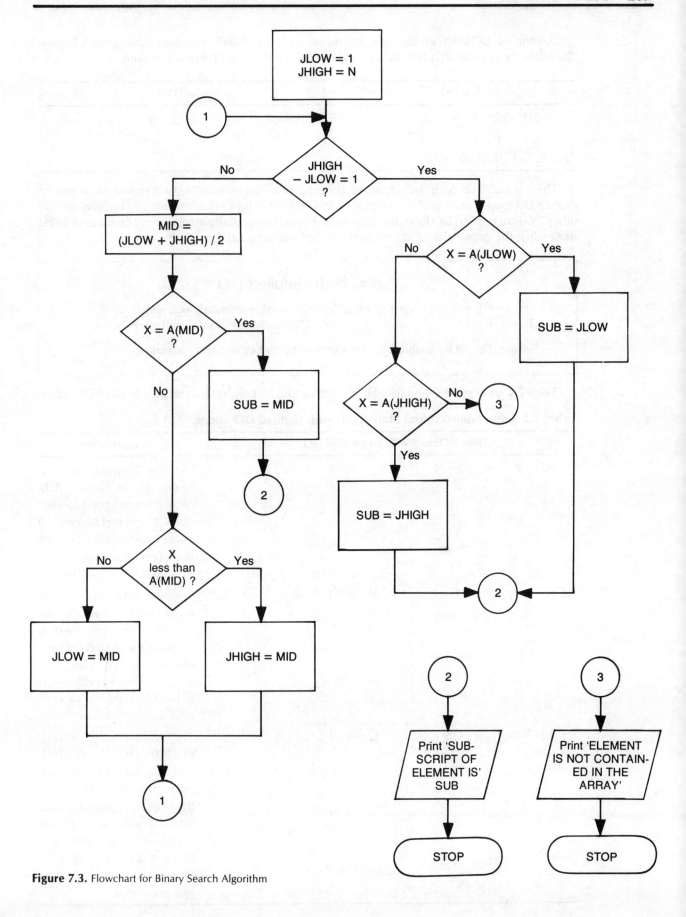

Figure 7.3. Flowchart for Binary Search Algorithm

An implied DO loop can also be incorporated within a PRINT statement. For example, to print the elements of array X(I) we may use either of the following program segments:

Explicit DO	Implied DO
``` DO 50 I = 1, 10 PRINT *, X(I) 50 CONTINUE ```	``` PRINT *, (X(I), I = 1, 10) ```

There is a difference, however, in the appearance of the outputs that are produced. When an explicit DO loop is used, each value of the array is printed on a separate line, one underneath the other. With an implied DO loop, the values are printed horizontally across a print line; a new line is used when the print fields of the current line become exhausted.

Syntax of the Implied DO

Input: READ *, (array variable, DO-variable = initial, exit, step)
Output: PRINT *, (array variable, DO-variable = initial, exit, step)

Note: The DO-variable appears as the subscript of the array variable.

Table 7.2 gives some examples of input and output statements that include implied DO loops.

Table 7.2 Some Input/Output Statements with Implied DO Loops

Input/Output with an Implied DO	Interpretation
`READ *, A, B,( X(K), K = 1, 10 )`	The first 2 data values entered on an input data record are assigned to variables A and B. The next 10 consecutive data values that are read are assigned to X(1), X(2), . . . , X(10).
`READ *, R, ( I(K), K = 1, 9, 2 ), Y`	The first data value on the input data record is assigned to R. The next 5 values are assigned consecutively to I(1), I(3), I(5), I(7), and I(9). The next value that is read is assigned to variable Y.
`PRINT *, ( OUT(L), L = 1, 6 )`	The values of OUT(1), OUT(2), OUT(3), OUT(4), OUT(5), and OUT(6) are printed horizontally across the print line, provided that the number of available print fields is not exhausted (if they are, printing continues on the next consecutive print line).

USING AN IMPLIED DO WITH FORMATTED INPUT/OUTPUT

When using an implied DO with format-directed input, the coding of the FORMAT statement will determine whether data are read from individual data records or from the same data record. If the format edit descriptor that corresponds to the subscripted variable appears with a repetition factor, then the elements of the array are read from the *same* physical data record; otherwise, each data element appears on a *separate* data record.

Similarly, if the format edit descriptor associated with an array that is being printed using an implied DO appears with a repetition factor, then the elements of the array are printed horizontally; otherwise, they are printed vertically, with each element of the array on a separate line.

Table 7.3 illustrates the use of an implied DO with format-directed input and output statements.

Table 7.3 Implied DO with Formatted Input/Output

Formatted Input/Output with an Implied DO	Interpretation

`READ (5,100) (ID(K),K = 1,4)`
`100 FORMAT (4I3)`
 	
or
	Four integer data values are read from the *same* data record and are assigned to I(1), I(2), I(3), and I(4).

`100 FORMAT (I3)`	Four integer data values are read from four *separate* data records and are assigned to I(1), I(2), I(3), and I(4).

`WRITE (6,200) (OUT(I),I = 1,5)`
`200 FORMAT (1X, 5F8.1)`
 	
or
	Five real values stored in array OUT are printed horizontally across the print line.

`200 FORMAT (1X, F8.1)`	Five real values stored in array OUT are printed vertically, one value on a print line.

EXAMPLE 7.12   An implied DO loop is to be used to read in 180 real data values and store them in array BETA. Using a format-directed input statement and an edit descriptor of F7.2, write the necessary program segment, assuming that:

(a) six data values are entered on each input data record

(b) a single data value is entered on each input data record

Solutions

(a)
```
      REAL BETA(180)
      READ (5, 100) ( BETA(I), I = 1, 180 )
  100 FORMAT (6F7.2)
```

Remark: Since six data values are entered per data record, the program would read *30* data records.

(b)
```
      REAL BETA(180)
      READ (5, 100) ( BETA(I), I = 1, 180 )
  100 FORMAT (F7.2)
```

Remark: Since one data value is entered per data record, the program would read *180* data records.

EXAMPLE 7.13   Rewrite each of the following statements without using an implied DO loop:
(a) `WRITE (6, 200) (A(I), B(I), I = 1, 3)`
(b) `READ (5, 100) (C(2 * K - 1), K = 1, 4)`
(c) `WRITE (6, 99) (X(I), I = 4, 10, 2)`
(d) `READ, '(4F10.2)', (A(L), L = 1, 12)`
(e) `WRITE (6, 300) (B, L(J), J = 1, 3)`

Solutions

(a) More than one subscripted variable may appear in an implied DO:

`WRITE (6, 200) A(1), B(1), A(2), B(2), A(3), B(3)`

(b) The subscript in an implied DO may be an expression:

`READ (5, 100) C(1), C(3), C(5), C(7)`

(c) The parameters of an implied DO may begin at a number other than 1 and may have an increment different from 1:

`WRITE (6, 99) X(4), X(6), X(8), X(10)`

(d) In this Fortran 77 format-directed READ statement the format editor appears within the apostrophes and specifies that data are entered in four fields per data record. Hence:

```
READ, '(4F10.2)', A(1), A(2), A(3), A(4)
READ, '(4F10.2)', A(5), A(6), A(7), A(8)
READ, '(4F10.2)', A(9), A(10), A(11), A(12)
```

(e) A nonsubscripted variable may appear in the implied DO:

`WRITE (6, 300)B, L(1), B, L(2), B, L(3)`

EXAMPLE 7.14   Read a list of 20 integer values into an array A. Copy the negative elements of array A into array N, and the nonnegative elements of array A into array P. Print the elements of arrays A, N, and P horizontally, each array on a separate print line. (Use formatted input/output, assuming that each element is either a one- or a two-digit integer value.)

Solution

See Program 7.9. The program illustrates formatted input/output in Fortran 77 using an implied DO loop. Each element of array A is compared with zero. A count is maintained of both nonnegative and negative elements of array A, and the current values of these counters (PKOUNT and NKOUNT) serve as the subscript values of arrays P and N.

```
* THIS PROGRAM WAS RUN ON A PRIME COMPUTER USING FORTRAN 77
        INTEGER A(20), N(20), P(20), NKOUNT, PKOUNT, I
        PKOUNT = 0
        NKOUNT = 0
        READ '( 20I3 )', (A(I), I = 1, 20 )
* NEXT COMPARE ELEMENT OF ARRAY A WITH ZERO
        DO 50 I = 1, 20
            IF ( A(I) .GE. 0 ) THEN
                PKOUNT = PKOUNT + 1
                P(PKOUNT) = A(I)
            ELSE
                NKOUNT = NKOUNT + 1
                N(NKOUNT) = A(I)
            ENDIF
   50 CONTINUE
* NOW PRINT OUT THE THREE ARRAYS
        PRINT *, ' '
        PRINT *, ' '
        PRINT *, 'THE ORIGINAL ARRAY'
```

```
          PRINT '( 1X, 20(I3, 2X) )', (A(I), I = 1, 20)
          PRINT *, ' '
          PRINT *, 'THE POSITIVE NUMBERS'
          PRINT *, ' '
          PRINT '( 1X, 20(I3, 2X) )', (P(I), I = 1, PKOUNT)
          PRINT *, ' '
          PRINT *, ' '
          PRINT *, 'THE NEGATIVE NUMBERS'
          PRINT *, ' '
          PRINT '( 1X, 20(I3, 2X) )', (N(I), I = 1, NKOUNT)
          STOP
          END
```

Program 7.9

Output:

```
THE ORIGINAL ARRAY
-11   22  -33   44   55  -66   77  -88   99   11  -22   33   44  -55   66   77   88   99   11  -22

THE POSITIVE NUMBERS

 22   44   55   77   99   11   33   44   66   77   88   99   11

THE NEGATIVE NUMBERS

-11  -33  -66  -88  -22  -55  -22
**** STOP
```

AN ABBREVIATED FORM OF THE IMPLIED DO

When a new array is being constructed by reading data values and assigning them to consecutive subscripted variables, from the lowest dimensioned subscript to the highest dimensioned subscript, the following abbreviated form of the implied DO may be used:

```
          REAL X(10)
          READ *, X
```

Notice that the READ statement contains only the variable which represents the name of the array. When the READ statement is executed, data values (exactly the correct number must be supplied) will be assigned in consecutive fashion to each subscripted variable of array X, from X(1) to X(10). Similarly, we may write the statement PRINT *, X which will print *each* element of the stored array, in sequential fashion, from X(1) to X(10).

Short Form of the Implied DO

Syntax: READ *, *array name*   or   PRINT *, *array name*
Effect: To consecutively store or print each element of the array, beginning with the variable having the lowest subscript value and ending with the highest subscripted variable. This form can be used only when the entire array is to be read or printed.

7.6 Multidimensional Arrays

A list of numbers can be represented by an array variable having a single subscript that indicates the position that a particular array element occupies in the stored list. Arrays defined in terms of one subscript are referred to as *one-dimensional* arrays. Arrays defined in terms of more than one subscript are called *multidimensional* arrays.

A table of values cannot be represented by a one-dimensional array. For instance, consider Table 7.4, which gives three exam scores for each of five students.

Table 7.4 Exam Scores for Five Students

	Student ID	Exam 1	Exam 2	Exam 3
	1234	84	67	89
	4536	76	87	92
Rows	3890	73	68	81
	1987	93	88	90
	5466	86	79	85

Columns

To reference a particular element of the table, we need to specify the horizontal row number *and* the vertical column number. An array may be defined in terms of more than one subscript. Table 7.4, for example, could be stored in an array $A(I, J)$, where I represents the row number and J indicates the column number. The value of $A(2, 4)$, for example, is 92 since this element occupies the position determined by the intersection of the second row and the fourth column. An array that is defined in terms of two subscripts is called a *two-dimensional* array. While most versions of Fortran limit arrays to those having a maximum of three subscript variables, Fortran 77 permits the use of arrays having up to seven subscript variables.

EXAMPLE 7.15   Refer to Table 7.4 in completing the following problems. Assume that the contents of the table are stored as a two-dimensional array using the array variable A and that the first subscript represents the row number and the second subscript corresponds to the column number.

(a) What are the values of $A(2, 3)$ and $A(3, 2)$?

(b) Name the subscripted variable that stores the score for Exam 1 for the student whose ID number is 5466.

(c) Explain the purpose and determine the output of the following program segment:

```
    DO 50 J = 2, 4
         KSUM = KSUM + A(2, J)
 50 CONTINUE
    X = KSUM / 3.0
    PRINT *, X
```

(d) Write a program segment that displays the contents of the array in a table-like format.

Solutions

(a) $A(2, 3) = 87$ and $A(3, 2) = 73$.

(b) $A(5, 2)$.

(c) The subscript variable J represents the column number, which varies in the DO loop from $J = 2$ (Exam 1) to $J = 4$ (Exam 3), while the row number (2) remains constant. Thus, the DO loop finds the sum of the exam scores for the student whose ID number is 4536. After leaving the DO loop, the sum is divided by 3 and the result is assigned to variable X, which therefore represents the average exam score for this student.

(d) Printing the contents of an array in a table-like arrangement can be accomplished easily by using the implied DO loop construction, in which the DO-variable in the implied DO represents the column number. By using an outer DO loop to control the row number, the implied DO may be utilized to print each horizontal line of the stored table in succession. To increase program clarity, IROW and JCOL are used as subscripts.

```
*       HOLD THE ROW NUMBER FIXED
        DO 50 IROW = 1, 5
*. . . . .PRINT A HORIZONTAL LINE
           PRINT *, ( A(IROW, JCOL), JCOL = 1,4)
    50 CONTINUE
```

When the DO statement is executed initially, the value of IROW is set at 1. The implied DO in the PRINT statement directs the computer to print the values of $A(1, 1)$, $A(1, 2)$, $A(1, 3)$, and $A(1, 4)$ horizontally. During the next execution of the explicit DO statement, the value of

IROW is incremented to 2. The implied DO then displays the values of A(2, 1), A(2, 2), A(2, 3), and A(2, 4) horizontally across the next consecutive print line. The process continues for IROW = 3, 4, and 5.

Let's consider how to store a two-dimensional array. There are several ways in which this may be accomplished. The method used must be consistent with the manner in which the input data are prepared and arranged for entry to the computer. For our purposes let's assume that the data to be stored as array K are obtained from a table that consists of two rows and four columns, as in Table 7.5.

Table 7.5 Data Elements for Array K

Memory Cell	K(1, 1)	K(1, 2)	K(1, 3)	K(1, 4)	} Row 1
Data Value	8	29	17	65	
Memory Cell	K(2, 1)	K(2, 2)	K(2, 3)	K(2, 4)	} Row 2
Data Value	34	198	74	40	

Column 1   Column 2   Column 3   Column 4

Note the following:

1. *A single data value appears on each data record.*

   If the data are organized into a series of eight data records such that each record contains a single value, then each data record corresponds to a single array element. If the data records are arranged so that the data appear in the order

   8
   29
   17
   65
   34
   198
   74
   40

   then the corresponding program segment that stores these elements as array K is

```
      INTEGER K(2, 4), IROW, JCOL
*     KEEP ROW NUMBER FIXED
      DO 50 IROW = 1, 2
*. . . .STORE DATA ROW BY ROW
         DO 75 JCOL = 1, 4
            READ *, K(IROW, JCOL)
50       CONTINUE
75 CONTINUE
```

   The following set of READ statements performs the same function as the nested DO loop in the preceding program segment:

```
      READ *, K(1, 1)
      READ *, K(1, 2)
      READ *, K(1, 3)
      READ *, K(1, 4)
      READ *, K(2, 1)
      READ *, K(2, 2)
      READ *, K(2, 3)
      READ *, K(2, 4)
```

2. *A row of data values appears on each data record.*

   If the data are organized into two data records such that each data record contains a row of four data values:

8, 29, 17, 65
34, 198, 74, 40

then the following program segment may be used to store the data as array K:

```
      INTEGER K(2, 4), IROW, JCOL
*   . . .KEEP ROW NUMBER FIXED
      DO 50 IROW = 1, 2
*   . . . . .READ AN ENTIRE ROW OF THE TABLE
          READ *, ( K(IROW, JCOL), JCOL = 1, 4)
   50 CONTINUE
```

The following set of READ statements has the same effect as the preceding program segment:

```
READ *, K(1, 1), K(1, 2), K(1, 3), K(1, 4)
READ *, K(2, 1), K(2, 2), K(2, 3), K(2, 4)
```

3. *Data are recorded consecutively on the input data record(s).*
   Sometimes it is convenient to arrange the data serially as a stream of values. In our present example the data would occupy a single data record:

8, 29, 17, 65, 34, 198, 74, 40

In this situation, the execution of the READ statement and the associated variable assignments may be controlled by a *nested* implied DO loop. The following READ statement would accomplish the desired input operation:

```
READ *,((K(IROW, JCOL),JCOL = 1,4),IROW = 1,2)
```

The components of the nested implied DO are identified in Figure 7.4.

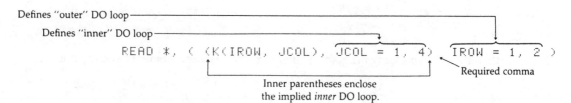

Figure 7.4 Components of a Nested Implied DO

The variable JCOL serves as the "inner" DO-variable and varies more rapidly than the "outer" DO-variable IROW. When the statement is first executed, the value of the outer DO-variable IROW is set at 1 and remains fixed, while the inner DO-variable JCOL ranges in value from 1 to 4. Control then passes to the outer DO so that the value of IROW is incremented to 2. The inner DO-variable again takes on values from 1 to 4. The READ statement in Figure 7.4, which includes the nested implied DO, is equivalent to the following READ statement:

```
READ *, K(1,1), K(1,2), K(1,3), K(1,4),
        K(2, 1), K(2,2), K(2,3), K(2,4)
```

When constructing an implied DO in an input/output statement, keep in mind that the DO list closest to the array variable represents the DO-variable and the range of the *inner* DO loop and varies more rapidly than the subscript furthest from the array name, which represents the DO-variable of the outer DO loop. Also note that the array variable and the expression that defines the inner DO must be enclosed within the same pair of inner parentheses. A comma is used to separate this parenthesized expression from the expression that defines the outer DO loop.

The short form of the implied DO may also be used to input and output multidimensional arrays. In the short form, only the array name is listed in the input or output statement. If, as in the preceding examples, the statement `INTEGER K(2, 4)` is used to define an array K, then the statement

```
READ *, K
```

can be used to store the data table shown as Table 7.5.

There is an important consideration when using this abbreviated form of the implied DO: elements are read and printed in *column* order. When using this form, the data would have to be arranged on the data record as follows:

8, 34, 29, 198, 17, 74, 65, 40

The statement `READ *, K` is equivalent to the statement

```
READ *, K(1, 1), K(2,1), K(1,2), K(2,2),
          K(1,3), K(2,3), K(1,4), K(2,4)
```

EXAMPLE 7.16 Write a PRINT statement using a nested implied DO that is equivalent to the statement

```
PRINT *, X
```

where X is defined as an array having three rows and five columns.
Solution

When the short form of the implied DO is used in a PRINT statement, the output is produced in *column* order so that the short-form PRINT statement is equivalent to

```
PRINT *, X(1, 1), X(2, 1), X(3, 1), X(1, 2),
          X(2, 2), . . . ,X(3, 5)
```

This may be expressed using the following nested implied DO:

```
PRINT *, ( X(IROW, JCOL), IROW = 1, 3), JCOL = 1, 5)
```

EXAMPLE 7.17 Rewrite each of the following statements without using implied DO loops:
(a) `READ (5, 100) ( A(M, N), M = 2, 3), N = 4, 5)`
(b) `WRITE (6, 200) ( (X(I, J), I = J + 1, 4), J = 1, 2)`
(c) `PRINT, '(1X, 3I12)', ( (J(K, L), L = 2, 4), K = 1, 2)`

Solutions

(a) `READ (5, 100) A(2, 4), A(3, 4), A(2, 5), A(3, 5)`
(b) `WRITE (6, 200) X(2, 1), X(3, 1), X(4, 1), X(3, 2), X(4, 2)`
(c) Three horizontal print fields are specified by the format editor descriptor 3I12. As a result:

```
PRINT, '(1X, 3I12)', J(1, 2), J(1, 3), J(1, 4)
PRINT, '(1X, 3I12)', J(2, 2), J(2, 3), J(2, 4)
```

EXAMPLE 7.18 Using the data in Table 7.4, write a program that computes each student's average and determines which student obtained the highest average. In addition, print the average for each exam.

Solution

See Program 7.10.

```
* THIS PROGRAM CREATES A TWO DIMENSIONAL ARRAY AND ACCESSES THAT ARRAY TO
* GENERATE A REPORT
* A MAXIMUM OF 50 STUDENTS IN A FORTRAN CLASS TAKE THREE EXAMS.
* THE PROGRAM COMPUTES EACH STUDENT'S AVERAGE AND DETERMINES WHICH STUDENT
* OBTAINED THE HIGHEST AVERAGE. IN ADDITION THE PROGRAM COMPUTES THE AVERAGE
* FOR EACH TEST
*
* THIS PROGRAM WAS RUN ON A PRIME 850 COMPUTER USING FORTRAN 77
*
         INTEGER A(50, 4)
*
* INITIALIZE HIGH
       HIGH = 0.0
*
* DETERMINE NUMBER OF STUDENTS IN THE CLASS
       READ *, N
*
* READ VALUES INTO THE ARRAY
       DO 30 I = 1, N
       READ *, (A(I, J), J = 1, 4)
   30 CONTINUE
*
* FIND THE AVERAGE FOR EACH STUDENT AND THE STUDENT WITH THE HIGHEST AVERAGE
       DO 90 I = 1, 5
           TOTAL = 0.0
           DO 80 J = 2, 4
               TOTAL = TOTAL + A(I, J)
   80      CONTINUE
           AVG = TOTAL / 3
           PRINT *,'THE AVERAGE FOR STUDENT NUMBER ', A(I, 1), '=', AVG
           IF (AVG .GT. HIGH) THEN
*. . . . . . . .THE VARIABLE HIGH IS USED TO STORE THE HIGHEST AVERAGE AND
*. . . . . . . .THE VARIABLE IHIGH IS USED TO STORE THE NUMBER OF THE STUDENT
*. . . . . . . .WITH THE HIGHEST AVERAGE
               HIGH = AVG
               IHIGH = I
           ENDIF
   90 CONTINUE
       PRINT *, ' '
       PRINT *, ' '
       PRINT *,'THE STUDENT WITH THE HIGHEST AVERAGE IS STUDENT NUMBER '
      -, A(IHIGH, 1)
       PRINT *, 'THE HIGHEST AVERAGE IS ', HIGH
       PRINT *, ' '
       PRINT *, ' '
*
* FIND THE AVERAGE FOR EACH TEST
       DO 100 J = 2, 4
           TOTAL = 0.0
           DO 110 I = 1, N
               TOTAL = TOTAL + A(I, J)
  110      CONTINUE
           AVERAGE = TOTAL / N
           PRINT *, 'AVERAGE FOR TEST', J - 1, '= ', AVERAGE
  100 CONTINUE
       STOP
       END
```

Program 7.10.

Output:

```
    THE AVERAGE FOR STUDENT NUMBER        1234=    80.0000
    THE AVERAGE FOR STUDENT NUMBER        4536=    85.0000
    THE AVERAGE FOR STUDENT NUMBER        3890=    74.0000
    THE AVERAGE FOR STUDENT NUMBER        1987=    90.3333
    THE AVERAGE FOR STUDENT NUMBER        5466=    83.3333


    THE STUDENT WITH THE HIGHEST AVERAGE IS STUDENT NUMBER          1987
    THE HIGHEST AVERAGE IS     90.3333

    AVERAGE FOR TEST          1=    82.4000
    AVERAGE FOR TEST          2=    77.8000
    AVERAGE FOR TEST          3=    87.4000
    **** STOP
```

7.7 The DATA and PARAMETER Statements

THE DATA STATEMENT

A READ statement supplies data to program variables when an input operation is performed *during program execution*. A DATA statement provides a means by which data can be "built into" the program at the time the program is written. For example, the following program segment uses a DATA statement to incorporate the initial values of the elements of the array AGE within the program itself:

```
      INTEGER AGE(10)
 DATA←──────DATA AGE /32, 52, 24, 18, 30, 41, 21, 29, 32, 39/
statement                      Data values are enclosed
                               by a pair of slashes.
```

The data assignments AGE(1) = 32, AGE(2) = 52, AGE(3) = 24, and so on, are made *during program compilation*. A DATA statement is particularly useful for establishing values of constants and for initializing the values of program variables such as counters. Some common forms that the DATA statement may take are illustrated in Table 7.6.

EXAMPLE 7.19 Write a DATA statement that accomplishes the same function as the following program segment:

```
          DO 50 K = 1, 25
              X(K) = 0.0
       50 CONTINUE
```

Solution

```
      DATA (X(K), K = 1, 25) / 25 * 0.0 /
```

THE PARAMETER STATEMENT

Fortran 77 provides a convenient facility by which a constant value may be referenced in a program by a programmer-determined symbolic name. The PARAMETER statement

```
      PARAMETER (PI = 3.1415926)
```

defines the symbolic name PI to be equal to the constant value 3.1415926. The PARAMETER statement is another example of a nonexecutable program statement and therefore must be placed before all executable program statements (and before any nonexecutable program statements that make use of the PARAMETER statement).

One common use of the PARAMETER statement is to establish the size of an array. For example, consider the following set of declaration statements:

```
      INTEGER K, L, N
      REAL ALPHA, BETA(100), GAMMA
        .  .  .
      DO 50 K = 1, 100
         READ *, BETA(K)
        .  .  .
        .  .  .
```

Table 7.6 Some DATA Statements and Their Interpretations

DATA Statement	Interpretation
`DATA KOUNT /0/, PI /3.141593/`	The value of KOUNT is set at 0, and the value of PI is set at 3.141593, during program compilation.
`DATA KOUNT, PI /0, 3.141593/`	Same as above.
`DATA NAME /'LAWRENCE S. LEFF'/`	The string variable NAME is assigned the character value LAWRENCE S. LEFF during program compilation.
`INTEGER KOUNT(12)` `DATA KOUNT / 12 * 0 /`	An array KOUNT is defined to have 12 elements. The DATA statement stores a 0 in each of the 12 elements.
`INTEGER KOUNT(12)` `DATA (KOUNT(I), I = 7, 12) / 6 * 0 /`	An implied DO is used in the DATA statement (this is *not* permitted in some implementations of Fortran). The DATA statement stores a 0 in the elements KOUNT(7), KOUNT(8), . . . , KOUNT(12).
`REAL SUM1, SUM2, ARRAY(50)` `DATA SUM1, SUM2, ARRAY / 52 * 0.0 /`	SUM1 and SUM2 are real variables, and ARRAY is defined as a real array having a size of 50. The DATA statement initializes the values of SUM1, SUM2, and each of the 50 elements of ARRAY at 0.

Array BETA contains a maximum of 100 elements. It would not be unusual for there to be several places in the program where the processing is based on the number 100. For example, the range of the DO-variable in the DO loop that inputs elements of array BETA is defined in terms of this value. Suppose that the program is to be modified so that the array may now store 150 elements. This increase would necessitate changes being initiated in *several* places in the program. Alternatively, a PARAMETER statement can be used to establish the size of an array:

```
INTEGER K, L, N, SUB
PARAMETER (SUB = 100)
REAL ALPHA, BETA(SUB), GAMMA
    . . .
DO 50 K = 1, SUB
    READ *, BETA(K)
    . . .
    . . .
```

The DATA Statement

The DATA statement is a nonexecutable statement that appears in a program between the set of data and array declaration statements and the set of executable program statements. It informs the Fortran compiler that a specified set of constant values is to be assigned to a corresponding set of program variable names. The variables are assigned these values during program compilation rather than during program execution.

DATA statements are particularly useful for the following purposes:

- assigning values to variable names whose values then remain fixed throughout program execution
- initializing the values of variable counters and accumulators

Syntax: D A T A *variable /constant/, variable /constant/, . . .*

or

D A T A *variable list /constant list/*

Note: The *variable list* may include:

- unsubscripted and subscripted variable names
- array names (which imply that *each* element of the array is to be assigned a constant)
- implied DO loops (which can be used to specify a selected sequence of elements within an array)

The *constant list:*

- must contain constant values that agree in type and number with the corresponding variables
- may contain constants expressed in the form n * value, where n is a positive integer that indicates the number of times the value is to be used for variable assignments

If the size of the array has to be changed, then only a single statement (the PARAMETER statement) will require modification (provided, of course, that throughout the program the dimensioned size of the array is referred to as SUB rather than as 100). Keep in mind that the value of a variable specified in the PARAMETER statement cannot be adjusted during program execution.

7.8 Some Closing Remarks

In this chapter we examined how a single variable name (called an *array*) could be used to refer to an entire list of data values (a one-dimensional array) or to a table of values that uses a row and column format (a two-dimensional array). Individual array elements can be referenced by writing the array name followed by a subscript that indicates the position of the element in the list or table. Array elements that represent a table value must be described by two subscript values: the first represents the row number, and the second gives the column number.

Forgetting to declare an array, using illegal subscript values, exceeding the declared size of an array, and attempting to store a value of a different type from that of the array are common programming errors.

Unlike earlier versions of Fortran, Fortran 77 permits integer subscripts having values less than 1. It also allows the size of an array to be specified in terms of an upper and a lower bound. The statement

```
INTEGER ZIPCOD (11200 : 11299)
```

defines the array ZIPCOD to have integer elements, and the subscripts to range in value from 11200 to 11299, inclusive. The number of elements in the array may be calculated by finding the difference between the upper and lower bounds and then adding 1: $11299 - 11200 + 1 = 100$.

Sorting represents an important application of subscripted variables. In addition to numeric data, alphanumeric data may also be sorted (for example, alphabetizing can be done). This will be discussed in Chapter 8, which discusses character data manipulation in detail.

The inclusion of an implied DO loop in a READ statement allows input data to be prepared using a minimum number of physical data records. Rather than entering each data array element on a separate data record, data values may be entered on the same physical data record, with successive data items separated by a comma or blank space. It is usually convenient to use an implied DO to store a two-dimensional array by entering the table data by row, with each data record corresponding to a row of table values.

An implied DO in a list-directed PRINT statement allows the contents of an array to be printed horizontally across the print page. Output is also produced horizontally when an implied DO is used in a format-directed output statement that defines the print fields with the help of a repetition factor. Similarly, data are read horizontally across a data record when an implied DO is used in a format-directed READ statement whose corresponding format statement includes a repetition factor in its specification of the input field.

The DATA and PARAMETER statements were introduced as programming aids. Both are nonexecutable program statements. The DATA statement is particularly useful for initializing the values of program variables such as counters, summers, and array elements. The PARAMETER statement can be used to define a constant value that will be used in a program by introducing a symbolic name. When it is anticipated that the size of an array may change, the PARAMETER statement may be used to help define the size of an array. If the size of the array changes, only the PARAMETER statement needs modification.

Review Exercises

A star preceding the number of a problem indicates that a solution to that problem is given at the back of the book.

* **1.** Rewrite each of the following statements without using an implied DO loop:
  (a) `READ *, ( A(J), J = 1, 9, 2)`
  (b) `READ(5, 100) (C, D(K), K = 1, 3)`
  (c) `READ(5, 100) C, ( D(K), K = 1, 3)`
  (d) `READ(5, 100) ( D(K), K = 1, 3), C`
  (e) `PRINT *, ( P(J), A, Q(J), J = 3, 5)`
  (f) `PRINT *, ( A(3 * K + 1), K = 1, 3)`
  (g) `READ , '(5F9.4)', ( X(K), K = 1, 10)`
  (h) `PRINT , '(1X, 4I9)', ( N(I, J), J = 2, 5), I = 1, 2)`
  (i) `PRINT *, ( Z(K, L), K = 1, 5, 2), L = 5, 6)`

* **2.** Rewrite each of the following input/output statements using an implied DO loop:
  (a) `INTEGER X(10)`
      `READ *, X`
  (b) `PRINT *, Y(2), Y(4), Y(6), Y(8), Y(10), Y(12)`
  (c) `PRINT *, A, Z(1), A, Z(3), A, Z(5), A, Z(7)`

* **3.** Rewrite each of the following input/output statements using a nested implied DO loop:
  (a) `REAL A(3, 5)`
      `READ *, A`
  (b) `PRINT *, Z, B(2, 7), B(2, 8), B(3, 7), B(3, 8)`
  (c) `PRINT *, Z, B(2,7), Z, B(2, 8), Z, B(3, 7), Z, B(3, 8)`

* **4.** An integer array GAMMA contains 20 elements. Write a Fortran program segment designed to accomplish (a) through (h):
  *(a) replaces every element with its absolute value.
  (b) prints the value of each array variable having an odd-valued subscript.

*(c) initializes each element of the array at 0.

(d) reads in another integer array, KLONE, which has 20 elements, and determines whether the two arrays are identical.

*(e) creates a second array, DELTA, whose elements consists of those elements of GAMMA that have values between 0 and 65, and prints the contents of DELTA using an implied DO.

(f) reads in an integer value and determines the number of times this value occurs in array GAMMA.

*(g) constructs and then prints a new array formed by interchanging the contents of GAMMA(1) and GAMMA(20), GAMMA(2) and GAMMA(19), and so on.

(h) uses the subscripted variable KOUNT(GAMMA(I)) to determine the number of 1's, 2's, 3's, 4's, and 5's contained in array GAMMA. (Assume that the elements of array GAMMA consist only of whole numbers between 1 and 5, inclusive.)

5. ALPHA is a two-dimensional array defined by the statement `INTEGER ALPHA(10, 10)`. Assume data is gathered from a table consisting of 10 rows and 10 columns. Write a Fortran program segment that uses a DO loop to accomplish each of the following:

    (a) prints the value of every subscripted variable of ALPHA in which the row number and the column number are the same (ALPHA(1, 1), ALPHA(2, 2), . . . , ALPHA(10, 10)).

    *(b) calculates and prints the sum of the elements that correspond to the fourth column of the data table.

    (c) calculates and prints the average of the elements that correspond to the seventh row of the data table.

    *(d) exchanges, in sequence, each element of the second row with each element of the ninth column. For example, the first exchange should occur between ALPHA(2, 1) and ALPHA(1, 9), the second between ALPHA(2, 2) and ALPHA(2, 9), and so on.

* 6. A list of integer values ends with a trailer value of -999. Store the list as an array. Without sorting the array, determine the position number of the largest data value in the original list. Print the original array, the value of the largest data value in the list, and its position number. (Assume that the list consists of a maximum of 100 values.)

7–23. Write a Fortran program that satisfies the conditions of each problem. Whenever appropriate, make up your own sample test data.

7. Read a data list into real ARRAY1. Construct an integer array, ARRAY2, by applying the following rule: If an element of ARRAY1 is less than 0, then assign -1 to the corresponding element of ARRAY2; if an element of ARRAY1 is equal to 0, then assign 0 to the corresponding element of ARRAY2; if an element of ARRAY1 is greater than 0, then assign $+1$ to the corresponding element of ARRAY2. Print the elements of ARRAY1 and ARRAY2 horizontally using an implied DO. Assume that the original data list contains fewer than 100 values and ends with a trailer value of -999.9.

* 8. Another well-known sorting algorithm is the *bubble* sort, which is based on comparing adjacent elements of an array in succession. To sort an array having N elements into ascending order, you must compare X(1) with X(2), X(2) with X(3), X(3) with X(4), and so forth. If, for any comparison, X(I) is greater than X(I + 1), the contents of these variables are switched. After the first pass the largest valued element of the list will have been "bubbled up" to the array variable having the highest valued subscript. Repeat this procedure using the first N − 1 elements. The array is sorted when no exchanges are made in a given pass.

9. Read a list of N whole numbers, where N is the first data item in the list. Store the even numbers in one array and the odd numbers in another array. Print the elements of each array horizontally across the print line. (You may assume that N is less than or equal to 25.)

*10. Using the flowchart presented in Figure 7.3 as a guide, prepare a Fortran program that performs a binary search.

*11. This sequence of numbers:

$$1, 1, 2, 3, 5, 8, 13, 21, \ . \ . \ .$$

is called a *Fibonacci sequence*. Each term, beginning with the third term (2), represents the sum of the preceding two terms. Write a program that generates the first 20 terms of the Fibonacci sequence horizontally on the print line.

12. Read a series of 25 numbers into an array. Print the value that is closest to the average of the list.

13. Read a list having N elements that has already been sorted in ascending order into an array A. Read in another value X and *insert* it into its proper position in the sorted array (do *not* resort the entire list of numbers). Accomplish this by comparing the number X with each element of the array, working from the highest valued subscript to the lowest. In other words, begin by comparing X with A(N). If X is less than A(N), then move A(N) to A(N + 1). Next, compare X with A(N − 1), and so on. The value X is inserted into its proper position when X is greater than or equal to A(I). Assume that the number of elements N is less than or equal to 50.

14. A sequence of numbers is *monotone increasing* if each member is greater than the number that immediately precedes it. Read into an array a list of whole numbers that is preceded by a header label. Determine the greatest number of consecutive terms in the array for which the resulting sequence of numbers is monotone increasing. For example, in the data list

10 (header value), 8, 11, 13, 9, 19, 23, 31, 28, 17, 35

the greatest number of terms for which the list is monotone increasing is four (9, 19, 23, and 31). Assume that the list contains a maximum of 100 values.

15. A data list consists of a series of student ID numbers, with each ID number followed by the student's numeric grade average. Store the ID numbers of only those students who have averages of 90 or greater in one array, and their averages in the corresponding elements of a second array. Print, in table form, an honor roll list consisting of the students' ID numbers and grade averages. The averages should be printed in descending order, from the highest average to the lowest qualifying average. Assume from past experience that the honor roll will contain a maximum of 150 students.

16. Read a list of 20 whole numbers into an array. The list may contain repetitions of the same integer value. Print, in table form, a list that consists of every distinct value in the list and its *frequency* (that is, the number of times the value appears in the list).

17. Modify Problem 16 so that, after the original array is printed, a second array is printed with all repetitions of a given value deleted. The contents of each array should be printed horizontally.

*18. Your job is to prepare a program that grades test answers that are suitably coded for computer input. The exam consists of 15 "true/false" types of questions. A student enters the digit 0 to indicate a false response, and the digit 1 to specify a true response. The instructor provides an answer key that is read and stored in array ANS. Process a class set of exam score data records. Each data record contains a student ID number followed by 15 "true/false" answers (use an implied DO to read the data). Store the student ID in an array and the number of correct answers as the corresponding element in another array. Print the test results in ascending ID number order.

   Assume that the class has a maximum of 40 students. The data record having an ID number of 9999 represents a trailer record. Your program should include a data validation routine.

*19. Read a sorted list of integer values having N elements into an array ALPHA. Read a second sorted list of integer values having M elements (M being less than N) into an array BETA. Assume that both arrays are sorted in ascending order. *Merge* the two arrays into a single array that is sorted in ascending sequence. Do *not* simply append array BETA to array ALPHA and then sort the combined list. Instead, selectively take elements of ALPHA and BETA so that the new array is sorted in the same sequence as the original arrays. (See the illustration that accompanies this problem.)

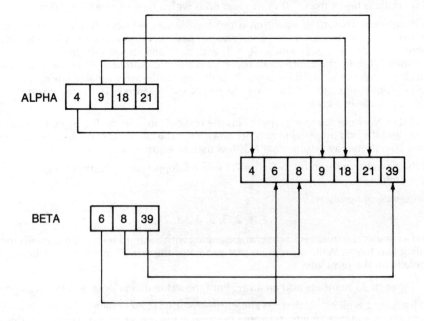

20. The sieve of Eratosthenes provides a method by which a list of prime numbers greater than 2 can be generated. The algorithm does *not* depend on testing for the divisibility of possible factors of a given number. Instead, the method is based on filling an array with consecutive whole numbers from 1 to

the last value of the interval under consideration and then blanking out the values of array elements that are multiples of previously listed values. This can be accomplished as follows:

1. Initialize an array, say PRIME(I), so that each element contains a zero.
2. Fill array PRIME with numbers such that PRIME(I) = I for all odd integer values of I from 3 to N, where N represents the end value of the interval being considered.
3. Identify all array elements greater than 3 that store an integer multiple of 3, and destroy the contents of those array variables by assigning a value of zero to them.
4. Identify all array elements greater than 5 that store an integer multiple of 5, and destroy the contents of those array variables by assigning a value of zero to them. Repeat for 7, 9, 11, . . . up to the square root of N.

At the end of this process, each nonzero array element will be a prime number.

Translate this algorithm into a Fortran coded program that generates and prints all prime numbers (using an implied DO) from 1 to 400.

*21. Read a binary number, assuming that the binary digits are entered individually as data and are stored in an integer array BINARY. Print the binary number so that its digits appear intact, one adjacent to the other. Also print the base-10 equivalent of the binary number. Assume that the binary number contains a maximum of 12 binary digits and that a trailer value is used in the input operation.

22. In mathematics a rectangular array of elements consisting of m rows and n columns is called an $m \times n$ matrix:

$$\text{matrix } \mathbf{A} = \begin{pmatrix} a_{11} & a_{12} & a_{13} & \cdots & a_{1n} \\ a_{21} & a_{22} & a_{23} & \cdots & a_{2n} \\ \cdot & & & & \\ \cdot & & & & \\ \cdot & & & & \\ a_{m1} & a_{m2} & a_{m3} & \cdots & a_{mn} \end{pmatrix}$$

where a_{ij} is the array element that occupies the ith row and jth column.

If two matrices have the same number of rows and the same number of columns, they are said to have the same *dimension*. Two matrices may be added (or subtracted) provided that they have the same dimension. If **A** and **B** are two matrices having the same dimension, then their sum is a matrix, say **C**, that has the same dimension and whose elements are found by adding corresponding elements of **A** and **B**:

$$c_{ij} = a_{ij} + b_{ij}$$

for all i, $1 \le i \le n$, and all j, $1 \le j \le n$. For example, if

$$\mathbf{A} = \begin{pmatrix} 5 & 9 \\ 3 & 0 \end{pmatrix} \quad \text{and} \quad \mathbf{B} = \begin{pmatrix} 1 & -1 \\ 4 & 2 \end{pmatrix}$$

then

$$\mathbf{C} = \mathbf{A} + \mathbf{B} = \begin{pmatrix} 5+1 & 9+(-1) \\ 3+4 & 0+2 \end{pmatrix} = \begin{pmatrix} 6 & 8 \\ 7 & 2 \end{pmatrix}$$

Write a program that inputs two matrices having the same dimension and outputs the elements of the matrix that is the sum of the original matrices.

23. If **A** is an $m \times p$ matrix and **B** is a $p \times n$ matrix, then the produt of **A** and **B**, denoted as **AB**, is the $m \times n$ matrix **C**, whose elements are calculated by multiplying the elements in row i of **A** by the elements in column j of **B**, so that

$$c_{ij} = a_{i1}b_{1j} + a_{i2}b_{2j} + a_{i3}b_{3j} + \cdots + a_{ik}b_{kj}$$

for all $1 \le i \le m$ and $1 \le j \le n$. For example, if

$$\mathbf{A} = \begin{pmatrix} 8 & 1 \\ 10 & 3 \\ 2 & 0 \end{pmatrix} \quad \text{and} \quad \mathbf{B} = \begin{pmatrix} 5 & -2 & 1 & 0 \\ 4 & 0 & 3 & 6 \end{pmatrix}$$

then

$$c_{11} = 8(5) \quad + 1(4) = 40 \quad + 4 \ = 44$$
$$c_{12} = 8(-2) + 1(0) = -16 + 0 \quad = -16$$
$$\cdot$$
$$\cdot$$
$$\cdot$$
$$c_{21} = 10(5) \quad + 3(4) = 50 \quad + 12 = 62$$

$$c_{21} = 10(5) + 2(4) = 50 + 8 = 58$$

$$c_{31} = 2(5) + 0(4) = 10 + 0 = 10$$

$$c_{34} = 2(0) + 0(6) = 0 + 0 = 0$$

Write a program that inputs an $m \times p$ matrix, say **A**, and inputs a $p \times n$ matrix, say **B**, and prints the $m \times n$ matrix that is their product.

CHAPTER 8
Character and Logical Data

COMPUTER AXIOM

Meaningful data come in many different forms: numbers, letters, special characters, and combinations of these.

COROLLARY

The laws of physics require that computers represent all types of data in their internal memory in numeric form as sequences of binary digits. By working with these binary coded values, computers are able to manipulate and process alphanumeric data.

8.1 Character Data

Recall from Chapter 2 that character (or string) data consist of combinations of digits, letters, and special symbols (including blanks). The number of characters in a string is referred to as the *length* of the character string. The length of the character data item `'COMPUTERS ARE DUMB'` is 18 (16 letters plus 2 blank spaces). When declaring a character variable, the maximum length of the string that the variable may represent must also be specified. On many computer systems, the greatest number of characters that a string may be declared to have is 256.

Table 8.1 gives some illustrations of character data declaration statements.

Table 8.1 Some Character Data Declaration Statements and Their Interpretations

Character Data Declaration	Interpretation
`CHARACTER NAME * 15, ADRESS * 24`	NAME and ADRESS are character (string) variables that may represent strings having maximum lengths of 15 and 24 characters, respectively.
`CHARACTER SEX`	The string variable SEX represents a string having exactly 1 character. In general, if the length of a character variable is omitted, it is interpreted as 1.
`CHARACTER * 10, A, B, C`	The character variables A, B, and C each store a string having a maximum of 10 characters.
`CHARACTER ALPHA(100) * 12`	An *array* ALPHA is declared that has a maximum size of 100 elements. Each array element may store a string having a maximum of 12 characters.

Let's consider how the following character data assignments will be handled by a computer:

```
CHARACTER COLOR(4) * 5
DATA COLOR /'RED', 'BLUE', 'LAVENDER', 'BLACK'/
```

_____

_____

_____

During program compilation, the character strings listed in the DATA statement will be assigned in sequence to COLOR(1), COLOR(2), COLOR(3), and COLOR(4). The storage of these character variables in computer memory may be pictured as follows:

Computer Memory

	1	2	3	4	5
COLOR(1)	R	E	D		
COLOR(2)	B	L	U	E	
COLOR(3)	L	A	V	E	N
COLOR(4)	B	L	A	C	K

Notice that, if the length of the character string is less than the declared length of the string, then the character string is stored (and printed) left-justified, with blanks entered in the rightmost unused positions. If, however, the length of the character string exceeds the declared length of the string, then the rightmost "extra" characters of the string are truncated so that the string "fits" into its allocated storage location.

Declaring a Character Array

An array whose elements are character strings may be declared using the CHARACTER data type declaration statement:

`CHARACTER` *array name* (size) * *length*

where *length* refers to the maximum number of characters that can be assigned to each array element. The maximum number of elements in the array is defined by the *size*.

8.2 Comparing Character Strings

In Chapter 1 we mentioned briefly that all data must be reduced to sequences of binary digits (1's and 0's) when stored in computer memory. It is possible to compare the stored (that is, binary) values of any pair of characters. For example, in one popular coding system, the letters "A" and "B" are represented as sequences of eight binary digits:

$$A = 1\,1\,0\,0\,0\,0\,0\,1$$
$$B = 1\,1\,0\,0\,0\,0\,1\,0$$

Since the binary coded value of A is less than the binary coded value of B, the character 'A' is considered to be "less than" the character 'B'.

In general, the system that a computer uses to organize characters in ascending numeric sequence based on their binary coded stored values is referred to as a *collating sequence*. Although collating sequences generally vary from one Fortran compiler to another, all share the following features:

- Beginning with the letter "A," each succeeding letter is represented by a greater binary number than the preceding letter. Hence:

'A' .LT. 'B' .LT. 'C' .LT. 'D' . . . .LT. 'Z'

- Beginning with the digit 0, each succeeding digit is represented by a greater binary number than the preceding digit. Hence:

'0' .LT. '1' .LT. '2' .LT. '3' . . . .LT. '9' . . .

- The binary representation of a blank has a smaller value than the binary representation of the letter "A" and the digit 0. Consequently:

' ' .LT. 'A'   and   ' ' .LT. '0'

A blank is therefore evaluated as "less than" each letter and each digit.

All Fortran compilers yield the same results when comparing strings that contain all letters or all digits. When character strings contain only letters, the rules for determining their order (less than or greater than) are the same as the rules for determining the order of words in a dictionary. For example, since the string 'BAR' comes *before* 'BUS' in a dictionary, we may conclude that the comparison

'BAR' .LT. 'BUS'

is true. Strings that include only numeric digits are ordered according to their numeric relationship. For example, the following comparison would be evaluated by the computer as true:

'111' .LT. '112'
'999' .GT. '991'

So far we have not considered the possibility that two strings may not have the same length. If two strings that are being compared do not have the same number of characters, a sufficient number of trailing blanks are appended to the shorter string so that the two strings have equal numbers of characters. To compare 'BAR' with 'BARN', the computer will pad the first string with one trailing blank *before* making the comparison. The string 'BARƀ' will then be compared with the string 'BARN', one character at a time, beginning with the leftmost character of each string. If the leftmost characters are different, then the collating sequence determines which character (and therefore which string) is greater. If the leftmost characters are identical, as in our example, then the characters in the next consecutive pair are compared. This pattern continues until the characters in a pair are different. If the two strings are identical in every character position, the strings will be evaluated as being equal. In our example the string 'BARƀ' is "less than" the string 'BARN' since the fourth character position determines the relation between the strings, and in all collating sequences a blank is "less than" a letter.

Similarly, when comparing all numeric strings that have different lengths, a sufficient number of trailing blanks are added to the shorter string so that the resulting strings have the same length. For example, in comparing '3410' with '67', the computer pads the second string with two trailing blanks *before* making the comparison. The string '3410' is then compared with the string '67ƀƀ'. The pattern of comparisons begins with the leftmost character. If they are the same, then the characters in the next consecutive pair are compared. If they are different, as in our example, then the collating sequence will determine which character (and therefore which string) is greater. Since '3' is "less than" '6', the computer considers the string '3410' to be "less than" the string '67ƀƀ'.

It becomes a tricky matter when strings containing combinations of letters, digits, and special characters must be compared. Fortran 77 does *not* include rules for making such comparisons. Thus, the result of comparing the string 'A2C' with the string 'AA3' will vary from one implementation of Fortran 77 to another. WATFIV, on the other hand, includes a specific collating sequence that standardizes the results of comparing mixed strings from one WATFIV compiler to another.

The WATFIV "dictionary" sequence is as follows:

1. a blank (the lowest valued character)
2. special characters: $(+ \$ *) - / , ' =$
3. letters in alphabetical order
4. digits in numerical order (highest valued characters)

In WATFIV the string 'A2C' would be evaluated as "greater than" 'AA3' since the second character would determine the ordering of the strings and WATFIV specifies that digits have a higher value than letters.

Table 8.2 provides some additional illustrations.

Table 8.2 Some Examples of Logical Comparisons

Logical Comparison	Result	Explanation
'ABC' .LT. 'XYZ'	True	'A' precedes 'X' in all Fortran collating sequences.
'508' .GT. '199'	True	Since the numeric strings have the same length, all Fortran collating sequences assign the greater binary value to the string having the greater numerical value.
'75' .LT. '129'	False	Since the numeric strings have different lengths, a trailing blank is added to the shorter string and the two strings are compared character by character, beginning with the leftmost character. The string '75β' is "greater than" '129' since in all collating sequences '7' is "greater than" '1'. Hence, '75' is "greater than" '129'.
'XYZ' .LT. '987'	Machine dependent	Fortran 77 does not specify the relative ordering of different character types. The results will vary among Fortran systems.
'19.84' .LT. '190.7'	Machine dependent	See above (a decimal point is being compared with a digit).
'2,001' .EQ. '2001'	Machine dependent	See above (a comma is being compared with a digit).

8.3 Logical Data

LOGICAL CONSTANTS

In addition to numeric and character data, a variable may represent *logical* data. A *logical variable* is a variable that can assume either of two logical values: .TRUE. or .FALSE. The values .TRUE. and .FALSE. are referred to as logical *constants* and must begin and end with a period. The keyword LOGICAL is used to declare logical variables.

A logical assignment statement takes this form:

logical variable = *logical* expression *or* constant

The logical constant may be either .TRUE. or .FALSE., while the logical expression may be any logical statement (comparison condition) that evaluates to either true or false. The evaluation of a logical assignment statement parallels the evaluation of an arithmetic Fortran assignment statement. The expression on the right side of the equal sign is evaluated, and the result (.TRUE. or

.FALSE.) is assigned to the memory location named by the logical variable on the left side of the equal sign.

Logical Data Declaration

Syntax: `LOGICAL` *variable list*
Example: `LOGICAL FLAG, SWITCH, STAR(10)`
Interpretation: FLAG and SWITCH are defined to be logical variables that may be assigned the value .TRUE. or .FALSE. An array STAR is defined to have a maximum of ten elements, each of which represents a logical value.

Table 8.3 illustrates the evaluation of logical assignment statements when it is assumed that the variable VALUE has been declared to be a logical variable.

Table 8.3 Some Logical Assignment Statements and Their Interpretations

Logical Assignment Statement	Interpretation
`VALUE = .TRUE.`	The logical variable VALUE is assigned the logical constant .TRUE.
`VALUE = 12 .GT. 5`	The logical expression on the right side of the equal sign is evaluated, and the result (true) is assigned to the logical variable VALUE. In other words, after this statement is executed, `VALUE = .TRUE.`
`VALUE = 'CAR' .GT. 'CART'`	The logical expression on the right side of the equal sign is evaluated, and the result is assigned to the logical variable VALUE. Since 'CAR' is "less than" 'CART' in all Fortran collating sequences, the logical constant .FALSE. is assigned to VALUE.
`VALUE = GRADE .GE. 90.0`	The logical expression is evaluated using the current value of the variable GRADE. If the result of the comparison is true, the logical constant .TRUE. is assigned to VALUE; otherwise, this variable will assume the value .FALSE.

EXAMPLE 8.1 Determine the output of the following program:

```
INTEGER K, L
CHARACTER * 12, NAME1, NAME2
LOGICAL SAME
DATA NAME1, NAME2, K, L /'JONES', 'SMITH', 0, 0/
SAME = NAME1 .EQ. NAME2
```

```
IF (SAME .EQV. .TRUE.) THEN
  K = K + 1
ELSE
  L = L + 1
ENDIF
PRINT *, SAME, K, L
STOP
END
```

Solution

When the logical assignment statement SAME = NAME1 .EQ. NAME2 is evaluated during program execution, the value .FALSE. will be assigned to the logical variable SAME since the stored values of the character variables ('JONES' and 'SMITH') are not identical.

The block IF is evaluated as follows: The condition within the parentheses in the IF statement is evaluated. Since the value of SAME is .FALSE., the IF condition evaluates as false. Program control passes to the statement in the ELSE block; the value of L is incremented by 1. The current values of the program variables SAME, K, and L are then printed:

F   0   1

Notice that a single letter is printed for the value of the logical variable. In general, the letter "T" is printed if the value of the logical variable is .TRUE. and "F" is printed if the value of the variable is .FALSE. The value of K remains initialized at 0, while the value of L was incremented during program execution from 0 to 1.

LOGICAL OPERATORS

Example 8.2 illustrates the fact that logical conditions may be established which involve the use of the logical operators .AND. and .OR. with logical variables.

EXAMPLE 8.2 Determine the output of the following program, which processes three unequal integer values. Use this data list: 9, 7, 3, 8, 19, 5, 10, 11, 12.

```
INTEGER A, B, C, I
LOGICAL COND1, COND2
DO 50 I = 1, 3
    READ *, A, B, C
    PRINT *, A, B, C
    COND1 = A .GT. B
    COND2 = A .GT. C
    IF ( COND1 .AND. COND2) THEN
        PRINT *, A, 'IS THE LARGEST'
    ELSE IF ( COND1 .OR. COND2 ) THEN
        PRINT *, A, 'IS NOT THE SMALLEST'
    ELSE
        PRINT *, A, 'IS THE SMALLEST'
    ENDIF
50 CONTINUE
    STOP
    END
```

Solution

In general, the truth or falsity of a statement that involves the logical operators .AND. and .OR. may be summarized as follows:

CONDITION1	.AND.	CONDITION2	RESULT
.TRUE.		.TRUE.	.TRUE.
.TRUE.		.FALSE.	.FALSE.
.FALSE.		.TRUE.	.FALSE.
.FALSE.		.FALSE.	.FALSE.

CONDITION1	.OR.	CONDITION2	RESULT
.TRUE.		.TRUE.	.TRUE.
.TRUE.		.FALSE.	.TRUE.
.FALSE.		.TRUE.	.TRUE.
.FALSE.		.FALSE.	.FALSE.

Let's trace the data through the program. Note that the program echo-prints the three data values.

Data Set	A	B	C	COND1	COND2	Description of Output
1	9	7	3	.TRUE.	.TRUE.	9 7 3 9 IS THE LARGEST
2	8	19	5	.FALSE.	.TRUE.	8 19 5 8 IS NOT THE SMALLEST
3	10	11	12	.FALSE.	.FALSE.	10 11 12 10 IS THE SMALLEST

COMPARING LOGICAL VARIABLES

It may be necessary to compare two logical variables. For example, if BEGIN and START are defined to be logical variables, their truth values may be compared by writing:

```
IF ( BEGIN .EQV. START ) THEN
   _____
   
   _____
```

Notice that the relational operator .EQV. is used. It is the logical equivalent of the operator .EQ. (the logical equivalent of the operator .NE. is .NEQV.).

A comparison based on whether the value of the logical variable BEGIN is .TRUE. may be expressed in one of two ways:

```
1. IF ( BEGIN ) THEN
      _____
```

```
2. IF ( BEGIN .EQV. .TRUE. ) THEN
      _____
      
      _____
```

There is also a third way of writing this type of comparison, based on using the logical .NOT. operator:

```
3. IF ( .NOT. BEGIN) THEN
   _____
   _____
```

In the first two approaches, if the value of BEGIN is .TRUE. then the condition in the IF statement evaluates as true and the set of statements contained in the IF block will be executed. In the third statement, if the value of BEGIN is *.FALSE.*, then the condition evaluates as .TRUE. since the negation (.NOT.) of .FALSE. is .TRUE. .

8.4 Using a Program Flag

The value of a logical variable may be used to indicate or *flag* a current processing condition. This may be illustrated by an enhanced version of the bubble sort program that was assigned as Exercise 8 in Chapter 7. Instead of sorting numeric data, the bubble sort algorithm is now applied to the sorting of string data; a list of ten names will be arranged in alphabetical order. Alphabetizing a list of names is directly analogous to arranging a list of numbers in ascending numerical order.

The bubble sort program (discussed in Exercise 8 of Chapter 7) is inefficient since it does not take into account the possibility that the list may be sorted before the completion of the last pass through the list. In the version of the bubble sort program presented here, a logical variable is used as a program flag to signal whether any switches have been made during a single pass through the set of names. If no switches have been made, the list must be sorted.

The name SWITCH will be given to this program flag variable. The value of SWITCH will be set at .FALSE. before *each* new pass begins. If a swap of adjacent elements is made during a particular pass, the logical variable SWITCH will be assigned the value .TRUE. . Before another pass is made, the value of SWITCH will be tested. If it evaluates as true, another pass will be executed (since a switch was made during the preceding pass); otherwise, the list must be sorted (since no exchanges were made in the preceding pass) and the list is printed.

The program also illustrates how the outer DO loop, which controls the initiation of the next pass, may be replaced by a counter and a GOTO statement. The program that accomplishes this is presented as Program 8.1. Study this program carefully.

```
* AN ENHANCED VERSION OF THE BUBBLE SORT


* AN ENHANCED VERSION OF THE BUBBLE SORT
* PROGRAM ALPHABETIZES A LIST OF 10 NAMES
* THIS PROGRAM WAS RUN ON A PRIME 850 COMPUTER USING FORTRAN 77
      INTEGER I, K
      CHARACTER * 15 NAME, TEMP
      LOGICAL SWITCH
      DIMENSION NAME(10)
*
* INITIALIZE VALUE OF SWITCH AT TRUE
      SWITCH = .TRUE.
* THE VARIABLE K WILL SERVE THE SAME FUNCTION AS THE OUTER
* DO VARIABLE IN THE ORIGINAL VERSION OF THE BUBBLE SORT
      K = 1
* READ LIST OF NAMES
      DO 30 I = 1, 10
         READ *, NAME(I)
   30 CONTINUE
* PRINT LIST OF NAMES
      PRINT *, 'THE ORIGINAL ARRAY'
      PRINT *, ' '
      PRINT *, (NAME(I), I = 1, 10)
```

```
*  PERFORM PROCESSING PROVIDED VALUE OF SWITCH REMAINS .TRUE.
*
     10 IF (SWITCH) THEN
* . . . . SET SWITCH AT .FALSE. AT THE BEGINNING OF EACH NEW PASS
             SWITCH = .FALSE.
             DO 50 I = 1, 10 - K
                 IF ( NAME(I) .GT. NAME(I + 1) ) THEN
* . . . . . . . . SWAP ADJACENT ELEMENTS
                     SWITCH = .TRUE.
                     TEMP = NAME(I)
                     NAME(I) = NAME(I + 1)
                     NAME(I + 1) = TEMP
                 ENDIF
     50      CONTINUE
             K = K + 1
             GOTO 10
         ELSE
* . . . . LIST IS SORTED SINCE NO SWAPS WERE MADE AS INDICATED
* . . . . BY THE VARIABLE SWITCH HAVING THE VALUE .FALSE.
*
* . . . . PRINT SORTED LIST OF NAMES
             PRINT *, ' '
             PRINT *, ' '
             PRINT *, 'THE SORTED ARRAY'
             PRINT *, ' '
             PRINT *, (NAME(I), I = 1, 10)
         ENDIF
         STOP
         END
```

} *serves same function as an outer DO loop*

Program 8.1

Output:

```
'DON'
'ARLENE'
'JEFF'
'STEVE'
'MARK'                    Data list
'MARTY'
'BEV'
'SHIRLEY'
'JEAN'
'BOB'
 THE ORIGINAL ARRAY

 DON            ARLENE          JEFF            STEVE
 MARK           MARTY           BEV             SHIRLEY
 JEAN           BOB


 THE SORTED ARRAY

 ARLENE         BEV             BOB             DON
 JEAN           JEFF            MARK            MARTY
 SHIRLEY        STEVE
 **** STOP
```

8.5 Manipulating Character Strings

The process of joining strings so that one string is attached to another is known as *concatenation*. To indicate that two strings are to be concatenated, we write

$$character\ string\ 1\ //\ character\ string\ 2$$

where the double slash (//) is called a *character* or *concatenator operator*.

Example	Resulting String
`'JOHN' // 'SMITH'`	`'JOHNSMITH'`
`'JOHN' // 'ßSMITH'`	`'JOHN SMITH'`
`'MR.ß' // 'JOHNß' // 'SMITH'`	`'MR. JOHN SMITH'`

EXTRACTING SUBSTRINGS

A *substring* is a group of characters that appear adjacent to one another in a given string. The string '987ABC' has many substrings, including '987', 'ABC', '7AB', and '987ABC' (the original string). The string '97B' is not a substring, however, since the three characters are not written consecutively in the original string.

A substring can be extracted from a given string by specifying the initial and the final column position of the desired substring. In general, the expression

> *string variable*(I : F)

Effect: Returns the set of characters in the string that occupy column positions I through F.

returns the set of characters of the specified string variable beginning in the Ith column position and ending in column position F, where I and F are integer values and I is between 1 and F ($1 \leq I \leq F \leq$ string length).

If SAMPLE = '987ABC', then the expression SAMPLE(1 : 3) will reference the characters in column positions 1 to 3, inclusive. Thus, SAMPLE(1 : 3) names the substring '987'. The substring call SAMPLE(3 : 6) will return the substring '7ABC'. An individual character in a substring may be identified by using the same pair of numbers in the initial and final character positions of the expression that calls a substring. In other words, the expression

> *string variable*(I : I)

Effect: Returns the character in the string that occupies column position I.

references the single character that occupies the Ith column position of the given string variable expression. SAMPLE(5 : 5), for example, will reference the character 'B', where SAMPLE = '987ABC'.

EXAMPLE 8.3 Write a program that reads a WORD having a maximum of 12 characters. Determine the number of occurrences of the letter X (if any).

Solution:

See Program 8.2.

```
* THIS PROGRAM WAS RUN ON A PRIME 850 COMPUTER USING A FORTRAN 77 COMPILER
      INTEGER KOUNT, I
      CHARACTER WORD * 12
      KOUNT = 0
      READ *, WORD
      DO 50 I = 1, 12
         IF ( WORD(I : I) .EQ. 'X' ) THEN
* WORD CONTAINS AN X IN COLUMN POSITION I
            KOUNT = KOUNT + 1
         ENDIF
   50 CONTINUE
      PRINT *, 'WORD = ', WORD
      PRINT *, 'THE LETTER X OCCURS ', KOUNT, ' TIMES'
      STOP
      END
```

Program 8.2.

Here's the output when the word 'XEROX' serves as data:

```
'XEROX'
WORD = XEROX
THE LETTER X OCCURS          2 TIMES
**** STOP
```

LENGTH OF A STRING

Fortran provides a built-in function that determines the length of a string. The general form of this function is as follows:

String LENgth Function

LEN(*character string* or *string variable expression*)

If the argument is a character string, the LEN function returns an integer value that represents the actual number of characters in the string. For example, LEN('COMPUTERS ARE LOGICAL') returns the integer value 21. If NAME is a string variable, the function LEN(NAME) does *not* return the number of characters in the particular string that the variable currently represents. Instead, the function returns an integer value that corresponds to the maximum length of the string variable as specified by the character data declaration statement.

EXAMPLE 8.4 Given:

```
CHARACTER MYTH * 15
DATA MYTH /'APHRODITE'/
```

evaluate each of the following expressions:

(a) LEN('APHRODITE')   (d) LEN(MYTH(1 : 5))
(b) LEN(MYTH)   (e) LEN(MYTH(4 : 4))
(c) LEN('ZEUS' // 'JUPITER')

Solutions

(a) 9
(b) 15 (Although the current value of the string variable MYTH contains nine characters, the LEN function returns the maximum *declared* length of the variable.)
(c) 11 (The LEN function returns the length of the concatenated string.)
(d) 5 (The LEN function returns the length of the specified substring.)
(e) 1

EXAMPLE 8.5 Suppose that a string variable SOURCE is declared to have a maximum of 20 characters in a data declaration statement. Write a program that reads in a character string value for SOURCE and determines the length of this string.

Solution

See Program 8.3.

```
          INTEGER LENGTH, K

          INTEGER LENGTH, K
          CHARACTER SOURCE * 20
    *
          READ *, SOURCE
    * THE FIRST OCCURRENCE OF A BLANK SIGNALS THE END
    * OF THE CHARACTER STRING
    *
          DO 50 K = 1, LEN(SOURCE)
              IF ( SOURCE (K : K) .NE. ' ') THEN
                  LENGTH = LENGTH + 1
              ELSE
    *. . . . . . . . THE END OF THE STRING HAS BEEN REACHED
                  PRINT *, SOURCE, 'LENGTH = ', LENGTH
    *. . . . . . . . EXIT THE LOOP
                  GOTO 60
              ENDIF
      50 CONTINUE
    * IF DO LOOP IS EXITED THEN NO TRAILING BLANKS WERE FOUND
          PRINT *, SOURCE, 'LENGTH = ', LEN(SOURCE)
      60 CONTINUE
          STOP
          END
```

Program 8.3

Here's the output when the word 'CAT' serves as the SOURCE string:

```
'CAT'
CAT                      LENGTH =           3
**** STOP
```

Suppose that a person's FIRST name and LAST name are entered as separate data items. The character variables FIRST and LAST are each declared to have a maximum length of 13 characters. To print the person's name as one string, we would merely use this command: PRINT *, FIRST // LAST. However, consider the appearance of the output if the FIRST name consists of fewer than 13 characters. For example, if the data entered were 'JOHN', 'SMITH', the output would appear as follows:

Column Positions of Output

1	2	3	4	5	6	7	8	9	10	11	12	13	14	15	16	17	18	19	20	21	22	23	24	25	26
J	O	H	N	ƀ	ƀ	ƀ	ƀ	ƀ	ƀ	ƀ	ƀ	ƀ	S	M	I	T	H	ƀ	ƀ	ƀ	ƀ	ƀ	ƀ	ƀ	ƀ

The extra blank spaces between the first and last names do not make for easy reading.

EXAMPLE 8.6   Read in as separate data items a person's FIRST and LAST names. Declare these string variables to have a maximum of 13 characters each. Print the concatenation of these variables so that exactly one blank space separates the FIRST and LAST names.

Solution

The program solution is based on comparing each character position of the FIRST name field with a blank. If a blank is encountered in the Kth column position (where K ≤ 13), then the string expression FIRST(1:K) will end with one trailing blank. The desired string is found by concatenating FIRST(1:K) with LAST. If no blank is encountered, then the FIRST name data value fills the entire 13-character position field. In this case, the concatenation of the FIRST and LAST names must include a blank inserted between the names. See Program 8.4.

```
* THIS PROGRAM WAS RUN ON A PRIME 850 COMPUTER USING A FORTRAN 77 COMPILER
      CHARACTER * 13, FIRST, LAST
      INTEGER K
      READ *, FIRST, LAST
* FIND FIRST OCCURRENCE OF A BLANK IN FIRST FIELD
      DO 50 K = 1, LEN(FIRST)
          IF (FIRST(K : K) .EQ. ' ') THEN
              PRINT *, FIRST (1 : K) // LAST
              GOTO 60
          ENDIF
   50 CONTINUE
* IF DO LOOP IS EXITED THEN FIRST FIELD DOES NOT INCLUDE
* ANY TRAILING BLANKS
*
      PRINT *, FIRST // ' '// LAST
   60 CONTINUE
      STOP
      END
```

Program 8.4

If 'ARLENE' and 'PODOS' are entered as data, the output will be:

```
'ARLENE' 'PODOS'
ARLENE PODOS
**** STOP
```

8.6 Additional Character Functions

INDEX FUNCTION

In text editing (word processing) applications it is sometimes necessary to search a given string for the occurrence of a specified substring. Fortran 77 offers the INDEX function for this purpose. The general form of this function is as follows:

| I N D E X (*string, substring*) | *INDEX Function:* Returns column position of the first character of the first occurrence of the specified substring. |

The Fortran intrinsic function INDEX requires two arguments, separated by a comma. The first argument identifies the string expression that is being examined. The second argument represents the substring that is being sought. The INDEX function returns an integer value that corresponds to the column position where the substring begins. If the INDEX function returns a value of 0, the string does not contain the specified substring.

Example	Value Returned
INDEX('SMART', 'R')	4
INDEX('SMART', 'Z')	0
INDEX('SMART', 'ART')	3
INDEX('I LOVE YOU', 'YOU')	8
SOCSEC = '414-36-9978' INDEX(SOCSEC, '36')	5
INDEX(SOCSEC, '4')	1
	(*Note:* The position of the *first* occurrence of the indicated substring will be returned.)

Examples 8.7 and 8.8 illustrate how to replace a specified substring with a different string expression. For example, given the line of text:

'HE LOVES TO DEBUG PROGRAMS'

the examples that follow consider how to replace a *substring* of such a line of text (say 'LOVES') with another substring (say 'HATES'). The target string (for example, 'LOVES') has the same number of characters as the replacement string (for example, 'HATES').

EXAMPLE 8.7 For a given line of TEXT consisting of a maximum of 80 characters, write a program that reads in the TARGET substring, the replacement substring, and their lengths (assume that the substrings have the same length). Print the original line of TEXT and the EDITED line of text.

Solution

The program solution is based on using the INDEX function to identify the beginning column POSition of the target substring. The EDITED text is obtained by concatenating the substring formed from the first column position of the text to the beginning of the target substring, the replacement substring, and the remainder of the original line of TEXT. Provision is made for the possibility that the target string is the entire line of TEXT or is the concluding set of characters of a full 80-character line of TEXT. See Program 8.5.

```
* PROGRAM REPLACES TARGET STRING WITH REPLACEMENT SUBSTRING


* PROGRAM REPLACES TARGET STRING WITH REPLACEMENT SUBSTRING
* THIS PROGRAM WAS RUN ON A PRIME 850 COMPUTER USING FORTRAN 77
*
* PROGRAM VARIABLE NAMES:
*       TARGET = SUBSTRING TO BE REPLACED
*       NEW    = SUBSTRING TO BE INSERTED
*       LENGTH = LENGTH OF TARGET AND NEW SUBSTRINGS
*       TEXT   = LINE OF TEXT
*       EDITED = REVISED LINE OF TEXT
*       POS    = STARTING COLUMN POSITION OF TARGET SUBSTRING
*
      INTEGER LENGTH, POS
      CHARACTER * 80, NEW, TARGET, TEXT, EDITED
*
      READ *, TEXT
      READ *, TARGET
      READ *, NEW
      READ *, LENGTH
      POS = INDEX(TEXT,TARGET(1 : LENGTH))
*
* IF LENGTH OF TARGET STRING IS 80 THEN ENTIRE LINE OF TEXT IS REPLACED
      IF (LENGTH .EQ. 80) THEN
          PRINT *, TEXT
          PRINT *, NEW
          GOTO 100
      ENDIF
      IF ( POS + LENGTH .LE. 80 ) THEN
          J = POS + LENGTH
          EDITED = TEXT(1 : POS -1) // NEW(1 : LENGTH) // TEXT (J : 80)
          PRINT *, TEXT
          PRINT *, EDITED
      ELSE
          EDITED = TEXT (1 :  POS - 1) // NEW
          PRINT *, TEXT
          PRINT *, EDITED
      ENDIF
  100 CONTINUE
      STOP
      END
```

Program 8.5

Output:

```
          'HE LOVES TO DEBUG PROGRAMS'
          'LOVES'
          'HATES'
          5
           HE LOVES TO DEBUG PROGRAMS
           HE HATES TO DEBUG PROGRAMS
          **** STOP
```

EXAMPLE 8.8 Modify Program 8.5 so that the lengths of the substrings involved in the exchange are not specified. You need not assume that the two substrings have the same length. Assume, however, that the EDITED text line will have a maximum of 120 characters.

Solution

After determining the length of the TARGET and NEW strings, the revised program parallels the approach illustrated in the solution to Example 8.7. See Program 8.6.

The ICHAR and CHAR intrinsic Fortran functions involve the collating sequences of characters. Their behavior is therefore machine dependent. Although collating sequences vary from one computer to another, each computer arranges the members of its character set into ascending sequence. The position of the first character in this sequence (often a blank) is indicated by a zero. If there are N characters in the collating sequence, the last character in the sequence occupies the $(N - 1)$th position.

```
* THIS PROGRAM WAS RUN ON A PRIME 850 COMPUTER USING FORTRAN 77


* THIS PROGRAM WAS RUN ON A PRIME 850 COMPUTER USING FORTRAN 77
      INTEGER LENGTH, LENGTH2, POS
      CHARACTER * 120, NEW, EDITED, TARGET * 80, TEXT * 80
*
      READ *, TEXT
      READ *, TARGET
      READ *, NEW
* FIND LENGTH OF TARGET
      LENGTH = 0
      DO 50 K = 1, 80
          IF (TARGET (K : K) .NE. ' ') THEN
              LENGTH = LENGTH + 1
          ENDIF
   50 CONTINUE
*
* FIND LENGTH OF NEW
      LENGTH2 = 0
      DO 60 K = 1, 120
          IF ( NEW(K : K) .NE. ' ') THEN
              LENGTH2 = LENGTH2 + 1
          ENDIF
   60 CONTINUE
      POS = INDEX(TEXT,TARGET(1 : LENGTH))
* IF LENGTH OF TARGET STRING IS 80 THEN ENTIRE LINE OF TEXT IS REPLACED
      IF (LENGTH .EQ. 80) THEN
          PRINT *, TEXT
          PRINT *, NEW
          GOTO 100
      ENDIF
      IF ( POS + LENGTH .LE. 80 ) THEN
          J = POS + LENGTH
          EDITED = TEXT(1 : POS -1) // NEW(1 : LENGTH2) // TEXT (J : 80)
          PRINT *, TEXT
          PRINT *, EDITED
      ELSE
          EDITED = TEXT (1 :  POS - 1) // NEW
          PRINT *, TEXT
          PRINT *, EDITED
      ENDIF
  100 CONTINUE
      STOP
      END
```

Program 8.6

Output:

```
          'HE LOVES TO DEBUG PROGRAMS'
          'DEBUG'
          'CORRECT'
           HE LOVES TO DEBUG PROGRAMS
           HE LOVES TO CORRECT PROGRAMS
          **** STOP
```

The ICHAR function returns an integer value that corresponds to the relative position of a character in the collating sequence established by the particular Fortran compiler. The function takes this general form:

ICHAR(*character*)	*ICHAR Function:* Returns the position of the specified character in the computer's collating sequence.

If the character ' ' (blank) is assumed to occupy the first position of a collating sequence, then the value returned by ICHAR(' ') will be 0.

The CHAR function allows a character to be identified, given its position in the collating sequence. The CHAR and ICHAR functions may therefore be considered to be inverse functions. The CHAR function takes an integer argument and returns the character which occupies that relative position in the computer's collating sequence. For example, CHAR($\emptyset$) = $\not{b}$. The general form of the CHAR function is as follows:

> CHAR(*integer value*)

CHAR Function: Returns the character having the specified position in the computer's collating sequence.

The argument of the CHAR function may be any integer value in the range of 0 to N − 1, where N represents the number of characters in the collating sequence.

8.7 Notes on Format-Directed Input/Output of Character and Logical Data

In format-directed input/output statements, the A field descriptor is used to describe a field that contains character (alphanumeric) data, while the L (logical) field descriptor specifies a field that contains a logical value.

Format Edit Descriptor	Interpretation
Aw	Specifies an input/output field *w* columns in width that contains a character string.
Lw	Defines an input/output field having a length of *w* columns in width that contains logical data. When used to describe an input data field, the computer will interpret only the *first* character in the field. If it finds a 'T' in this position, then the logical constant .TRUE. is assigned to the corresponding logical variable. If any other character is read in the beginning column position of the field, then the logical constant .FALSE. is assigned to the corresponding logical variable.

For example, the set of statements

```
CHARACTER NAME * 10
LOGICAL SWITCH, FLAG, OPEN
READ (5, 100) NAME, SWITCH, FLAG, OPEN
100 FORMAT (A10, 2X, L5, 2X, L5, 2X, L5)
```

may be interpreted as follows: The string variable NAME is assigned the character data contained in the first 10 columns of the input data record; the next 2 columns are ignored; SWITCH is a logical variable whose value will be determined by the *first* character of the data value entered in the next 5-column field. If a 'T' is encountered, the value .TRUE. will be assigned to SWITCH; otherwise, SWITCH will be set at .FALSE. . After skipping the next two columns, the logical variable FLAG will be assigned a value determined by the first character of the data value entered in the next 5-column field. Similarly, the logical variable OPEN will be assigned a logical value.

For example, suppose that the actual input data record was as follows:

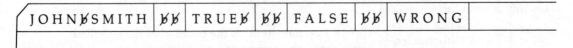

| J O H N $\not{b}$ S M I T H | $\not{b}\not{b}$ | T R U E $\not{b}$ | $\not{b}\not{b}$ | F A L S E | $\not{b}\not{b}$ | W R O N G |

During an input operation the following data assignments would occur:

```
NAME  =  JOHN SMITH
SWITCH =  .TRUE.
FLAG  =  .FALSE.
OPEN  =  .FALSE. (Since the first character is not
              a 'T', the truth value of the variable defaults to .FALSE.)
```

Recall that the edit descriptors included within a FORMAT statement that repeat consecutively may be written in a more compact form by introducing a repetition factor. The FORMAT statement given previously may be written as

```
100 FORMAT (A10, 3(2X, L5))
```

8.8 Some Closing Remarks

One of the most dramatic differences between Fortran 77 and previous implementations of Fortran is the variety of intrinsic functions found in Fortran 77 that facilitate the manipulation of character data. The emphasis in this chapter was on presenting and illustrating these functions.

After reviewing character data declaration statements, we discussed the comparison of string expressions. The relational operators .LT., .LE., .EQ., .NE., .GT., and .GE. may be used for comparing both numeric and nonnumeric string expressions. The result of comparing two strings will depend on the collating sequence that a particular computer follows. All collating sequences organize strings that consist entirely of letters into a "dictionary" order. If string 1 comes before string 2 in this dictionary sequence, then string 1 is considered to be less than string 2.

All numeric strings that have the same length are ordered by their actual numeric values. The numeric string having the smaller value is considered to be less than the other string. If two numeric strings have different lengths, the shorter string is padded with trailing blanks to give it the same length as the other string. The two strings are then compared character by character (that is, digit by digit), not by their overall numerical values. Thus, '98' would be considered to be *greater* than '1000'. Keep in mind that, in all collating sequences, blanks come before letters and digits.

Logical data were also discussed. There are exactly two logical constant values: .TRUE. and .FALSE. . A logical variable must be declared in a logical data declaration statement. A logical assignment statement may be used to store a logical constant in the memory location named by the logical variable.

The value of a logical variable may be printed. If the value is .TRUE., then the letter "T" is printed; otherwise, the value is .FALSE. and the letter "F" is printed.

Although not presented in the body of this chapter, intrinsic functions that compare two strings and return a logical constant based on the results of the comparison are provided by Fortran 77. The comparisons are made based on the ASCII (American Standard Code for Information Interchange) binary coding system for stored characters. This is specified by the ANSI Fortran 77 standard and is therefore the same for every Fortran 77 compiler regardless of the actual internal coding system used by the particular computer (for example, IBM computers use EBCDIC).

For the sake of completeness, these *lexical* intrinsic functions are given in Table 8.4.

Table 8.4 Lexical Functions Provided by Fortran 77

Lexical Function	Returns a Value of .TRUE. If:
LGT *(string 1, string 2)*	String 1 follows (is greater than) string 2.
LGE *(string 1, string 2)*	String 1 follows string 2 or is equal (identical) to string 2.
LLT *(string 1, string 2)*	String 1 comes before (is less than) string 2.
LLE *(string 1, string 2)*	String 1 comes before string 2 or is equal (identical) to string 2.

Programs that manipulate text data tend to be especially prone to error. When writing programs involving logical and character data, you should do the following:

- Verify that each logical and character variable has been declared. Be sure that the maximum lengths of character strings have been properly specified.
- Include appropriate input data validation routines. In a batch system, echo-print string data items.
- Use the logical relational operators .EQV. and .NEQV. when comparing logical variables. Do *not* use .EQ. or .NE. .

- Exercise extreme care in using the INDEX function. Check that the string arguments are written in their correct order. Provide for the possibility that the INDEX function may return a value of zero, indicating that the substring is not found within the string.
- Remember that the LEN function returns the declared maximum length of an argument that is a string *variable*. In general, when inserting substrings make certain that the declared maximum length of the resulting text string is not exceeded.
- Check the logic of your program by walking appropriate sample test data through the program. Be sure to choose sets of data that anticipate all possible program paths.

Review Exercises

A star preceding the number of a problem indicates that a solution to that problem is given at the back of the book.

* **1.** Read a character string having a maximum of 12 characters. Print the characters of the string in reverse order *vertically*, one character on a print line.

* **2.** Modify Problem 1 so that trailing blanks are eliminated and the characters are printed in reverse order *horizontally* across a print line. (*Hint:* Store each character, except trailing blanks, as an element in a character array. Print the character array using an implied DO loop.)

3. Read in a line of text having a maximum of 80 characters. Replace each blank space that is embedded in the text (that is, discount trailing blanks) by a hypen ('-'). Print the original and the revised line of text.

4. Read in a line of text having a maximum of 80 characters. Eliminate all embedded and trailing blanks from the line of text, and consolidate the line so that all characters are written consecutively. Print the original and the revised line of text.

5. A word is a *palindrome* if its spelling does not change when the letters of the word are written in reverse order. *Deed* and *Radar* are examples of palindromes. Read in a word having a maximum of 9 characters. Print whether the word is a palindrome.

* **6.** The INDEX function indicates the position of the *first* occurrence of a specified substring. It is possible that the substring may occur more than once in the original string. Read a SOURCE string and a TARGET substring. Determine the numbers and positions of all occurrences of the TARGET substring in the SOURCE string. Assume that the SOURCE string has a maximum of 40 characters.

7. Read a line of text having a maximum of 80 characters. Read TARGET and REPLACement substrings. Replace *all* occurrences of the TARGET substring with the REPLACement substring. Assume that the revised line of TEXT will not exceed 120 characters.

8. Read a line of text having a maximum of 80 characters. Read a TARGET substring. Print the original line of TEXT and a revised line of TEXT formed by deleting each occurrence of the TARGET substring from the line of text. Be sure to consolidate the revised line of text in order to eliminate the blanks created by the deletions.

9. Read a string that consists of a group of words with successive words separated by a blank space. Print in table form each word and the number of vowels contained in the word.

10. Read in a string having a maximum of 8 characters that represents a Roman numeral. Print the Roman numeral and its value. The string may consist of combinations of the letters C, L, X, V, I, where

$$C = 100, \quad L = 50, \quad X = 10, \quad V = 5, \quad I = 1$$

Keep in mind that XI = 11 since $10 + 1 = 11$. On the other hand, IX = 9 since $10 - 1 = 9$. In general, when the symbol for a smaller number appears to the immediate left of a symbol representing a greater value, the assigned value is determined by *subtracting* the smaller from the larger. Also, when a symbol for a smaller number is sandwiched between two symbols representing numbers having greater values, the middle symbol is grouped with the symbol to its right. Thus, XIV is interpreted as $X + IV$ ($= 14$) rather than $XI + V$ ($= 16$).

Test your program using the following sample test data:

XXXII
CLXVI
XCIV
CCXLVIII

*11. Prepare a coded message by replacing each letter of a line of text according to the following scheme:

Original	A	B	C	D	E	F	G	H	I	J	K	L	M
Replacement	Z	Y	X	W	V	U	T	S	R	Q	P	O	N

Original	N	O	P	Q	R	S	T	U	V	W	X	Y	Z
Replacement	M	L	K	J	I	H	G	F	E	D	C	B	A

Assume that the line of text has a maximum of 80 characters. Print the original and the coded line of text.

*12. Enter a character string that consists of a calendar date in the following form:

'name of month⁄ɓday number,ɓyear'.

Print the date in this form:

'month number-day number-last two digits of the year'.

For example:

Sample Input	Output
October 12, 1984	10-12-84
January 28, 1987	01-28-87

13. Read a list of ten names (last name only) into a character array and a corresponding set of birth dates into another character array. Assume as in Problem 13 that the dates have this form:

'name of month⁄ɓday number,ɓyear'

*(a) Print in table form the list of names and corresponding birth dates, sorted in ascending order of month of birth. Assume that each person was born in a different month.

(b) Revise the program written in part (a) by lifting the assumption that each person was born in a different month. If two people were born in the same month, compare the day number field. (To avoid erroneous results, be sure to enter birth dates as data using two digits for the day number. For example, enter the seventh day of the month as 07 rather than 7.)

14. Print in table form each digit and letter and its corresponding position in your computer's collating sequence.

15. Read a binary number having a maximum of 12 binary digits and print its base-10 equivalent. Solve this problem by using the following approach: Read the binary data value as a character string and determine the actual number of binary digits in the value; use the INDEX and ICHAR functions (see Problem 14) to examine each character of the string and determine whether it is a binary 0 or a binary 1; store each character of the string as an individual element of an integer array BINARY. The base-10 equivalent of the binary number may be found by multiplying each element of array BINARY by an appropriate power of 2 and finding the sum of these products. (*Note:* Although there may be better ways of solving this problem, use the algorithm suggested since it illustrates several concepts presented in this chapter.)

CHAPTER 9
Fortran Subprograms and Program Structure

+---+
| **COMPUTER AXIOM** |
| |
| Using several small programs to accomplish a complex task is |
| often more effective than using one very large program. |
+---+

+---+
| **COROLLARY** |
| |
| *When approaching a complicated problem, think "small" rather*|
| *than "big." Try to identify each of the small, ordinary tasks*|
| *necessary to accomplish the big job. A "miniprogram" can then*|
| *be written to achieve each of these smaller tasks. Later these*|
| *miniprograms can be coordinated to form a single program.* |
+---+

9.1 Some Additional Fortran Library Functions

One of the most attractive features of Fortran is the availability of a wide variety of built-in mathematically oriented functions. Some of these have already been discussed (see Section 5.10 of Chapter 5).

The Fortran functions used to evaluate trigonometric, exponential, and logarithmic functions are summarized in Table 9.1. The argument and the value returned by the function are typed as real for each function listed. The angle measure that serves as the argument for each trigonometric function must be expressed in radians. To convert from degrees to radians, the following relationship may be used:

$$\text{number of radians} = \text{number of degrees} \times \frac{3.14159}{180}$$

where 3.14159 is an approximation of the value of the constant pi (π). The Arcsine, Arccosine, and Arctangent functions are *inverse* trigonometric functions. For example, the statement

```
Y = Arcsine (X)
```

may be interpreted as "Assign to variable Y the measure of the angle (expressed in radians) whose sine has a value of X." For example, if Y = arcsine (1.0), the value 1.57080 ($\pi/2.0$) will be assigned to Y since the measure of the angle whose sine has a value of 1.0 is 90 degrees, which, expressed in radians, is approximately 1.57080.

EXAMPLE 9.1 Express each of the following formulas as a Fortran assignment statement using the function's specific name:

(a) $y = e^{x^2}$
(b) $w = a \sin(bx + t)$
(c) $h = \ln \sqrt{x}$
(d) $r = \log(x^2 + 3x)$

Solutions

(a) `Y = EXP(X * X)`

(b) `W = A * SIN(B * X + T)`

(c) In mathematics, the notation "ln" is used to distinguish the natural log function (base e) from the common log function (base 10).

$$H = ALOG(SQRT(X))$$

(d) `R = ALOG10(X * X + 3 * X)`

Table 9.1 A Partial Listing of Fortran 77 Exponential, Logarithmic, and Trigonometric Library Functions

Fortran 77 Generic Name	Explanation	Fortran IV Specific Name	Restriction on Argument
EXP	Returns the value of the constant e (= 2.7182818. . .) raised to a power represented by the function's argument: $$EXP\ (argument) = e^{argument}$$	EXP (X)	Real
LOG	Returns the value of the *natural* logarithm (base e) of a given argument.	ALOG (X)	Real and greater than zero
LOG10	Returns the value of the *common* logarithm (base 10) of a given argument.	ALOG10 (X)	Real and greater than zero
SIN	Returns the value of the sine of an angle measure.	SIN (X)	Real and expressed in radians
COS	Returns the value of the cosine of an angle measure.	COS (X)	Real and expressed in radians
TAN	Returns the value of the tangent of an angle measure.	TAN (X)	Real and expressed in radians; function is undefined for arguments that are odd multiples of $\pi/2$.
ASIN	Returns the angle, expressed in radians, whose sine has the value of the function's argument.	ASIN (X)	Real
ACOS	Returns the angle, expressed in radians, whose cosine has the value of the function's argument.	ACOS (X)	Real
ATAN	Returns the angle, expressed in radians, whose tangent has the value of the function's argument.	ATAN (X)	Real

EXAMPLE 9.2   When the measures of three sides of a triangle are given, the law of cosines may be used to determine the measure of any angle of the triangle. To find the measure of angle A of triangle ABC the following relationship may be used:

$$\cos A = \frac{b^2 + c^2 - a^2}{2bc}$$

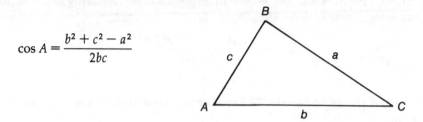

where a, b, and c represent the lengths of the sides of $\triangle ABC$.

Read values for a, b, and c. Enter the values such that side a is the *largest* of the three values. Determine the measure of angle A (the largest angle of the triangle), and print its measure in *degrees*. In addition, classify the triangle as acute, right, or obtuse.

Solution

The problem requires that we use the Arccosine function to determine the measure of the required angle. The value of the expression

$$COSARG = \frac{b^2 + c^2 - a^2}{2bc}$$

where COSARG represents the argument of the Arccosine function must be calculated for the data values provided for a, b, and c. If the result is equal to zero, angle A must be equal to 90 degrees and the triangle is a right triangle. If COSARG is not equal to zero, we may proceed to calculate the radian measure of the angle using the Arccosine function and then to convert it into degrees. After the degree measure of angle A is printed, the degree measure must be compared to 90. If it is less than 90, the triangle is ACUTE; otherwise, it is obtuse. The pseudocode solution is as follows:

Pseudocode Solution

```
            READ ASIDE, BSIDE, CSIDE
            Calculate COSARG
            IF COSARG is equal to 0 THEN
               PRINT 'ANGLE A = 90 DEGREES'
               PRINT 'TRIANGLE ABC IS A RIGHT TRIANGLE'
               STOP
            ELSE
               RADIAN = ACOS (COSARG)
               DEGREE = RADIAN * 180.0 / 3.141593
               PRINT 'ANGLE A =', DEGREE, 'DEGREES'
            ENDIF
      * TO DETERMINE THE TYPE OF TRIANGLE
            IF DEGREE is less than 90 THEN
               PRINT 'TRIANGLE IS ACUTE'
            ELSE
               PRINT 'TRIANGLE IS OBTUSE'
            ENDIF
            STOP
```

See Program 9.1.

```
$JOB    WATFIV
C* * * * * * * * * * * * *LAW OF COSINES* * * * * * * * * * * *  **
C*                                                                *
C*           TO DETERMINE THE MEASURE OF AN ANGLE OF A TRIANGLE   *
C*                GIVEN THE LENGTHS OF EACH OF ITS SIDES           *
C*          PROGRAM VARIABLES                                      *
C*                   COSARG = VALUE OF THE COSINE OF THE ANGLE     *
C*                   RADIAN = RADIAN MEASURE OF THE DESIRED ANGLE  *
C*                   DEGREE = DEGREE MEASURE OF THE DESIRED ANGLE  *
C*                   ASIDE, BSIDE, CSIDE = 3 SIDES OF THE TRIANGLE *
C*                                                                 *
C* THIS PROGRAM WAS RUN ON AN IBM COMPUTER USING WATFIV           *
C* IN THIS VERSION OF FORTRAN, THE ARCOS FUNCTION IS USED TO      *
C* DETERMINE THE MEASURE OF ANGLE A.                              *
C* * * * * * * * * * * * * * * * * * * * * * * * * * * * * * * * * *
C      NOTE:  ALL VARIABLES ARE IMPLICITLY DEFINED TO BE REAL
C
1          READ , ASIDE, BSIDE, CSIDE
C. . .ECHO PRINT DATA VALUES
2          PRINT , ASIDE, BSIDE, CSIDE
3          PRINT , ' '
4          COSARG = (BSIDE ** 2 + CSIDE ** 2 - ASIDE ** 2) /
1                   (2.0 * BSIDE * CSIDE)
C      NOTE: PREVIOUS LINE CONTAINED A LINE CONTINUATION ENTRY
C            IN COLUMN 6
C
C
5          IF (COSARG .EQ. 0) THEN
6             DEGREE = 90.0
7             PRINT , 'ANGLE A = ', DEGREE, 'DEGREES'
8             PRINT , 'TRIANGLE ABC IS A RIGHT TRIANGLE'
9             STOP
10         ELSE
11            RADIAN = ARCOS (COSARG)
12            DEGREE = RADIAN * 180.0 / 3.141593
13            PRINT , 'ANGLE A = ', DEGREE, 'DEGREES'
14         ENDIF
C TO DETERMINE THE TYPE OF TRIANGLE
15         IF (DEGREE .LT. 90) THEN
16            PRINT , 'TRIANGLE ABC IS AN ACUTE TRIANGLE'
17         ELSE
18            PRINT , 'TRIANGLE ABC IS AN OBTUSE TRIANGLE'
19         ENDIF
20         STOP
21         END

$ENTRY
12.0000000           12.0000000           12.0000000

ANGLE A =          59.9999600 DEGREES
TRIANGLE ABC IS AN ACUTE TRIANGLE
```

Program 9.1

9.2 Programmer-Defined Functions

The program language instructions that define Fortran's library of built-in functions are invisible to the programmer, as they are supplied by the Fortran compiler. Fortran also provides a facility by which you can invent your own functions. Special-purpose functions needed by a programmer may be defined in a self-contained segment of the program, called a *subprogram*. A subprogram is nothing more than a block of related statements, insulated from the rest of the program, that performs a specific processing task.

The program unit that controls the execution of the subprogram is known as the *main* or *calling* program. The general idea is that, once a function is given a name and defined in a subprogram, it may be referenced by its programmer-determined name at various places in the main program, and its value immediately returned, just as if the built-in function ABS, SQRT, or SIN were being used. When a subprogram is activated, it is said to be *called* or *invoked*. Let's find out how this can be accomplished.

Suppose that at several places in the main program it is necessary to find the sum of all integer values from 1 to a variable integer value, inclusive. At each place in the program where this task must be performed, we can code statements that accomplish this operation. Greater economy in programming code and effort may be achieved by referencing the same set of statements each time this function is needed. Let's agree to call the function that performs this task ADDING (the rules for naming functions are the same as those for naming Fortran variables). The function ADDING will be defined so that, for any given integer value K, ADDING(K) returns the sum of all integer values from 1 to K, inclusive.

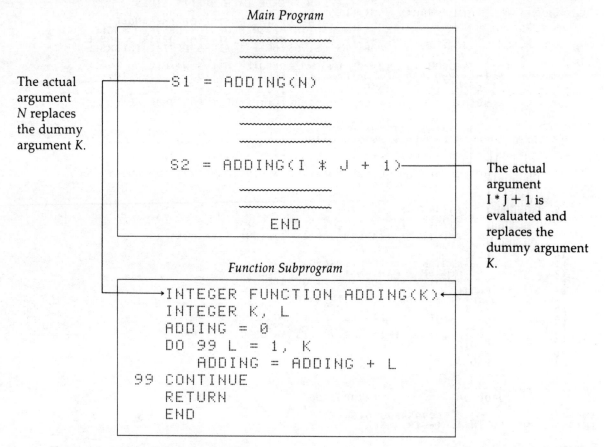

Figure 9.1 Outline of Subprogramming Process

Figure 9.1 gives a skeletal outline of this process. In Figure 9.1 the subprogram begins with the function definition statement

```
INTEGER FUNCTION ADDING(K)
```

where INTEGER defines the type of number that will be assigned to the FUNCTION having the name ADDING and the *dummy* argument K. The dummy variable K is a temporary placeholder for the actual argument that will be transmitted to the function subprogram when the statement that invokes the function subprogram is executed.

In our example, when the assignment statement

```
S1 = ADDING(N)
```

is executed in the main program, program control passes to the function subprogram. The current value of N replaces the variable K in the subprogram. After the DO loop in the subprogram is exited, the function ADDING has been assigned a value that corresponds to the sum of all integer values from 1 to N, inclusive. When the RETURN statement is executed, program control returns to the main program and execution of the main program resumes where it left off, except that the function call has returned the desired sum to the main program via the function name ADDING.

When the assignment statement

```
S2 = ADDING(I * J + 1)
```

is encountered, program control again passes to the function subprogram ADDING. This time the *actual* argument is an integer *expression*. This is legal, provided that it has been evaluated in the main program so that the resulting integer value replaces the dummy argument K in the function subprogram. Notice that, within the function subprogram, the function name ADDING is used with*out* its argument. In general, a function appears with its argument(s) only in the original function call statement and in the function definition statement that begins every function subprogram.

A program may contain more than one subprogram. The END statement must be the last statement of the main program and of each subprogram. Thus, each of these program units is compiled individually and is treated as a self-contained program. The variables used in each subprogram are defined *locally,* meaning that the computer allocates distinct storage areas for each set of variables in each subprogram. This implies that the variables used in each program unit require their own data declaration statements. Although a variable in one program unit may have the same name as a variable in a different program unit, the computer treats them as *different* variables that do not necessarily represent the same quantity. A variable X, for instance, used in a main program does *not* necessarily refer to the same memory location as a variable X that appears in a function subprogram (the two variables will, of course, refer to the same quantity if they are corresponding actual and dummy arguments).

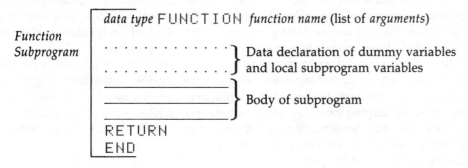

Figure 9.2 General Form of Function Subprogram

Figure 9.2 shows the general form of a function subprogram. In the function definition statement, the *data type* refers to the data type of the value returned by the function; FUNCTION is a required keyword; *function name* is a programmer-determined name that must conform to the rules for naming Fortran variables. If the data type is omitted from the function definition statement, the function is typed implicitly using the first letter of its name. (If the first letter begins with I through N, the function is typed INTEGER; otherwise, it is typed REAL.)

A function subprogram communicates a single value to the calling program through the function name. It follows that within the body of the subprogram there must be at least one assignment statement of the form

$$\textit{function name} = \text{expression}$$

The END statement marks the *physical* end of a subprogram, while the RETURN statement signals the *logical* conclusion of a subprogram. When a RETURN statement is executed, program control is transferred back to the calling program. The logic of a subprogram may require more than one RETURN statement. When a RETURN statement is followed by the END statement, the RETURN statement may be omitted. If the END statement is encountered during the execution of a subprogram, program control reverts to the calling program.

ARGUMENT ASSOCIATIONS

In general, a function may consist of a list of arguments, in which case the actual and dummy argument lists must correspond exactly in terms of number, order, and typing of their arguments. For example, if the actual arguments for the function SOLVE are N, A, and B, where N is an integer

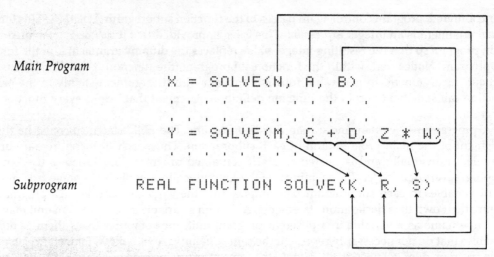

Figure 9.3 Use of Dummy Arguments

variable, and A and B are real variables, the function definition statement must have a dummy argument list consisting of an integer variable followed by two real variables. This is illustrated in Figure 9.3. Notice that the use of *dummy* arguments permits SOLVE function call statements having differently valued arguments to reference the same subprogram.

When forming actual and dummy argument lists, keep in mind that arguments which occupy corresponding positions in the two argument lists are paired together so that they refer to the same quantity in computer memory. Be careful. An actual argument list may include constants, variables, individual subscripted variables, array names, and variable expressions. A dummy argument list may include only nonsubscripted variables and array names; it may *not* include constants, individual array elements, or variable expressions.

Consider the following examples:

Function Call	Function Definition Statement
(a) X = TEST(A, B(3), 5)	FUNCTION TEST(R, S, K)
(b) X = TEST(A, B, C)	FUNCTION TEST(Y, W)
(c) X = TEST(A, B/C, D)	FUNCTION TEST(X, Y, Z(3))
(d) X = TEST(A, B, C)	FUNCTION TEST(R + S, T, W)
(e) X = TEST(A, B, C)	FUNCTION TEST(Y, 5.0, Z)
(f) X = TEST(A, B, C)	FUNCTION TEST(A, B, C)

The statements listed in (a) and (f) are legal. Example (b) is illegal since the lists do not have the same number of arguments. The dummy argument list of example (c) includes a subscripted variable, which is illegal. Example (d) includes as one of the dummy arguments a variable expression, which is not permitted. Example (e) uses a constant as a dummy argument; this is illegal.

PASSING ARRAYS

An entire array may be passed from one program module to another by using the array name as an argument in the function call. The corresponding dummy argument will store the array in the function subprogram. Although the array has been declared in the calling program module (for example, the main program), the dummy array must be declared (typed and dimensioned) in the subprogram, as shown in the following example:

```
Main Program                      Subprogram
REAL A(100)             ┌────────→REAL FUNCTION FUNCT(X)
  . . . . . . .         │         DIMENSION X(100)
  . . . . . . .         │
T = FUNCT(A)────────────┘
```

Notice that in the subprogram the dummy argument X represents the array A, which is being passed from the main program. Only the array name appears as an argument in both the actual and dummy argument lists. The dummy array must be dimensioned in the subprogram.

An alternative approach to setting the dimension of the dummy array is to use *adjustable dimensions*. If the size of the array is included as one of the arguments in the actual argument list, its corresponding dummy argument variable may be used to dimension the array. This is illustrated below, where the variable N is used to represent the size of the array A.

Main Program	Subprogram
`T = FUNCT(A, N)`	`REAL FUNCTION FUNCT(X, N)`
	`DIMENSION X(N)`

EXAMPLE 9.3   A program is designed to manipulate arrays, each having the same number of elements. The argument list of a user-defined function COMPAR consists of two array names and a single integer value that represents the number of elements in each array.

Write a function subprogram that returns the logical value .TRUE. to the main program if the two arrays are identical; otherwise, it returns the value .FALSE. .

Solution

```
*  *  *  *  *  *  *  *  *FUNCTION SUBPROGRAM*  *  *  *  *  *  *  *  *
*                                                                 *
      LOGICAL COMPAR(ARRAY1, ARRAY2, N)
      INTEGER I, N
      REAL ARRAY1(N), ARRAY2(N)
      DO 50 I = 1, N
         IF ( ARRAY1(I) .NE. ARRAY2(I) ) THEN
            COMPAR = .FALSE.
            RETURN
         ENDIF
   50 CONTINUE
      COMPAR = .TRUE.
      RETURN
      END
*                                                                 *
*  *  *  *  *  *  *  *  *  *  *  *  *  *  *  *  *  *  *  *  *  *  *  *
```

Program Notes: In this problem, two arrays are being passed to the function subprogram. Their corresponding dummy arguments have been given the names ARRAY1 and ARRAY2. The dummy argument N refers to the number of elements in each array. Notice that each dummy array name is dimensioned in the subprogram using the *variable* N. The dimensioned size of an array may be specified in a function subprogram using a variable value, *provided that the variable appears as one of the arguments of the function definition.*

The logic of the program requires two RETURN statements. The first RETURN statement is used to send program control back to the main program if two corresponding elements of the arrays are not equal. Notice that the value of COMPAR is set at .FALSE. in the IF block before this RETURN statement is reached. The second RETURN statement is placed outside the DO loop and corresponds to the situation in which the arrays are equal; that is, if the DO loop is exited normally, this implies that the corresponding elements in each pair are the same. Before the second RETURN statement is reached, the value of COMPAR is set at .TRUE. .

How can we be certain that the subprogram written for Example 9.3 is correct? The only way we can be sure is by examining how it behaves once it is put into service. To test the correctness of a subprogram we must provide a calling program that exercises the subprogram. This program must "drive" the subprogram by passing values to it, and then providing appropriate output that indicates whether the subprogram is performing its intended function.

In this example, our *driver* program will input an array having five integer elements, called TEST1. A function call using this array name as both arguments of the function COMPAR will be made. Thus, the value returned by the subprogram should be the logical value .TRUE. . Next, the driver program will generate another array, say TEST2, whose elements are formed by adding 1 to each element of the original array, TEST1. Another function call will be made using TEST1 and TEST2 as the arguments of COMPAR. Thus, the logical value .FALSE. should be returned by the subprogram.

```
      $JOB    WATFIV
      C DRIVER PROGRAM FOR EXAMPLE 9.3
 1            INTEGER TEST1(5), TEST2(5), K
 2            LOGICAL COMPAR
 3            READ , (TEST1(K), K = 1, 5)
 4            PRINT , 'OUTPUT SHOULD BE TRUE. . . .'
 5            PRINT , COMPAR(TEST1, TEST1, 5)
 6            PRINT , ' '
      C CREATE ARRAY TEST2
 7            DO 50 K = 1, 5
 8                TEST2(K) = TEST1(K) + 1
 9        50  CONTINUE
10            PRINT , 'OUTPUT SHOULD BE FALSE. . . .'
11            PRINT , COMPAR(TEST1, TEST2, 5)
12            STOP
13            END
      C
      C
      C *  *  *  *  *  *  FUNCTION SUBPROGRAM  *  *  *  *  *  *  *  *  *

14            LOGICAL FUNCTION COMPAR (ARRAY1, ARRAY2, N)
15            INTEGER ARRAY1(N), ARRAY2(N), I
16            DO 50 I = 1, N
17                IF ( ARRAY1(I) .NE. ARRAY2(I) ) THEN
18                    COMPAR = .FALSE.
19                    RETURN
20                ENDIF
21        50  CONTINUE
22            COMPAR = .TRUE.
23            RETURN
24            END
      C *  *  *  *  *  *  *  *  *  *  *  *  *  *  *  *  *  *  *  *  *  *  *  *
```

Thus the output of the program:

```
OUTPUT SHOULD BE TRUE. . . .
          T

OUTPUT SHOULD BE FALSE. . . .
          F
```

reveals that the subprogram is working correctly.

STRUCTURED PROGRAMMING GUIDELINE

Large programs generally feature more than one subprogram. Do *not* wait until the entire program is completed before testing it. After each subprogram is written, test it by using an appropriate *driver* program. This practice tends to increase the overall efficiency of the programming process, while producing highly reliable programs.

Example 9.4 illustrates how the use of a function subprogram can reduce the amount of program code needed to accomplish the goal of the program.

EXAMPLE 9.4   A program is to manipulate three distinct arrays, ALPHA, BETA, and GAMMA. Write a complete program that reads 10 real values into array ALPHA, 15 real values into array BETA, and 20 real values into array GAMMA. Determine and print the average value of the elements of each array.

Solution

We will offer two program solutions to this problem. The first does not use a function subprogram. After reading and storing the elements of each array using an implied DO loop, a separate set of program statements is used to calculate the average of the elements of each array. The program is presented as Program 9.2.

```
       $JOB    WATFIV
       C PROGRAM WITHOUT A FUNCTION SUBPROGRAM
       C THIS PROGRAM WAS RUN ON AN IBM COMPUTER USING WATFIV
       C
 1             REAL ALPHA(10), BETA(15), GAMMA(20), SUM
 2             INTEGER I
 3             SUM = 0.0
 4             READ , (ALPHA(I), I = 1, 10)
 5             READ , (BETA(I), I= 1, 15)
 6             READ , (GAMMA(I), I = 1, 20)
       C TO FIND THE AVERAGE OF ELEMENTS OF ARRAY ALPHA
 7             DO 10 I = 1, 10
 8               SUM = SUM + ALPHA(I)
 9          10 CONTINUE
10             PRINT , 'AVERAGE OF ALPHA ELEMENTS =', SUM / 10.0
       C TO FIND THE AVERAGE OF ELEMENTS OF ARRAY BETA
11             SUM = 0.0
12             DO 20 I = 1, 15
13               SUM = SUM + BETA(I)
14          20 CONTINUE
15             PRINT , 'AVERAGE OF BETA ELEMENTS = ', SUM / 15.0
       C TO FIND THE AVERAGE OF ELEMENTS OF ARRAY GAMMA
16             SUM = 0.0
17             DO 30 I = 1, 20
18               SUM = SUM + GAMMA(I)
19          30 CONTINUE
20             PRINT , 'AVERAGE OF GAMMA ELEMENTS =', SUM / 20.0
21             STOP
22             END
```

Program 9.2

If a subprogram is used, only one set of statements is needed to determine the average of the elements in each array. The function subprogram uses an argument list consisting of the array name and its number of elements, and then determines the required average. This is shown in Program 9.3.

```
       $JOB    WATFIV
       C PROGRAM WITH A FUNCTION SUBPROGRAM
       C THIS PROGRAM WAS RUN ON AN IBM COMPUTER USING WATFIV
       C
       C* * * * * * * * * * MAIN PROGRAM* * * * * * * * * * *
 1             REAL ALPHA(10), BETA(15), GAMMA(20), AVG
 2             INTEGER I
       C
 3             READ , (ALPHA(I), I = 1, 10)
 4             READ , (BETA(I), I= 1, 15)
 5             READ , (GAMMA(I), I = 1, 20)
       C FUNCTION CALLS IN PRINT STATEMENT FOLLOW
 6             PRINT , 'AVERAGE OF ALPHA ELEMENTS =', AVG(ALPHA, 10)
 7             PRINT , 'AVERAGE OF BETA ELEMENTS = ', AVG(BETA, 15)
 8             PRINT , 'AVERAGE OF GAMMA ELEMENTS =', AVG(GAMMA, 20)
 9             STOP
10             END
       C
       C
       C* * * * * * * * * * FUNCTION SUBPROGRAM* * * * * * * * * *
       C
11             REAL FUNCTION AVG(ARRAY, N)
12             INTEGER N
13             REAL ARRAY(N), SUM
14             SUM = 0.0
15             DO 50 I = 1, N
16               SUM = SUM + ARRAY(I)
17          50 CONTINUE
18             AVG = SUM / FLOAT(N)
19             RETURN
20             END
```

Program 9.3

Example 9.5 illustrates that one function subprogram may call another function subprogram. (A function subprogram may *not* call itself.)

EXAMPLE 9.5 Determine the value returned to the main program if the values passed to the FUNC subprogram given below are 5.0 and 2.0.

```
* * * * * * * MAIN PROGRAM
      READ *, C, D
      X = FUNC (C, D)
      PRINT *, C, D, X
      STOP
      END
*
* * * * * * * * FUNC SUBPROGRAM* * * * * * *
*
      REAL FUNCTION FUNC(X, Y)
      REAL X, Y
      FUNC = QUOT(X, Y) + QUOT (Y, X)
      RETURN
      END
*
* * * * * * * * QUOT SUBPROGRAM* * * * * * *
*
      REAL FUNCTION QUOT(A, B)
      REAL A, B
      QUOT = A / B
      RETURN
      END
```

Solution

In the FUNC subprogram 5.0 replaces X and 2.0 replaces Y. When the statement that references the QUOT function is executed, the next subprogram is called.

$$QUOT(5.0, 2.0) = 5.0 / 2.0 = 2.5$$

and

$$QUOT(2.0, 5.0) = 2.0 / 5.0 = 0.4$$

Hence

$$FUNC = 2.5 + 0.4 = 2.9$$

As the following program output shows, 2.9 is passed back to the main program.
   Output:

```
5. 2.
      5.00000        2.00000        2.90000
**** STOP
```

In Example 9.6 a subprogram is used to determine the actual length of a string. The overall purpose of the program is to find the position of the first occurrence of a specified substring in a given string without using the INDEX function. The dummy variable in the function substring will be given the name STRING. It will be necessary to call the function to find the actual lengths of the SOURCE string and the TARGET string. The declared length of the actual string variable argument may be communicated to the corresponding dummy variable by using the following notation in the CHARACTER data declaration statement in the function subprogram:

```
CHARACTER STRING * (*)
```

where STRING is the dummy string variable argument. The parentheses and the enclosed asterisk direct the computer to pass the length of the actual string variable argument as defined in the corresponding CHARACTER data declaration statement in the main program.

EXAMPLE 9.6 Write a program that finds the position of the first occurrence of a TARGET substring in a given SOURCE string *without* using the INDEX function. Read the SOURCE and TARGET strings. Assume that each has a maximum length of 25 characters, and that the first occurrence of a blank space in each signals the end of the string.

Solution

A function SIZE will be defined in a subprogram to find the actual length of a string by searching for the first occurrence of a blank. The dummy argument name STRING will be used to pass the actual string variable.

In the main program a function reference (SIZE) is made in order to determine the actual lengths of the SOURCE and TARGET strings. The variable S represents the actual number of characters in the SOURCE string; the variable T represents the actual length of the TARGET string. A DO loop is used to test sequentially whether each block of T consecutive characters in the SOURCE string, beginning in the first character position, is equal to the TARGET string. If, for example, the TARGET string consists of three characters, the substring occupying the first three character positions of the SOURCE string is compared to the TARGET string; then the substring in character positions 2 to 4 of the SOURCE string is compared to the TARGET string; next, the substring in character positions 3 to 5 of the SOURCE string is compared to the TARGET string; and so on.

Study Program 9.4 carefully, and convince yourself that the DO parameters are correctly set.

```
* THIS PROGRAM WAS RUN ON A PRIME 850 COMPUTER USING FORTRAN 77
*
*
* * * * * * * * * MAIN PROGRAM* * * * * * * * *
*
      CHARACTER * 25, SOURCE, TARGET
      INTEGER I, T, S, END, SIZE
*
      READ *, SOURCE, TARGET
*
* ECHO PRINT DATA VALUES
*
      PRINT *, SOURCE, TARGET
*
* SIZE REFERENCES FUNCTION SUBPROGRAM
*
* FIND LENGTH OF SOURCE STRING
      S = SIZE(SOURCE)
      PRINT *, 'THE LENGTH OF THE SOURCE STRING IS ', S
* FIND LENGTH OF TARGET STRING
      T = SIZE(TARGET)
      PRINT *, 'THE LENGTH OF THE TARGET STRING IS ', T
*
      DO 50 I = 1, S - T + 1
         END = I - 1 + T
         IF (SOURCE(I : END) .EQ. TARGET(1 : T) ) THEN
            PRINT *, 'SUBSTRING BEGINS IN POSITION     ', I
            GOTO 60
         ENDIF
   50 CONTINUE
      PRINT *, 'SUBSTRING IS NOT CONTAINED IN ORIGINAL STRING'
   60 CONTINUE
      STOP
      END
*
*
* * * * * * * * * *FUNCTION SUBPROGRAM* * * * * * * * * * * * *
*
      INTEGER FUNCTION SIZE(STRING)
      CHARACTER STRING * (*)
      INTEGER I
      DO 75 I = 1, LEN(STRING)
```

```
             IF ( STRING(I:I) .EQ. ' ') THEN
                 SIZE = I - 1
                 GOTO 80
             ENDIF
      75 CONTINUE
*  IF DO LOOP IS EXITED THEN NOT TRAILING BLANK FOUND
         SIZE = LEN(STRING)
      80 CONTINUE
         RETURN
         END
```

Program 9.4

Here is the sample output when the SOURCE string is 'CANTALOUPE' and the TARGET string is 'ANT':

```
'CANTALOUPE'
'ANT'
CANTALOUPE              ANT
THE LENGTH OF THE SOURCE STRING IS        10
THE LENGTH OF THE TARGET STRING IS         3
SUBSTRING BEGINS IN POSITION               2
**** STOP
```

With regard to array and character variables in dummy argument lists, keep the following points in mind:

- It is recommended that the declared length of a dummy character variable in a subprogram be expressed using a parenthesized asterisk. For example:

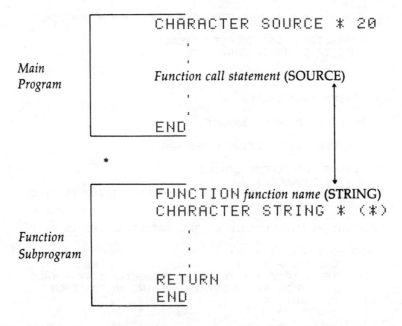

If the dummy character variable corresponds to the actual character variable SOURCE, it will be declared in the subprogram to have a length of 20 characters.
- If an *array* name is used as a dummy argument, its data type and size must be declared within the subprogram. An integer valued variable may be used to declare the size of the array, provided that the variable appears in the list of dummy arguments and the array is dimensioned so that its size is consistent with the size of the actual array.

Alternatively, the size of an array may be declared in a manner analogous to that used to declare the length of a dummy string variable:

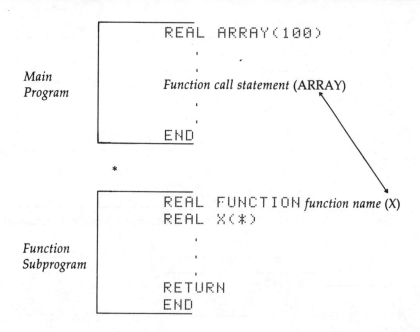

The computer interprets the parenthesized asterisk to mean that the dummy REAL array X is to be dimensioned at the same value as the corresponding actual array is dimensioned in its array declaration statement in the main program. This convention can be used for numeric arrays and for character arrays provided that the elements of the actual and dummy character arrays are declared to have the same length.

9.3 Creating Subroutine Subprograms

A subroutine subprogram is similar in concept and form to a function subprogram. Both represent independent program units that are called into action by the main program or by another subprogram. A *function* subprogram is restricted in the sense that it must return a single value to the calling program unit. A *subroutine*, on the other hand, can return several values, or it need not return any value; it may be used, for example, to adjust the values of program variables or to initiate the execution of an input/output routine.

Another fundamental difference is that a function subprogram communicates its value back to the calling statement through the *name of the function*. A subroutine passes values back to the calling program through its *arguments*.

THE GENERAL FORM OF A SUBROUTINE

A subroutine is referenced by a CALL statement whose general form is as follows:

CALL *subroutine name* (argument list)

The subroutine name is determined by the programmer but must conform to the rules for naming program variables. A subroutine name is merely a label; no data type is associated with it.

Figure 9.4 illustrates the general structure of a subroutine. Every subroutine begins with an identification statement, which starts with the keyword SUBROUTINE, followed by the name of the subroutine and a list of its arguments, if any. As with function subprograms, control passes back to the main program whenever a RETURN or END statement is encountered.

Main Program

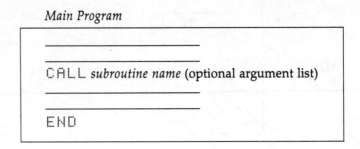

Subroutine Subprogram

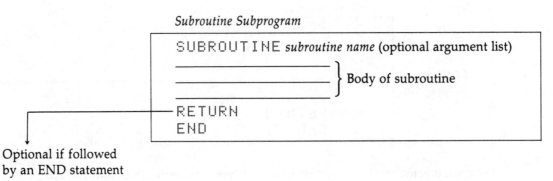

Optional if followed
by an END statement

Figure 9.4 General Structure of a Subroutine

SOME ILLUSTRATIONS

When a subprogram is used to calculate and then return a single value, either a function or a subroutine structure may be used. Consider the situation in which, at numerous places in the main program, there is a need to precede the printing of output values by displaying the column heading

THE RESULTS ARE:

followed by six blank lines. It would be tedious to code this in the main program; a subroutine can be used instead. At each point in the main program where the required output operation is needed, we can insert the statement CALL HEADNG where HEADNG is a programmer-defined subroutine name. The corresponding subroutine subprogram would be coded as follows;

```
* * * * * * * * * *SUBROUTINE* * * * * * * * * * *
*                                                 *
      SUBROUTINE HEADNG
      INTEGER I
      PRINT *, 'THE RESULTS ARE:'
      PRINT *, '_____'
      DO 50 I = 1, 6
         PRINT *, ' '
   50 CONTINUE
      RETURN
      END
*                                                 *
* * * * * * * * * * * * * * * * * * * * * * * * * *
```

Notice that in this subroutine an argument list is *not* provided, because no values are being passed between the main program and the subroutine program.

As another illustration, let's consider an example where values are passed between the main program and the subroutine program. Suppose that the CALL statement in the main program reads as follows:

```
CALL ANSWER(A, B, SUM, PROD)
```

The subroutine name is ANSWER, and the argument list consists of the variables A, B, SUM, and PROD. The idea is that, for given values of A and B, the subroutine calculates and returns their sum and product. The corresponding Fortran program would be coded as follows:

```
* THIS PROGRAM ILLUSTRATES THE USE OF ARGUMENT LISTS TO PASS
* VALUES BETWEEN THE MAIN PROGRAM AND THE SUBROUTINE PROGRAM.
* THIS PROGRAM WAS RUN ON A PRIME 850 COMPUTER USING FORTRAN 77
*
*MAIN ROUTINE
      REAL A, B, SUM, PROD
      READ *, A, B
      CALL ANSWER (A, B, SUM, PROD)
      PRINT *, A, B, SUM, PROD
      END
*
* SUBROUTINE
      SUBROUTINE ANSWER (X, Y, ADD, MULT)
      REAL X, Y, ADD, MULT
      ADD = X + Y
      MULT = X * Y
      RETURN
      END
```

When the data 4.0 (A) and 3.0 (B) are used, here is the output:

```
4.0 3.0
      4.00000        3.00000        7.00000       12.0000
**** STOP
```

Notice that the values are being passed between the main program and the subroutine according to the following correspondences:

```
CALL ANSWER(A, B, SUM, PROD)

SUBROUTINE ANSWER(X, Y, ADD, MULT)
```

To appreciate more fully this exchange of data between the main program and the subroutine subprogram, let's represent the situation in computer memory. When the CALL statement is executed, the current contents of the memory cells labeled A, B, SUM, and PROD are *copied* in corresponding order into the memory cells having the dummy variable names X, Y, ADD, and MULT. If the current contents of A, B, SUM, and PROD are assumed to be 4.0, 3.0, 0.0, and 0.0, respectively, the current status of computer memory may be pictured as follows:

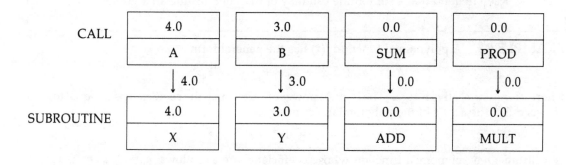

After the subroutine has been executed, the contents of memory locations X, Y, ADD, and MULT are copied back into the corresponding memory locations A, B, SUM, and PROD:

~~4.0~~ 4.0	~~3.0~~ 3.0	~~0.0~~ 7.0	~~0.0~~ 12.0
A	B	SUM	PROD

↑ 4.0   ↑ 3.0   ↑ 7.0   ↑ 12.0

SUBROUTINE

4.0	3.0	7.0	12.0
X	Y	ADD	MULT

It is important to keep in mind that, after the subroutine has been executed, the current value of *each* dummy variable will replace the current value of the corresponding actual variable. If, for example, the values of dummy variables X and Y were unintentionally altered in the subroutine, their new values would wipe out the original values of A and B when program control was transferred back to the main program.

Some computers simply change the *address* of memory cells that store argument values when program control is transferred between the calling program and the subroutine, particularly when arrays are being passed. In our example, such a computer would use four memory cells rather than eight storage locations to accomplish the passing of values between the main program and the subroutine. When control was transferred to the subroutine, the addresses of the memory cells that stored the values 4.0 (A), 3.0 (B), 0.0 (SUM), and 0.0 (PROD) would be changed to X, Y, ADD, and MULT; the values that resided in these cells would remain. As the subroutine executed, the contents of these memory cells might change. When control was transferred back to the main program, the same four memory cells would be relabeled with the original corresponding set of actual argument variables (A, B, SUM, and PROD).

Communicating Between Main Program and Subroutine

Data values are passed from the main program to a subroutine *and* from a subroutine back to the main program through argument lists. As with function subprograms, actual and dummy argument lists must match exactly with each pair of corresponding arguments agreeing in type.

As a result of the two-way communication between the argument lists of the main program and subroutine subprogram, it is possible, either intentionally or unintentionally, to change any or all argument values in the main program. Be careful!

Keep in mind that a subroutine call may or may not include an argument list.

EXAMPLE 9.7 A polynomial function $f(x)$ has the general form

$$f(x) = a_0 + a_1x^1 + a_2x^2 + \cdots + a_nx^n$$

where n is a nonnegative integer. The highest power of x for which the coefficient is unequal to zero zero is called the *degree* of the polynomial. For example,

$$f(x) = 3 + 2x + 9x^2 - x^3 + 7x^5$$

is a fifth-degree polynomial function whose coefficients are as follows: $a_0 = 3$, $a_1 = 2$, $a_2 = 9$, $a_3 = -1$, $a_4 = 0$, and $a_5 = 7$.

The value of the polynomial function, say at $x = 2$, can be found by replacing x with 2:

$$f(2) = 3 + 2(2) + 9(2)^2 - (2)^3 + 0(2)^4 + 7(2)^5 = 259$$

Read in the DEGREE of a particular polynomial function, the value of each of its COEFFicients (a_0 to a_n), and the value of x for which the polynomial is to be evaluated. The polynomial evaluation should be accomplished in a subroutine. Print the RESULT of the evaluation in the main program. Assume that the degree of the polynomial is less than or equal to 10.

Solution

The program that follows stores the coefficients of the polynomial in an array COEFF, which is dimensioned using upper and lower bounds (0 : 10) so that it may accommodate a subscript value of 0. The inputting of the coefficients and the evaluation of the polynomial in the subprogram can therefore be accomplished in a DO loop. See Program 9.5.

```
* * * * * * *EVALUATING A POLYNOMIAL FUNCTION* * * * * * *


* * * * * * *EVALUATING A POLYNOMIAL FUNCTION* * * * * * *
*
*
* THIS PROGRAM WAS RUN ON A PRIME 850 COMPUTER USING FORTRAN 77
*
        INTEGER DEGREE, INDEX
        REAL COEFF(0:10), X, RESULT
*
* . . READ DEGREE OF POLYNOMIAL
        READ *, DEGREE
*
* . . READ COEFFICIENTS INTO AN ARRAY COEFF
        READ *, (COEFF(INDEX), INDEX = 0, DEGREE)
*
* . . READ THE VALUE OF X FOR WHICH THE FUNCTION IS
* . . TO BE EVALUATED AT
*
        READ *, X
        CALL POLY (DEGREE, COEFF, X, RESULT)
        PRINT *, 'FUNCTION VALUE AT ', X, 'EQUALS', RESULT
        STOP
        END
*
*
* * * * * * *SUBROUTINE POLY* * * * * * *
*
*
        SUBROUTINE POLY (N, A, XVAL, FUNVAL)
        INTEGER K, N
        REAL A(0:10), XVAL, FUNVAL
        FUNVAL = 0.0
        DO 99 K = 0, N
            FUNVAL = FUNVAL + A(K) * XVAL ** K
   99 CONTINUE
        RETURN
        END
```

Program 9.5

Program Notes: The program is organized so that three separate data records are required. The first data record contains the DEGREE of the polynomial (an integer value between 1 and 10, inclusive). The second data record includes the value of each COEFFicient of the polynomial (if a term is "missing," its coefficient has a value of zero). The third data record contains the particular value X for which the function is to be evaluated.

WHY USE SUBPROGRAMS?

- Subprograms can reduce the amount of repetitious coding (see Example 9.4), thereby not only simplifying the programmer's job, but also reducing the memory storage requirements of the program.
- Subprograms tend to be portable. Once a subprogram is written, it can be easily incorporated within another program with little or no modification. For example, each time that it is necessary to sort a data list or to find the actual length of a character string by searching for the first occurrence of a trailing blank, why scratch your head and begin to write the program anew? The preferred approach is to write frequently needed program routines as subprograms and then to "plug" them into programs whenever they are needed.
- Subprograms tend to improve program readability and reliability. The use of subprograms tends to encourage a *modular* design approach to program development. A large program can often be organized into a set of program *modules* (that is, subprograms) that can be individually coded, tested, and debugged. These program modules can then be pieced together, and their action coordinated by a main program in a manner somewhat analogous to the way the body's central nervous system controls the movements of our arms and legs. (Section 9.5 of this chapter elaborates on this point.)
- Programs built on subprograms are easy to change since it is a relatively simple matter to identify and work with the subprogram involved. This is an important consideration, not only in the debugging process, but also when it becomes necessary to expand or modify the capabilities of the program in some way after it has been placed into service.
- Organizing a program into a set of independent "miniprograms" (that is, subprograms) allows more than one programmer to work on a given programming project at the same time.
- In a professional setting the use of subprograms and a modular design approach to program development allows the programmer to capitalize on the *virtual storage* capability of mainframe computer systems. To accommodate large programs that exceed the available storage capacity of main memory, modern operating systems permit such programs to be split between main memory and virtual (secondary) storage, which is usually a magnetic disk. The active part of the program resides in main memory, while the part that is not currently needed remains waiting in secondary storage. As needed, program segments are exchanged between main and virtual (disk) memory, so that at no time does the entire program reside in main memory. Organizing a program into a set of independent subprograms helps to facilitate this process.

9.4 COMMON and EQUIVALENCE Statements

THE COMMON STATEMENT

The computer knows that a variable in a calling program refers to the same quantity as a variable in the subprogram that it invokes if the two variables occupy corresponding positions in the actual and dummy argument lists. An alternative way of declaring that variables used in different program modules are synonyms for the same quantity is through the use of a COMMON statement, which takes the general form

COMMON *variable list*

A COMMON is a nonexecutable data declaration statement that must appear before any executable program statement in *both* the calling and the referenced subprogram. For example, these COMMON statements:

Calling Program	Subprogram
`COMMON A, B, K(5)`	`COMMON R, T, L(5)`

establish a common storage area in main memory that is partitioned as illustrated in Figure 9.5. Thus variables A and R refer to the same quantity since they name the identical memory location. The same holds true for variables B and T, and for corresponding elements of arrays K and L. Arrays may be declared within the COMMON statement. Since the COMMON statement does its work during compile time (that is, establishes a block of common storage to be shared by variables that occupy corresponding positions in the COMMON statement), an array may *not* be declared in a COMMON statement using a variable dimension value.

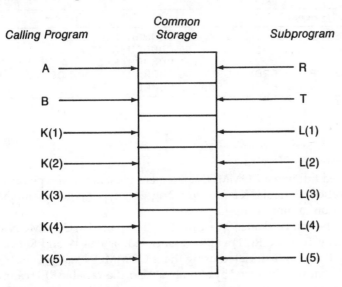

Figure 9.5 Partitioning of Common Storage Area

COMMON statements may be used to advantage in simplifying argument lists. Variables associated through the use of a COMMON statement are *not* included in argument lists. In fact, some programmers prefer to eliminate argument lists entirely and use COMMON statements instead. See Program 9.6.

```
* THIS PROGRAM ILLUSTRATES THE USE OF THE COMMON STATEMENT.

* THIS PROGRAM ILLUSTRATES THE USE OF THE COMMON STATEMENT.
* THIS PROGRAM WAS RUN ON A PRIME 850 COMPUTER USING FORTRAN 77
* MAIN ROUTINE *
*
      REAL A, B, SUM, PROD
      COMMON A, B, SUM, PROD
      READ *, A, B
      CALL ANSWER
      PRINT *, A, B, SUM, PROD
      END
*
* SUBROUTINE
      SUBROUTINE ANSWER
      REAL X, Y, ADD, MULT
      COMMON X, Y, ADD, MULT
      ADD = X + Y
      MULT = X * Y
      RETURN
      END
```

Program 9.6

Output:

```
4.0 3.0
       4.00000        3.00000        7.00000        12.0000
**** STOP
```

As already mentioned, COMMON statements establish variable correspondences during compile time by setting aside common storage areas. More complicated data transfers in memory are required when argument lists are used to pass values between the various subprograms with a corresponding increase in the number of machine language instructions required to accomplish the task. Consequently, the use of COMMON statements can result in economies in internal storage requirements and in program execution times.

EXAMPLE 9.8   For each of the following, determine whether there is an error. Assume implicit data typing of variables.

Calling Program	Subprogram
(a) COMMON A, B, K	(a) COMMON X, Y, Z
(b) COMMON A(N), Y	(b) COMMON A(50), B
(c) COMMON T(20), S, W	(c) COMMON R(25)
(d) COMMON BLUE, RED, GRAY BLACK	(d) SUBROUTINE COLOR (C1, C2, C3)
CALL COLOR(RED, ORANGE, TAN)	COMMON A, B, C, D

Solutions

(a) Variables associated through a COMMON statement must agree in type since they share the same memory location. Variables K and Z do not agree in type (assuming implicit data typing).
(b) A variable dimension cannot be used in array A.
(c) There is no error. The first 20 elements of array R will be paired in COMMON storage with the 20 elements of array T; S and R(21) will be associated, as will W and R(22). The remaining elements of array R are not associated using these COMMON statements.
(d) The variable GRAY must be followed by a comma. Also, the variable RED cannot appear in the COMMON statement and then be used as an argument of a subroutine call. If variables BLUE, RED, GRAY, and BLACK are character variables, then A, B, C, and D must also be typed as character variables.

LABELED (NAMED) COMMON

The type of COMMON statement we have been discussing is sometimes referred to as the *blank* or *unlabeled* COMMON since it creates an unnamed storage area that is not restricted to particular program units; instead, all program modules that have a COMMON share the same island of memory locations, which is external to the section of memory allocated to the particular program unit.

Sometimes it may be desirable to use COMMON to associate variables of selected program modules. Fortran 77 provides a facility by which common storage areas may be referenced by name. For example, consider the following set of COMMON statements:

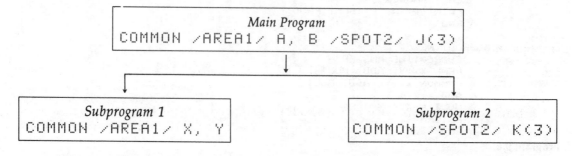

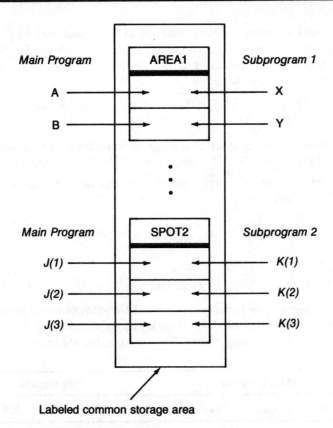

Figure 9.6 Association of Variables in Common Storage

Two distinct common areas, named AREA1 and SPOT2, are declared. The variable associations in common storage are pictured in Figure 9.6. The general form of the *labeled* or *named* COMMON is as follows:

```
COMMON /NAME1/ list₁ /NAME2/ list₂ /NAME3/ list₃ . . .
```

Notice that the name of each common storage area is enclosed by slashes and is followed by the list of variables to be associated in this common area. Remember that the correspondences are established by the order in which the variables are written in the named COMMON statements. As another point of interest, COMMON statements are cumulative. For example, the COMMON statements

```
COMMON A, B, C
COMMON D, E
```

are equivalent to

```
COMMON A, B, C, D, E
```

Also, the statements

```
COMMON /BLOCK1/ R, S
COMMON A, B
COMMON /BLOCK1/E
```

are equivalent to

```
COMMON /BLOCK1/ R, S, E
COMMON A, B
```

A blank COMMON may *not* include both numeric and alphanumeric (that is, character) values. When both numeric and character variables are to be associated by means of common storage, character variable memory locations that are to be shared may be established using a named COMMON statement. For example, if A and B are real variables and CHAR1 and STRING are character variables, it would be incorrect to include these variables in the same blank COMMON statement. Instead, we could write

```
COMMON /ALPHA/ CHAR1, STRING
COMMON A, B
```

where ALPHA is a named common block of storage reserved for character data.

Here are a few additional guidelines for using the COMMON statement:

- Blank and named common storage areas may be declared in the same COMMON statement. The statements

```
COMMON K(15), J
COMMON /OUT/ X(20), Y(30)
```

may be written as

```
COMMON K(15), J /OUT/ X(20), Y(30)
```

- The number of memory cells defined in a *blank* COMMON in the main program may be greater than the number of storage locations allocated by the COMMON statement in the invoked subprogram. For example, the statements

Main Program	Subprogram
COMMON A(3), B, C(4)	COMMON D, E(5)

create the following variable associations in memory:

|←————————Common storage————————→|

A(1) D	A(2) E(1)	A(3) E(2)	B E(3)	C(1) E(4)	C(2) E(5)	C(3)	C(4)

- The total number of memory cells defined in a *named* common storage area must be the same in every subprogram that references the same named common area.

THE EQUIVALENCE STATEMENT

An EQUIVALENCE statement is a nonexecutable program statement that may be used to establish that variables in the *same* program unit refer to the same storage locations and are therefore equivalent.

The statement

```
EQUIVALENCE (EXAM1, GRADE1, SCORE1)
```

establishes that the variables EXAM1, GRADE1, and SCORE1 refer to the same quantity within the same program module. This is sometimes useful when, in various parts of a complicated program, you may wish to use different mnemonic variable names to refer to the same quantity.

A more significant application of the EQUIVALENCE statement is in conserving memory space. It may happen, for example, that in a program two arrays having 5000 elements each will be needed, but never at the same time. After the processing involving one array is completed, the other array may be used with no reference being made to both arrays as the processing progresses. Instead of reserving 10,000 memory locations (5000 for each array), an EQUIVALENCE statement such as

```
REAL A(5000), B(5000)
EQUIVALENCE (A(1), B(1))
```

may be used, which reserves the same 5000 memory locations for both arrays. Since the elements of arrays are always stored in consecutive order, the computer interprets the equivalenced pair (A(1), B(1)) to mean that each successive pair of elements of the two arrays are equivalenced (that is, share the same memory locations) in corresponding subscript order. Incidentally, it would be incorrect to write

```
EQUIVALENCE (A, B)
```

since only variables and subscripted variables (*not* array names) may be equivalenced.

As a further illustration, consider the following set of statements:

```
INTEGER K(9), L(4), N, J, M
EQUIVALENCE (K(1), L(1)), (K(5), N), (K(6), J, M)
```

This set of statements establishes that in the same program unit the first four elements of array K and the four corresponding elements of array L share the same memory locations. The same holds true for K(5) and N, as well as for variables K(6), J, and M.

What happens to K(7), K(8), and K(9), as these are not equivalenced? Since an array is stored in a block of consecutive memory locations, these elements are also found in the shared storage area but are not associated with any other variables. This situation can be illustrated graphically as follows:

K(1)	K(2)	K(3)	K(4)	K(5)	K(6)	K(7)	K(8)	K(9)
L(1)	L(2)	L(3)	L(4)	N	J			
					M			

Common storage area

Notice that more than two variables may be equivalenced. The general form of the EQUIVALENCE statement is

$$EQUIVALENCE \ (list_1), (list_2), \ . \ . \ .$$

where each list contains variables that name the same memory location. As usual, you should not mix variable types in forming equivalence variable lists.

An EQUIVALENCE statement may also be used in conjunction with a COMMON. For example, the statements

```
INTEGER J, K, L(3), M(7), N(2)
COMMON J, K, L
EQUIVALENCE (J, M(1)), (K, N(2))
```

establish a common storage area having the following variable associations:

J	K	L(1)	L(2)	L(3)		
M(1)	M(2)	M(3)	M(4)	M(5)	M(6)	M(7)
N(1)	N(2)					

Variables that appear in a COMMON statement may not be included in the *same* list of equivalenced variables, as this may result in giving the Fortran compiler conflicting instructions when it allocates storage space. When you construct your own COMMON and EQUIVALENCE statements, you will be well advised to map out variable associations using a diagram. This will help prevent situations in which the variable storage assignments are physically impossible.

EXAMPLE 9.9 Explain why each of the following sets of statements is illegal:

```
(a) REAL A, B, C, D(2)
    COMMON A(3), B, C(2)
    EQUIVALENCE (A(2), D(1)), (B, D(2))
(b) INTEGER K, L, M(6)
    COMMON K(5), L(4)
    EQUIVALENCE (K(2), M(3))
```

Solutions

(a) The COMMON statement specifies that A(1), A(2), A(3), B, C(1), and C(2) be assigned in sequence to the first seven memory locations in COMMON storage. Since the elements of arrays must be stored in sequence, if A(2) and D(1) are equivalenced, then D(2) must immediately follow and will therefore be associated with A(3). This contradicts the equivalenced pair (B, D(2)).

(b) The COMMON statement specifies that the first nine memory locations in common storage be assigned to elements of arrays K and L in sequence, with K(1) occupying the first memory cell. The EQUIVALENCE statement associates K(2) and M(3), implying that K(1) and M(2) must share the same memory cell. What about M(1)? The block of common storage cannot accommodate M(1) since K(1) occupies the initial memory location as defined by the COMMON statement.

EXAMPLE 9.10 Determine the output of the following program:

```
CHARACTER * 6, DATE
CHARACTER * 2, MONTH, DAY, YEAR
EQUIVALENCE (MONTH, DATE(1:2) )
EQUIVALENCE (DAY, DATE (3:4) )
EQUIVALENCE (YEAR, DATE (5:6) )
DATE = '060981'
PRINT *, 'MONTH =', MONTH
PRINT *, 'DAY = ', DAY
PRINT *, 'YEAR = ', YEAR
END
```

Solution

This program provides a simple illustration of the EQUIVALENCE statement in which a simple string variable is equivalenced with a string variable that returns the indicated substring of the character variable DATE.

The output would be as follows:

```
MONTH =06
DAY =  09
YEAR = 81
**** STOP
```

EXAMPLE 9.11 Read a character string having a maximum of 12 characters. Print the character string so that any trailing blanks are eliminated and the characters are printed in reverse order horizontally across a print line.

Solution

The key to this problem is to store each character of the string as an element of an array. This can be accomplished by equivalencing the string variable with a character array. The array is declared so that its size agrees with the declared length of the string variable and each character element has a length of one. In memory, each array element will refer to a single character of the string variable in corresponding order. For example, the third element of the array will be aligned in memory with the third character of the stored string. The actual length of the stored string can be determined using the Index function. The length serves as a parameter of the implied DO loop which prints the elements of the array in reverse order.

```
      INTEGER I, K, LENGTH
      CHARACTER WORD * 12, ARRAY(12) * 1
      EQUIVALENCE (ARRAY, WORD)
*
*     INPUT THE STRING VARIABLE VALUE WORD
*
      READ (*, 100) WORD
  100 FORMAT(A12)
*
*     DETERMINE THE LENGTH OF THE STRING
*
      I = INDEX (WORD, ' ')
      IF (I .EQ. 0) THEN
         LENGTH = 12
      ELSE
         LENGTH = I - 1
      ENDIF
*
*     PRINT ELEMENTS OF ARRAY HORIZONTALLY IN REVERSE ORDER
*
      PRINT *, (ARRAY(K), K = LENGTH, 1, -1)
      STOP
      END
```

Program Notes: You may wish to compare this solution to the solution to Exercise 8.2 which solves the same problem but does not take advantage of the EQUIVALENCE statement.

9.5 Problem Solving Approaches

The most challenging aspect of preparing a computer solution to a problem is the development of the algorithm that describes the type and sequence of operations which solve the problem. Formulating an algorithm typically requires a thoughtful and creative analysis of the problem, while coding a specified algorithm into Fortran tends more to be of a mechanical process.

When you are confronted with a programming problem that you have not encountered before, the algorithm that defines the solution to the problem may not be obvious. A flowchart analysis may not be helpful since, in order to build a flowchart, a good part, if not all, of the solution algorithm must already be known. What can you do? First, make sure that you understand the nature and requirements of the problem. Then try one or more of the following heuristics (see Section 1.2 of Chapter 1), which may prove helpful in developing the needed algorithm:

- *Search for a similar problem* that you have already solved or that someone else has solved. For example, look for a similar model problem in this book. Examine the techniques used to solve that problem, and determine whether they can be modified to help you formulate the algorithm that solves your problem.
- *Think of an easier problem that is related to your problem.* Determine whether the algorithm that solves the simpler problem can illuminate the solution path to your problem.
- *Tackle the problem by subdividing it into a set of smaller problems* that are more manageable than the original problem. Most programs, for example, consist of

three major tasks: input, processing, and output. In complex programs, these functions can be further resolved into a set of component tasks. Each of these subtasks corresponds to a program module. Thus, there is a close relationship between problem solving and Fortran subprograms. When analyzing complex problems, think in terms of reducing the larger (global) problem into a set of relatively independent smaller problems, each of which can be solved within a subprogram. Since the purpose of the subprogram is generally narrowly defined, the algorithm required to accomplish each subprogram task can be developed easily. Tools such as *structure charts* can help you to identify the component parts of a problem.

STRUCTURE CHARTS

A flowchart is not the only diagrammatic tool that can be used to help develop a solution to a problem. *Structure chart* analysis can be helpful in analyzing a problem for which the algorithm is not known. A structure chart is a tree type of diagram that, by working backward from the given problem, seeks to identify the underlying set of component tasks that must be accomplished for the given problem to be solved. Consider, for example, the plight of a housewife who must plan a busy day. She might organize her chores for the day under three categories: morning chores, afternoon chores, and evening chores. Under each heading she might list the corresponding set of required tasks, as in Figure 9.7. Notice that each task can be broken down into one or more component tasks until the original task is reduced to a set of basic tasks that completely defines the solution to the original problem.

An analogous approach may be taken in planning the computer solution to a problem. Figure 9.8 shows the general form of a structure chart. The global task represents the end result or purpose of the program. The first level of program modules typically includes an *input* module, a *processing* module, and an *output* module. Under each of these modules, the required tasks are identified in a hierarchical fashion. The pattern of program modules that unfolds as a result of this type of diagrammatic analysis serves to define the algorithm necessary to solve the original problem (global task).

Notice that the structure chart is read from top to bottom and shows the logical relationships between self-contained program units. A coded program that follows this type of analysis is said to

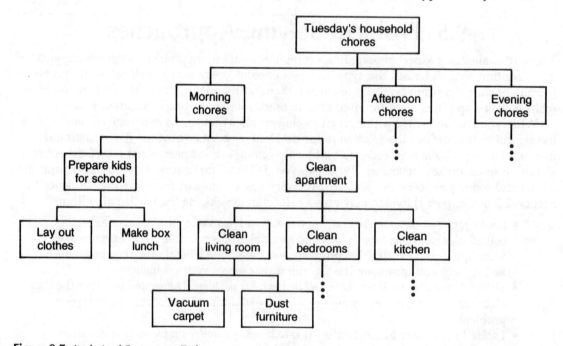

Figure 9.7 Analysis of Component Tasks

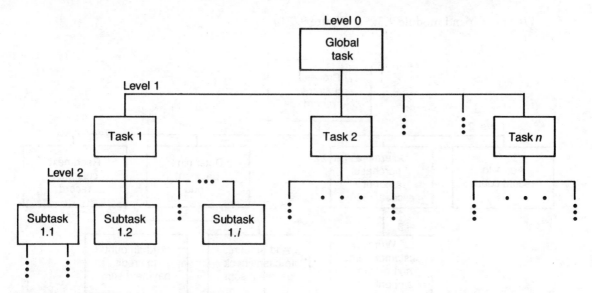

Figure 9.8 General Form of Structure Chart

be designed using a *top-down, modular design* approach, and it is generally agreed that programs which follow this approach are easier to read, test, and debug. They also tend to be more reliable and are easier to change. (See Problem 20 at the end of this chapter, which asks you to apply this methodology to the solution of a statistics-related problem.)

EXAMPLE 9.12   A certain department store uses the following coding system to indicate the method of customer payment:

> code 1 = payment by cash/check
> code 2 = payment by credit card
> code 3 = trailer record

Assume for simplicity that a customer transaction record includes only the following items: customer name, amount of purchase, and payment code. Design a structure chart that determines and prints:

(a) the number of customer transaction records processed
(b) the sum of the payments made by cash/check and by credit card
(c) the total amount of customer payments
(d) the name and amount for any purchase that exceeds $500

Solution

See Figure 9.9(a)–(c).

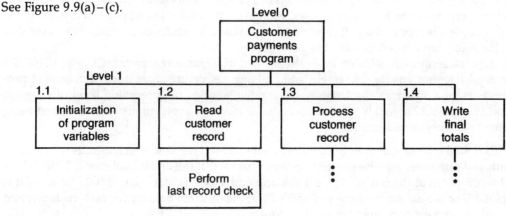

Figure 9.9(a)

We now expand module 1.3. See Figure 9.9(b).

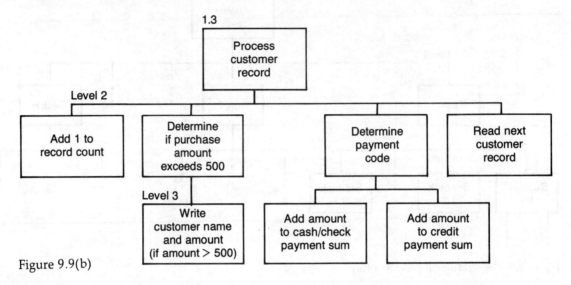

Figure 9.9(b)

We now expand module 1.4. See Figure 9.9(c).

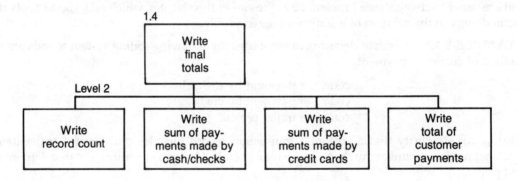

Figure 9.9(c) Structure Chart for Example 9.11, Showing Modular Expansion

THE METHOD OF STEPWISE REFINEMENT

Still another effective problem solving strategy is based on describing in general terms (usually in the form of a pseudocode) the major functions of a program as a sort of "rough" draft. A revised draft is then prepared, which expands upon the initial draft by inserting steps of increasing detail. When this process is repeated a sufficient number of times, a pattern of statements evolves that defines the algorithm needed to solve the problem.

This type of analysis is referred to as the *method of stepwise refinement*. Clearly, there is a relationship between stepwise refinement and building a structure chart since each level of program modules in a structure chart represents a refinement of the preceding level of program modules. Example 9.12 shows how a pseudocode solution to a problem may be developed using the method of stepwise refinement.

EXAMPLE 9.13 Read in a series of customer credit account records, which include the month's payments and purchases and the previous month's balance. If the unpaid balance is $500 or less, interest is computed at the rate of 1.5%. If the unpaid balance is more than $500, the interest is $7.50 plus 1% of the amount in excess of $500. Print the updated balance for each customer and the sum of the interest computed for each customer.

Solution

Step 1. Give a general description of the processing required:

> Start
> Read customer record
> Process customer record
> Print sum of interest
> Stop

Step 2. Begin to refine the solution in a stepwise fashion. The program must be designed to process more than a single customer record. A repetition sequence is needed that reads and processes records until the EOF record is read.

> Start
> Read first customer record
> DO WHILE not EOF
> > Process customer record
> > Read next record
> END OF DO WHILE loop
> Print sum of interest
> Stop

Step 3. Continue stepwise refinement by elaborating on the processing required.

> Start
> Read first customer record
> DO WHILE not EOF
> > Calculate unpaid balances
> > IF unpaid balance is less than 500 THEN
> > > Calculate interest at 1.5% of unpaid balance
> > ELSE
> > > Calculate interest at 7.50 plus 1% of the difference between the unpaid balance and 500
> > END of IF sequence
> > Accumulate interest totals
> > Calculate updated balance
> > Print customer account record
> > Read next customer record
> END of DO WHILE loop
> Print sum of customer interest
> Stop

After an appropriate number of stepwise refinements, this solution can be coded easily into Fortran.

9.6 Some Closing Remarks

The emphasis in this chapter was on problem analysis and program organization. Sometimes a problem seems overwhelming because it requires the performance of many tasks, some of which may or may not seem related. In approaching a large or complex problem, it is often helpful to first identify each of its component tasks. Structure charts and the method of stepwise refinement can be useful in this process. Next, a subprogram can be designed to accomplish each of these subtasks. A main program can then be written that coordinates the calling of each subprogram.

Although simply stated, the approach just described represents one of the most effective and powerful problem solving strategies. It is based on a common-sense approach: "If you can't solve a large problem, cut it down to size by dividing it into smaller problems each of which you already know how to solve." In programming jargon, we refer to this as a top-down, modular design approach.

Which is better to use, flowcharts or structure charts? In planning a solution to a problem, either technique can be used to advantage. The methods share — and accomplish — the same two goals:

- to provide an established and effective method for planning *before* coding
- to supplement the resulting computer program with a document that describes the logic used in the program without making reference to a particular programming language

There is, however, a fundamental difference between flowcharts and structure charts. A structure chart focuses on *what* tasks are to be performed, while a flowchart describes *how* a particular task is to be accomplished. Problems that involve a straightforward application of a known algorithm tend to lend themselves to a flowchart analysis. A problem for which the algorithm is not known at the outset, or whose complexity would obscure the logic of a flowchart approach, can usually be handled best by a structure chart analysis.

Sometimes it may be appropriate to use more than one problem solving technique. For example, after designing a structure chart, a flowchart or pseudocode analysis may prove helpful in specifying how a task identified in a particular structure chart module is to be accomplished.

Throughout our presentation we have stressed the importance of program clarity and of framing solutions in terms of the three fundamental programming sequences: simple, selection, and repetition. The fact that program solutions should be readable from top to bottom implies that the use of the GOTO should be minimized and that program control should pass to a programming sequence and leave it only at its entry and exit points. We have used the term *structured programming* to refer to these ideas. One might say that the top-down modular design approach to problem analysis and program development is the "glue" that binds the concepts of structured programming together.

Review Exercises

A star preceding the number of a problem indicates that a solution to that problem is given at the back of the book.

* **1.** Describe the variable memory allocations in common storage that are created by each of the following sets of statements:

(a)
```
REAL R, S(5), T
COMMON R(3), T
EQUIVALENCE (R(1), S(1))
```
(b)
```
INTEGER J(2), K(6), L(5), M
REAL A(4), B(3)
COMMON J, L
EQUIVALENCE (J(1), M), (J(2), K(1)), (A(1), B(1))
```

* **2.** Determine the error in each of the following:

(a)
```
INTEGER L, M
REAL A, B, C(4)
COMMON L, A(3), M, B(2)
EQUIVALENCE (A(2), C(1))
```
(b)
```
REAL A(3), B(2), C(4), D
COMMON A, D, B
EQUIVALENCE (C(1), B(1)), (D, C(4))
```

3-5. Write a function subprogram to accomplish each of the following. Also code an appropriate driver program.

* **3.** Given the real argument X and the integer argument N, the subprogram returns the value of

$$X + \frac{X^2}{2} + \frac{X^3}{3} + \cdots + \frac{X^N}{N}$$

4. Given the unequal real arguments A, B, and C, the subprogram returns the value that is less than one value but greater than the other value.

5. Given as arguments a real array A and its size, the subprogram returns the average of the elements of the array.

6–10. Write a subroutine subprogram to accomplish each of the following:

* **6.** Given an array having 100 real data elements, the subprogram returns the array with the data "smoothed" by relacing each element X(I), except the first and the last element, by

$$\frac{X(I-1) + X(I) + X(I+1)}{3}$$

* **7.** Given an array having 25 integer elements, the subprogram returns the array with each of its elements initialized at zero.

8. Given an array, the number of elements in the array, and a variable that represents the maximum value of an array element (assume that the array consists of positive integer values), the subprogram returns the maximum value of the array.

* **9.** Given an integer array having 50 nonzero elements, the subprogram returns the number of even and the number of odd elements in the array.

* **10.** Given the arguments STRING and T, where STRING is a character string having a maximum of 26 characters and T is a character variable that represents a single character, the subprogram returns the number of occurrences of T in STRING.

* **11.** Print a table of the values of SIN(X), COS(X), AND TAN(X) for all values of X, in increments of 10 degrees between 0 and 90 degrees, inclusive. The tangent of 90 degrees is undefined. Instead of attempting to evaluate the tangent function at 90 degrees, print UNDEFINED. (Remember to convert degrees to radians before evaluating the trigonometric functions.)

12. On a certain Fortran compiler, the arguments of the Arcsine, Arccosine, and Arctangent functions must be nonnegative. Modify the program developed in Example 9.2 so that it will run successfully on this compiler.

13. A projectile launched at an angle of θ (theta) degrees has a horizontal range given by the formula

$$\text{range} = \frac{2v^2}{g} \sin \theta \cos \theta$$

where v = initial velocity and g = 32.2 ft/sec² (acceleration due to gravity).

Read in the initial velocity. Print, in table form, θ and the corresponding range for values of θ from 0 to 90 degrees in intervals of 15 degrees. In addition, your program should determine and print the angle in this interval at which the range is a maximum.

14. The value of SIN(X) may be calculated using the series expansion

$$SIN(X) = X - \frac{X^3}{3!} + \frac{X^5}{5!} - \frac{X^7}{7!} + \cdots$$

For a given value of X expressed in radians, find the number of terms needed in order for the function value SIN(X) and the calculated series expansion value to differ by less than 0.001. Calculate the factorial of a number in a function subprogram.

15. After developing a pseudocode solution based on the structure chart given in Example 9.12, prepare the corresponding Fortran program.

16. The amount of radioactive decay is expressed in terms of the half-life of the substance involved. The polonium isotope, for example, has a half-life of approximately 140 days. If we begin with 40 milligrams of polonium, then, after 140 days, there are 20 mg of polonium; after 280 days, 10 mg of polonium remain; and so on. The general relationship for the amount of radioactive substance that remains during the decaying process is given by

$$SUBST = IAMT \times e^{(-0.6931)\,T/HLIFE}$$

where: e = the base of the natural log function, IAMT = the initial amount of the radioactive substance, HLIFE = the half-life rating, T = the number of elapsed units of time, which must be expressed in the same units of time as the half-life, SUBST = the amount of the radioactive substance that remains after T units of time have elapsed.

For an initial amount of polonium of 40 mg, print the amount of the substance that remains after each 7-day interval from 0 to 140 days.

17. Write a main program that accepts as input three positive real values, A, B, and C. In a subprogram determine whether the three numbers can represent the lengths of the sides of a triangle (check whether each value is less than the sum of the other two). If the values cannot represent the lengths of the sides of a triangle, then program control should pass back to the main program, which will print an appropriate message and stop execution. If the numbers can represent the lengths of the sides of a triangle, then program control should pass to another subprogram, which will find the area of the triangle using the formula

$$AREA = \sqrt{S(S - A)(S - B)(S - C)}$$

where

$$S = (A + B + C) / 2.0$$

Program control should now pass back to the main program, which will print the output under appropriate column headings.

*18. Modify the program written for Problem 17 so that the following additional subprograms are included:
    (a) a subprogram for validating that each of the input data values is positive
    (b) a subprogram for determining whether the triangle is acute, right, or obtuse (a triangle is acute if $C^2 < A^2 + B^2$, right if $C^2 = A^2 + B^2$, and obtuse if $C^2 > A^2 + B^2$, where C is the longest side of the triangle)
    Also, your program should process a series of data records. Use as a trailer record values of 0.0 for A, B, and C.

19. Read in an integer value less than 100. Print the number and its representation in Roman numerals.

*20. An unsorted list of real numbers ends with a trailer value of -999.9 and contains a maximum of 100 values. Read the list into an array. Draw a structure chart, and use a top-down modular approach in designing a program that does the following:
    (a) Finds the mean (average) and standard deviation. The standard deviation may be calculated using the formula,

$$STDEV = \sqrt{\frac{\Sigma (X(I))^2}{N} - (MEAN)^2}$$

where Σ = summation symbol, and N = number of elements.

    (b) After sorting the array, finds the range and the median. The range is the difference between the largest and smallest values in the array. The median of a sorted list of number is the middle value. If, for example, the list is 4, 18, 21, 59, and 62, the median is 21; if the list contains an even number of values, such as 4, 18, 21, 27, 59, and 62, the median is found by taking the average of the center values: $(21 + 27)/2 = 24$.
    (c) Finds the mode that is the most frequently occurring value in the array. A list may have more than one mode.

21. Read a decimal (base-10) positive integer. Convert the number into its binary (base-2) equivalent, storing each binary digit as a distinct element of an array BINARY. Print the original number and its binary equivalent. Use formatted output and an implied DO loop so that elements of BINARY are printed adjacent to one another on the same horizontal line. (*Hint:* The highest power of 2 that must be used in expressing a base-10 number as the sum of powers of 2 may be found using this relationship:

$$POWER = LOG(NUMBER) / LOG(2.0)$$

Assume that the original number is less than or equal to 1024.)

CHAPTER 10
External File Processing

┌───┐
│ **COMPUTER AXIOM**   │
│ It is easier to tell a computer to fetch a large volume of data │
│ stored on a machine-readable storage medium than it is to key │
│ in the data set each time that the program is run.   │
├───┤
│ **COROLLARY**   │
│ *When large volumes of data must be processed both at the* │
│ *present time and in the future, rather than keying the data in* │
│ *during each session at the computer, they should be*   │
│ *"permanently" saved on a secondary storage device such as* │
│ *magnetic tape or magnetic disk. Fortran 77 includes special* │
│ *commands that allow information to be stored on secondary* │
│ *storage devices and retrieved when needed.*   │
└───┘

10.1 Organizing Data on Magnetic Media

A payroll for a large company is produced typically by a computer. Think of the waste of time it would be to have to key in during each payroll period the names and related information (such as social security number and wage rate) for each employee. A more efficient procedure is to "permanently" store this information on a magnetic tape or magnetic disk so that it can be read by the computer whenever the payroll program is run. In this type of data processing application, employee information must be organized in a common hierarchical arrangement of field → record → file. Data items such as employee name, social security number, and wage rate are entered in reserved areas called *fields*. The collection of fields that pertain to a particular employee is called a *record*. The set of employee payroll records forms a *file*.

Before proceeding further, you should review the material in Sections 1.4 and 1.9 of Chapter 1. These sections contrast sequential and direct access file organizations and illustrate the field-record-file concept. Although Fortran 77 provides for the handling of both sequential and direct access files, in this chapter we will restrict our attention to manipulating external files that are organized sequentially. It will help to keep in mind that the commands needed to create files, or to copy a file from a secondary storage medium into the computer's main memory, must be generated from within a Fortran program.

10.2 File-Related Commands (Fortran 77)

OPEN AND CLOSE STATEMENTS

A program instruction is needed that identifies the file under consideration and establishes a communications link between main memory and the secondary storage device in which the file resides. This is accomplished by the OPEN statement, which takes this general form:

> OPEN (list of *specifiers*)

Effect: Identifies and links an external file to main memory

A list of specifiers consists of the parameters that define the file. For example, the statement

```
OPEN (UNIT = 13, FILE = 'PROD', STATUS = 'NEW')
```

includes three specifiers, separated by commas. The first specifier (UNIT = *device number*) is required in all OPEN statements since it identifies the auxiliary storage device that is to be used. The device number (13 in our example) must be a nonnegative integer value that references a particular input/output device in the computer system being used. It is permissible to write the device number without preceding it by UNIT = . In some systems an asterisk is used to identify an I/O device, such as a disk drive, that is preconnected for a particular file organization.

The second specifier (FILE = '*file name*') identifies the particular file that is to be accessed or created. The character expression within the single apostrophes is the file name. If this specifier is omitted and a file is not currently connected, then, by default, a system-determined file is accessed.

The specifier STATUS = '*status parameter*' indicates whether the file already exists, is to be created, or is to be deleted. If the parameter NEW is used, as in our example, the file does not exist and is being created. If the file has already been created and is being retrieved, the parameter OLD is used. Sometimes it is desirable to create a temporary file and then to erase it. The parameter SCRATCH is used for this purpose. If the STATUS = specifier uses the parameter UNKNOWN or if this specifier is omitted, the status defaults to a system-determined condition.

Here are some additional specifiers:

ACCESS = 'SEQUENTIAL ' or 'DIRECT'
> Default selection is SEQUENTIAL.

FORM = 'FORMATTED' or 'UNFORMATTED'
> Default selection is FORMATTED for a sequential file and UNFORMATTED for a direct access file.

RECL = n, where n is an integer that corresponds to the record length in a direct access file.

ERR = s, where s is the statement label to which program control transfers in the event of an error.

After a file is processed, a CLOSE statement is used to sever the connection between a file and its input/output device. It takes this general form:

> CLOSE (list of *specifiers*)

Effect: Disconnects a file from an I/O device.

Like the OPEN statement, the UNIT = specifier is required, while the ERR = specifier is optional. The STATUS = specifier may have a designated value of KEEP or DELETE. The parameter KEEP maintains the data on the file for possible use at some later date; the DELETE value erases the data on the file. The value KEEP may not be used if SCRATCH appears in the list of values of specifiers in the OPEN statement, as these values are contradictory. If the STATUS = specifier is omitted, then the value defaults to KEEP, provided that SCRATCH was not used in the OPEN statement; if SCRATCH appears in the OPEN statement, then the default value is DELETE.

READ AND WRITE STATEMENTS

After a file is defined by means of an OPEN statement, READ and WRITE statements are used to manipulate the file. The READ statement "looks" into an external file and copies its contents into main memory. The WRITE statement creates a file by copying data stored in main memory to an external file. The general forms of these input/output statements are as follows:

> READ (*control* list) *input variable* list
> WRITE (*control* list) *output variable* list

Effect: To retrieve (READ) or create (WRITE) data from or to an external file.

The control list includes the specifier UNIT = , which associates a file with an input/output device. Recall that the device number may be written without being preceded by UNIT = . The following specifiers may also be included:

FMT = s, where s is the statement label of a FORMAT statement that defines the column layout of an input or output record.

REC = n, where n is a nonnegative integer that identifies the number of the record to be processed in a direct access file.

ERR = s, where s is the statement label of an executable program statement to which program control is transferred when an error condition is encountered.

END = s, where s is the statement label of an executable program statement to which program control is transferred when the end-of-file record is read. This specifier is not appropriate for a WRITE statement or for a direct access file.

```
* * * * * * * * * * * * * * * * * * * * * * * * * * * * * * * * * * * * * *
* PROGRAM TO CREATE A SEQUENTIAL FILE                                     *
* THIS PROGRAM WAS RUN ON A PRIME 850 COMPUTER USING FORTRAN 77           *
* AUTHOR ARLENE PODOS                                                     *
*                                                                         *
*        VARIABLE NAMES                                                   *
*            PRODNO   = MODEL NUMBER OF PRODUCT                           *
*            DESCR    = DESCRIPTION OF PRODUCT                            *
*            QUANT    = QUANTITY ON HAND OF PRODUCT                       *
*            PRICE    = UNIT PRICE OF PRODUCT                             *
*            KOUNT    = A COUNTER TO DETERMINE HOW MANY RECORDS ARE       *
*                       WRITTEN TO THE PRODUCT FILE                       *
* * * * * * * * * * * * * * * * * * * * * * * * * * * * * * * * * * * * * *
*
* DATA DECLARATIONS FOLLOW
      CHARACTER DESCR * 20
      REAL PRICE
      INTEGER KOUNT, QUANT, PRODNO
*
* INITIALIZATION
      OPEN (UNIT = 13, FILE = 'PROD', STATUS = 'NEW')
      KOUNT = 0
      READ (*, 100) PRODNO, DESCR, QUANT, PRICE
  100 FORMAT (I3, A20, I3, F5.2)
*
* WHILE LOOP BEGINS
   50 CONTINUE
      IF (PRODNO .NE. 999) THEN
          WRITE (13, 200) PRODNO, DESCR, QUANT, PRICE
  200     FORMAT(I3, A20, I3, F5.2)
          KOUNT = KOUNT + 1
          READ (*, 300) PRODNO, DESCR, QUANT, PRICE
  300     FORMAT (I3, A20, I3, F5.2)
          GOTO 50
      ENDIF
*
* THE WHILE LOOP HAS BEEN EXITED. PERFORM TERMINATION ROUTINES
*
* INSERT A TRAILER RECORD TO MARK THE END OF THE FILE
      PRODNO = 999
      DESCR = ' '
      QUANT = -1
      PRICE = 0.0
      WRITE (13,400) PRODNO, DESCR, QUANT, PRICE
  400 FORMAT (I3, A20, I3, F5.2)
* PRINT CONTROL TOTALS
      PRINT *, 'COUNT =', KOUNT
      CLOSE (UNIT = 13)
      STOP
      END
```

Program 10.1

It may help to keep in mind that we READ *from* an existing external file into main memory, and WRITE *to* a file on an external storage medium from main memory.

Program 10.1 illustrates how to create a sequential file. In the initialization routine the OPEN statement instructs the computer that a file to be named PROD is to be created (since status = 'NEW') and connected to device 13. The READ statement:

```
READ (*, 100) PRODNO, DESCR, QUANT, PRICE
```

reads four quantities that are entered using a keyboard terminal (device = *) according to the specification provided by the FORMAT statement having the statement label 100. In the WHILE loop that follows, the WRITE statement:

```
WRITE (13, 200) PRODNO, DESCR, QUANT, PRICE
```

writes a record onto the file PROD, with the layout of the record organized according to the FORMAT statement having the statement label 200.

Notice that, after the WHILE loop is exited, a trailer record having PRODNO = 999 is written to the file as the last record. When the file must be subsequently read, this record will serve to signal the end of the file.

Here is a listing of the file created in Program 10.1:

```
95LOOSE LEAF PAPER    100 1.00


95LOOSE LEAF PAPER    100 1.00
99FORTRAN BOOKS       20010.00
102MAGIC MARKERS      150 1.25
105SCOTCH TAPE        400 0.29
109SCISSORS           25510.00
999                    -1 0.00
```

The file that was created in Program 10.1 is processed in Program 10.2. After a record has been read from the file, the quantity (QUAN) is multiplied by the price (PRICE) to obtain the value (VALUE). The results are printed in table form as illustrated.

```
* * * * * * * * * * * * * * * * * * * * * * * * * * * * * * * * * * * *
* PROGRAM TO PRINT CONTENTS OF  A SEQUENTIAL FILE                    *
* THIS PROGRAM WAS RUN ON A PRIME 850 COMPUTER USING FORTRAN 77      *
*                                                                    *
* AUTHOR ARLENE PODOS                                                *
*                                                                    *
*        VARIABLE NAMES                                              *
*             PRODNO   = MODEL NUMBER OF PRODUCT                     *
*             DESCR    = DESCRIPTION OF PRODUCT                      *
*             QUANT    = QUANTITY ON HAND OF PRODUCT                 *
*             PRICE    = UNIT PRICE OF PRODUCT                       *
*             VALUE    = QUANTITY TIMES THE UNIT PRICE               *
* * * * * * * * * * * * * * * * * * * * * * * * * * * * * * * * * * * *
*
* DATA DECLARATIONS FOLLOW
      CHARACTER DESCR * 20
      REAL PRICE, VALUE
      INTEGER KOUNT, QUANT, PRODNO
*
* INITIALIZATION
      OPEN (UNIT = 13, FILE = 'PROD', STATUS = 'OLD')
      READ (13, 100) PRODNO, DESCR, QUANT, PRICE
100 FORMAT (I3, A20, I3, F5.2)
* WRITE HEADINGS
      WRITE (*, 150)
150 FORMAT (1X, 'PROD NO', 6X, 'DESCRIPTION', 11X, 'QUANTITY', 3X, 'PR
     -ICE', 3X, 'VALUE' )
      WRITE (*, 175)
175 FORMAT ( 1X )
*
```

```
*  WHILE LOOP BEGINS
    50 CONTINUE
       IF (PRODNO .NE. 999) THEN
            VALUE = QUANT * PRICE
            WRITE (*, 200) PRODNO, DESCR, QUANT, PRICE, VALUE
  200       FORMAT (3X, I3, 6X, A20, 6X, I3, 6X, F5.2, 6X, F7.2)
            READ (13, 300) PRODNO, DESCR, QUANT, PRICE
  300       FORMAT(I3, A20, I3, F5.2)
            GOTO 50
       ENDIF
*
       CLOSE (UNIT = 13)
       STOP
       END
```

Program 10.2

Output:

PROD NO	DESCRIPTION	QUANTITY	PRICE	VALUE
95	LOOSE LEAF PAPER	100	1.00	100.00
99	FORTRAN BOOKS	200	10.00	2000.00
102	MAGIC MARKERS	150	1.25	187.50
105	SCOTCH TAPE	400	0.29	116.00
109	SCISSORS	255	10.00	2550.00

```
**** STOP
```

FILE-MARKING STATEMENTS

If the same sequential tape file must be processed a second time during the same programming session, the tape must be physically rewound on the tape drive unit. The command

$$REWIND \ u$$

where *u* is the device unit number, rewinds the tape so that the tape drive is ready to process the first record of the file. If the sequential file is stored on a disk drive, this command will position the read/write access arm assembly of the disk drive over the first record of the file.

A sequential file must end with a record that marks the end of the file. The command

$$ENDFILE \ u$$

where *u* is the device unit number, automatically writes an end-of-file record and inserts it at the end of the sequential file that is currently being processed on input/output device number *u*. The record created by this statement does not contain any data; when encountered during an input operation it signals that the last actual data record of the file has been read.

When it is desirable to backspace one record in order to reread the same data record, the command

$$BACKSPACE \ u$$

where *u* is the device number, may be used. For example, the program segment

```
        READ (13, 100) ALPHA
    100 FORMAT (F8.2)
        BACKSPACE 13
        READ (13, 100) BETA
```

reads a field from a record of a file connected to device 13 according to the FORMAT descriptor F8.2 and assigns the value to ALPHA. The backspace instruction permits the same value to be reread and assigned to BETA. After this program segment has been executed, ALPHA and BETA will have the same value.

10.3 Some Data Processing Applications

Sequential file organization is particularly important in applications in which a relatively large number of records contained in a file are processed. For example, each time a payroll is produced, each active record in the employee file must be read.

An employee *master file* contains employee records that store information of a biographical or relatively permanent nature such as employee name, social security number, address, wage rate, and year-to-present-date total earnings. A record that contains temporary information such as the number of hours an employee works during a given week is called a *transaction record*. A record used to initiate a change in the information contained in a corresponding master record is also considered to be a transaction record. The act of matching a set of transaction records against the corresponding record in a master file in order to perform some type of data processing function that includes making the information in the master records more current is called *master file updating*. Changing the number of dependents listed on an employee's master record, as well as adding new master records of recently hired employees, or deleting master records of employees no longer on the payroll, would require a master file update.

Master file updating requires the following:

1. A field that contains the same information on both the transaction and master records must be selected so that this field uniquely identifies the record. Such a field is called a *key* field. The field that contains a person's name would not be a good choice as a key field since two different people may have the same name. The field that stores an employee's social security number, however, may serve as a record key since two people cannot share the same social security number.
2. Both the master and transaction files must be sorted on the key field in the same sequence before initiating the master file updating procedure.
3. The master and transaction files must be compared in some systematic fashion so that a transaction record can be efficiently paired with its corresponding master record.
4. Each active master record must be processed and written to the new updated file regardless of whether there is a corresponding transaction record. This ensures that the newly created updated master file contains every record in sequence, including records for which no updating was necessary.

The algorithm used to pair records in a transaction file to the corresponding records in a master file is based on reading the first transaction record, followed by the first master record, and then comparing the key fields of the two records. There are several possibilities:

- If the record keys are equal, the transaction record is processed against the master record. The next transaction record is then read, followed by the next master record, and the keys are compared.
- If the record key of the transaction record is greater than the record key of the master record, the master record is written on the new updated master file and additional master records are read and written to the updated master file until the record keys of the transaction and master records agree.
- If the record key of the transaction record is less than the record key of the master record, either the transaction record is designed to initiate the addition of a new master record or an error condition exists.
- If the transaction file has been exhausted, the remaining records in the master file, if any, are written to the updated master file.
- If the master file has been exhausted, than any remaining transaction records that initiate an addition to the master file are processed; any transaction records that require a change to an existing master record will generate an error condition.

Program 10.3 illustrates a master file updating procedure in which the key fields in both files are the fields that store the product number (TPROD on the transaction record and MPROD on the master record). The variable TCODE is used to define the type of transaction.

TCODE	Type of Transaction
1	Record addition to the master file
2	Record deletion from the master file
3	Quantity added to inventory
4	Quantity subtracted from inventory
5	Change in price

If the record keys match, the appropriate processing, based on an examination of the transaction code (TCODE), is performed. If the record key of the transaction record is greater than the master record key, the master record is copied to the updated master file and another master record is read. If the transaction record key is less than the master record key and the transaction code is 1, the transaction record is added to the updated master file; otherwise, the message "RECORD NOT FOUND" is printed.

```
* * * * * * * * * * * * * * * * * * * * * * * * * * * * * * * * * * * * *
* PROGRAM TO UPDATE A SEQUENTIAL FILE
* THIS PROGRAM WAS RUN ON A PRIME 850 COMPUTER USING FORTRAN 77
* AUTHOR ARLENE PODOS
*
*
*         VARIABLE LIST
*
*             TPROD = PRODUCT NUMBER ON TRANSACTION FILE
*             MPROD = PRODUCT NUMBER ON OLD MASTER FILE
*            TDESCR = PRODUCT DESCRIPTION ON TRANSACTION FILE
*            MDESCR = PRODUCT DESCRIPTION ON OLD MASTER FILE
*            TQUANT = QUANTITY OF THE PRODUCT ON THE TRANSACTION FILE
*            MQUANT = QUANTITY OF THE PRODUCT ON OLD MASTER FILE
*            TPRICE = UNIT PRICE OF PRODUCT ON TRANSACTION FILE
*            MPRICE = UNIT PRICE OF PRODUCT ON OLD MASTER FILE
*             TCODE = TRANSACTION CODE
*
* * * * * * * * * * * * * * * * * * * * * * * * * * * * * * * * * * * * *
*
* DATA DECLARATIONS FOLLOW
      CHARACTER * 20, TDESC, MDESC
      CHARACTER MSG * 40
      REAL TPRICE, MPRICE
      INTEGER TQUANT, MQUANT, TPROD, MPROD, TCODE
*
* OPEN FILES
      OPEN (UNIT = 13, FILE = 'PROD', STATUS = 'OLD')
      OPEN (UNIT = 14, FILE = 'TRANS', STATUS = 'OLD')
      OPEN (UNIT = 15, FILE = 'NEWPR', STATUS = 'NEW')
*
* READ FIRST TRANS RECORD
      READ (14, 100) TPROD, TDESC, TQUANT, TPRICE, TCODE
  100 FORMAT (I3, A20, I3, F5.2, I1)
*
* READ FIRST MASTER RECORD
      READ (13, 200) MPROD, MDESC, MQUANT, MPRICE
  200 FORMAT (I3, A20, I3, F5.2)
*
   50 CONTINUE
      IF ((TPROD .NE. 999) .OR. (MPROD .NE. 999)) THEN
*
* . . . . .CHECK IF MASTER AND TRANS RECORDS ARE EQUAL
*
         IF (TPROD .EQ. MPROD) THEN
            GOTO (410, 420, 430, 440, 450), TCODE
*
  410       MSG = 'DUPLICATE ADD'
            GOTO 460
*
  420       MSG = 'DELETION PROCESSED'
* . . . . . .READ MASTER
            READ (13, 500) MPROD, MDESC, MQUANT, MPRICE
  500       FORMAT (I3, A20, I3, F5.2)
            GOTO 460
```

```
*
  430           MQUANT = MQUANT + TQUANT
                MSG = 'MERCHANDISE ADDED TO INVENTORY'
                GOTO 460
  440           MQUANT = MQUANT - TQUANT
                MSG = 'MERCHANDISE SUBTRACTED FROM INVENTORY'
                GOTO 460
*
  450           MPRICE = TPRICE
                MSG = 'PRICE CHANGE'
                GOTO 460
*
*
  460            CONTINUE
* . . . . . .WRITE STATUS OF TRANSACTION
                WRITE (*, 600) TPROD, MSG
  600           FORMAT (1X, 'TRANSACTION RECORD #   ', I3, 1X, A40)
* . . . . . .READ ANOTHER TRANSACTION RECORD
                READ (14, 700) TPROD, TDESC, TQUANT, TPRICE, TCODE
  700           FORMAT (I3, A20, I3, F5.2, I1)
*
*
* . . . . .CHECK IF TRANS IS GREATER THAN MASTER
* . . . .IF SO COPY MASTER RECORD TO NEW FILE
            ELSEIF (TPROD .GT. MPROD) THEN
* . . . .
                WRITE (15, 800) MPROD, MDESC, MQUANT, MPRICE
  800           FORMAT (I3, A20, I3, F5.2)
* . . . . . .WRITE MESSAGE ON REPORT
                WRITE (*, 900) MPROD
  900           FORMAT (1X, 'MASTER RECORD       #  ', I3, ' RECORD COPIED')
* . . . . . .READ NEXT MASTER RECORD
                READ (13, 1000) MPROD, MDESC, MQUANT, MPRICE
 1000           FORMAT (I3, A20, I3, F5.2)
            ELSE
*
*
* . . . . . .TRANS IS LESS THAN MASTER
                IF (TCODE .EQ. 1) THEN
* . . . . . . . .RECORD IS TO BE ADDED TO THE NEW FILE
                    WRITE (15, 1100) TPROD, TDESC, TQUANT, TPRICE
 1100               FORMAT (I3, A20, I3, F5.2)
                    MSG = 'RECORD ADDED'
                ELSE
                    MSG = 'RECORD NOT FOUND'
                ENDIF
* . . . . . .WRITE MESSAGE TO REPORT
                WRITE (*, 1200) TPROD, MSG
 1200           FORMAT (1X, 'TRANSACTION RECORD #   ', I3, 1X, A30)
* . . . . . .READ ANOTHER TRANS
                READ (14, 1300) TPROD, TDESC, TQUANT, TPRICE, TCODE
 1300           FORMAT (I3, A20, I3, F5.2, I1)
            ENDIF
            GOTO 50
        ENDIF
*
* . . TERMINATION ROUTINE. WRITE TRAILER RECORD TO NEW FILE
        CONTINUE
        TPROD = 999
        TDESC = ' '
        TQUANT = 000
        TPRICE = 00.00
        WRITE (15, 1400) TPROD, TDESC, TQUANT, TPRICE
 1400       FORMAT (I3, A20, I3, F5.2, I1)
                *
                * CLOSE FILES
                    CLOSE (UNIT = 13)
                    CLOSE (UNIT = 14)
                    CLOSE (UNIT = 15)
                    STOP
                    END
```

Program 10.3

Output: Sequential Update Program

Old master file:

```
25 LOOSE LEAF PAPER    100 | 1.00
29 FORTRAN BOOKS       200 |0.00
102 MAGIC MARKERS      150 | 1.25
105 SCOTCH TAPE        400 | 0.29
109 SCISSORS           255 |0.00
999                     -1 | 0.00
```

TRANS file:

```
099                         50    3
099                         40    4
100   MATH BOOKS          11 0.00 1
102   WHITE OUT           20  9.00 1
103                                2
105                                2
109                           12.00 5
999                       00000.000
```

Product number	Description	Quantity	Price Code

New master file:

```
95   LOOSE LEAF PAPER   100 | 1.00
99   FORTRAN BOOKS      210 |10.00
100  MATH BOOKS          11 |10.00
102  MAGIC MARKERS      150 | 1.25
109  SCISSORS           255 |12.00
999                       0 | 0.00
```

Processing Report

```
OK, SEG UPDATE
  MASTER RECORD         #   95 RECORD COPIED
  TRANSACTION RECORD #   99 MERCHANDISE ADDED TO INVENTORY
  TRANSACTION RECORD #   99 MERCHANDISE SUBTRACTED FROM INVENTORY
  MASTER RECORD         #   99 RECORD COPIED
  TRANSACTION RECORD #  100 RECORD ADDED
  TRANSACTION RECORD #  102 DUPLICATE ADD
  MASTER RECORD         #  102 RECORD COPIED
  TRANSACTION RECORD #  103 RECORD NOT FOUND
  TRANSACTION RECORD #  105  DELETION PROCESSED
  TRANSACTION RECORD #  109 PRICE CHANGE
  MASTER RECORD         #  109 RECORD COPIED
**** STOP

OK, CLOSE UPDATE.COMO
```

10.4 Some Closing Remarks

Fortran 77 offers increased file processing capabilities as compared to earlier Fortrans. For example, the OPEN and CLOSE statements, as well as some of the control specifiers, are not available in the old standard.

If your Fortran program is designed to process a limited set of data values, or will probably not be used repeatedly, then creating data files may not be appropriate. If, however, the same pool of data will be shared by many different programs, or if it will be used repeatedly by the same program at different times, then it will be worthwhile to maintain the data in an external file.

This chapter has merely touched upon file processing in Fortran. For example, we have not discussed some additional statements such as the INQUIRE statement, which can be used to determine the current status of a control specifier, or ways to create and manipulate direct access files. Such discussions are beyond the scope of this presentation and may be found in advanced textbooks and in the reference manuals for the computer system being used.

Review Exercises

A star preceding the number of a problem indicates that a solution to that problem is give at the back of the book.

1. Write the following programs:
    (a) A program that creates a student examination data file in which each record consists of a nine-digit student ID number, followed by five examination grades.
    (b) A program that retrieves the data file, calculates the average of examination grades, uses a subroutine to sort the records of the file into descending exam grade averages, and then writes the results of this internal processing to a new external file. Also, this program should delete the original student data file.

* 2. Write a program designed to identify customers whose magazine subscriptions have expired and to create a "personalized" form-letter file for these customers. Assume that an external customer file called 'CUST' already exists and each customer record contains the following data items: name (last name first name), customer account number, sex ('M' for male and 'F' for female), magazine code:

    '1' = Fortran
    '2' = mathematics
    '3' = golf
    '4' = tennis
    '5' = running

    and expiration date using this format: mmddyy.

    After reading in today's date, process the customer magazine subscription file by retrieving the file and calling three subprograms:
    (a) Use a subroutine (call it VALID) to validate the input data. Perform tests that verify:
        (1) whether the sex code is 'M' or 'F'
        (2) whether the magazine code ranges from '1' to '5'
        (3) whether the month, day, and year are valid
    (b) If there is no error in input data, use a subroutine (call it DATCHK) to determine whether the magazine subscription has expired. Compare today's date with the expiration date, first converting each to yymmdd format.
    (c) If the magazine subscription has expired, have control pass to a third subroutine (call it LETTER) that creates a customer LETTER data file (which is available for future processing). Each record in the file consists of the customer's name, account number, sex, magazine code, and expiration date.

* 3. In Problem 2 each customer's name, account number, and address are maintained in a customer ADDRESS file. After creating the LETTER file in Problem 2(c), write a program that retrieves the LETTER and ADDRESS files and produces mailing labels and letters for each customer record contained in the LETTER file. Use the account number field as the record key, and assume that both files are sorted according to this record key.

The format of the personalized customer letter is as follows:

```
                              XXXXXXXXX XX, 19XX
DEAR MR. (OR MS.) XXXXXXXXXXXXXXXXXXXX

·ACCORDING TO OUR RECORDS YOUR SUBSCRIPTION TO
XXXXXXXXXXXXXXX (MAGAZINE NAME) HAS EXPIRED. IF YOU
RENEW YOUR SUBSCRIPTION WITHIN THE NEXT MONTH YOU
WILL QUALIFY FOR A SPECIAL DISCOUNT. SEE DETAILS
INSIDE. WE HOPE YOU WILL TAKE ADVANTAGE OF OUR
SPECIAL OFFER.

                              SINCERELY YOURS

                              COLETTE DRIMMER
                              CIRCULATION MANAGER
```

(*Note:* Before printing the actual names and months, any trailing blanks associated with these stored variable data items must be eliminated.)

4. The customer ADDRESS file referred to in Problem 3 must be updated since some customers have changed their addresses, some new subscribers have been added, and some old subscribers have discontinued their subscriptions so that their records can be deleted. Write a program that updates the master customer ADDRESS file by processing an ADDRESS transaction file against it. Assume that both files are sorted on the account number field. Each transaction record includes the date on which the subscription expires and one of the following codes:

> 'A' = Add transaction record to the master file
> 'C' = Change a field on the master record
> 'E' = Subscription has expired

If the transaction code is 'E', delete the record if the subscription expired more than six months ago; otherwise, add the customer to a list of subscribers who must be sent a letter inviting them to renew their subscriptions. At the end of the master file updating procedure, print the following:

(1) the total number of transaction records processed
(2) the total number of master records in the old master file
(3) the total number of master records added and deleted
(4) the number of master records written to the newly created master file
(5) the list of customers who must be sent letters to renew their subscriptions.

As a control check, verify that the totals for (2) and (3) above agree with the number in (4).

A Comparison of the Major Versions of Fortran

The following table lists the features discussed in Chapters 1 – 10 that may not be available on all of the major Fortran compilers. This table offers a convenient summary of the major differences among various Fortrans and is *not* intended to serve as a definition of the instruction sets and features offered by Fortran IV (1966 standard), WATFIV, Fortran 77, and the Fortran 77 Subset.

Most versions of Fortran written for desktop computers are based on the ANSI Fortran 77 Subset Language. Each microcomputer-based Fortran, however, typically includes extensions that may be contained in the full ANSI Fortran 77 standard. For example, the IBM personal computer runs a P-system Fortran 77 version that include the following extensions to the subset:

- use of subscripted variables as subscripts
- integer expressions as DO loop parameters
- expressions in an output list
- expressions in a computed GOTO statement

Additionally, the IBM P-system Fortran 77 includes specialized compiler directives that go beyond the features of the full Fortran 77 standard. Apple Fortran, which runs under the Apple Pascal operating system, has similar features.

Microcomputer-based Fortrans generally do not feature list-directed I/O statements, do not accept complex data types, and offer a limited number of character data manipulation functions and special format codes.

Differences in Features among Various Fortrans

Chapter in This Book	Feature	Fortran IV	WATFIV	Fortran 77	Fortran 77 Subset
2	Format-free input and output	No	Yes	Yes	No
2	Asterisk in list-directed READ and PRINT statements	Not applicable	No	Yes	Not applicable
2	Symbol with which comments begin	C	C	C or *	C or *
2	CHARACTER data declaration supported	No	Yes	Yes	Yes
3	Mixed-mode arithmetic permitted	No	Yes	Yes	Yes
4	END-of-Data specification in READ statement	No	Yes	Yes	Yes

Differences in Features among Various Fortrans *(continued)*

Chapter in This Book	Feature	Fortran IV	WATFIV	Fortran 77	Fortran 77 Subset
4	Embedded edit descriptor within READ and PRINT statements	No	No	Yes	No
4	T edit descriptor	No	Yes	Yes	No
4	BN and BZ edit descriptors	No	No	Yes	Yes
4	Use of apostrophe in FORMAT statement in place of H descriptor	No	Yes	Yes	Yes
4	Complex data	Yes	Yes	Yes	No
4	Double-precision data type	Yes	Yes	Yes	No
5	Integer valued expression permitted in computed GOTO statement	No	No	Yes	No
5	Use of generic names for library functions	No	No	Yes	No
5	ERR specification in READ statement	No	Yes	Yes	No
5	DO CASE statement	No	Yes	No	No
5	WHILE . . . DO statement	No	Yes	No	No
5	Block IF statement	No	Yes	Yes	Yes
6	Negative integers permitted as DO loop parameters	No	No	Yes	Yes
6	Integer expressions permitted as DO loop parameters	No	No	Yes	No
6	Real valued variables and expressions permitted as DO loop parameters	No	No	Yes	No
6	Expressions permitted in output list	No	Yes	Yes	No

Differences in Features among Various Fortrans *(continued)*

Chapter in This Book	Feature	Fortran IV	WATFIV	Fortran 77	Fortran 77 Subset
6	Place where the comparison between values of the DO variable and its exit value occurs	End of loop	End of loop	Beginning of loop	Beginning of loop
7	Maximum number of subscripts	3	7	7	3
7	Arrays with upper and lower bounds	No	No	Yes	No
7	Negative subscripts	No	No	Yes	No
7	Integer subscript expressions	Limited to c c * K K ± c c * K ± d	Yes	Yes	Yes
7	Real valued subscripts	No	Yes	No	No
7	Implied DO in DATA statement	No	Yes	Yes	Yes
7	Use of a subscripted variable as a subscript, as in B(J(9))	No	Yes	Yes	No
7	PARAMETER statement	No	No	Yes	No
8	LOGICAL data type statement	No	Yes	Yes	Yes
8	Index function	No	No	Yes	No
8	Substring function	No	No	Yes	No
8	String comparisons	No	Yes	Yes	Yes
8	Concatenation	No	No	Yes	No
8	LEN function	No	No	Yes	No
9	Name (labeled) COMMON	No	Yes	Yes	Yes
10	Supports sequential and direct access file processing	Supports sequential file processing only	Yes	Yes	Yes

Answers to Selected Exercises

Note: The program solutions given are *not* intended to serve as *model* programs. Each program or program segment represents one possible approach to the given problem. Your program solution may be as good as the program solution displayed, or better. When an asterisk is omitted from a list-directed I/O statement, you may assume that the program is coded in WATFIV.

Chapter 1

1. (b) 2. (d) 3. (a) 4. (c) 5. (d) 6. (d) 7. (d) 8. (a) 9. (a) 10. (d) 11. (c) 12. (b)

Chapter 2

1. (b) 2. (b) 3. (c) 4. (b) 5. (d) 6. (c) 7. (a) 8. (b) 9. (d) 10. (d)

11.
```
REAL ALPHA
INTEGER BETA
CHARACTER GAMMA * 10
```

12.
```
REAL SIDE, AREA
READ *, SIDE
AREA = SIDE ** 2
PRINT *, AREA
STOP
END
```

14.
```
REAL PRICE, TAX
READ *, PRICE
TAX = PRICE * .07
PRICE = PRICE + TAX
PRINT *, TAX, PRICE
STOP
END
```

16.
```
REAL INCHES, CENT, METER
READ *, INCHES
CENT = INCHES * 2.54
METER = INCHES * .0254
PRINT *, CENT, METER
STOP
END
```

Chapter 3

1. (a) 6 (b) 9 (c) 3 (d) 4
2. (a) Multiplication sign (asterisk) must be inserted between the number and the left parenthesis.

   Correct answer: $Z = 2.0 * (X + Y)$

   (b) The expression contains two consecutive operators. Parentheses must be inserted.

   Correct answer: $R = D + E/(-F) * G$

   (c) An arithmetic expression is to the left of the equal sign.
   (d) Last right parenthesis is missing.

   Correct answer: $X = (Y ** 2 + Z ** (A + B))$

3. (a) $Y = A * X ** 2 + B * X + C$
   (b) $A = (X + 2.0 * Y + 3.0 * Z)/6.0$
   (c) $B = P ** K * Q ** (N - K)$
   (d) $X = ((A - B)/(C + D)) ** 3$
   (e) $A = E ** (0.5 * Q * T ** 2)$
   (f) $S = A * (1 - R ** N)/(1 - R)$
   (g) $X = W * A ** ((B + 1)/C)$
   (h) $B = (X * Y ** 2 - X ** 2 * Y)/(3.0 * X + Y)$
4. (a) $A = ((X + Z) ** 3 - (X * Z)) ** 0.5$
   (b) $C = X/((X ** 2 + Y ** 2 + Z ** 2) ** 0.5)$
   (c) $X = W ** ((Y + Z) ** 0.5)$
   (d) $R = S/((A * X + B) ** 0.5) - (S + T)/((C * X ** 2 + D) ** 0.5)$
   (e) $F = ((A + B) ** 0.33) ** ((C * X - D) ** 0.5)$

5. (a) A = 26.0 **(b)** A = 162.0 **(c)** A = 18.75 **(d)** A = 0.0 **(e)** A = 12.5
6. (a) M = 10 **(b)** M = 1 **(c)** M = 7 **(d)** M = 1 **(e)** M = 3

7.
```
REAL L, W, H, V, SAREA
READ *, L, W, H
PRINT *, L, W, H
V = L * W * H
SAREA = 2 * ( L*W+L*H+H*W )
PRINT *, V, SAREA
STOP
END
```

9.
```
READ *, K
L = ( K ** 2 - 1 ) / 2
M = ( K ** 2 + 1 ) / 2
PRINT *, K, L, M
STOP
END
```

11.
```
READ *, P, N, R, K
A = P * (1 + R/K) ** (N*K)
PRINT *, A
STOP
END
```

13.
```
READ *, I1
PRINT *, I1
R1 = I1/ 10.0
I2 = R1
R2 = R1 - I2
R2 = R2 * 100
I3 = R2 + I2
PRINT *, I3
STOP
END
```

Chapter 4

1. (a) I4 **(b)** F9.3 **(c)** A7 **(d)** E12.6
2. (a) ᵇᵇ81930 **(b)** ᵇᵇ819 **(c)** ᵇᵇ8.19 **(d)** ᵇᵇ819.3 **(e)** ᵇᵇ8.1
3. (a) L = ᵇᵇ31524 **(b)** L = 1524
   X = 16.89   X = 16.89
   K = ᵇᵇ987   K = ᵇᵇ9
  (c) The variable L, an integer, is described as F7.2 (real). The FORMAT code and the data type do not match. An error message would be generated.
4. (a) ᵇᵇᵇᵇ7134 **(b)** ✲✲✲
  (c) Format/data mismatch. A real value is assigned to an integer variable.
  (d) ᵇᵇ185.7 **(e)** 185.70 **(f)** ✲✲✲✲ **(g)** 51.44
  (h) ᵇᵇ.9873200E+04
     ᵇᵇ.98732E+04
     ᵇ.9873E+04
5. (a) The value 97503 is written on a new line.
  (b) ✲✲✲✲ is written on a new page.
  (c) ᵇᵇᵇ97503 is written on a new line.
  (d) 7503 is written on a new line.
  (e) ᵇᵇ97503 is written on a new line.
6. (a) 876.125 is written on a new page.
  (b) 1876.1250 is written after the print head advances two lines.
  (c) RESULT = ᵇᵇ1876.125.
  (d) 1876.13 is written on a new line.
  (e) ✲✲✲✲✲✲✲ is written on a new page.
  (f) 1876.12500 is written on a new line.
7.
```
    WRITE (6, 100)
100 FORMAT ('1', 19X, 'STUDENT ID', 20X, 'MIDTERM',
   -20X, 'FINAL', 20X, 'EXAM AVERAGE')
```
8. (a) 863   507.4   1329865
  (b) 635.07   98650
  (c) 863   1329.86
  (d) 86350.74   A new record is read.
  (e) No values are passed to the computer from this record since the computer is directed to skip two records.
  (f) 86350   650   74132.98

9. (a) LIST-DIRECTED OUTPUTƀƀIS EASIER TO USEƀƀƀƀƀBUT HARDER TO R

        A20   A16   A18

                        25   56
                        ↓   ↓

(b) LIST-DIRECTED OUTPUTƀƀIS EASIER TO USEƀƀƀƀƀƀƀƀƀƀƀƀƀƀƀƀƀƀƀBUT HARDER TO R

(c) LIST-DIRECTED OUTPUT
    IS EASIER TO USE
    (skip a line)
    ƀƀƀBUT HARDER TO R
    (skip 3 lines)

(d) (Begin on a new page and then skip two lines)

    10   30   47
    ↓   ↓   ↓

    LIST-DIRECTED OUTPUT IS EASIER TO USEƀƀƀƀBUT HARDER TO R

10. (a) E9.1   .1780
    (b) E11.2   2,163,200
    (c) E6.0   .000034
    (d) E9.3   436,900,000

11. (a) ƀ.1834E−05
    ƀ.186E+09
    −.720809E+04

(*Note:* Some computer systems do not allow six significant digits to the right of the decimal point. When this exercise was run using the WATFIV compiler, the output for T was as follows: ∗∗∗∗∗∗∗∗∗∗∗∗∗.)

(b) After skipping a line, print

    ƀ   19   29
                 ↓   ↓

    ƀƀ.1834E−05ƀƀƀƀƀƀƀ.186E+09ƀƀƀ.72081E+04

(c) Start on new page.
    ƀƀ.183400E−05
    ƀ

    19   31
    ↓   ↓

    ƀ.186E+09ƀƀƀƀƀ−.72080900E+04

13.
```
     * WRITE HEADINGS
           WRITE (*, 100)
       100 FORMAT ( 2X,'PART NUMBER', 6X,'UNIT COST', 6X,'QUANTITY ORDERED',
          - 6X, 'TOTAL COST')
           WRITE (*, 200)
       200 FORMAT (' ')
           SUM = 0.0
           KOUNT = 0
       300 READ (*,400, END = 900) IPART, COST, QUANT
       400 FORMAT (I5, 5X, F6.2, 6X, I3)
           TCOST = COST * QUANT
           SUM = SUM + TCOST
           KOUNT = KOUNT + 1
           WRITE (*, 500) IPART, COST, QUANT, TCOST
       500 FORMAT (' ', 5X, I5, 10X, F7.2, 13X, I3, 13X, F9.2)
           GOTO 300
       900 WRITE (*,950)
       950 FORMAT (' ')
           WRITE (*, 1000) SUM
      1000 FORMAT (' ', 'TOTAL COST FOR ALL PRODUCTS', 27X, F11.2)
           WRITE (*,1100) KOUNT
      1100 FORMAT (' ', 'TOTAL RECORDS PROCESSED', 36X, I3)
           STOP
           END
```

```
15.        READ *, N
           SUMX = 0.0
           SUMY = 0.0
           SUMXX = 0.0
           SUMXY = 0.0
      10 READ ( *, *, END = 500) X, Y
           SUMX = SUMX + X
           SUMY = SUMY + Y
           SUMXY = SUMXY + X * Y
           SUMXX = SUMXX + X * X
           GOTO 10
     500 B = (N * SUMXY - (SUMX * SUMY)) / (N * SUMXX - SUMX ** 2)
           A = (SUMY - B * SUMX) / N
           PRINT *, A, B
           STOP
           END
```

Chapter 5

```
1. IF (A / B .EQ. C / D) THEN
        PRINT , 'A, B, C, AND D ARE IN PROPORTION'
   ENDIF
2. IF ( A .LE. B) THEN
        KOUNT1 = KOUNT1 + 1
   ELSE
        KOUNT2 = KOUNT2 + 1
   ENDIF
3. IF ( C .LT. SQRT (A ** 2 + B ** 2)) THEN
        PRINT , 'TRIANGLE ABC IS ACUTE'
   ELSE IF (C .EQ. SQRT (A ** 2 + B ** 2)) THEN
        PRINT , 'TRIANGLE ABC IS RIGHT'
   ELSE
        PRINT , 'TRIANGLE ABC IS OBTUSE'
   ENDIF
4. IF ((K .GE. 100) .AND. (K .LE. 200) ) THEN
        L = 3 * K
        PRINT , L
   ENDIF
5. IF (( X .EQ. Y) .OR. (X .GT. 12.0) ) THEN
        PRINT , AVALUE
   ELSE IF ( (X .LT. Y) .OR. (X .EQ. 13. )) THEN
        PRINT , BVALUE
   ELSE
        PRINT , CVALUE
   ENDIF
6. IF (( ANGLE .LT. 0.0) .OR. (ANGLE .GT. 180.0))
   THEN
        PRINT , 'INVALID ANGLE'
   ENDIF
7. IF (SALES .LE. 100.00) THEN
        SALARY = 300.00
   ELSE IF (SALES .LE. 200.00) THEN
        SALARY = 300.00 + (.05 * PRICE * (SALES -
        100.00))
   ELSE
        SALARY = 350.00 + (.05 * PRICE * (SALES -
        100.00))
   ENDIF
8. IF ((A .LE. B) .OR. (A .LE. C)) THEN
        PRINT , 'INVALID DATA'
   ENDIF
```

9. ```
IF (X .LT. 0) THEN
      SIGNUM (X) = -1
ELSE IF (X .EQ. 0) THEN
      SIGNUM (X) = 0
ELSE
      SIGNUM (X) = 1
ENDIF
```

10.
```
       $JOB   WATFIV
 1   INTEGER SUM,KOUNT,N
 2   SUM = 0
 3   KOUNT = 1
 4   READ, N
 5   PRINT, 'N =',N
 6   100 IF (KOUNT .GT. N) THEN
 7   PRINT, 'THE SUM OF THE NUMBERS FROM 1 TO ',N, 'IS', SUM
 8   STOP
 9   ELSE
10   SUM = SUM + KOUNT
11   KOUNT = KOUNT + 1
12   ENDIF
13   GOTO 100
14   END
```

11.
```
        READ *, N
        PRINT *, N
        KOUNT = 1
* DO THE FOLLOWING. . .
     10 CONTINUE
        IF (MOD(N, 2) .EQ. 0) THEN
            N = N/2
        ELSE
            N = 3 * N + 1
        ENDIF
        PRINT *, N
        KOUNT = KOUNT + 1
* UNTIL THE CONDITION. . .
        IF (N .NE. 1) GOTO 10
        PRINT *, 'KOUNT = ', KOUNT
        STOP
        END
```

12.
```
       $JOB   WATFIV
 1   CHARACTER NAME * 20,MAXNAM * 20
 2   REAL AVG,MAX
 3   INTEGER EXAM1, EXAM2, FINAL
 4   MAX = 0
 5   MAXNAM = '   '
 6   100 READ ,NAME, EXAM1, EXAM2, FINAL
 7   IF (NAME. EQ. 'EOF') THEN
 8   PRINT, ' '
 9   PRINT, ' '
10   PRINT, 'THE STUDENT WITH THE HIGHEST AVERAGE IS', MAXNAM
11   PRINT, 'THE HIGHEST AVERAGE IS', MAX
12   STOP
13   ENDIF
14   AVG = (EXAM1 +2 * EXAM2 + 3 * FINAL) / 6.0
15   IF (AVG. GT. MAX) THEN
16   MAX = AVG
17   MAXNAM = NAME
18   ENDIF
19   PRINT, NAME,AVG
20   GOTO 100
21   END
```

18.
```
        CHARACTER * 20 NAME
        REAL OVT
        REGSUM = 0.0
        OVTSUM = 0.0
        READ (*, 100) NAME, RATE, IHOURS
    100 FORMAT (A20, F4.2, I2)
```
```

```
    200 CONTINUE
        IF (NAME .NE. 'EOF') THEN
            IF (IHOURS .GT. 35 ) THEN
                REG = 35 * RATE
                OVT = (IHOURS - 35) * RATE * 1.5
            ELSE
                REG = IHOURS * RATE
                OVT = 0.0
            ENDIF
            IF (OVT .GT. REG) THEN
                WRITE (*, 300) NAME, REG, OVT
    300         FORMAT (1X, A20, 10X, F7.2, 10X, F8.2, '**********')

            ELSE
                WRITE (*, 400) NAME, REG, OVT
    400         FORMAT (1X, A20, 10X, F7.2, 10X, F8.2)
            ENDIF
            REGSUM = REGSUM + REG
            OVTSUM = OVTSUM + OVT
            READ (*, 100) NAME, RATE, IHOURS
            GOTO 200
        ENDIF
        WRITE (*, 500) REGSUM, OVTSUM
    500 FORMAT (1X, 'TOTAL', 24X, F8.2, 9X, F9.2)
        STOP
        END
```

20.

```
 1          REAL A, B, C
 2      100 READ ,A, B, C
 3          IF (A .EQ. -999) THEN
 4              STOP
 5          ENDIF
   C
 6          IF( (C .LT. A+B).AND.(B .LT. A+C).AND.(A .LT. B+C))THEN
 7              IF ((A .EQ. B) .AND. (B .EQ. C) )THEN
 8                  PRINT ,A,B,C,'          EQUILATERAL TRIANGLE'
 9              ELSE
10                  IF ((A .EQ. B) .OR.(B. EQ. C).OR.(A .EQ. C)) THEN
11                      PRINT ,A,B,C,'          ISOSCELES TRIANGLE'
12                  ELSE
13                      PRINT,A, B, C ,'          SCALENE'
14                  ENDIF
15              ENDIF
16          ELSE
17              PRINT, A,B,C, '          NO TRIANGLE CAN BE FORMED'
18          ENDIF
19          GOTO 100
20          END
```

21.

```
        READ *, VALUE
        LARGE = 0.0
        SMALL = VALUE
    200 CONTINUE
        IF (VALUE .NE. -999.9 ) THEN
            IF (VALUE .LT. SMALL) THEN
                SMALL = VALUE
            ELSE IF (VALUE .GT. LARGE ) THEN
                LARGE = VALUE
            ENDIF
            READ *, VALUE
            GOTO 200
        ENDIF
        RANGE = LARGE - SMALL
        PRINT *, RANGE
        STOP
        END
```

```
 23.          INTEGER QUANT
              IBACK = 0
              IQUANT = 0
              READ *, IBALANCE
              READ *, ICODE, IACCT, QUANT
      100 CONTINUE
              IF (ICODE .NE. -1) THEN
                  IF ((ICODE .GT. 1) .OR. (ICODE .LT. -1 ) ) THEN
                      PRINT *, IACCT, ' ', ICODE, 'INVALID CODE '
                      PRINT *, ' '
                      PRINT *, ' '
                      GOTO 300
                  ENDIF
                  IF (QUANT .LE. IBALANCE) THEN
                      IQUANT = IQUANT + QUANT
                      IBALANCE = IBALANCE - QUANT
                      PRINT *, 'CUSTOMER ACCOUNT NUMBER : ', IACCT
                      PRINT *, 'NUMBER OF UNITS SHIPPED: ', QUANT
                      PRINT *, ' '
                      PRINT *, ' '
                  ELSE
                      IF (ICODE .EQ. 0) THEN
                          IBACK = IBACK + QUANT
                          PRINT *, 'CUSTOMER ACCOUNT NUMBER : ', IACCT
                          PRINT *, 'NUMBER OF UNITS SHIPPED : ', 0
                          PRINT *, 'NUMBER OF UNITS BACKORDERED', QUANT
                          PRINT *, ' '
                          PRINT *, ' '
                      ELSE
                          JQUANT = QUANT / 4
                          IF (JQUANT .LE. IBALANCE) THEN
                          IQUANT = IQUANT + JQUANT
                          IBALANCE = IBALANCE - JQUANT
                          JBACK = QUANT - JQUANT
                          IBACK = IBACK + JBACK
                          PRINT *, 'CUSTOMER ACCOUNT NUMBER : ', IACCT
                          PRINT *, 'NUMBER OF UNITS SHIPPED : ', JQUANT
                          PRINT *, 'NUMBER OF UNITS BACKORDERED ', JBACK
                          PRINT *, ' '
                          PRINT *, ' '
                      ELSE
                          IBACK = IBACK + QUANT
                          PRINT *, 'CUSTOMER ACCOUNT NUMBER : ', ACCT
                          PRINT *, 'NUMBER OF UNITS SHIPPED : ', 0
                          PRINT *, 'NUMBER OF UNITS BACKORDERED', QUANT
                          PRINT *, ' '
                          PRINT *, ' '
                      ENDIF
                  ENDIF
              ENDIF
      300     READ *, ICODE, IACCT, QUANT
              GOTO 100
          ENDIF
          PRINT *, ' '
          PRINT *, ' '
          PRINT *, 'UPDATED INVENTORY BALANCE ', IBALANCE
          PRINT *, 'TOTAL UNITS SHIPPED        ', IQUANT
          PRINT *, 'TOTAL UNITS BACKORDERED   ', IBACK
          STOP
          END
```

Chapter 6

```
1.    READ *, N
      DO 50 K = 1, N
          READ *, NUMBER
          PRINT *, NUMBER, NUMBER ** 3
   50 CONTINUE
          STOP
          END
2.    SUM = 0
      READ *, M, N
      IF (M .GT. N) THEN
          LIMIT = M
          INIT = N
      ELSE
          LIMIT = N
          INIT = M
      ENDIF
      DO 50 K = INIT, LIMIT
          SUM = SUM + K ** 2
   50 CONTINUE
      PRINT *, SUM
      STOP
      END
3.    READ *, M, N
      ISUM = 0
      DO 50 K = 1, N
          SUM = SUM + M
   50 CONTINUE
      PRINT *, SUM
      STOP
      END
4.    DO 50 K = 1, 25
          RMETER = K * 0.3048
          PRINT *, K, RMETER
          IF (MOD (K,5) .EQ. 0) THEN
              DO 60 L = 1, 3
                  PRINT *, ' '
   60         CONTINUE
          ENDIF
   50 CONTINUE
      STOP
      END

7.    SUM = 0.0
      DO 50 K = 1, 99, 2
          SUM = SUM + (1.0/ (K * 2 - 1))
          SUM = SUM - (1.0 / ( (K + 1) * 2 -1 ))
          IF (MOD (K + 1, 10) .EQ. 0) THEN
              PRINT *, 'TERM = ', K + 1, 'PI =', 4 * SUM
          ENDIF
   50 CONTINUE
      STOP
      END
```

```
8.      READ *, COST, SCRAP, N
        STDEP = (COST - SCRAP)/ N
        SUM = N * (N + 1) / 2
        DO 50 K = 1, N
            DEP = (N - K + 1) * (COST - SCRAP) / SUM
            PRINT *, K, STDEP, DEP
     50 CONTINUE
        STOP
        END


12.     READ *, N
        SUMXY = 0.0
        SUMX = 0.0
        SUMXX = 0.0
        SUMY = 0.0
        SUMYY = 0.0
        DO 50 K = 1,N
            READ *, X, Y
            SUMXY = SUMXY + X * Y
            SUMX = SUMX + X
            SUMY = SUMY + Y
            SUMXX = SUMXX + X ** 2
            SUMYY = SUMYY + Y ** 2
     50 CONTINUE
        A = N * SUMXY -  SUMX * SUMY
        B = SQRT (N * SUMXX - SUMX ** 2) * SQRT (N * SUMYY - SUMY **2)
        R = A / B
        PRINT *, R
        IF ((R .GT. 1.0) .OR. (R .LT. -1.0)) THEN
            PRINT *, 'INVALID COEFFICINENT'
        ELSEIF ( R .GE. .75) THEN
            PRINT *, 'X AND Y ARE CLOSELY RELATED'
        ELSE IF (R .GE. .25) THEN
            PRINT *, 'X AND Y MAY BE RELATED'
        ELSE IF (R .GE. - .24) THEN
            PRINT *, 'X AND Y ARE NOT STRONGLY RELATED'
        ELSE
            PRINT *, 'X AND Y ARE INVERSELY RELATED'
        ENDIF
        STOP
        END


13.     DO 50 K = 1, 250
            IF ( (MOD (K, 3) .EQ. 2) .AND. (MOD (K, 5 ) .EQ. 1) ) THEN
                PRINT *, K
        ENDIF
     50 CONTINUE
        STOP
        END


15.     READ *, I, J
        DO 50 M = 1, J
            LCM = M * I
            IF (MOD (LCM, J) .EQ. 0) THEN
                PRINT *, I, J, LCM
                GOTO 60
            ENDIF
     50 CONTINUE
     60 CONTINUE
        STOP
        END
```

Chapter 7

1. **(a)** READ *, A(1), A(3), A(5), A(7), A(9)
   (b) READ (5, 100) C, D(1), C, D(2), C, D(3)
   (c) READ (5, 100) C, D(1), D(2), D(3)
   (d) READ (5, 100) D(1), D(2), D(3), C
   (e) PRINT *, P(3), A, Q(3), P(4), A, Q(4), P(5),
   A, Q(5)
   (f) PRINT *, A(4), A(7), A(10)
   (g) READ '(5F9.4)', X(1), X(2), X(3), X(4), X(5)
   READ '(5F9.4)', X(6), X(7), X(8), X(9), X(10)
   (h) PRINT '(1X, 4I9)', N(1, 2), N(1, 3), N(1, 4), N(1, 5)
   PRINT '(1X, 4I9)', N(2, 2), N(2, 3), N(2, 4), N(2, 5)
   (i) PRINT *, Z(1, 5), Z(3, 5), Z(5, 5), Z(1, 6), Z(3, 6), Z(5, 6)
2. **(a)** INTEGER X(10)
   READ *, (X(I), I = 1, 10)
   (b) PRINT *, (Y(I), I = 2, 12, 2)
   (c) PRINT *, (A, Z(K), K = 1, 7, 2)
3. **(a)** REAL A(3, 5)
   READ *, ((A(IROW, JCOL), IROW = 3, 5), JCOL = 1, 5)
   (b) PRINT *, Z, ((B(IROW, JCOL), JCOL = 7, 8), IROW = 2, 3
   (c) PRINT *, ((Z, B(IROW, JCOL), JCOL = 7, 8), IROW = 2, 3
3. **(a)** REAL A(3, 5)
   READ *, ((A(IROW, JCOL), IROW = 3, 5),
   JCOL = 1, 5)
   (b) PRINT *, Z, ((B(IROW, JCOL), JCOL = 7, 8),
   IROW = 2, 3
   (c) PRINT *, ((Z, B(IROW, JCOL), JCOL = 7, 8),
   IROW = 2, 3

4. **(a)**
```
      INTEGER GAMMA(20)
      DATA GAMMA/1,-2,3,4,5,6,7,-8,9,0,1,2,3,4,5,6,7,8,9,0/
      PRINT , (GAMMA(I), I = 1, 20)
      DO 50 K = 1, 20
         IF (GAMMA(K) .LE. 0) THEN
            GAMMA(K) = -GAMMA(K)
         ENDIF
50    CONTINUE
      PRINT ,(GAMMA(K), K = 1, 20)
      STOP
      END
```

   (c)
```
      INTEGER GAMMA(20)
      DATA GAMMA/20 * 0/
      PRINT *, GAMMA
      STOP
      END
```

   (e)
```
      INTEGER GAMMA(20), DELTA(20)
      DATA GAMMA/ 5,-17,8,9,0,5,6,93,44,3,2,1,76,9,5,4,3,4,5,7/
      L = 0
      DO 50 K = 1, 20
         IF ((GAMMA(K) .GT. 0) .AND. (GAMMA(K) .LT. 65)) THEN
            L = L + 1
            DELTA (L) = GAMMA(K)
         ENDIF
50    CONTINUE
      PRINT *, (DELTA (K), K = 1, L)
      STOP
      END
```

```
(g)    INTEGER GAMMA(20), NEW(20)
       DATA GAMMA/ 1,-2,3,4,5,6,7,-8,9,0,1,2,3,4,5,6,7,8,9,0/
       DO 50 K = 1, 10
           NEW (K) = GAMMA (20 - K + 1)
           NEW (20 - K + 1) = GAMMA(K)
    50 CONTINUE
       PRINT *, NEW
       STOP
       END
```

5. (b)
```
       INTEGER ALPHA(10,10), TOTAL
       DO 50 K = 1, 10
           READ *, (ALPHA(K, J), J =1, 10)
    50 CONTINUE
       TOTAL = 0
       DO 60 K = 1, 10
           TOTAL = TOTAL + ALPHA(K, 4)
    60 CONTINUE
       PRINT *, 'THE TOTAL IS ', TOTAL
       STOP
       END
```

(d)
```
       INTEGER ALPHA(10,10)
       DO 50 K = 1, 10
           READ *, (ALPHA(K, J), J =1, 10)
    50 CONTINUE
       DO 100 K = 1, 10
           ITEMP = ALPHA (2, K)
           ALPHA (2, K) = ALPHA(K, 9)
           ALPHA (K, 9) = ITEMP
   100 CONTINUE
       DO 150 K = 1, 10
           PRINT *, (ALPHA(K, J), J = 1, 10)
   150 CONTINUE
       STOP
       END
```

6.
```
       INTEGER A, X(100), MAX, MAXK, K
       KOUNT = 0
       READ *, A
    10 CONTINUE
       IF (A .NE. -999) THEN
           KOUNT = KOUNT + 1
           X(KOUNT) = A
           READ *, A
           GOTO 10
       ENDIF
       MAX = X(1)
       MAXK = 1
       DO 50 K = 2, KOUNT
           IF (X(K) .GT. MAX) THEN
               MAX = X(K)
               MAXK = K
           ENDIF
    50 CONTINUE
       PRINT *, ( X(K), K = 1, KOUNT)
       PRINT *, ' '
       PRINT *, 'THE LARGEST DATA VALUE IS          ', MAX
       PRINT *, 'ITS POSITION IN THE DATA LIST IS    ', MAXK
       STOP
       END
```

8.

```
* * * * * * * * * * BUBBLE SORT ROUTINE* * * * * * * * * * * * * *
*                                                                *
*               X = ARRAY NAME (N ELEMENTS)                      *
*                                                                *
* THIS PROGRAM WAS RUN ON A PRIME 850 COMPUTER USING FORTRAN 77  *
*
      REAL X(50)
      READ *, N
* READ N ELEMENTS INTO ARRAY X
      DO 40 J = 1, N
          READ *,  X(J)
   40 CONTINUE
* PRINT CONTENTS OF ARRAY X BEFORE THE SORT
      PRINT *, 'THE ORIGINAL ARRAY'
      PRINT *, ' '
      DO 45 K = 1, N
          PRINT *, X(K)
   45 CONTINUE
* THE SORT ROUTINE BEGINS
      DO 75 K = 1, N - 1
*
* . . . .INITIALIZE COUNTER
          KOUNT = 0
          DO 50 I = 1, N - K
              IF ( X(I) .GT. X(I + 1) ) THEN
* . . . . . . . . . MAKE SWITCH
                  TEMP = X(I)
                  X(I) = X(I + 1)
                  X(I + 1) = TEMP
                  KOUNT = KOUNT + 1
              ENDIF
   50     CONTINUE
          IF (KOUNT .EQ. 0) GOTO 66
* RETURN TO OUTER DO LOOP
   75 CONTINUE
* PRINT CONTENTS OF ARRAY AFTER SORT
   66 PRINT *, ' '
      PRINT *, ' '
      PRINT *, 'THE SORTED ARRAY'
      PRINT *, ' '
      DO 90 I = 1, N
          PRINT *, X(I)
   90 CONTINUE
      STOP
      END
```

```
10.    REAL A (10), X
       DATA A/ 15, 16, 18, 20, 23, 25, 48, 50, 65, 90/
       READ *, X
       JLOW = 1
       JHIGH = 10
  10 CONTINUE
       IF (JHIGH - JLOW .EQ. 1) THEN
           IF (X .EQ. A(JLOW) ) THEN
               ISUB = JLOW
               PRINT *, 'SUBSCRIPT OF ELEMENT IS', ISUB
               GOTO 800
           ELSE IF (X .EQ. A(JHIGH)) THEN
               ISUB = JHIGH
               PRINT *, 'SUBSCRIPT OF ELEMENT IS ', ISUB
               GOTO 800
           ELSE
               PRINT *, 'ELEMENT IS NOT CONTAINED IN THE ARRAY'
               GOTO 800
           ENDIF
       ELSE
           MID = (JLOW + JHIGH) / 2
           IF ( X .EQ. A(MID)) THEN
               SUB = MID
               PRINT *, 'SUBSCRIPT OF ELEMENT IS', SUB
               GOTO 800
           ELSEIF (X .LT. A(MID)) THEN
               JHIGH = MID
           ELSE
               JLOW = MID
           ENDIF
           GOTO 10
       ENDIF
 800 CONTINUE
       STOP
       END


11.    INTEGER F(20)
       F(1) = 1
       F(2) = 1
       DO 50 K = 3, 20
           F(K) = F(K - 1) + F(K - 2)
  50 CONTINUE
       PRINT *, (F(K), K = 1, 20)
       STOP
       END


18.    INTEGER ANSKEY(15), ANSWER(16),  ID(30), SCORE(30)
       DATA ANSKEY/1,0,0,1,0,1,0,0,1,0,1,1,0,1,0/
       READ *, N
       DO 50 I = 1, N
           READ *,(ANSWER(K), K = 1, 16)
           ID(I) = ANSWER (1)
           KOUNT = 0
           DO 60 J = 1, 15
               IF (ANSKEY(J) .EQ. ANSWER(J + 1)) THEN
                   KOUNT = KOUNT + 1
               ENDIF
  60       CONTINUE
           SCORE (I) = KOUNT
  50 CONTINUE
       DO 75 K = 1, N - K
           IF (ID(K) .GT. ID(K + 1) ) THEN
               TEMP = ID(K)
               ID(K) = ID(K + 1)
               ID (K + 1) = TEMP
               TEMP = SCORE(K)
               SCORE (K) = SCORE(K + 1)
               SCORE (K + 1) = TEMP
           ENDIF
  75 CONTINUE
       DO 90 K = 1, N
           PRINT *, ID(K), SCORE(K)
  90 CONTINUE
       STOP
       END
```

```
19.     INTEGER A, B
        INTEGER ALPHA(4), BETA(3), GAMMA(7)
        DATA ALPHA/ 4, 9, 18, 21/
        DATA BETA / 6, 8, 39 /
        A = 1
        B = 1
        M = 4
        N = 3
        DO 50 K = 1, 7
            IF (ALPHA(A) .LT. BETA(B) ) THEN
                GAMMA(K) = ALPHA(A)
                A = A + 1
                IF (A .GT. M) THEN
                    ALPHA(M) = 99
                    A = A - 1
                ENDIF
            ELSE
                GAMMA(K) = BETA(B)
                B = B + 1
                IF(B .GT. N) THEN
                    BETA(N) = 99
                    B = B - 1
                ENDIF
            ENDIF
    50 CONTINUE
        PRINT *, (GAMMA (J), J = 1, 7)
        STOP
        END

21.     INTEGER BINARY(12)
        K = 0
        READ *, NUMBER
   100 CONTINUE
            IF (NUMBER .NE. -999) THEN
                K = K + 1
                BINARY(K) = NUMBER
                READ *, NUMBER
                GOTO 100
            ENDIF
        PRINT '(1X,12I1)', (BINARY(J), J = 1, K)
* CONVERT TO BASE 10
        ISUM = 0
        DO 50 J = K, 1, - 1
            ISUM = ISUM + (BINARY(J) * 2 **(K - J))
    50 CONTINUE
        PRINT *, ISUM
        STOP
        END

23.     INTEGER A(2,3), B(3, 5), C(2, 5)
        DO 50 I = 1, 2
            READ *,(A (I, J), J = 1, 3)
    50 CONTINUE
        DO 60 K = 1, 3
            READ *, (B(K, J), J = 1, 5)
    60 CONTINUE
        DO 100 I = 1, 2
            DO 110 J = 1, 5
                C(I, J) = 0
   110      CONTINUE
   100 CONTINUE
        DO 120 I = 1, 2
            DO 130 J = 1, 5
                DO 140 K = 1, 3
                    C(I, J) = C(I, J) + A(I, K) * B(K, J)
   140          CONTINUE
   130      CONTINUE
   120 CONTINUE
        DO 90 I = 1, 2
            PRINT *, (C(I, J), J =1, 5)
    90 CONTINUE
        STOP
        END
```

Chapter 8

```
1.      INTEGER I, LENGTH
        CHARACTER WORD * 12
        READ *, WORD
        I = INDEX (WORD, ' ')
        IF ( INDEX (WORD, ' ') .EQ. 0) THEN
            LENGTH = 12
        ELSE
            LENGTH = I - 1
        ENDIF
        DO 50 K = LENGTH, 1, -1
            PRINT *, WORD (K:K)
    50 CONTINUE
        STOP
        END

2.      CHARACTER WORD * 12
        CHARACTER ARRAY(12)
        READ *, WORD
        DO 50 K = 1, 12
            ARRAY(K) = WORD (K:K)
    50 CONTINUE
        IF ( WORD (12:12) .NE. ' ') THEN
            PRINT *, (ARRAY(K), K = 12, 1, -1)
        ELSE
* . . . . STRING CONTAINS TRAILING BLANKS
            K = 1
    60      CONTINUE
            IF ( ARRAY(K) .NE. ' ') THEN
                K = K + 1
                GOTO 60
            ENDIF
            LENGTH = K - 1
            PRINT *, (ARRAY (K), K = LENGTH, 1, -1)
        ENDIF
        STOP
        END

6.      CHARACTER * 40 SOURCE, TARGET
        READ *, SOURCE
        READ *, TARGET
        KOUNT = 0
* FIND LENGTH OF TARGET
        I = INDEX (TARGET, ' ')
        IF ( INDEX (TARGET, ' ') .EQ. 0) THEN
            T = 40
        ELSE
            T = I - 1
        ENDIF
*FIND LENGTH OF SOURCE
        I = INDEX (SOURCE, ' ')
        IF ( I .EQ. 0) THEN
            S = 40
        ELSE
            S = I - 1
        ENDIF
        DO 50 I = 1, S - T + 1
            END = I - 1 + T
            IF (SOURCE (I:END) .EQ. TARGET (1 : T)) THEN
                KOUNT = KOUNT + 1
                PRINT *, 'KOUNT = ', KOUNT, 'POSITION = ', I
            ENDIF
    50 CONTINUE
        STOP
        END
```

```
11.     CHARACTER ARRAY(26)
        CHARACTER LETTER
        CHARACTER *26 ALPHABET
        CHARACTER * 80 MESSAGE
        CHARACTER PRINT(80)
        EQUIVALENCE (ALPHABET, ARRAY)
        DATA ALPHABET /'ABCDEFGHIJKLMNOPQRSTUVWXYZ'/
        READ *, MESSAGE
        I = INDEX (MESSAGE, '  ')
        DO 50 K = 1, I
            IF (MESSAGE(K:K) .NE. ' ') THEN
                LETTER = MESSAGE (K:K)
                I2 = INDEX (ALPHABET, LETTER )
                PRINT (K) = ARRAY (27 - I2)
            ELSE
            PRINT(K) = ' '
            ENDIF
    50 CONTINUE
       PRINT *, (PRINT (K), K = 1, I)
       STOP
       END

12.     CHARACTER MONTHS(12) * 10
        CHARACTER MONTHN (12) * 2
        CHARACTER * 30 STRING,EDSTR
        CHARACTER * 2 MONTH, DAY, YEAR
        DATA MONTHS / 'JAN', 'FEB', 'MAR', 'APR', 'MAY', 'JUN', 'JUL', 'AU
       -G', 'SEP', 'OCT', 'NOV', 'DEC'/
        DATA MONTHN/'01', '02', '03', '04', '05', '06', '07', '08', '09',
       - '10', '11', '12' /
        READ * , STRING
        DO 50 K = 1, 12
            IF (STRING(1:3) .EQ. MONTHS(K) ) THEN
                MONTH = MONTHN (K)
                GOTO 60
            ENDIF
    50 CONTINUE
    60 I = INDEX (STRING, ' ')
       DAY = STRING (I+1:I+2)
       J = INDEX (STRING, ',')
       YEAR = STRING (J+4:J+5)
       EDSTR = MONTH//'-'//DAY//'-'//YEAR
       PRINT *, EDSTR
       STOP
       END

13. (a) CHARACTER MONTHS(12) * 10
        CHARACTER MONTHN (12) * 2
        CHARACTER * 20 NAME, STRING
        CHARACTER MNUMB(10) * 2
        CHARACTER * 20 S, TEMP
        DIMENSION NAME(10), STRING(10)
        DATA MONTHS / 'JAN', 'FEB', 'MAR', 'APR', 'MAY', 'JUN', 'JUL', 'AU
       -G', 'SEP', 'OCT', 'NOV', 'DEC'/
        DATA MONTHN/'01', '02', '03', '04', '05', '06', '07', '08', '09',
       - '10', '11', '12' /
        DO 40 K = 1, 10
            READ *, STRING(K)
    40 CONTINUE
       DO 45 K = 1, 10
           READ *, NAME(K)
    45 CONTINUE
       DO 100 L = 1, 10
       S = STRING(L)
           DO 50 K = 1, 12
               IF (S(1:3) .EQ. MONTHS(K) ) THEN
                   MNUMB (L) = MONTHN(K)
                   GOTO 100
               ENDIF
    50     CONTINUE
```

```
      100 CONTINUE
          DO 110 J = 10, 2, -1
              DO 120 K = J - 1, 1, -1
                  IF (MNUMB(J) .LT. MNUMB(K) ) THEN
                      TEMP = MNUMB(J)
                      MNUMB(J) = MNUMB(K)
                      MNUMB(K) = TEMP
                      TEMP = NAME(J)
                      NAME(J) = NAME(K)
                      NAME(K) = TEMP
                      TEMP = STRING(J)
                      STRING(J) = STRING(K)
                      STRING(K) = TEMP
                  ENDIF
      120     CONTINUE
      110 CONTINUE
          DO 130 K = 1, 10
              PRINT *, NAME(K), STRING(K)
      130 CONTINUE
          STOP
          END
```

Chapter 9

1. (a)

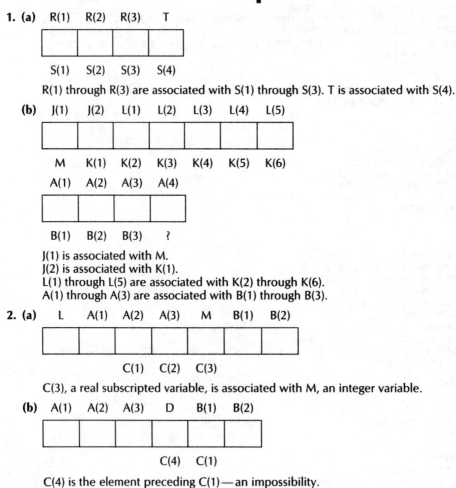

R(1) through R(3) are associated with S(1) through S(3). T is associated with S(4).

(b)

J(1) is associated with M.
J(2) is associated with K(1).
L(1) through L(5) are associated with K(2) through K(6).
A(1) through A(3) are associated with B(1) through B(3).

2. (a)

C(3), a real subscripted variable, is associated with M, an integer variable.

(b)

C(4) is the element preceding C(1)—an impossibility.

3.
```
      * * * * * *
      * MAIN PROGRAM
            READ *, X, N
            PRINT *, VALUE(X, N)
            STOP
            END
      * FUNCTION SUBPROGRAM
            REAL FUNCTION VALUE (X, N)
            SUM = 0.0
            DO 50 K = 1, N
                SUM = SUM + X ** K / K
         50 CONTINUE
            VALUE = SUM
            RETURN
            END
```

4.
```
            REAL ARRAY(3)
            READ *, (ARRAY(K), K = 1, 3)
            PRINT *, VALUE(ARRAY)
            STOP
            END
      *
            FUNCTION VALUE(ARRAY)
            REAL ARRAY(3)
            DO 50 K = 1, 2
                IF (ARRAY(K) .GT. ARRAY(K + 1) ) THEN
                    TEMP = ARRAY(K)
                    ARRAY(K) = ARRAY(K+1)
                    ARRAY (K + 1) = TEMP
                ENDIF
         50 CONTINUE
            VALUE = ARRAY(2)
            RETURN
            END
```

6.
```
            REAL X(100)
            READ *, (X(I), I = 1, 100)
            CALL SMOOTH(X)
            PRINT *, (X(I), I = 1, 100)
            STOP
            END
      *
            SUBROUTINE SMOOTH(X)
            REAL X(100), Y(100)
            Y(1) = X(1)
            Y(100) = X(100)
            DO 50 I = 2, 9
                Y(I) =( X(I - 1) + X(I) + X(I + 1) ) / 3.0
         50 CONTINUE
            DO 70 K = 1, 100
                X(K) = Y(K)
         70 CONTINUE
            RETURN
            END
```

7.
```
            INTEGER A(25)
            READ *, (A(K), K = 1, 25)
            PRINT *, A
            CALL ZERO (A)
            PRINT *, A
            STOP
            END
      *
            SUBROUTINE ZERO (A)
            INTEGER A(25)
            DO 50 K = 1, 25
            A(K) = 0
         50 CONTINUE
            RETURN
            END
```

```
9.      INTEGER A(50)
        READ *, (A(I), I = 1,50)
        CALL KOUNT (A, M, N)
        PRINT *, 'THERE ARE ', M, ' EVEN ELEMENTS'
        PRINT *, 'THERE ARE ', N, ' ODD ELEMENTS'
        STOP
        END
* * * * * * * *
        SUBROUTINE KOUNT (A, M, N)
        INTEGER A(50)
        M = 0
        N = 0
        DO 50 K = 1, 50
            IF (MOD (A(K), 2) .EQ. 0) THEN
                M = M + 1
            ELSE
                N = N + 1
            ENDIF
     50 CONTINUE
        RETURN
        END

10.     CHARACTER * 26 STRING
        CHARACTER T
        READ *, STRING, T
        N = 0
        CALL KOUNT (STRING, T, N)
        PRINT *, 'THERE ARE ', N, ' OCCURRENCES OF ', T, ' IN ', STRING
        STOP
        END
*
        SUBROUTINE KOUNT(TEXT, T, K)
        CHARACTER * 26 TEXT
        CHARACTER    T
        K = 0
        DO 50 J = 1, 26
            IF (TEXT (J:J) .EQ. T) K = K + 1
     50 CONTINUE
        RETURN
        END

11.     DO 50 K = 0, 90, 10
        RAD = K * 3.1416/180.0
            IF (K .NE. 90) THEN
                PRINT *, K, SIN(RAD), COS(RAD), TAN(RAD)
            ELSE
                PRINT *, K, SIN(RAD), COS(RAD), '      UNDEFINED'
            ENDIF
     50 CONTINUE
        STOP
        END
```

```
18.      LOGICAL SWITCH,PLUS
         CHARACTER * 6 TYPE
         READ *, A, B, C
    50 CONTINUE
         IF ( A .NE. 0.0) THEN
             CALL VALID (A,B,C,PLUS)
             IF ( .NOT. PLUS) THEN
                 PRINT *, A, B, C ,'ALL VALUES ARE NOT POSITIVE'
                 GOTO 70
             ENDIF
             CALL TRIANGLE (A, B, C, SWITCH,AREA)
             IF (.NOT. SWITCH) THEN
                 PRINT *, A, B, C, ' NO TRIANGLE CAN BE FORMED'
                 GOTO 70
             ENDIF
             CALL TYPEX (A, B, C, TYPE)
             PRINT *, A, B, C, 'REPRESENTS A TRIANGLE'
             PRINT *, 'AREA = ', AREA
             PRINT *, 'THE TRIANGLE IS ', TYPE
    70       READ *, A, B,C
             GOTO 50
         ENDIF
         STOP
         END
*
         SUBROUTINE TRIANGLE (A, B, C, SWITCH,AREA)
         LOGICAL SWITCH
         SWITCH = .FALSE.
         IF ((C .LT. A + B) .AND. (B .LT. A + C) .AND. (A .LT. B + C)) THEN
             SWITCH = .TRUE.
         ENDIF
         IF (SWITCH) CALL AREAX(A,B,C,AREA)
         RETURN
         END
*
         SUBROUTINE AREAX (A,B,C,AREA)
         S = (A + B + C) / 2.0
         AREA = SQRT(S * (S - A) * (S - B) * (S - C))
         RETURN
         END
*
         SUBROUTINE VALID (A,B,C,PLUS)
         LOGICAL PLUS
         PLUS = .FALSE.
         IF ( (A .GT. 0) .AND. (B .GT. 0) .AND. (C .GT. 0) ) PLUS = .TRUE.
         RETURN
         END
*
         SUBROUTINE TYPEX (A, B, C, TYPE)
         CHARACTER * 6 TYPE
         IF (A .GT. C) THEN
             TEMP = A
             A = C
             C = TEMP
         ENDIF
         IF ( B.GT.C) THEN
             TEMP = B
             B = C
             C = TEMP
         ENDIF
         IF (C **2 .LT. A **2 + B **2) THEN
             TYPE = 'ACUTE'
         ELSEIF (C **2 .EQ. A**2 + B**2) THEN
             TYPE = 'RIGHT'
         ELSE TYPE = 'OBTUSE'
         ENDIF
         RETURN
         END
```

19.
```
        CHARACTER ROMAN * 10
        CHARACTER ARRAY(10)
        EQUIVALENCE (ROMAN, ARRAY)
        L = 0
        READ *, NUMBER
        IF (NUMBER .GE. 50) THEN
            NUMBER = NUMBER - 50
            L = L + 1
            ARRAY (L) = 'L'
        ENDIF
   10 CONTINUE
        IF (NUMBER .GE. 10) THEN
            NUMBER = NUMBER - 10
            L = L + 1
            ARRAY (L) = 'X'
            GOTO 10
        ENDIF
        IF (NUMBER .GE. 5) THEN
            NUMBER = NUMBER - 5
            L = L + 1
            ARRAY (L) = 'V'
        ENDIF
   20 CONTINUE
        IF (NUMBER .GE. 1) THEN
            NUMBER = NUMBER - 1
            L = L + 1
            ARRAY (L) = 'I'
            GOTO 20
        ENDIF
* REPLACE LXXXX WITH XC
        I = INDEX (ROMAN, 'LXXXX')
        IF (I .NE. 0) THEN
            ROMAN (I:I+4) = 'XCUUU'
* THE LETTER U MARKS AN UNUSED POSITION. ALL OCCURRENCES OF THE LETTER
* U WILL LATER BE REMOVED.
        ENDIF
* REPLACE XXXX WITH XL
        I = INDEX (ROMAN, 'XXXX')
        IF ( I .NE. 0) THEN
            ROMAN (I:I+3) = 'XLUU'
        ENDIF
* REPLACE VIIII WITH IX
        I = INDEX (ROMAN, 'VIIII')
        IF (I .NE. 0) THEN
            ROMAN (I:I+4) = 'IXUUU'
        ENDIF
* REPLACE IIII WITH IX
        I = INDEX (ROMAN, 'IIII')
        IF (I .NE. 0) THEN
            ROMAN (I:I+3) = 'IVUU'
        ENDIF
* IF THE LAST ELEMENT OF THE ARRAY IS 'U', CHANGE 'U' TO ' '.
        IF (ARRAY(10) .EQ. 'U') ARRAY(10) = ' '
* REMOVE ALL OCCURRENCES OF THE LETTER 'U'
        I = INDEX (ROMAN, 'U')
  300 CONTINUE
        IF ( I .NE. 0 ) THEN
            DO 50 K = I, 9
                ARRAY(K) = ARRAY(K + 1)
   50       CONTINUE
                I = INDEX(ROMAN, 'U')
            GOTO 300
        ENDIF
        PRINT *, ROMAN
        STOP
        END
```

20. (Structure chart)

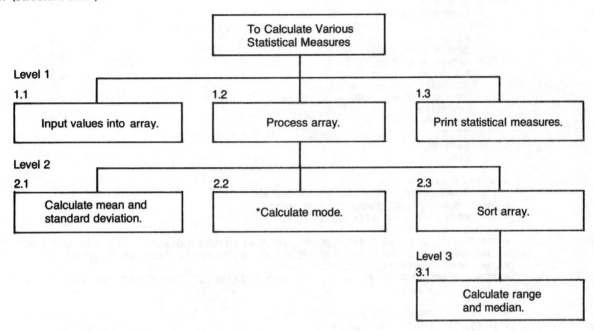

*To calculate the mode:
    Create an array B that contains all the elements of data array A, but does not accept repetitions of any elements. As part of the same process, create an array C that maintains the frequencies of each element of array B in corresponding order. This can be accomplished by comparing each successive element of array A, after A(1), with each previously stored element of array B. If the value of the current element of A is found in B, the count of that element in array C is incremented by 1. Otherwise, the value is assigned to the next consecutive element of array B and the corresponding element of array C is set at 1.
    At the end of this process, array C is scanned for the mode by determining the maximum value of the array. If the maximum value is 1, then each element of the array is the mode. If the maximum value is greater than 1, then the array may have one or more modes. In either case, after the mode(s) is (are) determined, it is (they are) placed into array D for subsequent printing.

20. (Program)

```
      REAL A(100), D(100)
* INPUT VALUES INTO ARRAY
      KOUNT = 0
      READ *, VALUE
   10 CONTINUE
      IF (VALUE .NE. -999.9) THEN
          KOUNT = KOUNT + 1
          A (KOUNT) = VALUE
          READ *, VALUE
          GOTO 10
      ENDIF
      N = KOUNT
* PROCESS ARRAY
      CALL SDEV(A,N, RMEAN, STDEV)
      CALL MODE (A,N,D,L,M)
      CALL SORT(A,N)
      CALL MEDIAN(A,N, RMED, RANGE)
* PRINT STATISTICAL MEASURES
      PRINT *, 'THE AVERAGE IS ', RMEAN
      PRINT*, 'THE STANDARD DEVIATION IS ',STDEV
      PRINT *, 'THE MODE IS ', (D(K), K = 1,M)
      IF (L .EQ. M) THEN
          PRINT *, 'EACH VALUE IN THE ARRAY OCCURS EXACTLY ONCE'
      ENDIF
      PRINT *, 'THE MEDIAN IS ', RMED
      PRINT *, 'THE RANGE IS ', RANGE
      STOP
      END
```

```
*
* * * * * * * *
      SUBROUTINE SDEV(A, N, RMEAN, STDEV)
* THIS SUBROUTINE COMPUTES THE STANDARD DEVIATION AND THE MEAN
      REAL A(100)
      SUM = 0.0
      SUMSQ = 0.0
      DO 20 K = 1, N
          SUM = SUM + A(K)
          SUMSQ = SUMSQ + A(K) ** 2
   20 CONTINUE
      RMEAN = SUM / N
      STDEV = SQRT ( ABS (SUMSQ / N - RMEAN **2))
      RETURN
      END
*
* * * * * * * * *
      SUBROUTINE MODE (A, N, D, L, M)
* THIS SUBROUTINE COMPUTES THE MODE
      REAL A(100), B(100), D(100)
      INTEGER C(100)
* THE ARRAY B STORES THE VALUES IN A, ELIMINATING ALL DUPLICATE VALUES
* THE ARRAY C STORES THE FREQUENCY OF EACH CORRESPONDING ELEMENT IN B
* THE ARRAY D STORES THE MODE VALUES
* PLACE FIRST VALUE OF A INTO B AND INITIALIZE THE FIRST ELEMENT OF C AT 1
      B(1) = A(1)
      C(1) = 1
* L IS THE INDEX FOR ARRAYS B AND C
* M IS THE INDEX FOR ARRAY D
      L = 1
      M = 0
      DO 10 K = 2, N
      DO 20 J = 1, L
          IF (A(K) .EQ. B(J)) THEN
              C(J) = C(J) + 1
              GOTO 25
          ENDIF
   20     CONTINUE
* DO LOOP HAS BEEN EXITED. NO MATCH HAS BEEN FOUND. PLACE NEW VALUE IN
* B AND SET COUNT IN C TO 1
      L = L + 1
      B(L) = A(K)
      C(L) = 1
   25 CONTINUE
   10 CONTINUE
* FIND MAXIMUM VALUE OF C
      RMAX = C(1)
      DO 30 K = 1, L
          IF ( C(K) .GT. RMAX) RMAX = C(K)
   30 CONTINUE
      IF (RMAX .EQ. 1.0) THEN
          DO 35 K = 1, L
              D(K) = B(K)
   35     CONTINUE
          M = L
      ELSE
          DO 40 K = 1, L
              IF (C(K) .EQ. RMAX) THEN
                  M = M + 1
                  D(M) = B(K)
              ENDIF
   40     CONTINUE
      ENDIF
      RETURN
      END
* *
* * * * * * * * *
      SUBROUTINE SORT(A, N)
* THIS SUBROUTINE SORTS THE ARRAY USING AN EXCHANGE SORT.
      REAL A(100)
```

```
        DO 50 J = N, 2, -1
            DO 60 K = J - 1, 1, -1
                IF (A(J) .LT. A(K) ) THEN
                    TEMP = A(J)
                    A(J) = A(K)
                    A(K) = TEMP
                ENDIF
    60      CONTINUE
    50 CONTINUE
        RETURN
        END
* * * * * * * * *
* * * * * * * * * *
        SUBROUTINE MEDIAN (A, N, RMED, RANGE)
* THIS SUBROUTINE COMPUTES THE MEDIAN AND THE RANGE
        REAL A(100)
        IF (MOD (N, 2) .EQ. 1) THEN
            RMED =   A(N / 2 + 1)
        ELSE
            RMED = ( A(N/2) + A(N/2 + 1) )/ 2
        ENDIF
        RANGE = A(N) - A(1)

        RETURN
        END
```

Chapter 10

2.
```
    * MAGAZINE SUBSCRIPTION PROGRAM
    * PROGRAMMER ARLENE PODOS
    * THIS PROGRAM WAS RUN ON A PRIME 850 COMPUTER USING FORTRAN 77
    *
    *
            CHARACTER * 1 SEX, MCODE
            CHARACTER * 20 NAME
            CHARACTER * 6 EXPDT, TDATE
            LOGICAL ERROR, EXPIRE
            INTEGER ACCTNO
    *
    *
    * INITIALIZATION RTN
    *
            OPEN (UNIT = 13, FILE = 'CUST', STATUS = 'OLD')
            OPEN (UNIT = 14, FILE = 'LETTER', STATUS = 'NEW')
    * . . INPUT TODAY'S DATE
            READ *, TDATE
    * . . INPUT CUSTOMER RECORD
            READ (13, 85) NAME, ACCTNO, SEX, MCODE, EXPDT
        85 FORMAT (A20, I5, 2A1, A6)
    *
    * WHILE LOOP BEGINS
        50 CONTINUE
            IF (NAME .NE. 'EOF') THEN
    *
    * . . . . INITIALIZE ERROR SWITCH
            ERROR = .FALSE.
    *
    * . . . . VALIDATE DATA
            CALL VALID (ERROR, NAME, ACCTNO, SEX, MCODE, EXPDT)
    *
    * . . . . IF THERE IS AN ERROR READ THE NEXT RECORD
            IF (ERROR) GOTO 60
    *
    * . . . . SET EXPIRE SWITCH
            EXPIRE = .FALSE.
    *
    * . . . . CHECK IF MAGAZINE HAS EXPIRED
            CALL DATCHK (EXPIRE, TDATE, EXPDT)
    *
```

```
*  . . . .  IF THE MAGAZINE HAS EXPIRED WRITE RECORD TO LETTER FILE
           IF (EXPIRE) THEN
                CALL LETTER (NAME, ACCTNO, SEX, MCODE, EXPDT)
           ELSE

                PRINT *, ' '
                PRINT *, ' '
                PRINT *, NAME
                PRINT *, 'MAGAZINE HAS NOT EXPIRED. DO NOT SEND LETTER'
           ENDIF
*
*  . . . .  READ NEXT RECORD
   60      READ (13,95) NAME, ACCTNO, SEX, MCODE, EXPDT
   95      FORMAT (A20, I5, 2A1, A6)
           GOTO 50
        ENDIF
* WRITE TRAILER RECORD
        NAME = 'EOF'
        ACCTNO = 99999
        SEX = 'X'
        MCODE = '9'
        EXPDT = '999999'
        WRITE (14, 1100) NAME, ACCTNO, SEX, MCODE, EXPDT
 1100 FORMAT (A20, I5, 2A1, A6)
        CLOSE (UNIT = 13)
        CLOSE (UNIT = 14)
        STOP
        END
*
*
* * * * * * * * * * * * * * * * * * * * * * * * * * * * * * * * *
        SUBROUTINE VALID (ERROR, NAME, ACCTNO, SEX, MCODE, EXPDT)
*
*
* THIS SUBROUTINE VALIDATES THE INPUT DATA. IF AN ERROR IS DETECTED, THE
* APPROPRIATE MESSAGE IS PRINTED AND THE ERROR SWITCH IS SET TO .TRUE. IF NO
* ERROR IS DETECTED THEN THE ERROR SWITCH REMAINS SET TO .FALSE.
*
*
        CHARACTER * 1 SEX, MCODE
        CHARACTER * 20 NAME
        CHARACTER * 6 EXPDT, TDATE
        INTEGER ACCTNO
        LOGICAL ERROR
        IF ( (SEX .NE. 'M') .AND. (SEX .NE. 'F')) THEN
            PRINT *, ' '
            PRINT *, ' '
            ERROR = .TRUE.
            PRINT *, NAME, SEX, '   INVALID SEX CODE'
        ENDIF
        IF ( (MCODE .LT. '1') .OR. (MCODE .GT. '5')) THEN
            IF (.NOT. ERROR) THEN
                PRINT *, ' '
                PRINT *, ' '
            ENDIF
            ERROR = .TRUE.
            PRINT *, NAME, MCODE, '   INVALID MAGAZINE CODE'
        ENDIF
        IF ((EXPDT (1:2) .LT. '01' ) .OR. (EXPDT(1:2) .GT. '12' ) ) THEN
            IF (.NOT. ERROR) THEN
                PRINT *, ' '
                PRINT *, ' '
            ENDIF
            ERROR = .TRUE.
            PRINT *, NAME, EXPDT (1: 2), ' INVALID MONTH'
        ENDIF
        IF ( (EXPDT (3:4) .LT. '01' ) .OR. ( EXPDT(3:4) .GT. '31' ) ) THEN
            IF (.NOT. ERROR) THEN
                PRINT *, ' '
                PRINT *, ' '
            ENDIF
```

```
                    ERROR = .TRUE.
                    PRINT *, NAME, EXPDT(3:4), ' INVALID DAY'
              ENDIF
              IF ( (EXPDT (5:6) .LT. '83' ) .OR. (EXPDT(5:6) .GT. '87' ) ) THEN
                    IF (.NOT. ERROR) THEN
                          PRINT *, ' '
                          PRINT *, ' '
                    ENDIF
                    ERROR = .TRUE.
                    PRINT *, NAME, EXPDT (5:6), ' INVALID YEAR'
              ENDIF
              RETURN
              END
*
*
* * * * * * * * * * * * * * * * * * * * * * * * * * * * * * * * * * * * *
              SUBROUTINE DATCHK(EXPIRE, TDATE, EXPDT)
*
*
* THIS SUBROUTINE CHECKS WHETHER OR NOT THE MAGAZINE HAS EXPIRED. IF
* TODAY'S DATE IS GREATER THAN OR EQUAL TO THE EXPIRATION DATE THEN THE
* MAGAZINE HAS EXPIRED AND THE SWITCH EXPIRE IS SET TO .TRUE. OTHERWISE
* EXPIRE REMAINS SET TO THE VALUE .FALSE. .   IN ORDER TO COMPARE THE TWO
* DATES (TDATE AND EXPDT) BOTH DATES MUST BE REARRANGED INTO YYMMDD FORMAT.
*
*
              CHARACTER * 6 EXPDT, TDATE, TNEW, ENEW
              LOGICAL EXPIRE
              TNEW = TDATE (5:6) // TDATE (1:2)//TDATE (3:4)
              ENEW = EXPDT (5:6) // EXPDT (1:2) // EXPDT(3:4)
              IF (TNEW .GE. ENEW) EXPIRE = .TRUE.
              RETURN
              END
*
*
* * * * * * * * * * * * * * * * * * * * * * * * * * * * * * * * * * * * *
              SUBROUTINE LETTER (NAME, ACCTNO, SEX, MCODE, EXPDT)
*
*
* THIS SUBROUTINE WRITES THE VALID RECORDS TO A LETTER FILE. THE
* LETTER FILE WILL BE ACCESSED IN A FUTURE PROGRAM.
*
*
              CHARACTER *1 SEX, MCODE
              CHARACTER *20 NAME
              CHARACTER *6 EXPDT
              INTEGER ACCTNO
              WRITE (14,1200) NAME, ACCTNO, SEX, MCODE, EXPDT
 1200 FORMAT (A20, I5, 2A1, A6)
              PRINT *, ' '
              PRINT *, ' '
              PRINT *, NAME
              PRINT *, 'RECORD WRITTEN TO NEW FILE'
              RETURN
              END
```

Output:

```
                    '062784


                    ANDREWS JENNIFER
                    RECORD WRITTEN TO NEW FILE


                    SMITH SCOTT
                    RECORD WRITTEN TO NEW FILE


                    JONES STACEY
                    RECORD WRITTEN TO NEW FILE
```

```
        BELL DIANE              K   INVALID SEX CODE
        BELL DIANE              6   INVALID MAGAZINE CODE
        BELL DIANE             13   INVALID MONTH
        BELL DIANE             54   INVALID DAY
        BELL DIANE             79   INVALID YEAR


        KENT LORRAINE
        MAGAZINE HAS NOT EXPIRED. DO NOT SEND LETTER
        **** STOP
```

Files Used in Program

Input file:

```
        ANDREWS JENNIFER       11111F1052784
        SMITH SCOTT            22222M5053184
        JONES STACEY           33333F3062184
        BELL DIANE             44444K6135479
        KENT LORRAINE          55555F5070384
        EOF                    99999X0000000
```

Output file:

```
        ANDREWS JENNIFER       11111F1052784
        SMITH SCOTT            22222M5053184
        JONES STACEY           33333F3062184
        EOF                    99999X9999999
```

3.

```
* PROGRAM TO PRODUCE A LETTER FOR A MAGAZINE SUBSCRIPTION SYSTEM
* PROGRAMMER ARLENE PODOS
* THIS PROGRAM WAS RUN ON A PRIME 850 COMPUTER USING FORTRAN 77
*
*
      CHARACTER * 1 SEX, MCODE
      CHARACTER *15 FIRST, LAST
      CHARACTER * 20 ANAME, MNAME
      CHARACTER * 6 EXPDT, TDATE
      CHARACTER * 20 ADDRESS1, ADDRESS2
      INTEGER AACCT, MACCT
*
*
* INITIALIZATION RTN
*
      OPEN (UNIT = 13, FILE = 'LETTER', STATUS = 'OLD')
      OPEN (UNIT = 14, FILE = 'ADDRES', STATUS = 'OLD')
* . . INPUT TODAY'S DATE
      READ *, TDATE
* . . READ FIRST RECORD FROM LETTER FILE
      READ (13, 85) MNAME, MACCT, SEX, MCODE, EXPDT
   85 FORMAT (A20, I5, 2A1, A6)
*
* READ FIRST RECORD FROM ADDRES FILE
      READ (14, 87) ANAME, AACCT, ADDRESS1, ADDRESS2
   87 FORMAT (A20, I5, 2A20)
* WHILE LOOP BEGINS
   50 CONTINUE
      IF ( (AACCT .NE. 99999) .OR. (MACCT .NE. 99999)) THEN
*
         IF (MACCT .EQ. AACCT) THEN
            CALL LETTER (MNAME, MACCT, SEX, MCODE, EXPDT, TDATE, TITLE
     -, LAST, FIRST, I2)
            CALL ADDRESS(ANAME, AACCT, ADDRESS1, ADDRESS2, TITLE, LAST
     -, FIRST, I2)
            READ (13, 85) MNAME, MACCT, SEX, MCODE, EXPDT
            READ (14, 87) ANAME, AACCT, ADDRESS1, ADDRESS2
         ELSE IF (MACCT .GT. AACCT) THEN
            READ (14, 87) ANAME, AACCT, ADDRESS1, ADDRESS2
         ELSE
```

```
*  . . .        MAILING FILE RECORD IS NOT MATCHED BY AN ENTRY IN THE ADDRESS FILE
                PRINT *, ' '
                PRINT *, ' '
                PRINT *, MNAME, MACCT
                PRINT *, 'RECORD NOT FOUND ON ADDRESS FILE'
                READ (13, 85) MNAME, MACCT, SEX, MCODE, EXPDT
            ENDIF
            GOTO 50
        ENDIF
        CLOSE (13)
        CLOSE (14)
        STOP
        END
*
* * * * * * * * * * * * * * * * * * * * * * * * * * * * * * * * * * * * * *
        SUBROUTINE LETTER (NAME, MACCT,  SEX, MCODE, EXPDT, TDATE, TITLE,
        - LAST, FIRST, I2)
*
*
* THIS SUBROUTINE PREPARES AND PRINTS A PERSONALIZED CUSTOMER LETTER.
* ARRAYS ARE SEARCHED TO DETERMINE THE NAME OF THE MAGAZINE ASSOCIATED WITH
* THE MAGAZINE CODE (MCODE) AND THE NAME OF THE MONTH ASSOCIATED WITH THE
* FIRST TWO CHARACTERS OF THE TDATE FIELD. THE INDEX FUNCTION IS USED TO
* DETERMINE THE LENGTH OF THE MONTH AND OF THE MAGAZINE AND TO EXTRACT THE
* LAST NAME FROM THE NAME FIELD.
*
*
        INTEGER MACCT
        CHARACTER *20 NAME
        CHARACTER ARRAY(20)
        CHARACTER * 15 LAST, FIRST
        CHARACTER * 4 TITLE
        CHARACTER * 12 MONTHP
        CHARACTER * 30 DATEPR
        CHARACTER * 1 SEX, MCODE
        CHARACTER *6 EXPDT, TDATE
        CHARACTER MONTHS(12) * 4
        CHARACTER MNUMB (12) * 2
        CHARACTER MNAME (5) * 20
        CHARACTER MAGN (5) * 1
        CHARACTER * 20 MAGPR
*
* . . INITIALIZE ARRAYS WITH CONSTANT VALUES
        DATA MONTHS / 'JAN', 'FEB', 'MAR', 'APR', 'MAY', 'JUNE', 'JULY', '
       -AUG', 'SEPT', 'OCT', 'NOV', 'DEC'/
        DATA MNUMB/ '01', '02', '03', '04', '05', '06', '07', '08', '09',
       -'10', '11', '12'/
        DATA MNAME/ 'FORTRAN', 'MATH', 'GOLF', 'TENNIS', 'RUNNING' /
        DATA MAGN /'1', '2', '3', '4', '5'/
*
* . . SEARCH FOR MONTH NAME
        DO 70 K = 1, 12
        IF ( TDATE (1:2) .EQ. MNUMB(k) ) THEN
                MONTHP = MONTHS (K)
                GOTO 80
            ENDIF
   70 CONTINUE
*
* . . SEARCH FOR MAGAZINE NAME
   80 DO 90 K = 1, 5
            IF (MCODE .EQ. MAGN(K) ) THEN
                MAGPR = MNAME (K)
                GOTO 100
            ENDIF
   90 CONTINUE
*
* EXTRACT FIRST AND LAST NAME FROM NAME
  100 I = INDEX (NAME, ' ')
        LAST = NAME (1: I - 1)
        DO 105 K = 1, 20
            ARRAY(K) = NAME (K:K)
```

```
   105 CONTINUE
       DO 110 K = I+1, 20
           IF (ARRAY(K) .EQ. ' ') GOTO 112
   110 CONTINUE
   112 FIRST = NAME (I+1:K)
       I2 = INDEX (FIRST, ' ')
*
* DETERMINE TITLE
       IF (SEX .EQ. 'M' ) THEN
           TITLE = 'MR. '
       ELSE
           TITLE = 'MS. '
       ENDIF
*
* DETERMINE LENGTH OF MAGAZINE NAME
       I = INDEX (MAGPR, ' ')
       IF (I .EQ. O) THEN
           LENGTH1 = 20
       ELSE
           LENGTH1 = I - 1
       ENDIF
*
* DETERMINE LENGTH OF MONTH NAME
       I = INDEX (MONTHP, ' ')
       IF ( I .EQ. O) THEN
           LENGTH2 = 4
       ELSE
           LENGTH2 = I - 1
       ENDIF
*
* . . WRITE LETTER
       DATEPR = MONTHP(1:LENGTH2) // ' '// TDATE(3:4)//', 19'//TDATE(5:6)
       PRINT *, '                              ', DATEPR
       PRINT *, 'DEAR ', TITLE, LAST
       PRINT *, ' '
       PRINT *, 'ACCORDING TO OUR RECORDS YOUR SUBSCRIPTION TO '
       PRINT *, MAGPR(1:LENGTH1)// ' MAGAZINE HAS EXPIRED. IF YOU RENEW'

       PRINT *, 'YOUR SUBSCRIPTION WITHIN THE NEXT MONTH YOU WILL'
       PRINT *, 'QUALIFY FOR A SPECIAL DISCOUNT. SEE DETAILS INSIDE.'
       PRINT *, 'WE HOPE YOU WILL TAKE ADVANTAGE OF OUR SPECIAL OFFER.'
       PRINT *, '                         SINCERELY YOURS'
       PRINT *, '                         COLETTE DRIMMER'
       PRINT *, '                         CIRCULATION MANAGER'
       PRINT *, ' '
       PRINT *, ' '
       PRINT *, ' '
       RETURN
       END

*
*

       SUBROUTINE ADDRESS (ANAME, AACCT, ADDRESS1, ADDRESS2, TITLE, LAST,
      -FIRST, I2)
*
*
* THIS SUBROUTINE PRINTS MAILING LABELS AS PART OF THE MASS MAILING PROCEDURE
*
*
       CHARACTER *20 ANAME, ADDRESS1, ADDRESS2
       INTEGER AACCT
       CHARACTER *15 FIRST, LAST
       CHARACTER *4 TITLE
       PRINT *, '* * * * * * * * * * * * * * * * * * * * * * * * *'
       PRINT *, ' '
       PRINT *, ' '
       PRINT *, ' '
       PRINT *, TITLE // FIRST (1:I2)// LAST
       PRINT *, ADDRESS1
       PRINT *, ADDRESS2
```

Input file:

```
ANDREWS JENNIFER      1111115 MAIN STREET      NEW YORK, NY 10007
SMITH SCOTT           2222220 BROAD STREET     CLARK, NJ 10003
JONES STACEY          3333340 IVY WALK         NEW YORK, NY 10089
BELL DIANE            4444450 ELM STREET       BROOKLYN, NY 11212
KENT LORRIANE         5555560 20TH STREET      NEW YORK, NY 11010
EOF                   99999EOF                 EOF
```

Sample Output for Program

```
                                        JUNE 28, 1984
        DEAR MS. ANDREWS

        ACCORDING TO OUR RECORDS YOUR SUBSCRIPTION TO
        FORTRAN MAGAZINE HAS EXPIRED. IF YOU RENEW
        YOUR SUBSCRIPTION WITHIN THE NEXT MONTH YOU WILL
        QUALIFY FOR A SPECIAL DISCOUNT. SEE DETAILS INSIDE.
        WE HOPE YOU WILL TAKE ADVANTAGE OF OUR SPECIAL OFFER.
                                 SINCERELY YOURS
                                 COLETTE DRIMMER
                                 CIRCULATION MANAGER



        * * * * * * * * * * * * * * * * * * * * * * * * * * *



        MS. JENNIFER  ANDREWS
        15 MAIN STREET
        NEW YORK, NY 10007


        * * * * * * * * * * * * * * * * * * * * * * * * * * *



                                        JUNE 28, 1984
        DEAR MR. SMITH

        ACCORDING TO OUR RECORDS YOUR SUBSCRIPTION TO
        RUNNING MAGAZINE HAS EXPIRED. IF YOU RENEW
        YOUR SUBSCRIPTION WITHIN THE NEXT MONTH YOU WILL
        QUALIFY FOR A SPECIAL DISCOUNT. SEE DETAILS INSIDE.
        WE HOPE YOU WILL TAKE ADVANTAGE OF OUR SPECIAL OFFER.
                                 SINCERELY YOURS
                                 COLETTE DRIMMER
                                 CIRCULATION MANAGER



        * * * * * * * * * * * * * * * * * * * * * * * * * * *



        MR. SCOTT  SMITH
        20 BROAD STREET
        CLARK, NJ 10003


        * * * * * * * * * * * * * * * * * * * * * * * * * * *
```

```
                                          JUNE 28, 1984
DEAR MS. JONES

ACCORDING TO OUR RECORDS YOUR SUBSCRIPTION TO
GOLF MAGAZINE HAS EXPIRED. IF YOU RENEW
YOUR SUBSCRIPTION WITHIN THE NEXT MONTH YOU WILL
QUALIFY FOR A SPECIAL DISCOUNT. SEE DETAILS INSIDE.
WE HOPE YOU WILL TAKE ADVANTAGE OF OUR SPECIAL OFFER.
                                 SINCERELY YOURS
                                 COLETTE DRIMMER
                                 CIRCULATION MANAGER



        * * * * * * * * * * * * * * * * * * * * * * * * * *



MS. STACEY  JONES
40 IVY WALK
NEW YORK, NY 10089



        * * * * * * * * * * * * * * * * * * * * * * * * * *
```

INDEX